黒鷺死体宅配便
the KUROSAGI corpse delivery service

story
EIJI OTSUKA

art
HOUSUI YAMAZAKI

original cover design
BUNPEI YORIFUJI

translation
TOSHIFUMI YOSHIDA

editor and english adaptation
CARL GUSTAV HORN

lettering and touch-up
IHL

contents

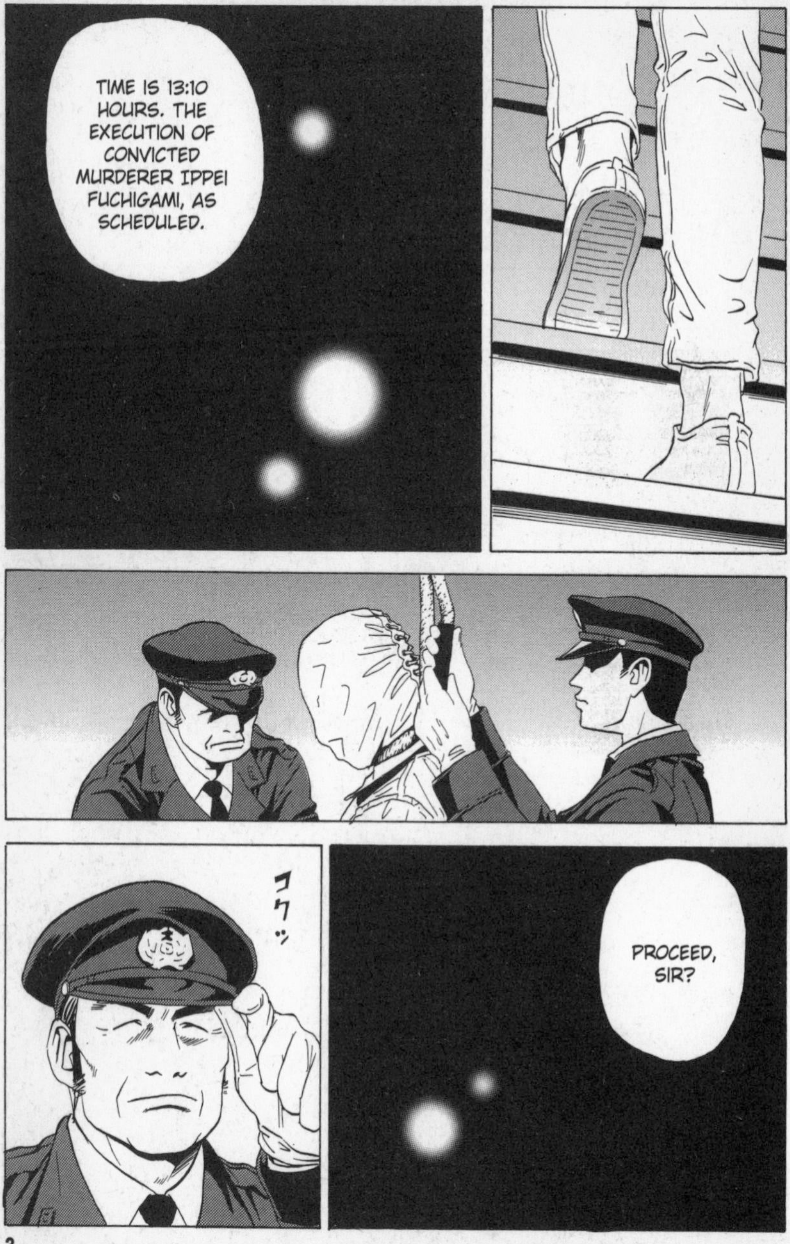
TIME IS 13:10 HOURS. THE EXECUTION OF CONVICTED MURDERER IPPEI FUCHIGAMI, AS SCHEDULED.
PROCEED, SIR?
コクッ

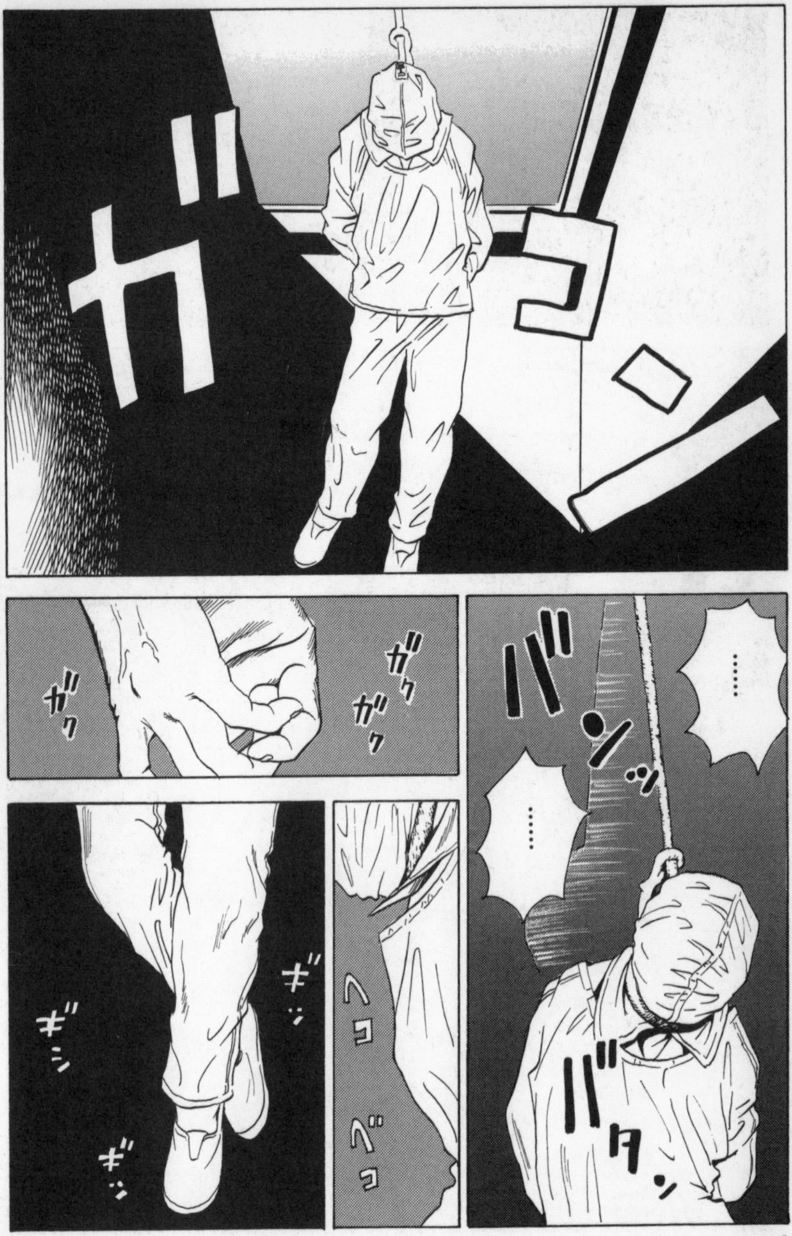

ガコン
バンッ
……
……
バタン
ガク
ガク
ガク
ヘコ
ベコ
ギッ
ギシ
ギッ

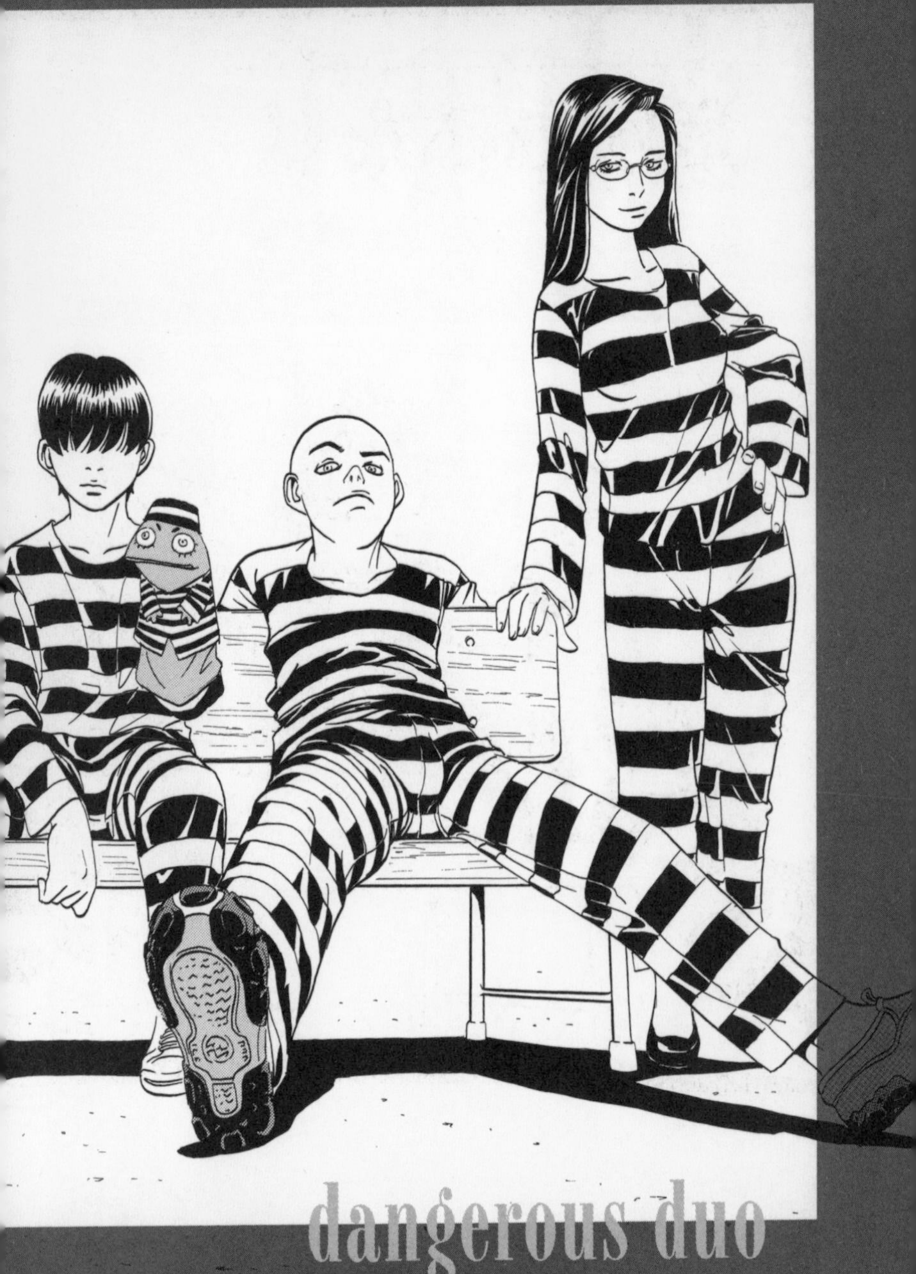
dangerous duo

1st delivery
危険なふたり

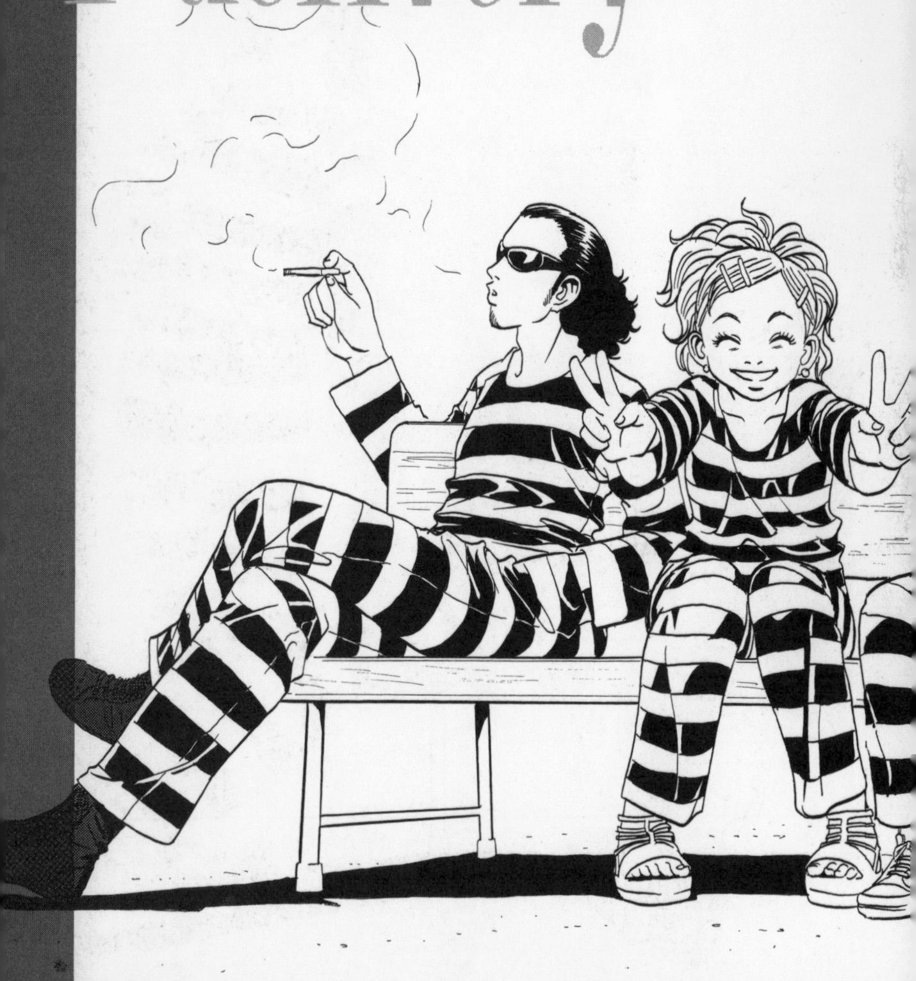

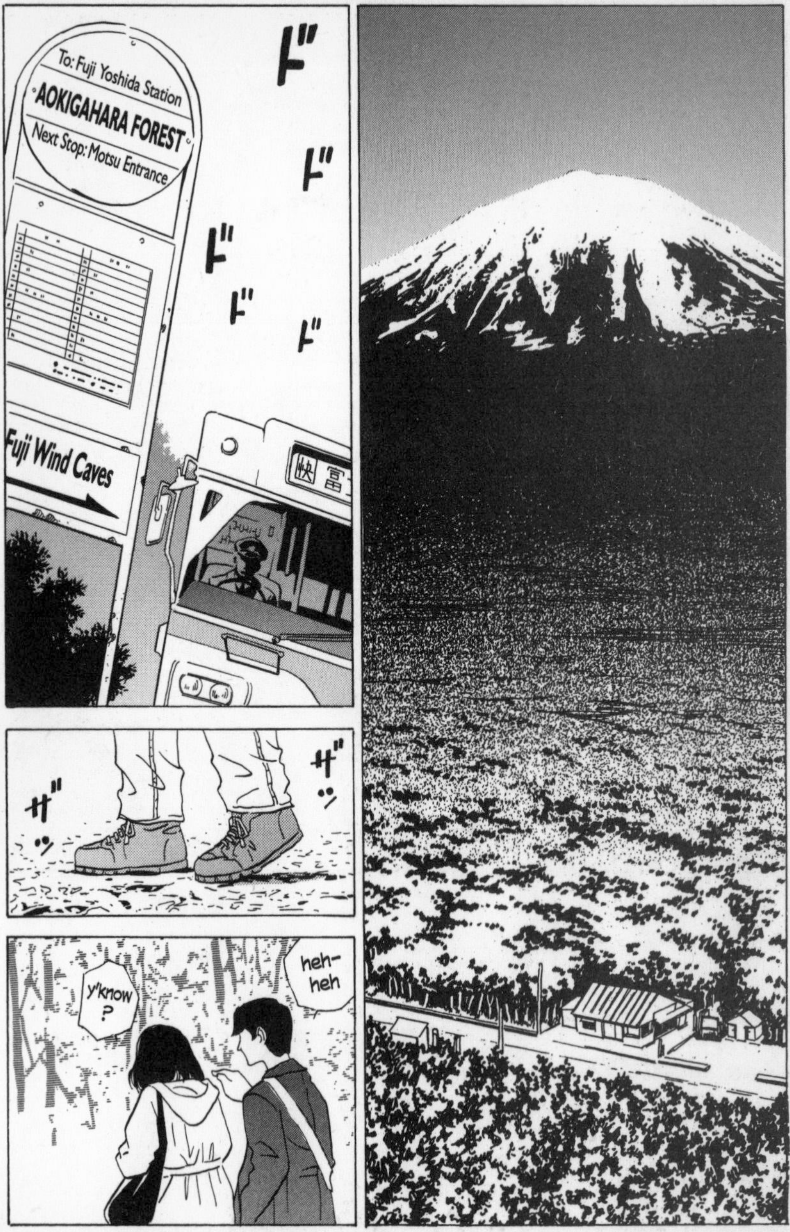

To: Fuji Yoshida Station
AOKIGAHARA FOREST
Next Stop: Motsu Entrance
Fuji Wind Caves
ド
ド
ド
ド
ド
ザッ
ザッ
heh-heh
y'know?

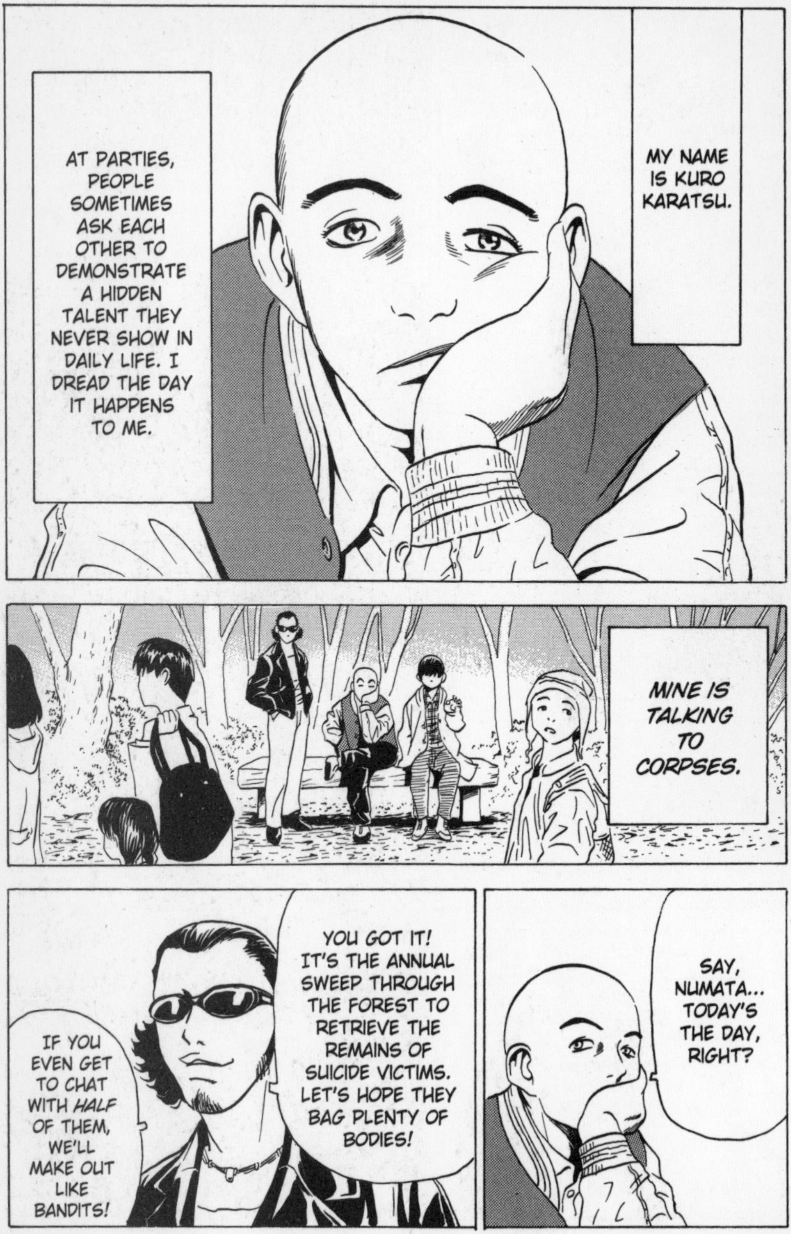
MY NAME IS KURO KARATSU.
AT PARTIES, PEOPLE SOMETIMES ASK EACH OTHER TO DEMONSTRATE A HIDDEN TALENT THEY NEVER SHOW IN DAILY LIFE. I DREAD THE DAY IT HAPPENS TO ME.
MINE IS TALKING TO CORPSES.
SAY, NUMATA... TODAY'S THE DAY, RIGHT?
YOU GOT IT! IT'S THE ANNUAL SWEEP THROUGH THE FOREST TO RETRIEVE THE REMAINS OF SUICIDE VICTIMS. LET'S HOPE THEY BAG PLENTY OF BODIES!
IF YOU EVEN GET TO CHAT WITH *HALF* OF THEM, WE'LL MAKE OUT LIKE BANDITS!

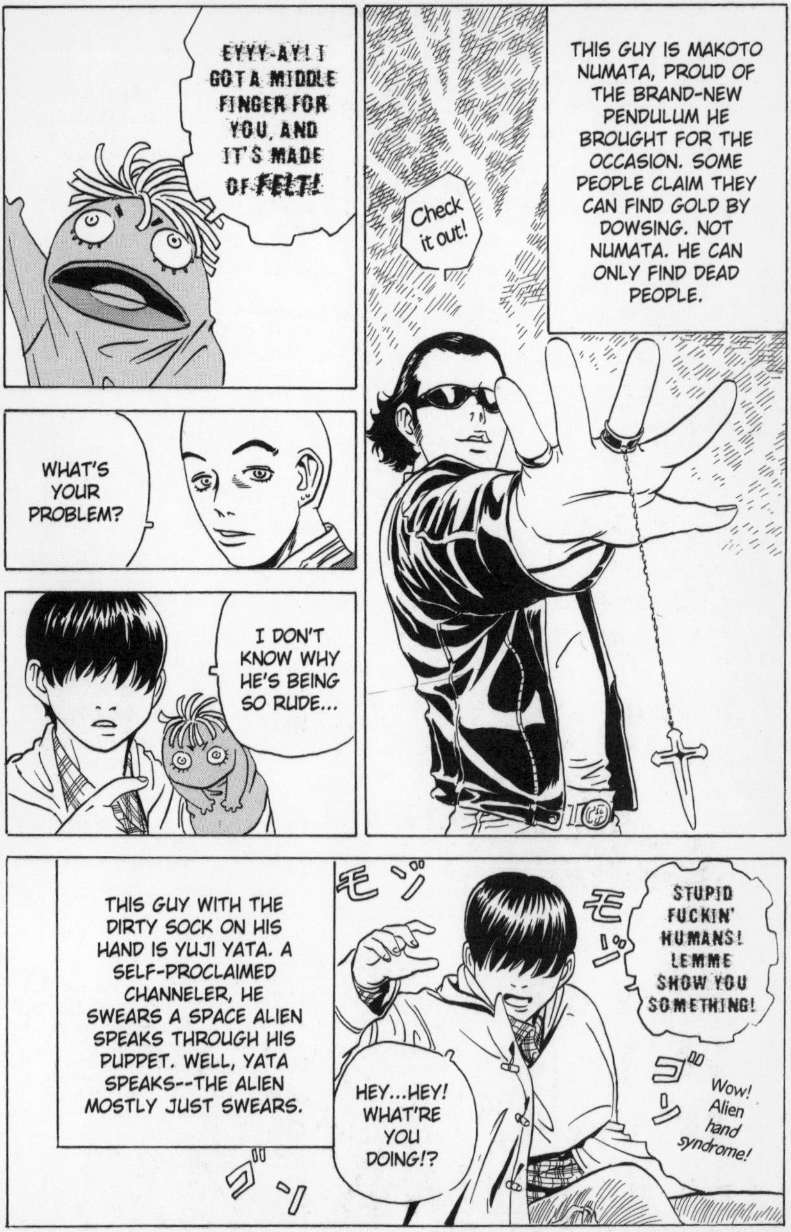

THIS GUY IS MAKOTO NUMATA, PROUD OF THE BRAND-NEW PENDULUM HE BROUGHT FOR THE OCCASION. SOME PEOPLE CLAIM THEY CAN FIND GOLD BY DOWSING. NOT NUMATA. HE CAN ONLY FIND DEAD PEOPLE.
Check it out!
EYYY-AY! I GOT A MIDDLE FINGER FOR YOU, AND IT'S MADE OF FELT!
WHAT'S YOUR PROBLEM?
I DON'T KNOW WHY HE'S BEING SO RUDE...
STUPID FUCKIN' HUMANS! LEMME SHOW YOU SOMETHING!
Wow! Alien hand syndrome!
HEY...HEY! WHAT'RE YOU DOING!?
THIS GUY WITH THE DIRTY SOCK ON HIS HAND IS YUJI YATA. A SELF-PROCLAIMED CHANNELER, HE SWEARS A SPACE ALIEN SPEAKS THROUGH HIS PUPPET. WELL, YATA SPEAKS--THE ALIEN MOSTLY JUST SWEARS.

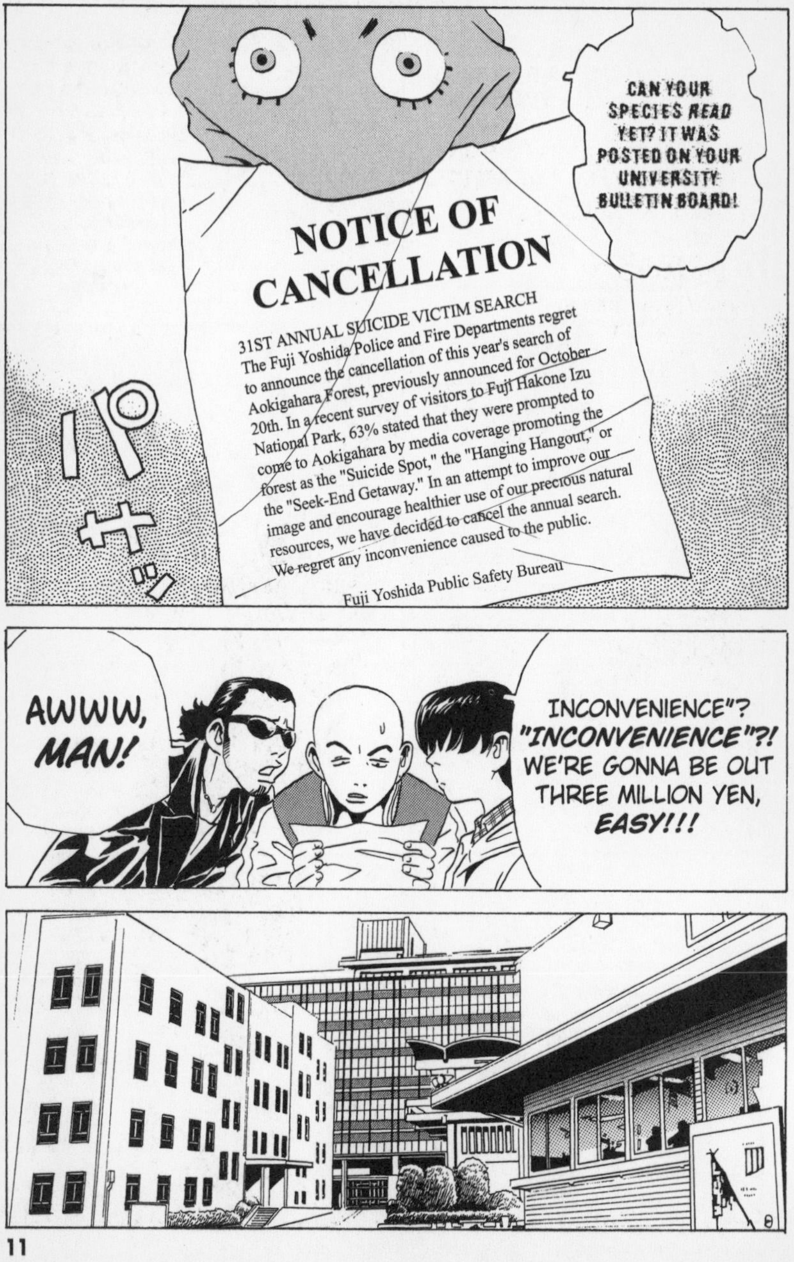
CAN YOUR SPECIES READ YET? IT WAS POSTED ON YOUR UNIVERSITY BULLETIN BOARD!
NOTICE OF CANCELLATION
31ST ANNUAL SUICIDE VICTIM SEARCH
The Fuji Yoshida Police and Fire Departments regret to announce the cancellation of this year's search of Aokigahara Forest, previously announced for October 20th. In a recent survey of visitors to Fuji Hakone Izu National Park, 63% stated that they were prompted to come to Aokigahara by media coverage promoting the forest as the "Suicide Spot," the "Hanging Hangout," or the "Seek-End Getaway." In an attempt to improve our image and encourage healthier use of our precious natural resources, we have decided to cancel the annual search. We regret any inconvenience caused to the public.
Fuji Yoshida Public Safety Bureau
パサッ
INCONVENIENCE"? "INCONVENIENCE"?! WE'RE GONNA BE OUT THREE MILLION YEN, EASY!!!
AWWW, MAN!

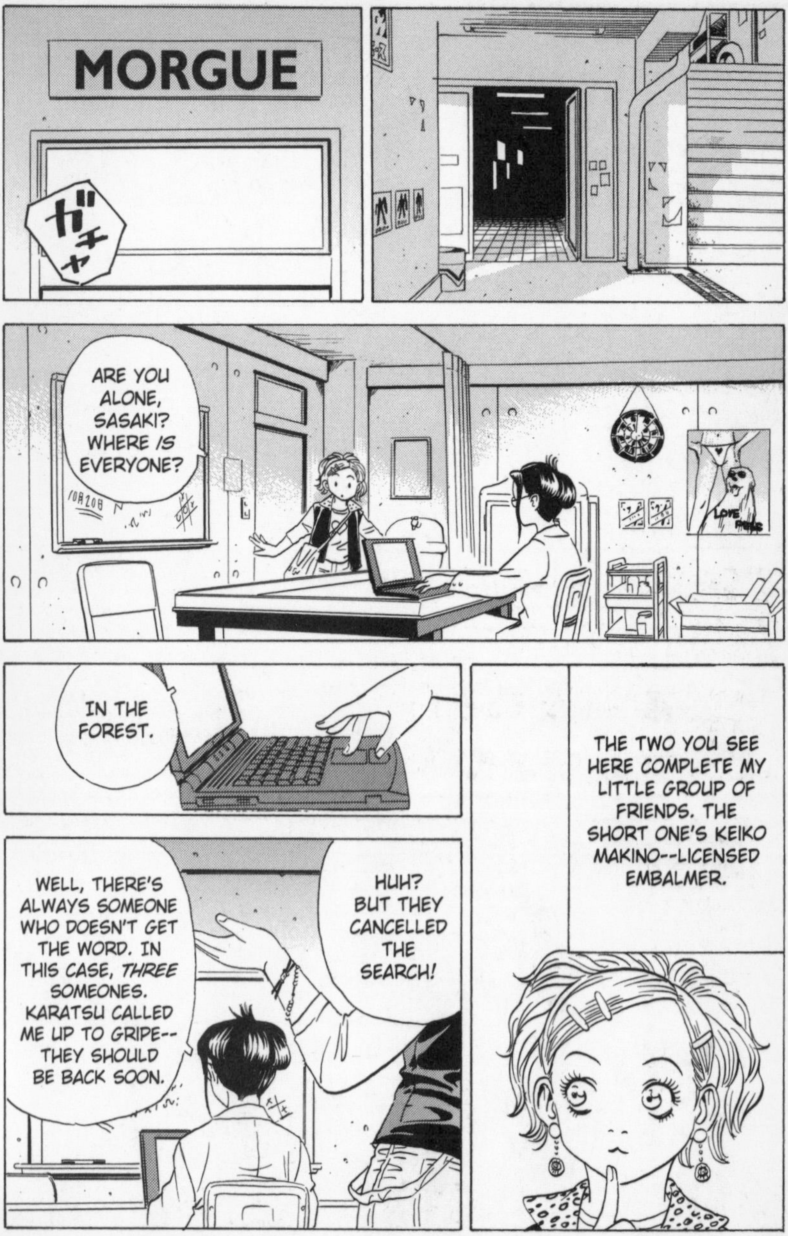
MORGUE
ガチャ
ARE YOU ALONE, SASAKI? WHERE *IS* EVERYONE?
THE TWO YOU SEE HERE COMPLETE MY LITTLE GROUP OF FRIENDS. THE SHORT ONE'S KEIKO MAKINO--LICENSED EMBALMER.
IN THE FOREST.
HUH? BUT THEY CANCELLED THE SEARCH!
WELL, THERE'S ALWAYS SOMEONE WHO DOESN'T GET THE WORD. IN THIS CASE, *THREE* SOMEONES. KARATSU CALLED ME UP TO GRIPE-- THEY SHOULD BE BACK SOON.

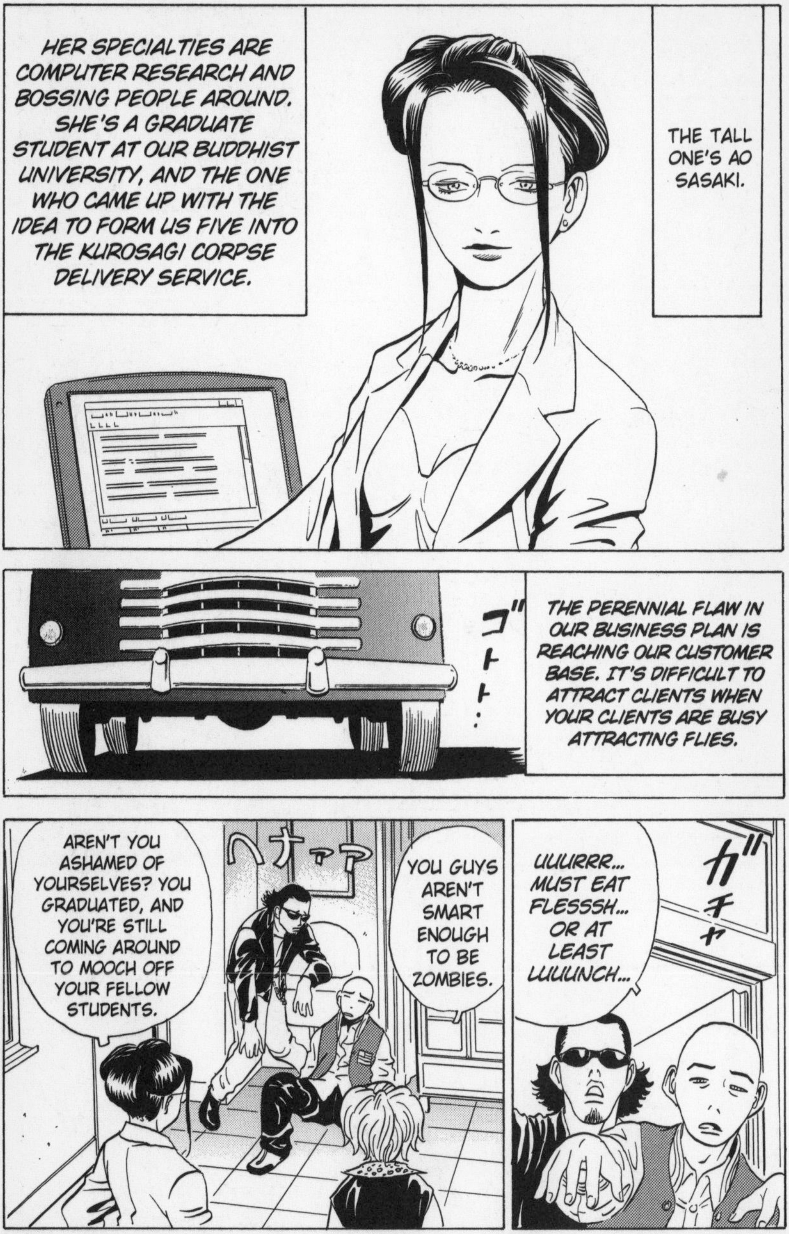
THE TALL ONE'S AO SASAKI.
HER SPECIALTIES ARE COMPUTER RESEARCH AND BOSSING PEOPLE AROUND. SHE'S A GRADUATE STUDENT AT OUR BUDDHIST UNIVERSITY, AND THE ONE WHO CAME UP WITH THE IDEA TO FORM US FIVE INTO THE KUROSAGI CORPSE DELIVERY SERVICE.
THE PERENNIAL FLAW IN OUR BUSINESS PLAN IS REACHING OUR CUSTOMER BASE. IT'S DIFFICULT TO ATTRACT CLIENTS WHEN YOUR CLIENTS ARE BUSY ATTRACTING FLIES.
ゴトト‥
ガチャ
UUURRR... MUST EAT FLESSSH... OR AT LEAST LUUUNCH...
YOU GUYS AREN'T SMART ENOUGH TO BE ZOMBIES.
ヘナァア
AREN'T YOU ASHAMED OF YOURSELVES? YOU GRADUATED, AND YOU'RE STILL COMING AROUND TO MOOCH OFF YOUR FELLOW STUDENTS.

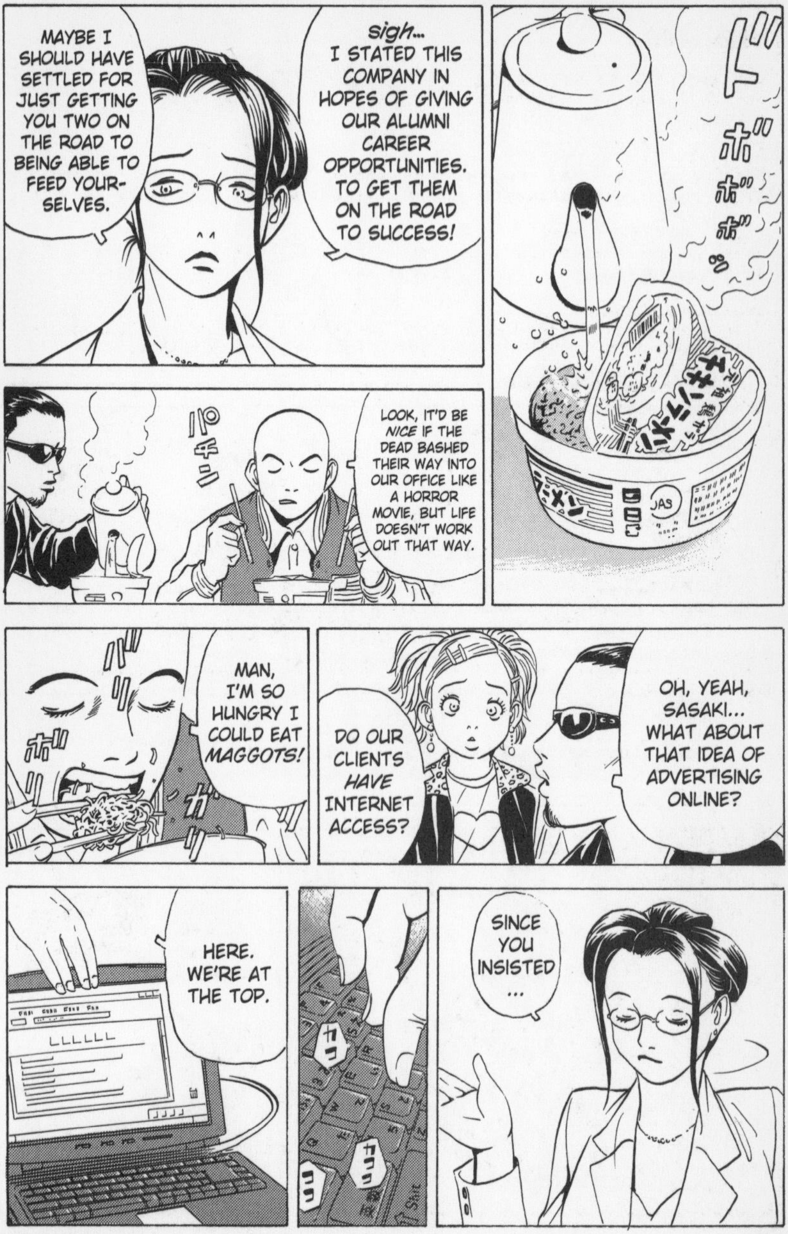
sigh... I STATED THIS COMPANY IN HOPES OF GIVING OUR ALUMNI CAREER OPPORTUNITIES. TO GET THEM ON THE ROAD TO SUCCESS!
MAYBE I SHOULD HAVE SETTLED FOR JUST GETTING YOU TWO ON THE ROAD TO BEING ABLE TO FEED YOUR-SELVES.
LOOK, IT'D BE NICE IF THE DEAD BASHED THEIR WAY INTO OUR OFFICE LIKE A HORROR MOVIE, BUT LIFE DOESN'T WORK OUT THAT WAY.
OH, YEAH, SASAKI... WHAT ABOUT THAT IDEA OF ADVERTISING ONLINE?
DO OUR CLIENTS HAVE INTERNET ACCESS?
MAN, I'M SO HUNGRY I COULD EAT MAGGOTS!
SINCE YOU INSISTED ...
HERE. WE'RE AT THE TOP.

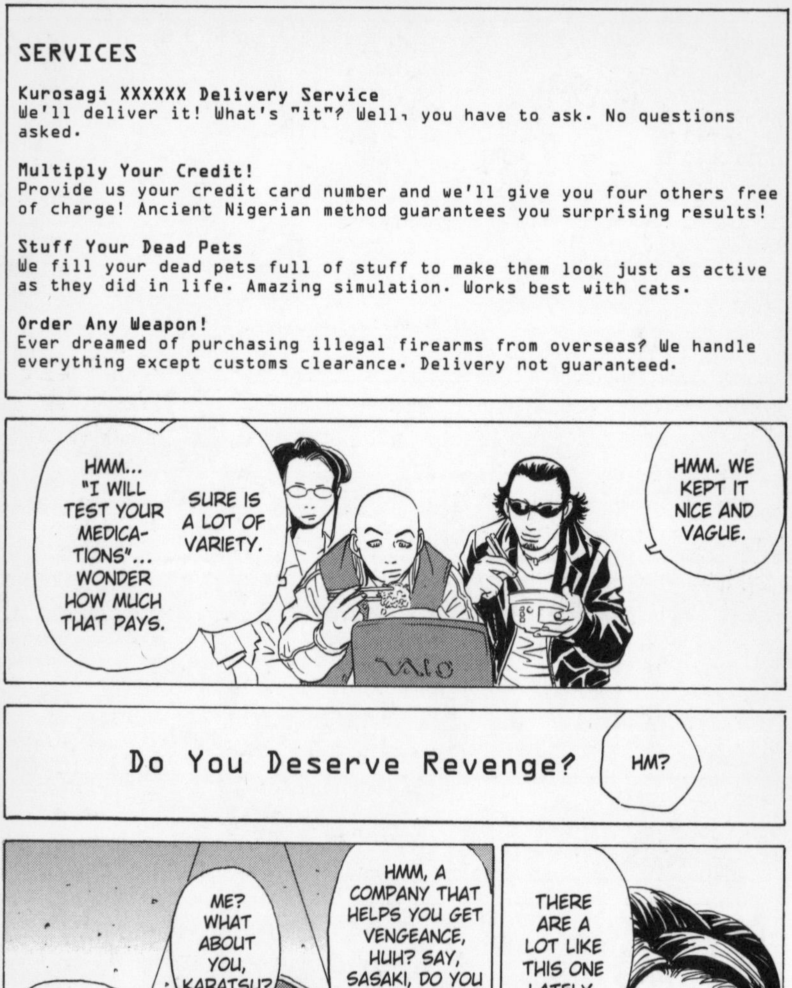
SERVICES
Kurosagi XXXXXX Delivery Service
We'll deliver it! What's "it"? Well, you have to ask. No questions asked.
Multiply Your Credit!
Provide us your credit card number and we'll give you four others free of charge! Ancient Nigerian method guarantees you surprising results!
Stuff Your Dead Pets
We fill your dead pets full of stuff to make them look just as active as they did in life. Amazing simulation. Works best with cats.
Order Any Weapon!
Ever dreamed of purchasing illegal firearms from overseas? We handle everything except customs clearance. Delivery not guaranteed.
HMM. WE KEPT IT NICE AND VAGUE.
SURE IS A LOT OF VARIETY.
HMM... "I WILL TEST YOUR MEDICATIONS"... WONDER HOW MUCH THAT PAYS.
HM?
Do You Deserve Revenge?
THERE ARE A LOT LIKE THIS ONE LATELY.
HMM, A COMPANY THAT HELPS YOU GET VENGEANCE, HUH? SAY, SASAKI, DO YOU HAVE ANYONE YOU'D WANT TO GET REVENGE ON?
ME? WHAT ABOUT YOU, KARATSU?
ME. HMM... MAYBE THAT GUY I HAD FOR "PRINCIPLES OF BUDDHISM" WHO MADE ME REWRITE MY THESIS THREE TIMES.

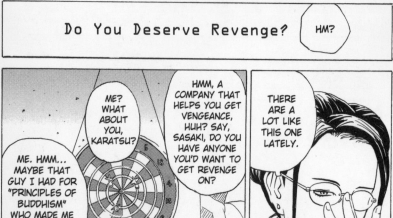

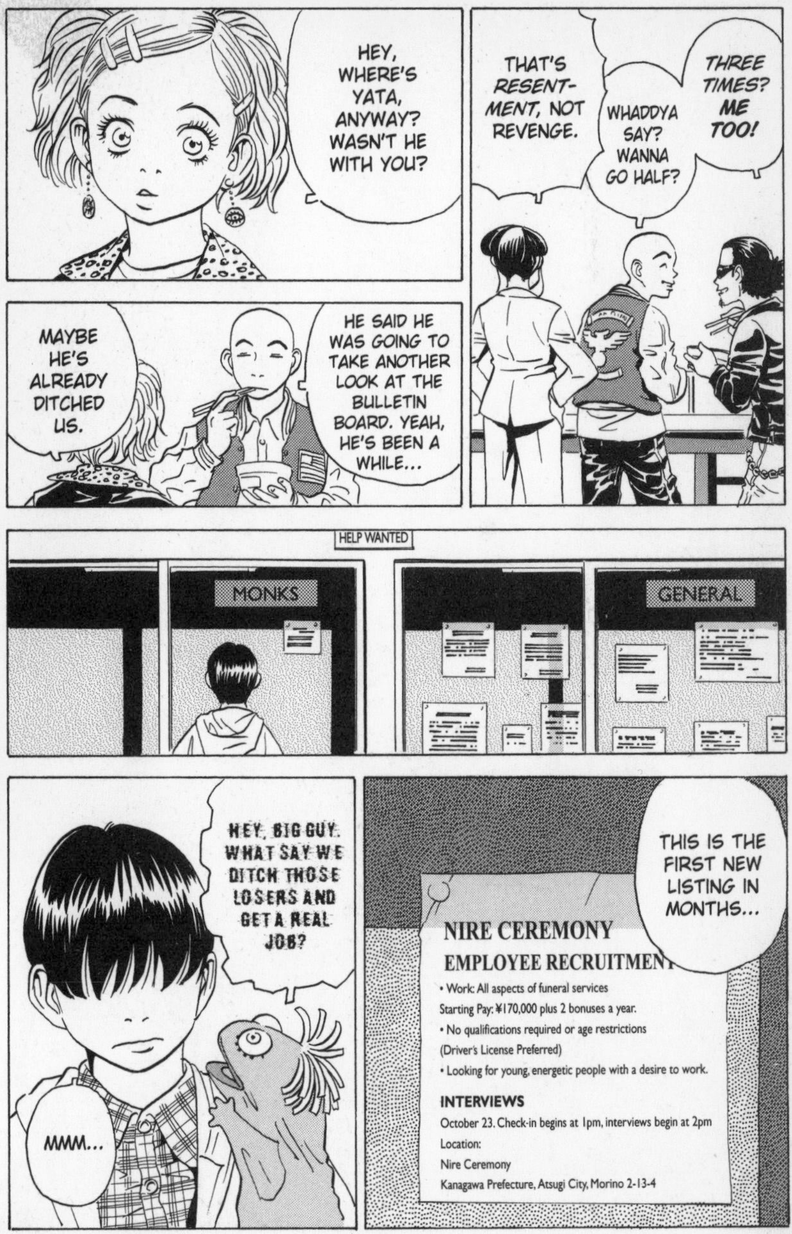
THREE TIMES? ME TOO!
WHADDYA SAY? WANNA GO HALF?
THAT'S RESENTMENT, NOT REVENGE.
HEY, WHERE'S YATA, ANYWAY? WASN'T HE WITH YOU?
HE SAID HE WAS GOING TO TAKE ANOTHER LOOK AT THE BULLETIN BOARD. YEAH, HE'S BEEN A WHILE...
MAYBE HE'S ALREADY DITCHED US.
HELP WANTED
GENERAL
MONKS
THIS IS THE FIRST NEW LISTING IN MONTHS...
NIRE CEREMONY
EMPLOYEE RECRUITMENT
• Work: All aspects of funeral services
Starting Pay: ¥170,000 plus 2 bonuses a year.
• No qualifications required or age restrictions
(Driver's License Preferred)
• Looking for young, energetic people with a desire to work.
INTERVIEWS
October 23. Check-in begins at 1pm, interviews begin at 2pm
Location:
Nire Ceremony
Kanagawa Prefecture, Atsugi City, Morino 2-13-4
HEY, BIG GUY. WHAT SAY WE DITCH THOSE LOSERS AND GET A REAL JOB?
MMM...

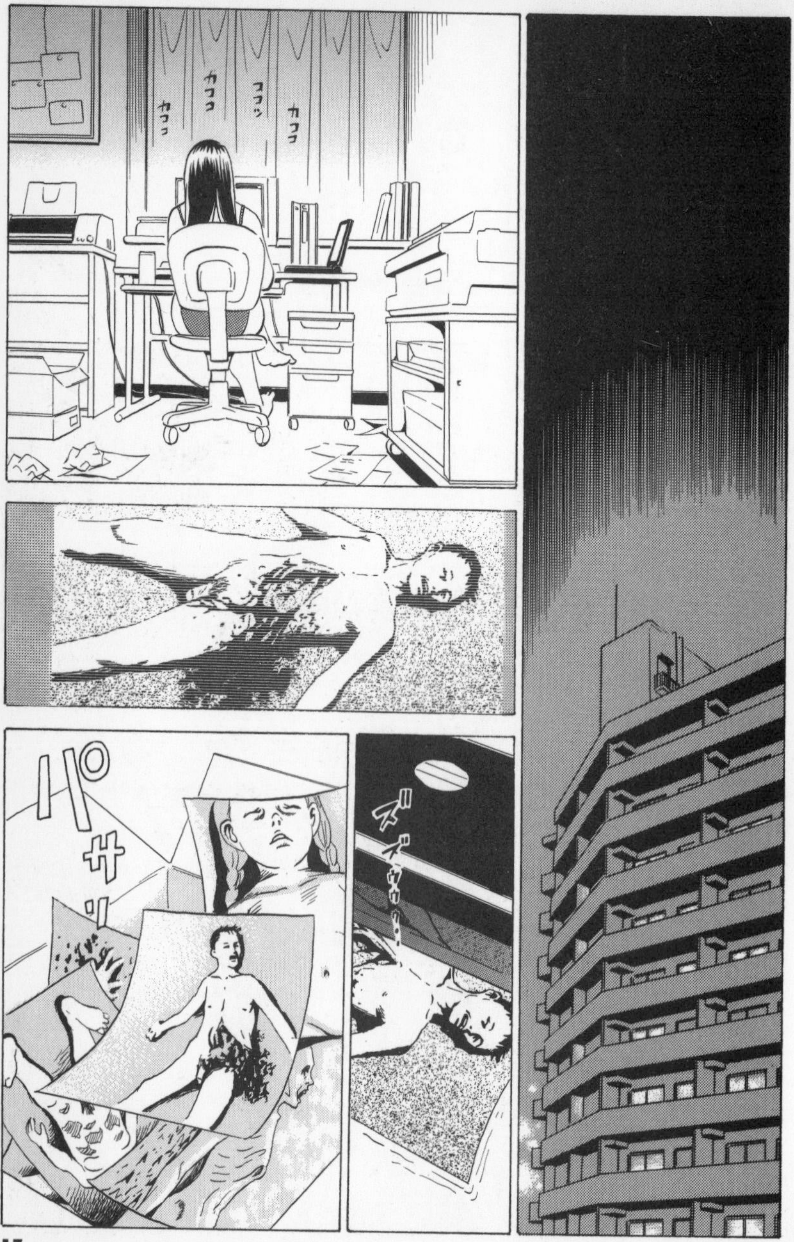
カココ
ココッ
カココ
カココ
ズズウウ…
パサッ

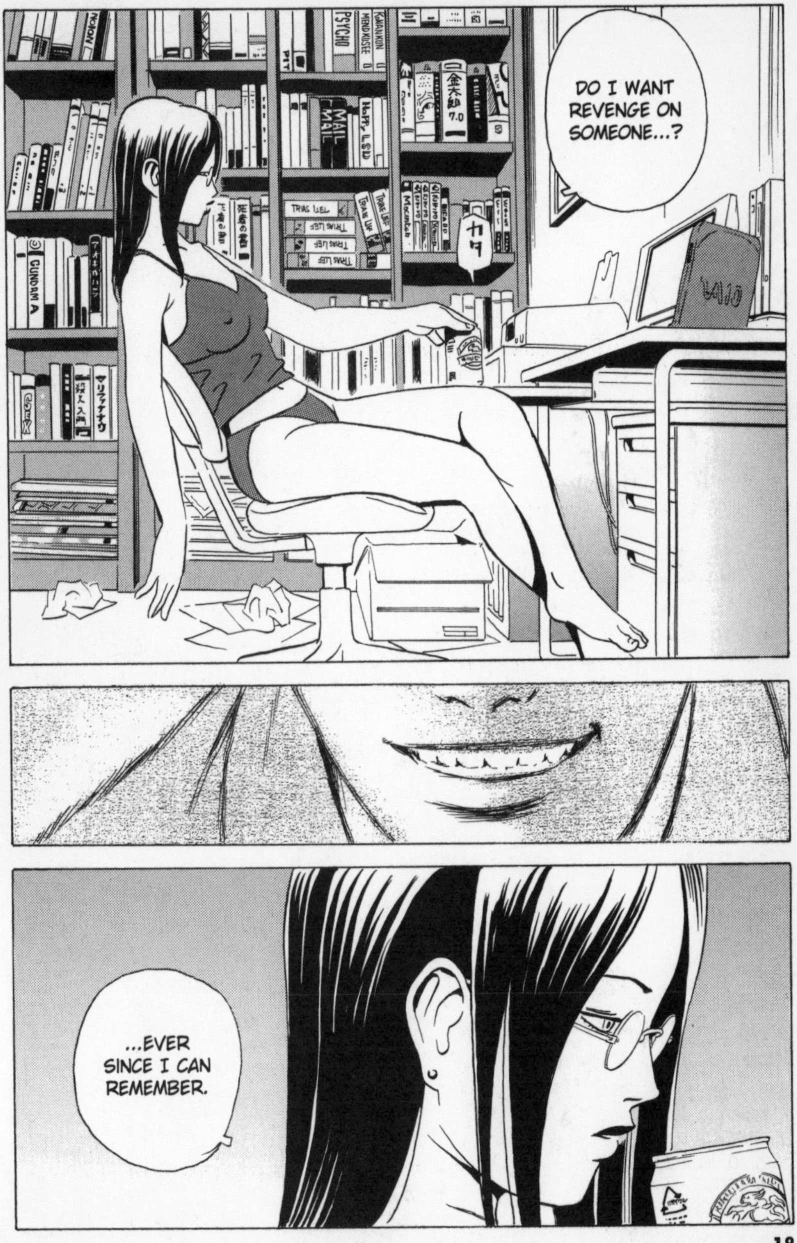
DO I WANT REVENGE ON SOMEONE...?
カタ
...EVER SINCE I CAN REMEMBER.

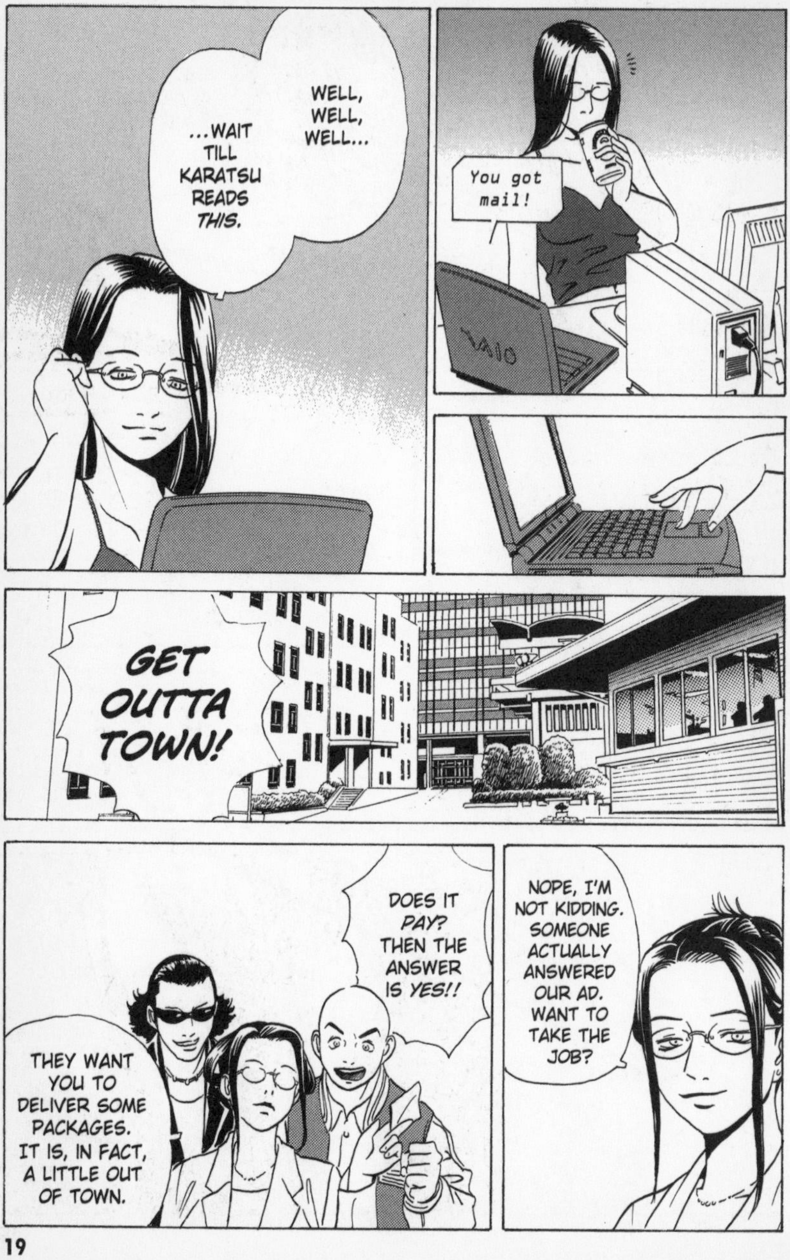
You got mail!
WELL, WELL, WELL...
...WAIT TILL KARATSU READS *THIS.*
GET OUTTA TOWN!
NOPE, I'M NOT KIDDING. SOMEONE ACTUALLY ANSWERED OUR AD. WANT TO TAKE THE JOB?
DOES IT *PAY?* THEN THE ANSWER IS *YES!!*
THEY WANT YOU TO DELIVER SOME PACKAGES. IT IS, IN FACT, A LITTLE OUT OF TOWN.

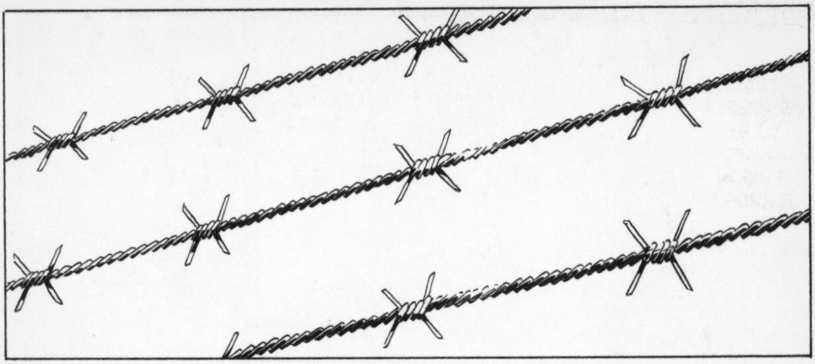

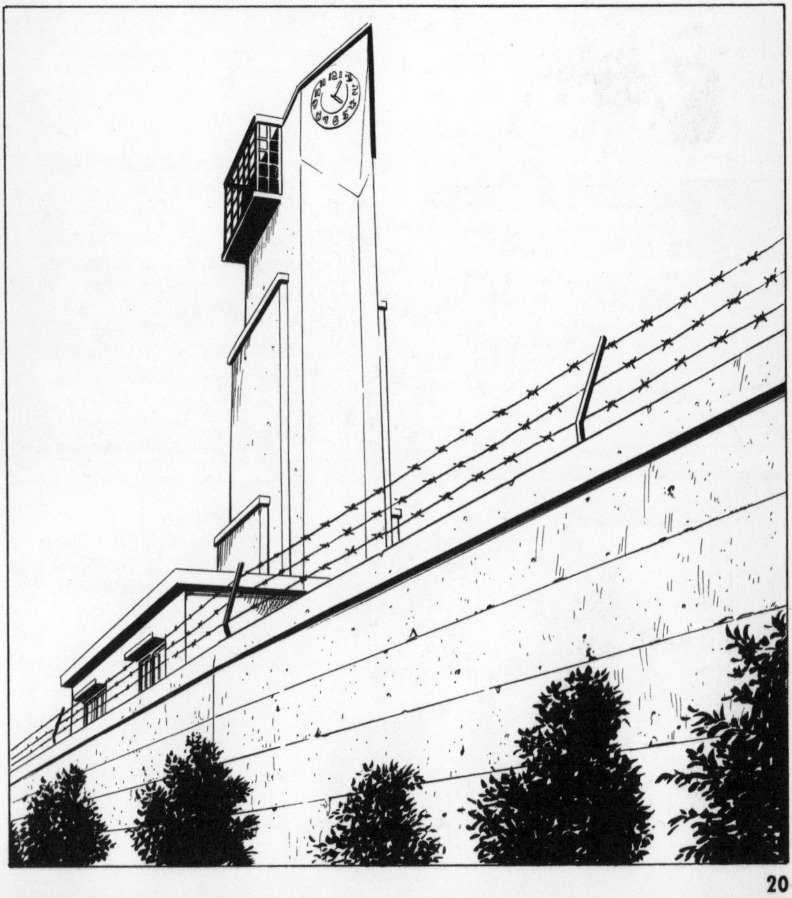

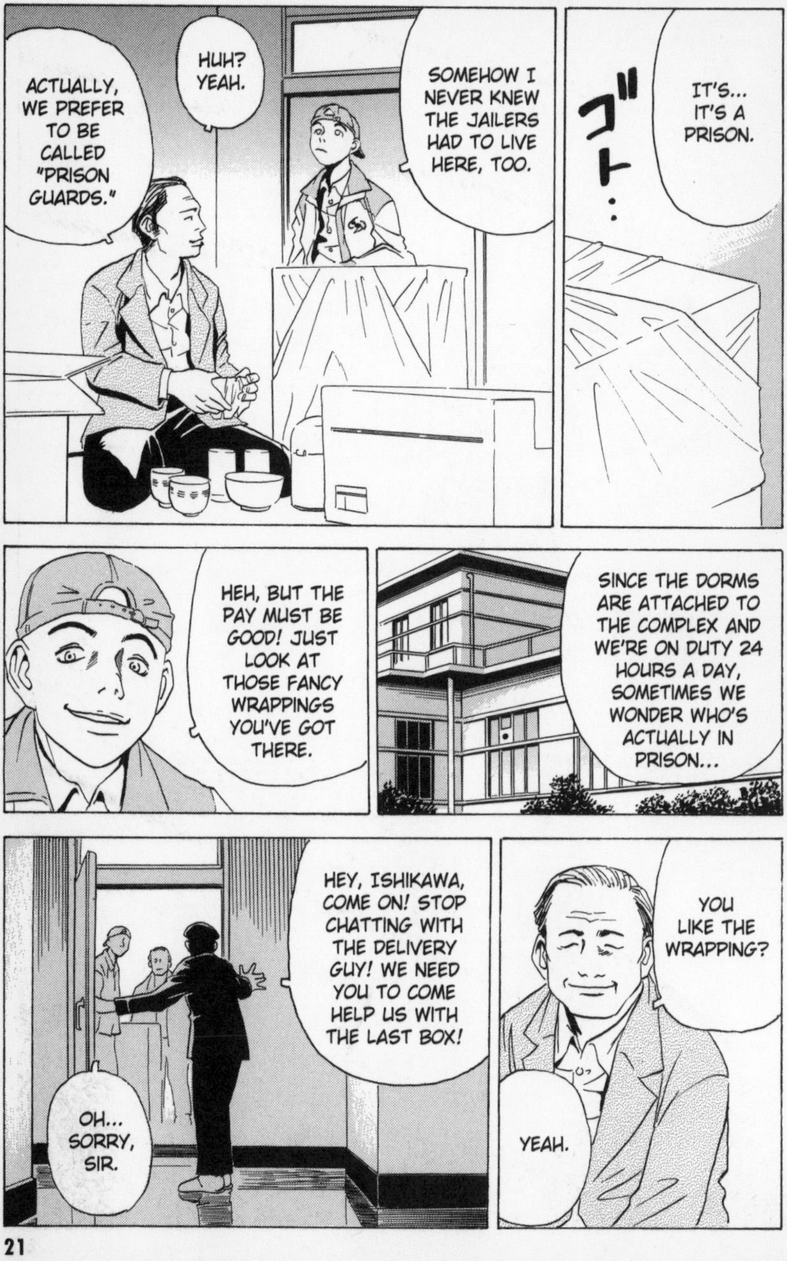
IT'S... IT'S A PRISON.
ゴト‥
SOMEHOW I NEVER KNEW THE JAILERS HAD TO LIVE HERE, TOO.
HUH? YEAH.
ACTUALLY, WE PREFER TO BE CALLED "PRISON GUARDS."
SINCE THE DORMS ARE ATTACHED TO THE COMPLEX AND WE'RE ON DUTY 24 HOURS A DAY, SOMETIMES WE WONDER WHO'S ACTUALLY IN PRISON...
HEH, BUT THE PAY MUST BE GOOD! JUST LOOK AT THOSE FANCY WRAPPINGS YOU'VE GOT THERE.
YOU LIKE THE WRAPPING?
YEAH.
HEY, ISHIKAWA, COME ON! STOP CHATTING WITH THE DELIVERY GUY! WE NEED YOU TO COME HELP US WITH THE LAST BOX!
OH... SORRY, SIR.

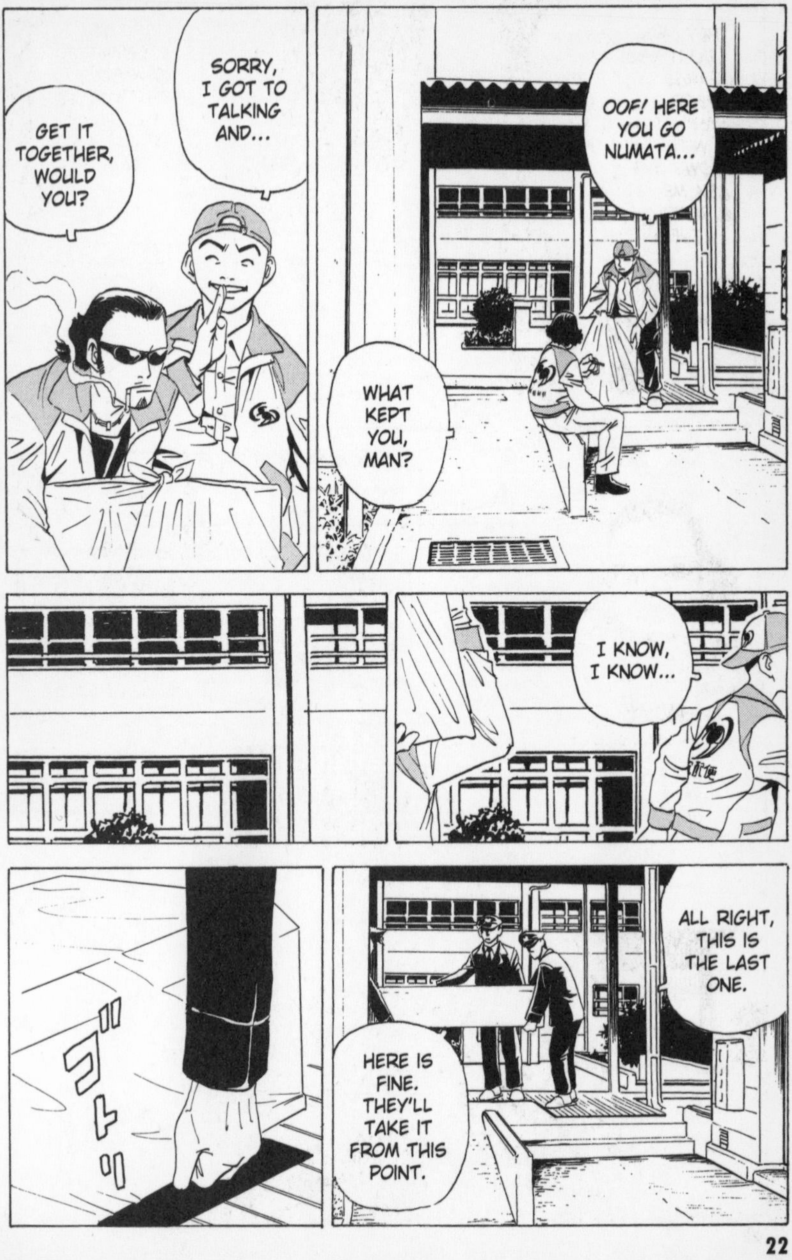
OOF! HERE YOU GO NUMATA...
WHAT KEPT YOU, MAN?
SORRY, I GOT TO TALKING AND...
GET IT TOGETHER, WOULD YOU?
I KNOW, I KNOW...
ALL RIGHT, THIS IS THE LAST ONE.
HERE IS FINE. THEY'LL TAKE IT FROM THIS POINT.
ゴトッ

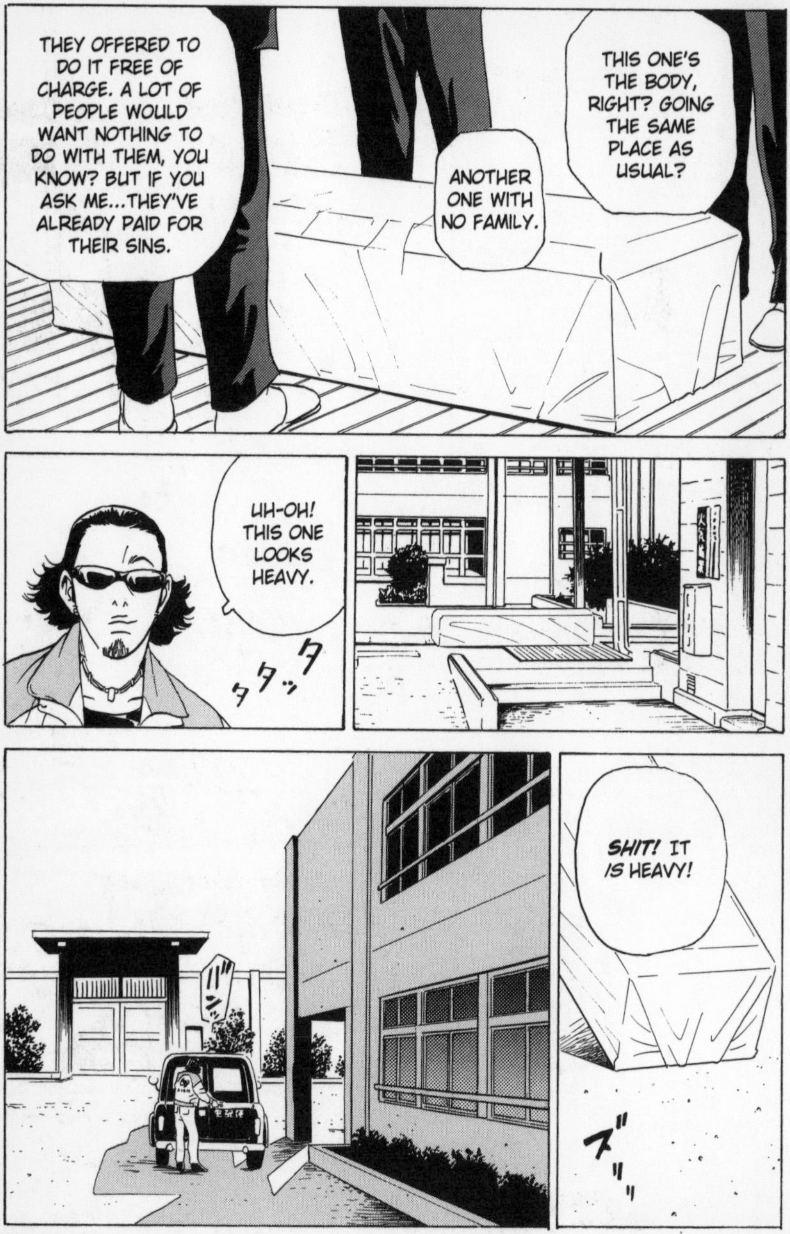
THIS ONE'S THE BODY, RIGHT? GOING THE SAME PLACE AS USUAL?
ANOTHER ONE WITH NO FAMILY.
THEY OFFERED TO DO IT FREE OF CHARGE. A LOT OF PEOPLE WOULD WANT NOTHING TO DO WITH THEM, YOU KNOW? BUT IF YOU ASK ME...THEY'VE ALREADY PAID FOR THEIR SINS.
UH-OH! THIS ONE LOOKS HEAVY.
タタッタ
SHIT! IT *IS* HEAVY!
ズリッ
バンッ

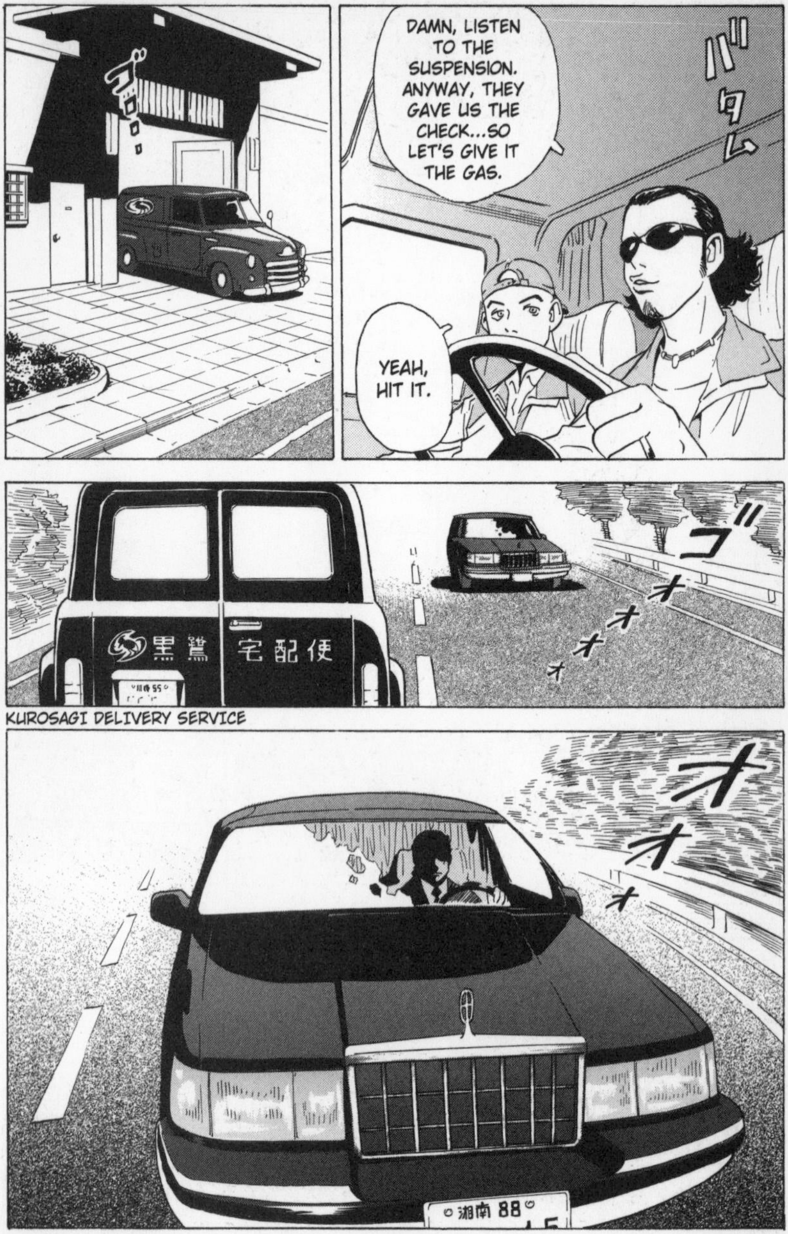
バタム
DAMN, LISTEN TO THE SUSPENSION. ANYWAY, THEY GAVE US THE CHECK...SO LET'S GIVE IT THE GAS.
YEAH, HIT IT.
黒鷺 宅配便
湘南 88

KUROSAGI DELIVERY SERVICE

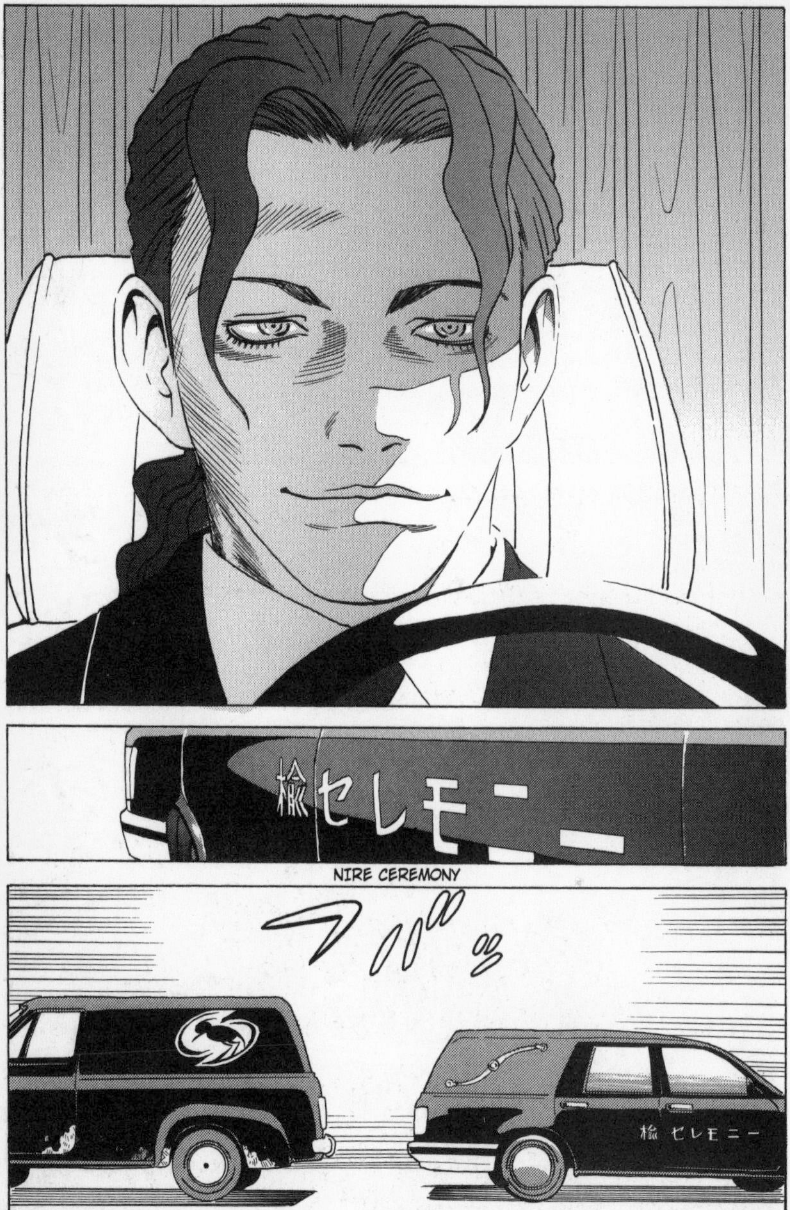
楡 セレモニー
NIRE CEREMONY
フバッ
楡 セレモニー

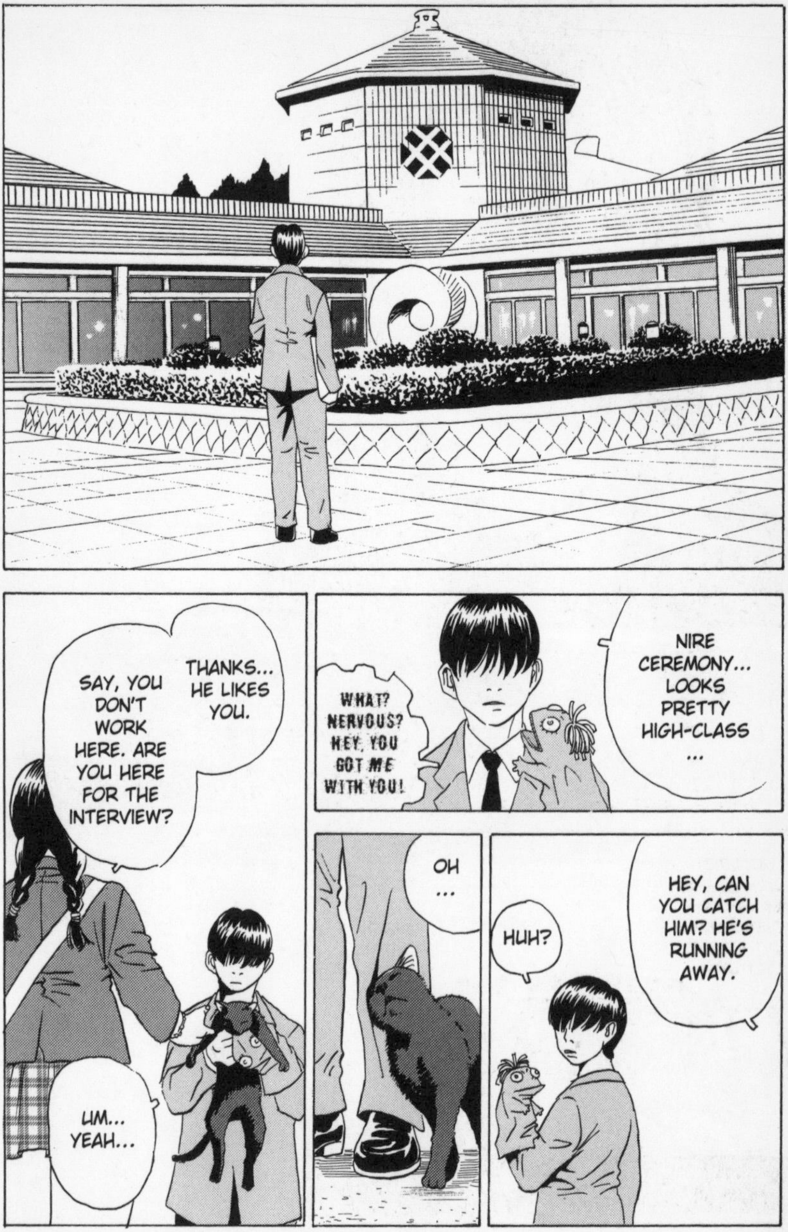
NIRE CEREMONY... LOOKS PRETTY HIGH-CLASS ...
WHAT? NERVOUS? HEY, YOU GOT *ME* WITH YOU!
HEY, CAN YOU CATCH HIM? HE'S RUNNING AWAY.
HUH?
OH ...
THANKS... HE LIKES YOU.
SAY, YOU DON'T WORK HERE. ARE YOU HERE FOR THE INTERVIEW?
UM... YEAH...

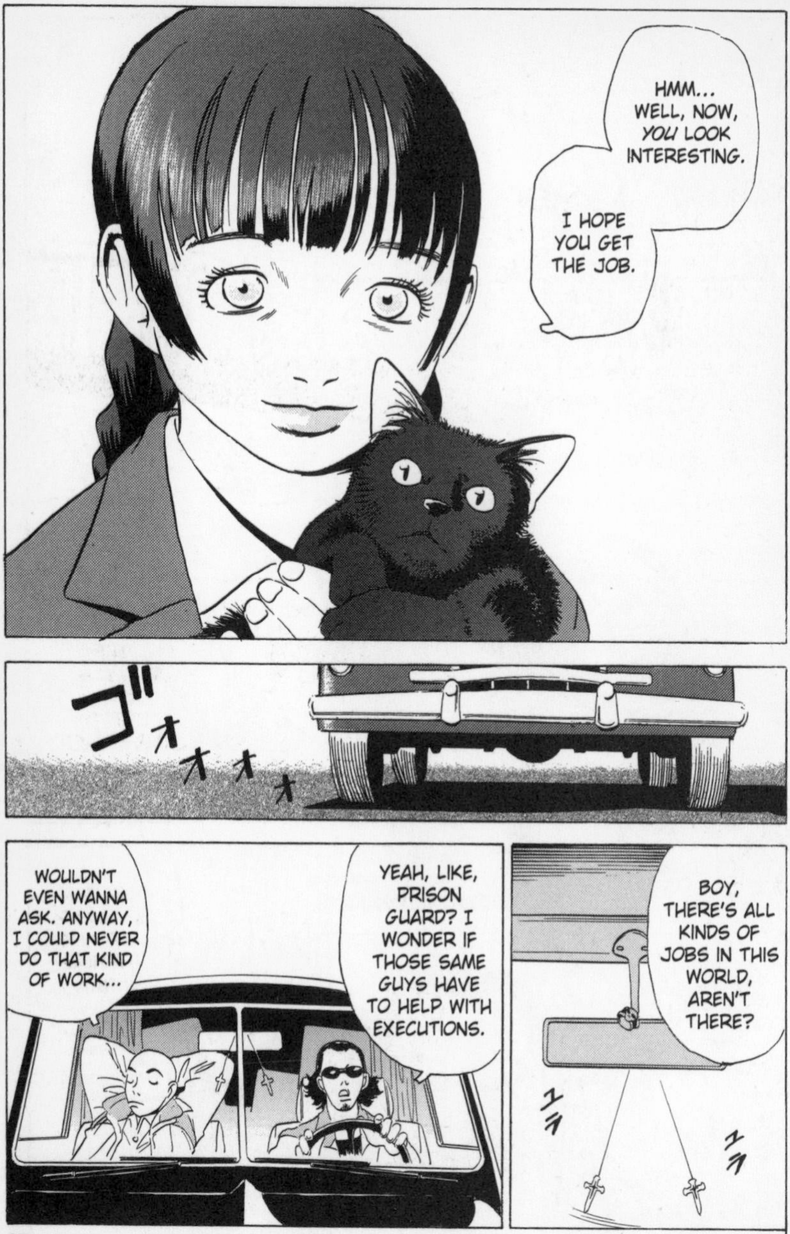
HMM... WELL, NOW, *YOU* LOOK INTERESTING.
I HOPE YOU GET THE JOB.
ゴォォォォ
BOY, THERE'S ALL KINDS OF JOBS IN THIS WORLD, AREN'T THERE?
ユラ
ユラ
YEAH, LIKE, PRISON GUARD? I WONDER IF THOSE SAME GUYS HAVE TO HELP WITH EXECUTIONS.
WOULDN'T EVEN WANNA ASK. ANYWAY, I COULD NEVER DO THAT KIND OF WORK...

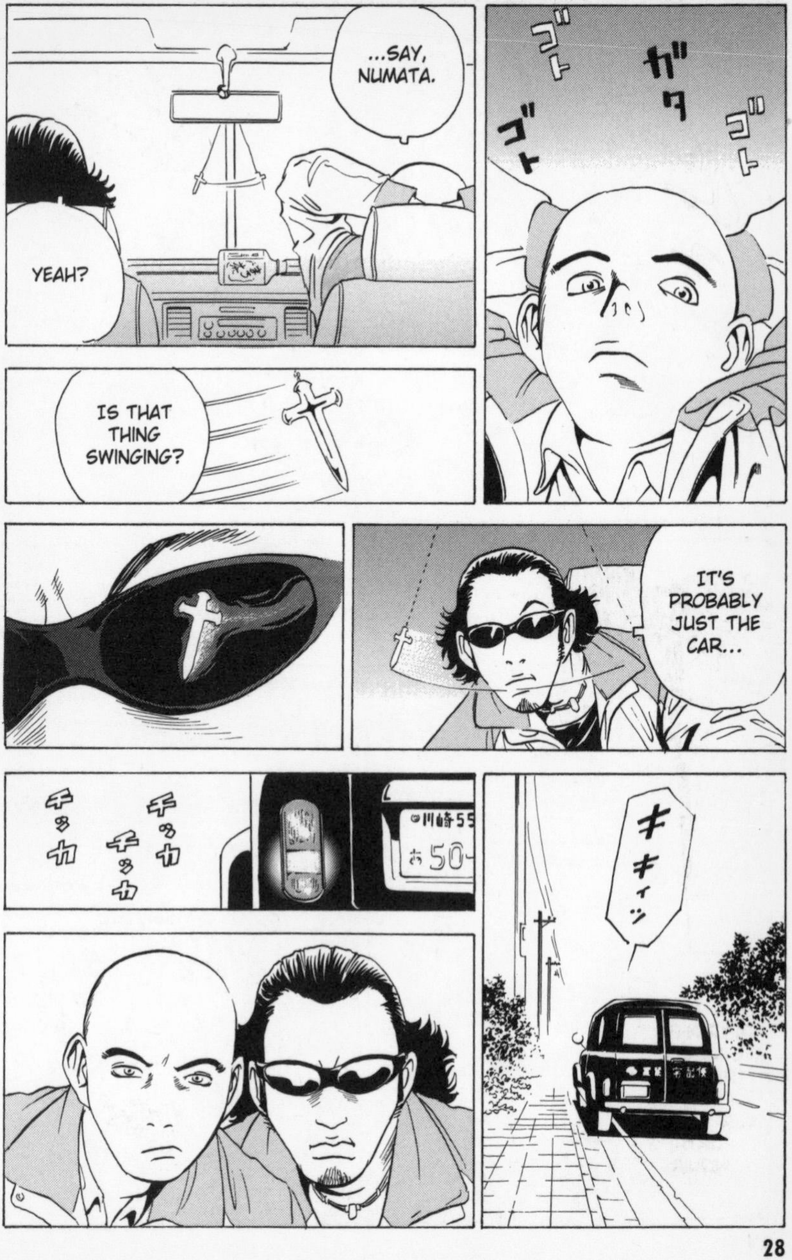
ゴト
ガタ
ゴト
ゴト
...SAY, NUMATA.
YEAH?
IS THAT THING SWINGING?
IT'S PROBABLY JUST THE CAR...
キキィッ
チッカ
チッカ
チッカ

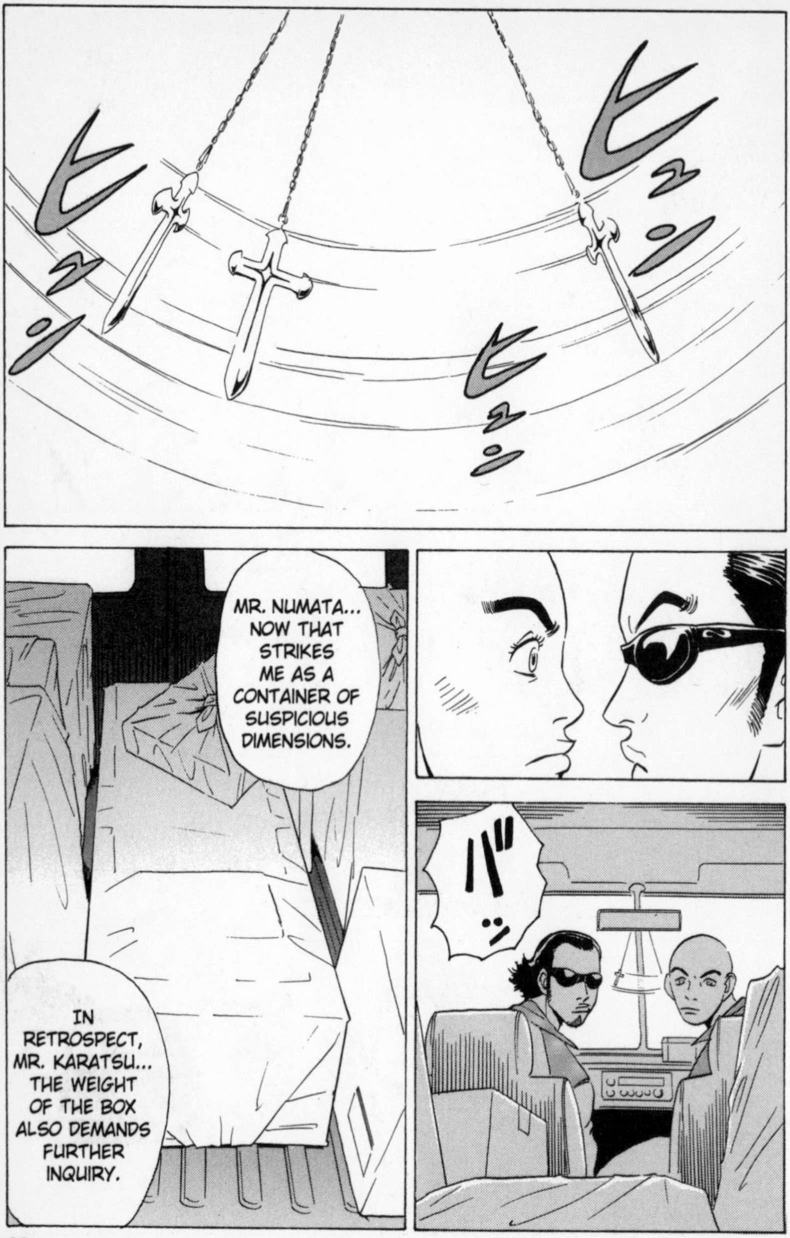
ヒュン
ヒュン
ヒュン
バッ
MR. NUMATA... NOW THAT STRIKES ME AS A CONTAINER OF SUSPICIOUS DIMENSIONS.
IN RETROSPECT, MR. KARATSU... THE WEIGHT OF THE BOX ALSO DEMANDS FURTHER INQUIRY.

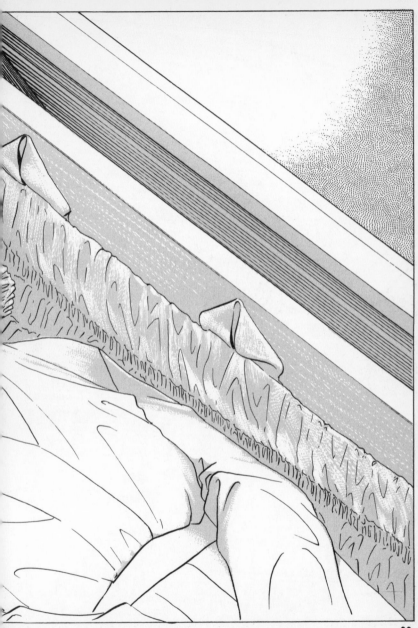

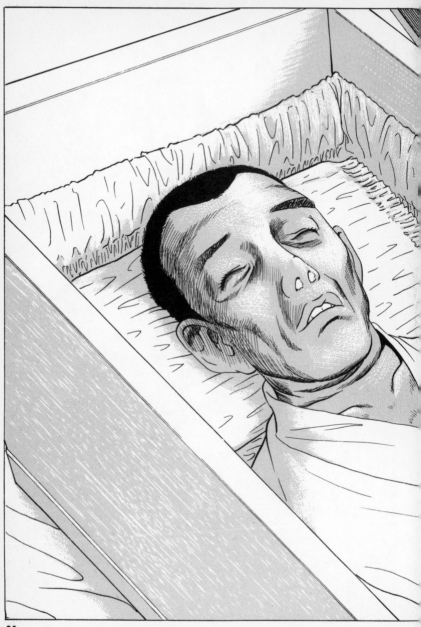

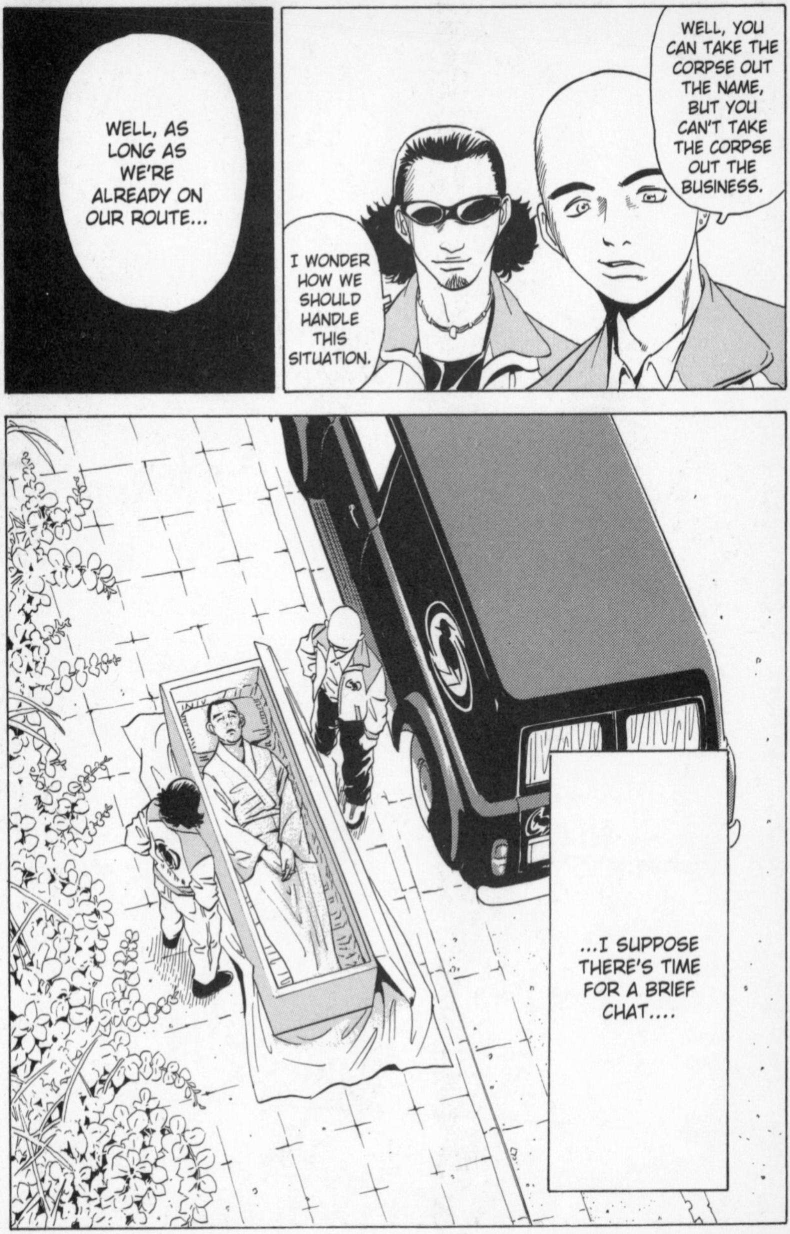
WELL, YOU CAN TAKE THE CORPSE OUT THE NAME, BUT YOU CAN'T TAKE THE CORPSE OUT THE BUSINESS.
I WONDER HOW WE SHOULD HANDLE THIS SITUATION.
WELL, AS LONG AS WE'RE ALREADY ON OUR ROUTE...
...I SUPPOSE THERE'S TIME FOR A BRIEF CHAT....

1st delivery: dangerous duo—the end

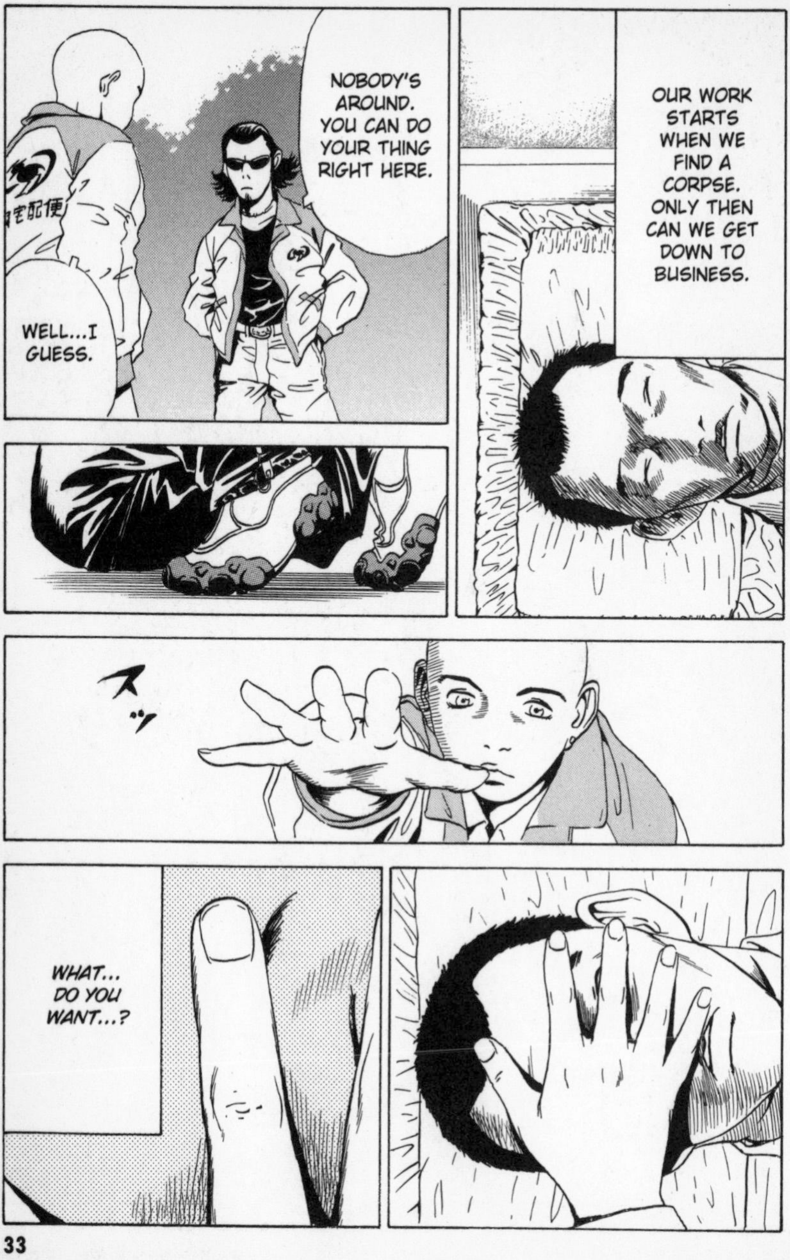
OUR WORK STARTS WHEN WE FIND A CORPSE. ONLY THEN CAN WE GET DOWN TO BUSINESS.
NOBODY'S AROUND. YOU CAN DO YOUR THING RIGHT HERE.
WELL...I GUESS.
スッ
WHAT... DO YOU WANT...?

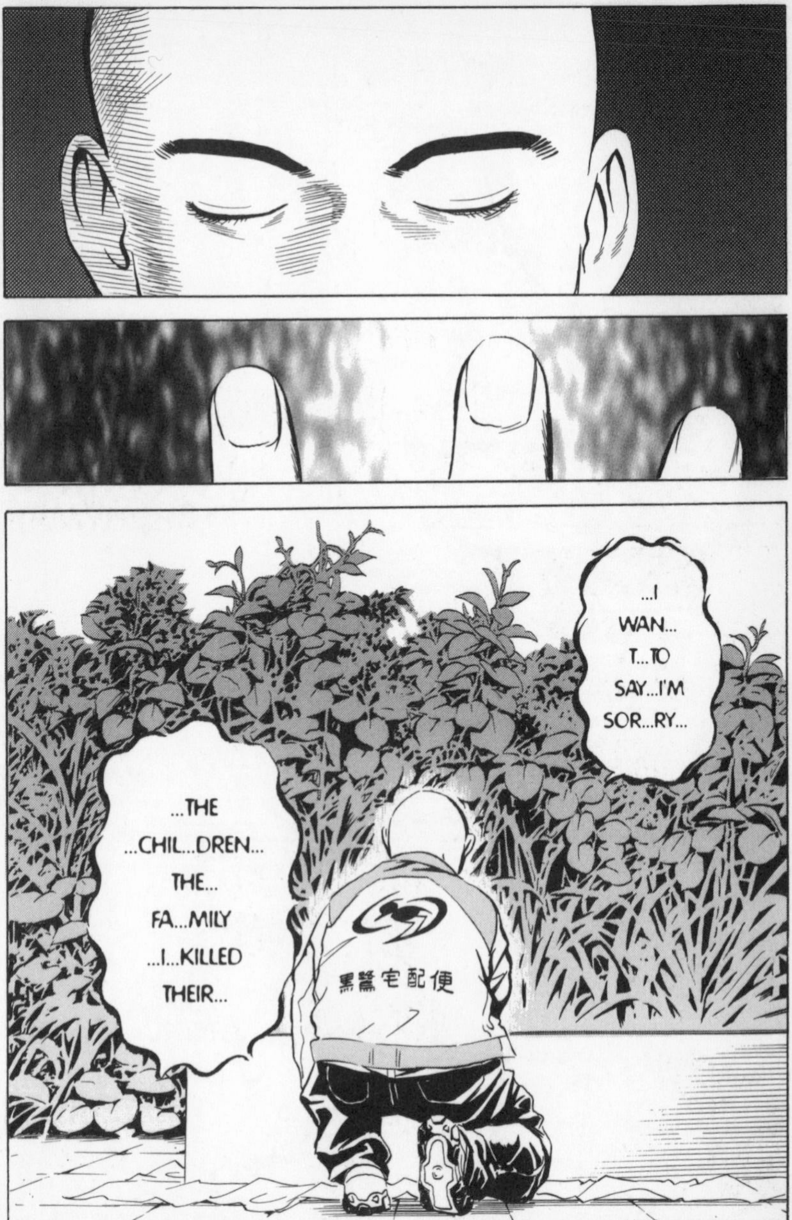
...I WAN... T...TO SAY...I'M SOR...RY...
...THE ...CHIL...DREN... THE... FA...MILY ...I...KILLED THEIR...
黒鷺宅配便

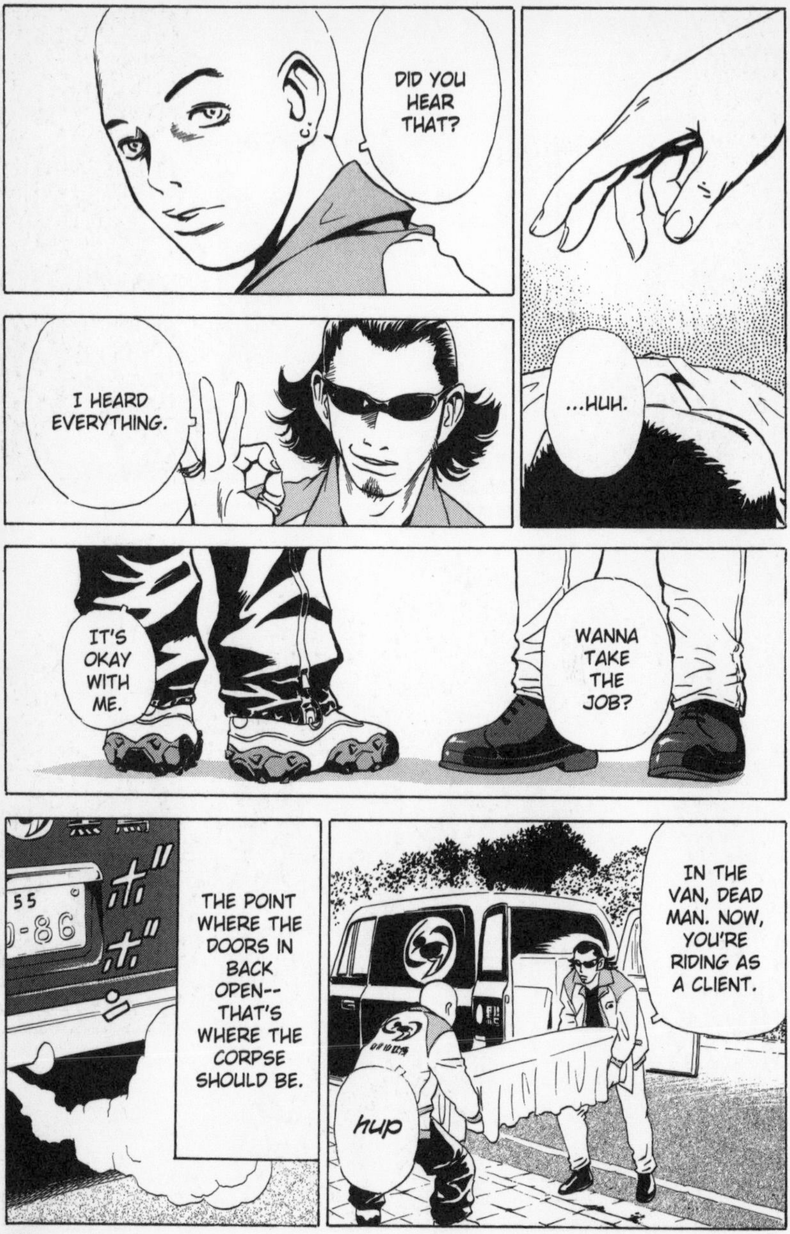
...HUH.
DID YOU HEAR THAT?
I HEARD EVERYTHING.
WANNA TAKE THE JOB?
IT'S OKAY WITH ME.
IN THE VAN, DEAD MAN. NOW, YOU'RE RIDING AS A CLIENT.
hup
THE POINT WHERE THE DOORS IN BACK OPEN-- THAT'S WHERE THE CORPSE SHOULD BE.

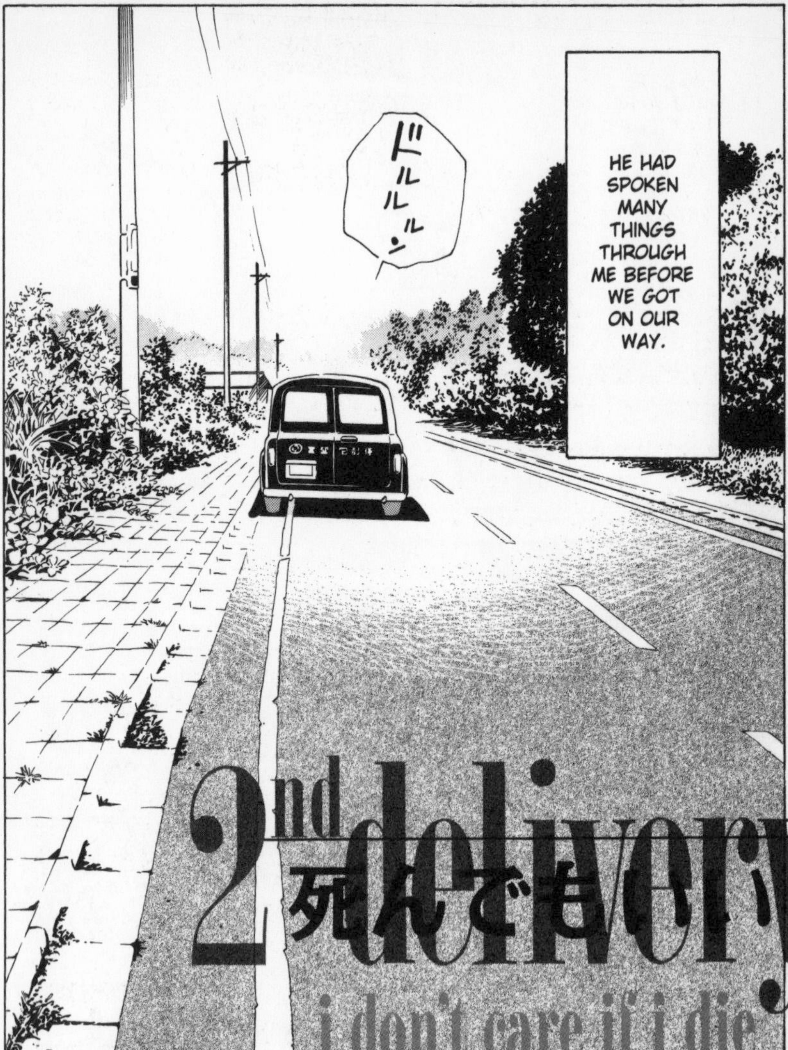
HE HAD SPOKEN MANY THINGS THROUGH ME BEFORE WE GOT ON OUR WAY.
ドルルルン
2nd delivery
死んでもいい
i don't care if i die

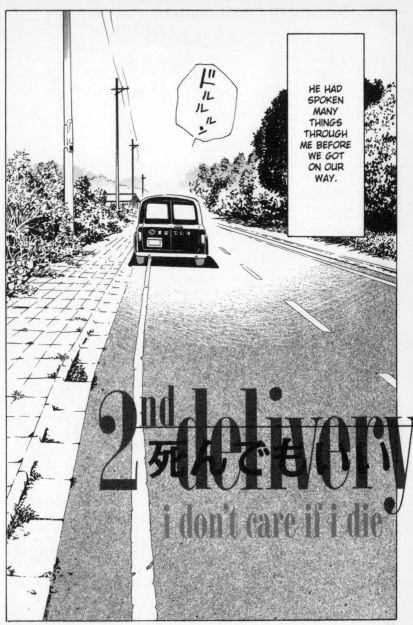

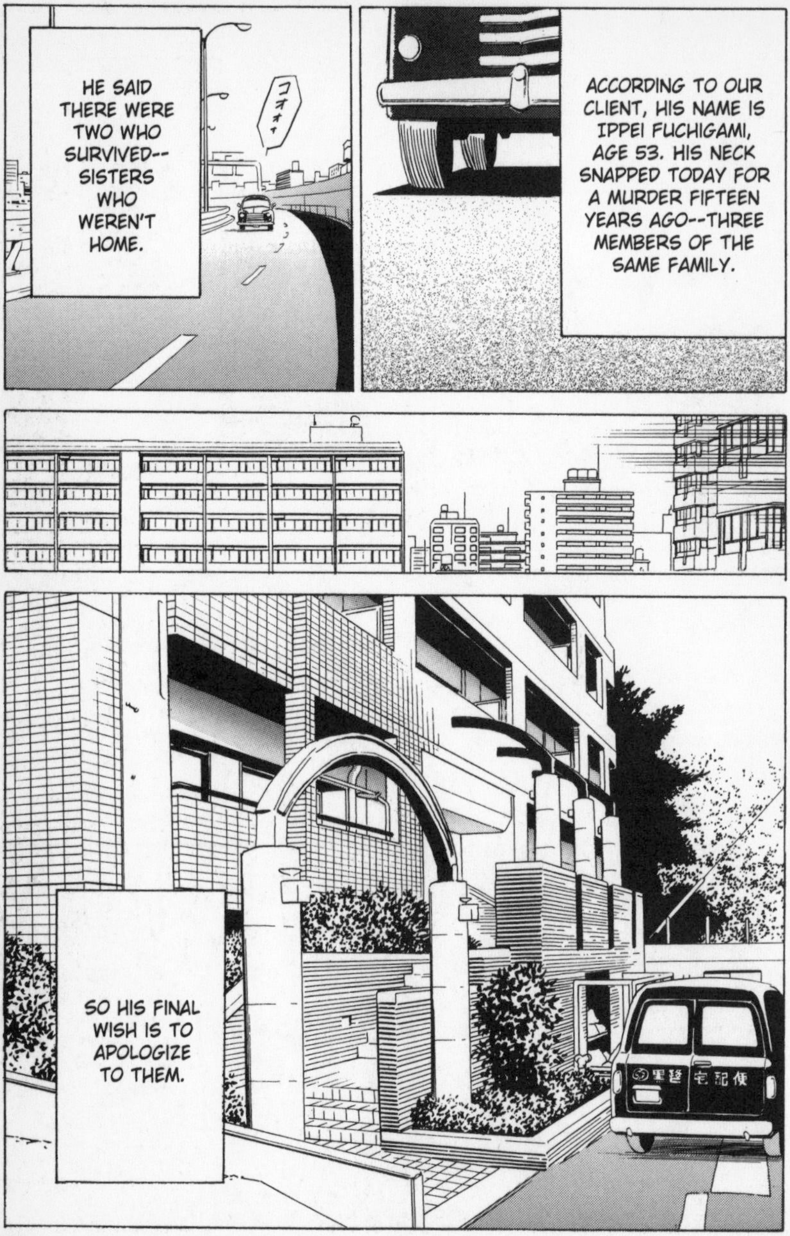
ACCORDING TO OUR CLIENT, HIS NAME IS IPPEI FUCHIGAMI, AGE 53. HIS NECK SNAPPED TODAY FOR A MURDER FIFTEEN YEARS AGO--THREE MEMBERS OF THE SAME FAMILY.
HE SAID THERE WERE TWO WHO SURVIVED--SISTERS WHO WEREN'T HOME.
コオォ
SO HIS FINAL WISH IS TO APOLOGIZE TO THEM.

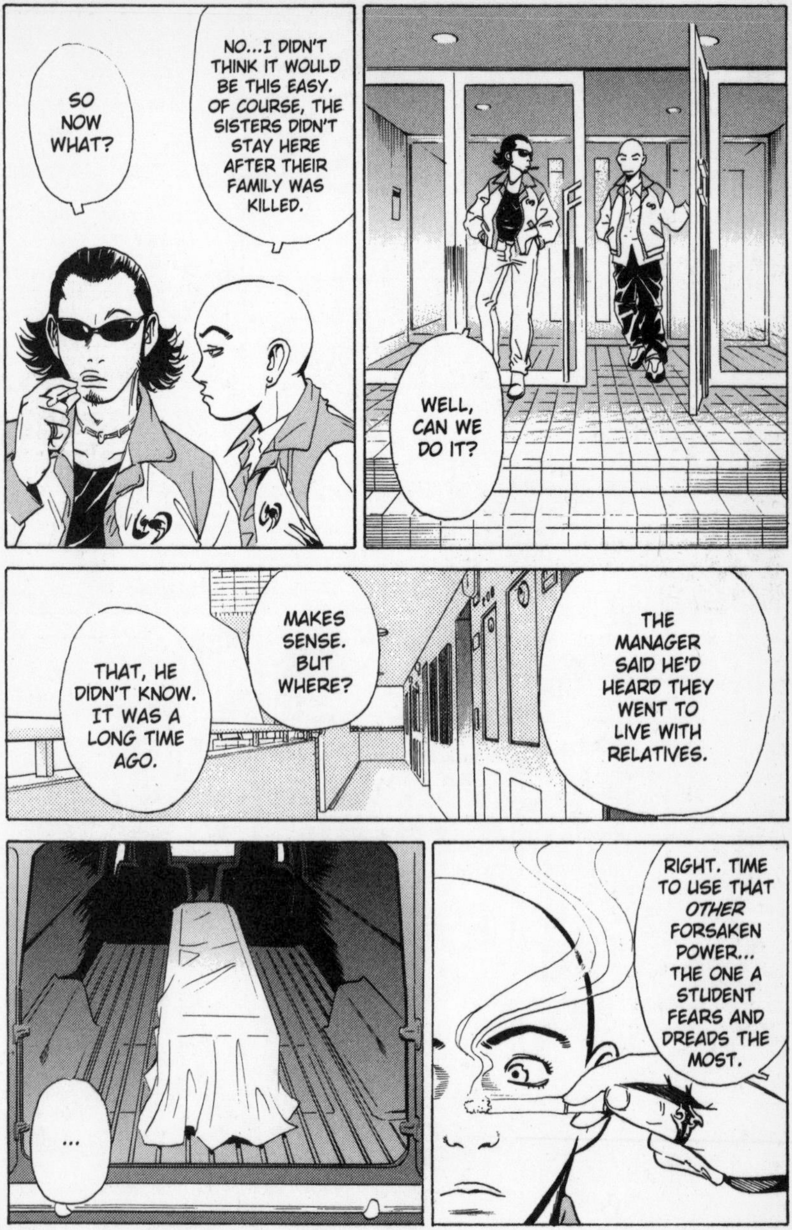

WELL, CAN WE DO IT?
NO...I DIDN'T THINK IT WOULD BE THIS EASY. OF COURSE, THE SISTERS DIDN'T STAY HERE AFTER THEIR FAMILY WAS KILLED.
SO NOW WHAT?
THE MANAGER SAID HE'D HEARD THEY WENT TO LIVE WITH RELATIVES.
MAKES SENSE. BUT WHERE?
THAT, HE DIDN'T KNOW. IT WAS A LONG TIME AGO.
RIGHT. TIME TO USE THAT *OTHER* FORSAKEN POWER... THE ONE A STUDENT FEARS AND DREADS THE MOST.
...

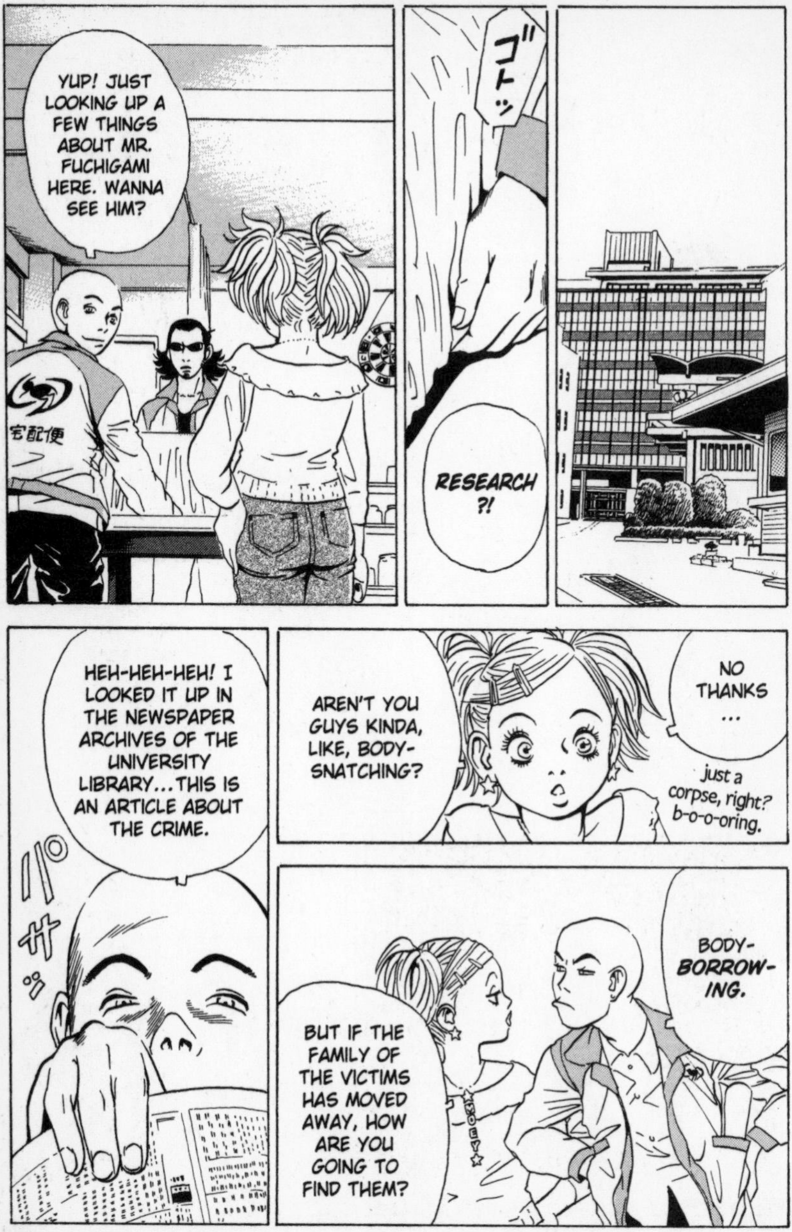
ゴトッ
RESEARCH ?!
YUP! JUST LOOKING UP A FEW THINGS ABOUT MR. FUCHIGAMI HERE. WANNA SEE HIM?
NO THANKS ...
just a corpse, right? b-o-o-oring.
AREN'T YOU GUYS KINDA, LIKE, BODY-SNATCHING?
BODY-BORROW-ING.
BUT IF THE FAMILY OF THE VICTIMS HAS MOVED AWAY, HOW ARE YOU GOING TO FIND THEM?
HEH-HEH-HEH! I LOOKED IT UP IN THE NEWSPAPER ARCHIVES OF THE UNIVERSITY LIBRARY...THIS IS AN ARTICLE ABOUT THE CRIME.
パサッ

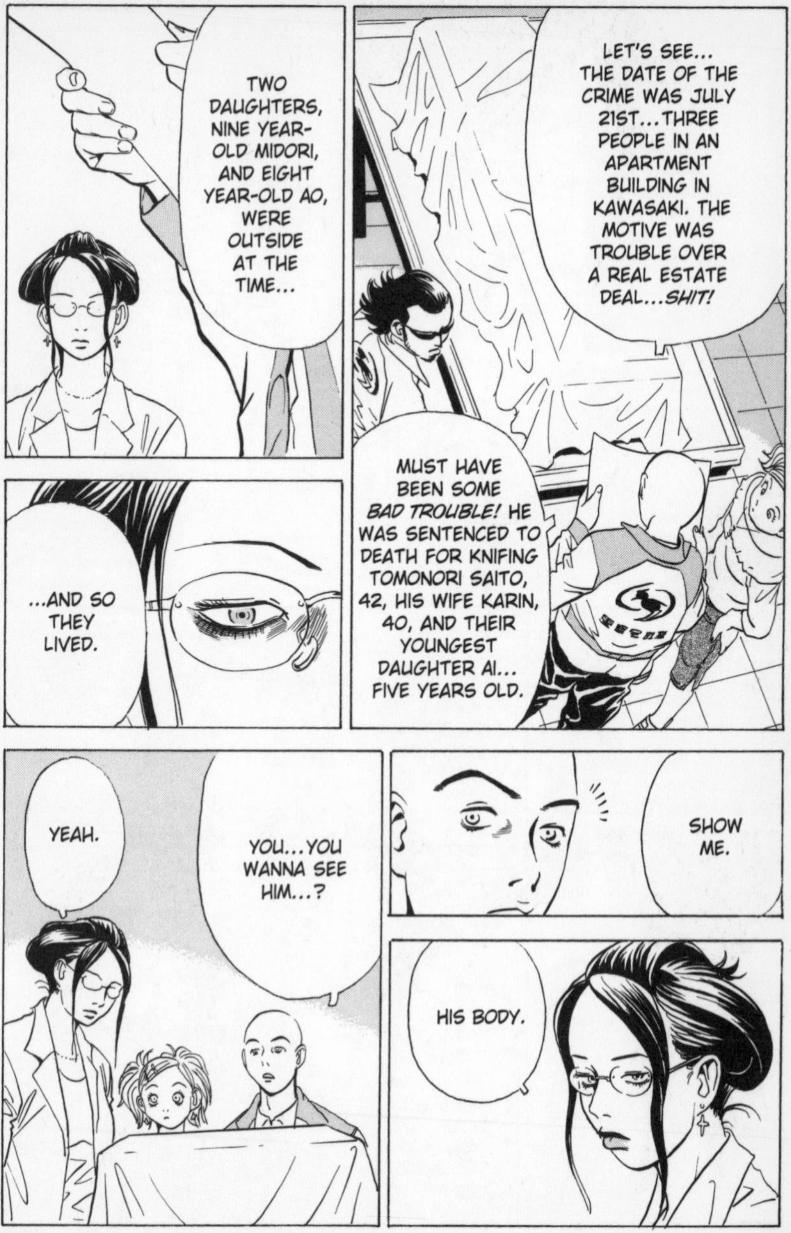
LET'S SEE... THE DATE OF THE CRIME WAS JULY 21ST... THREE PEOPLE IN AN APARTMENT BUILDING IN KAWASAKI. THE MOTIVE WAS TROUBLE OVER A REAL ESTATE DEAL... *SHIT!*
TWO DAUGHTERS, NINE YEAR-OLD MIDORI, AND EIGHT YEAR-OLD AO, WERE OUTSIDE AT THE TIME...
MUST HAVE BEEN SOME *BAD TROUBLE!* HE WAS SENTENCED TO DEATH FOR KNIFING TOMONORI SAITO, 42, HIS WIFE KARIN, 40, AND THEIR YOUNGEST DAUGHTER AI... FIVE YEARS OLD.
...AND SO THEY LIVED.
SHOW ME.
HIS BODY.
YOU... YOU WANNA SEE HIM...?
YEAH.

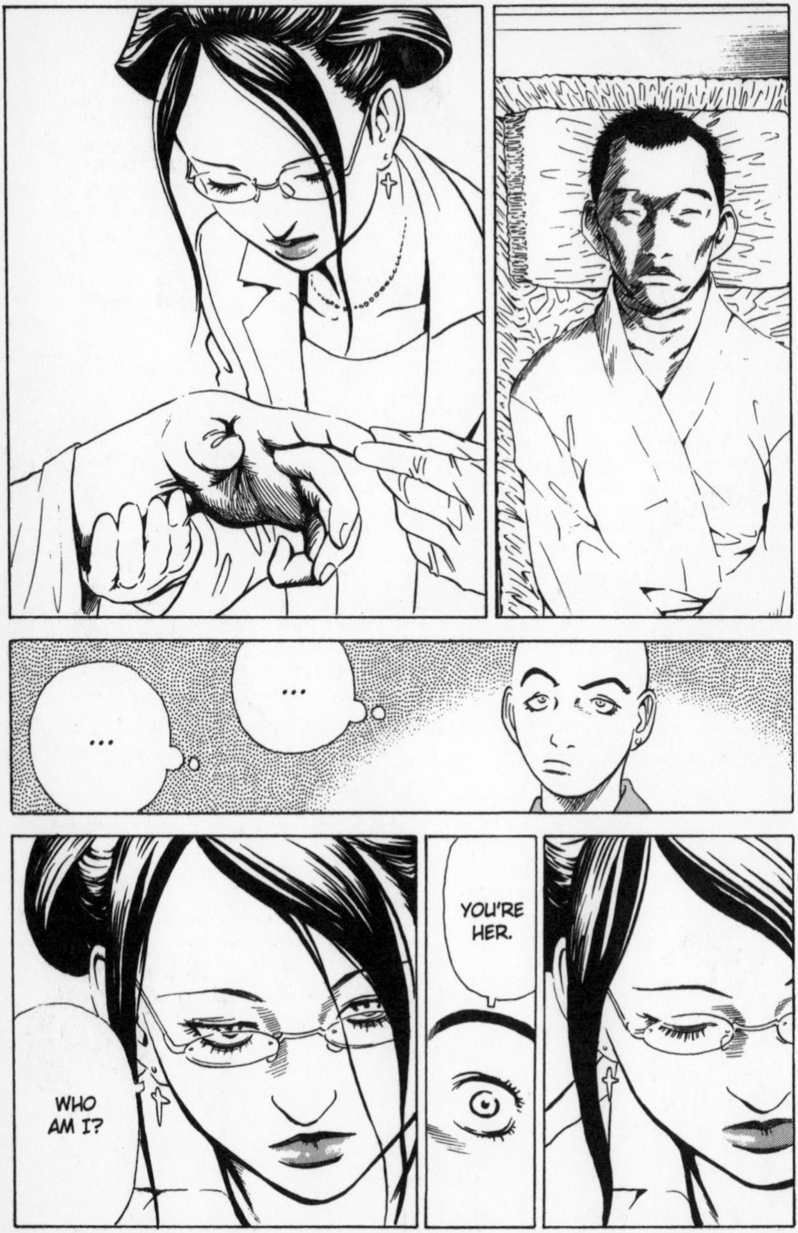
...
...
YOU'RE HER.
WHO AM I?

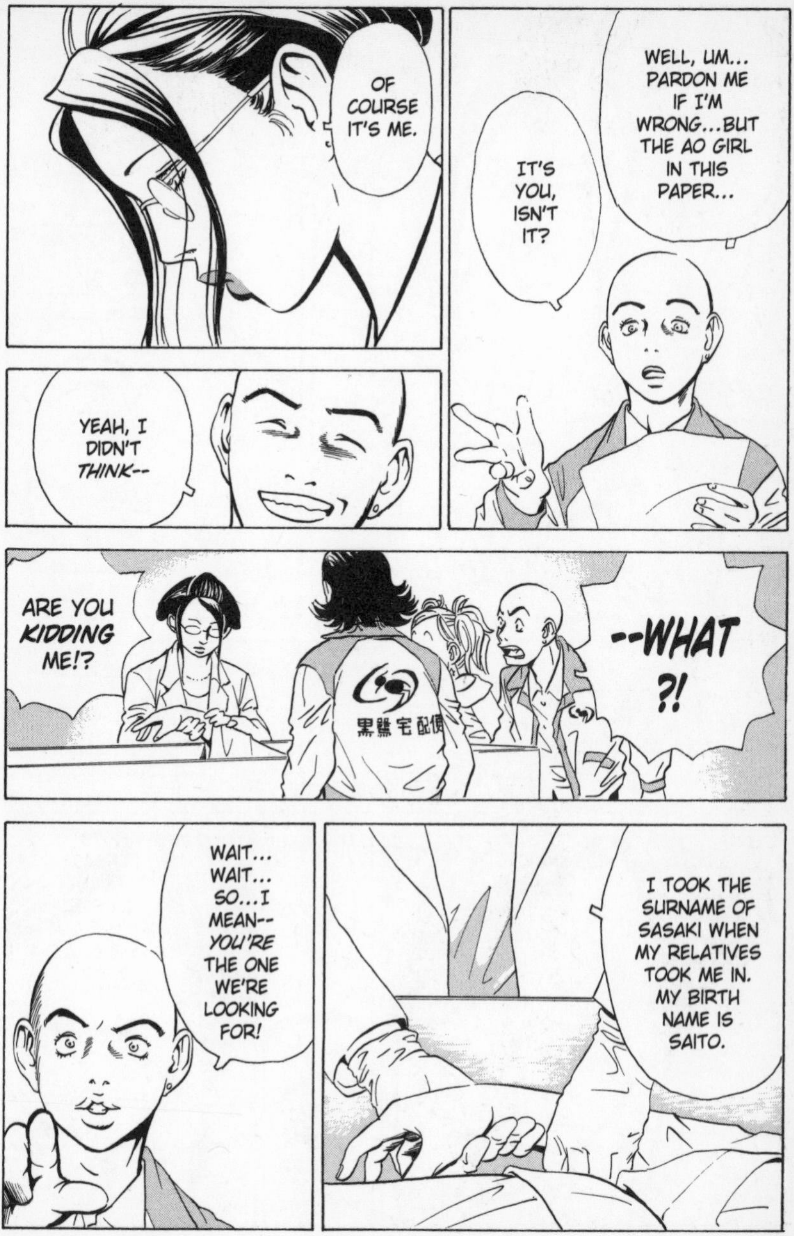
WELL, UM... PARDON ME IF I'M WRONG...BUT THE AO GIRL IN THIS PAPER...
IT'S YOU, ISN'T IT?
OF COURSE IT'S ME.
YEAH, I DIDN'T *THINK*--
--*WHAT* ?!
ARE YOU *KIDDING* ME!?
I TOOK THE SURNAME OF SASAKI WHEN MY RELATIVES TOOK ME IN. MY BIRTH NAME IS SAITO.
WAIT... WAIT... SO...I MEAN-- *YOU'RE* THE ONE WE'RE LOOKING FOR!

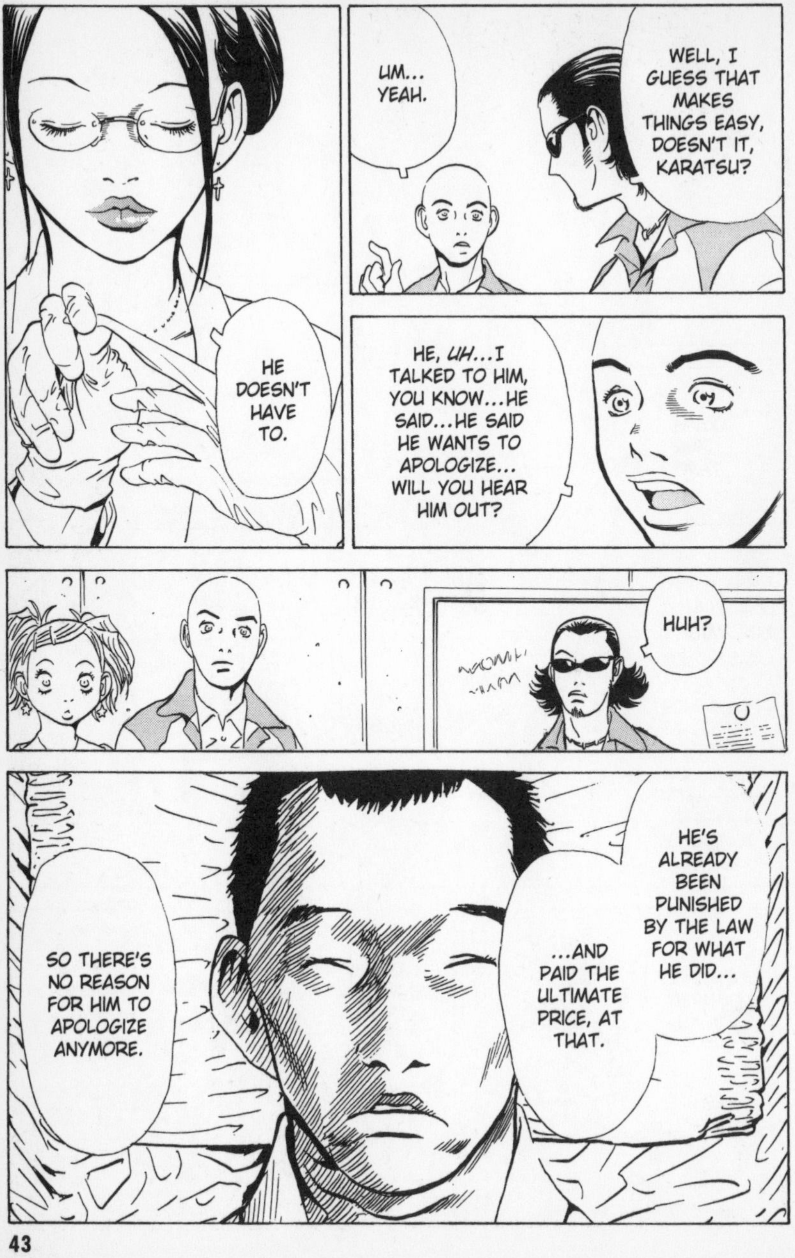
WELL, I GUESS THAT MAKES THINGS EASY, DOESN'T IT, KARATSU?
UM... YEAH.
HE, *UH*...I TALKED TO HIM, YOU KNOW...HE SAID...HE SAID HE WANTS TO APOLOGIZE... WILL YOU HEAR HIM OUT?
HE DOESN'T HAVE TO.
HUH?
HE'S ALREADY BEEN PUNISHED BY THE LAW FOR WHAT HE DID...
...AND PAID THE ULTIMATE PRICE, AT THAT.
SO THERE'S NO REASON FOR HIM TO APOLOGIZE ANYMORE.

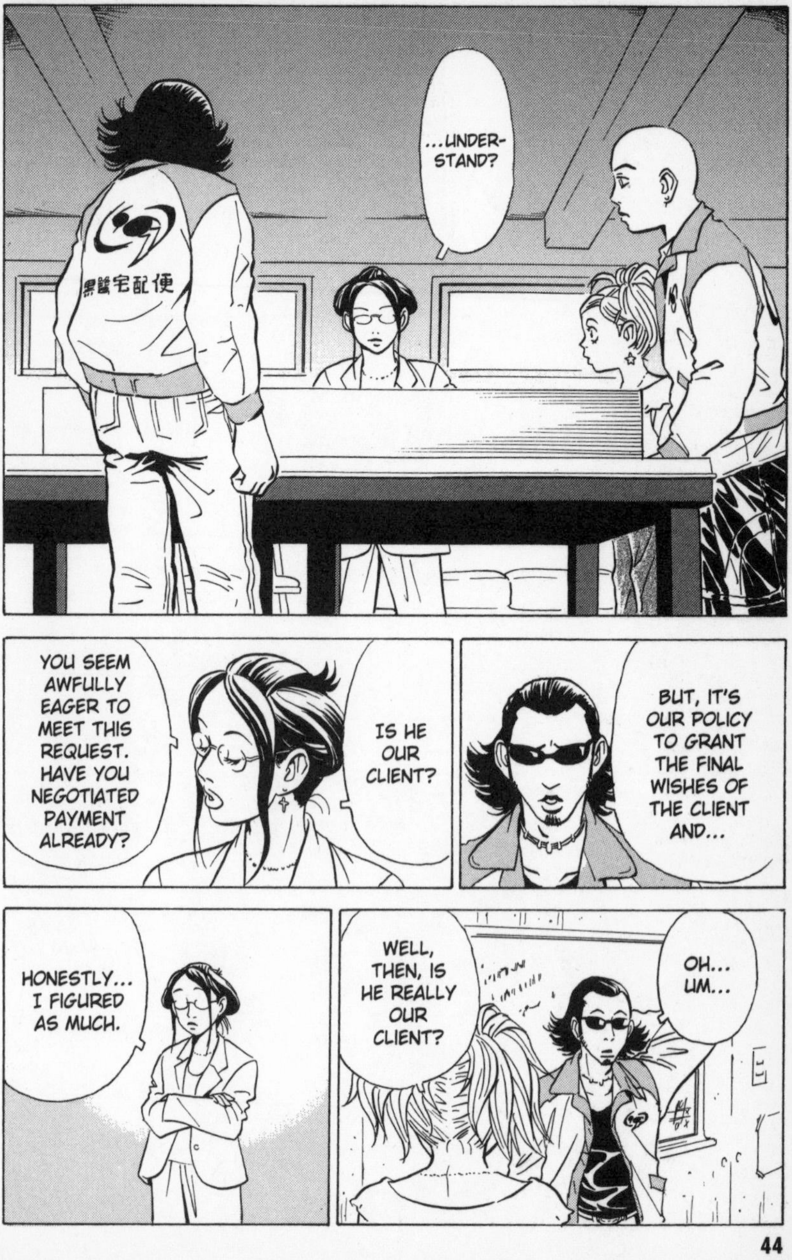
...UNDER-STAND?
黒鷺宅配便
BUT, IT'S OUR POLICY TO GRANT THE FINAL WISHES OF THE CLIENT AND...
YOU SEEM AWFULLY EAGER TO MEET THIS REQUEST. HAVE YOU NEGOTIATED PAYMENT ALREADY?
IS HE OUR CLIENT?
OH... UM...
WELL, THEN, IS HE REALLY OUR CLIENT?
HONESTLY... I FIGURED AS MUCH.

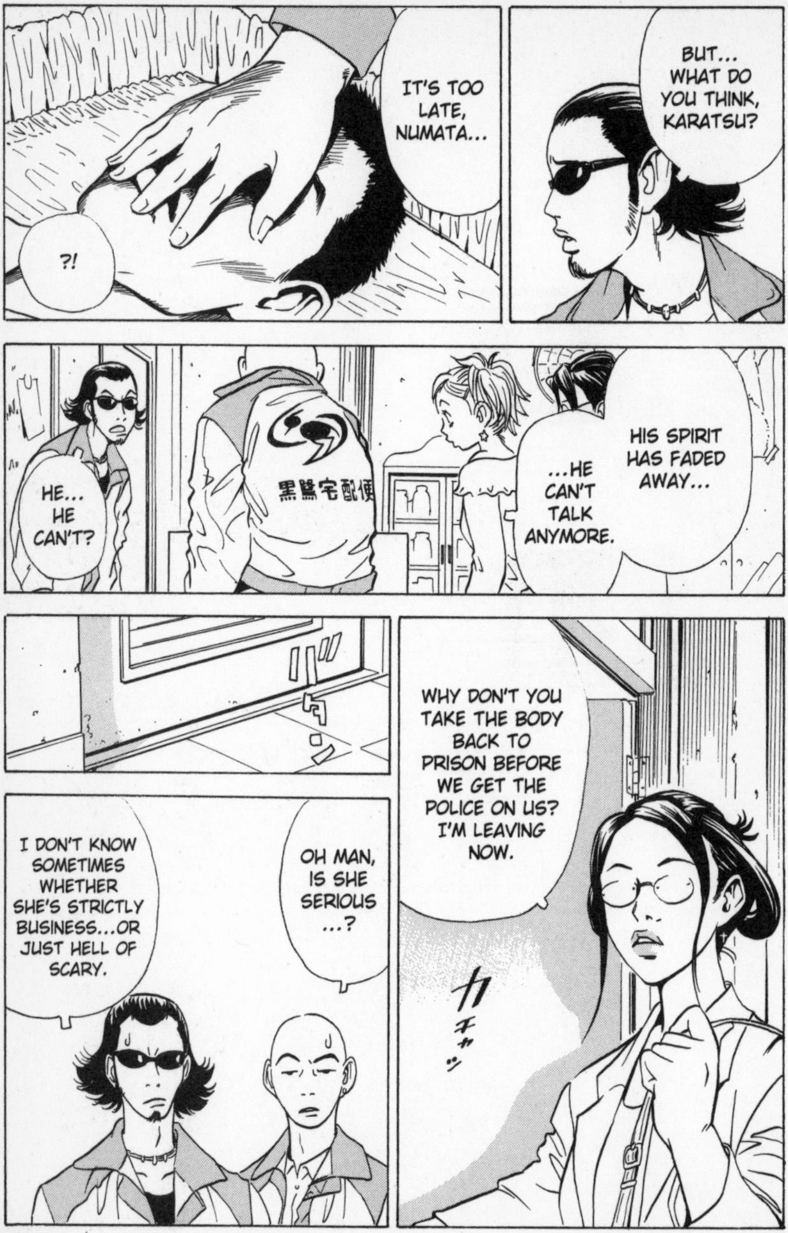
BUT... WHAT DO YOU THINK, KARATSU?
IT'S TOO LATE, NUMATA...
?!
HIS SPIRIT HAS FADED AWAY...
...HE CAN'T TALK ANYMORE.
黒鷺宅配便
HE... HE CAN'T?
WHY DON'T YOU TAKE THE BODY BACK TO PRISON BEFORE WE GET THE POLICE ON US? I'M LEAVING NOW.
カチャッ
OH MAN, IS SHE SERIOUS ...?
I DON'T KNOW SOMETIMES WHETHER SHE'S STRICTLY BUSINESS...OR JUST HELL OF SCARY.

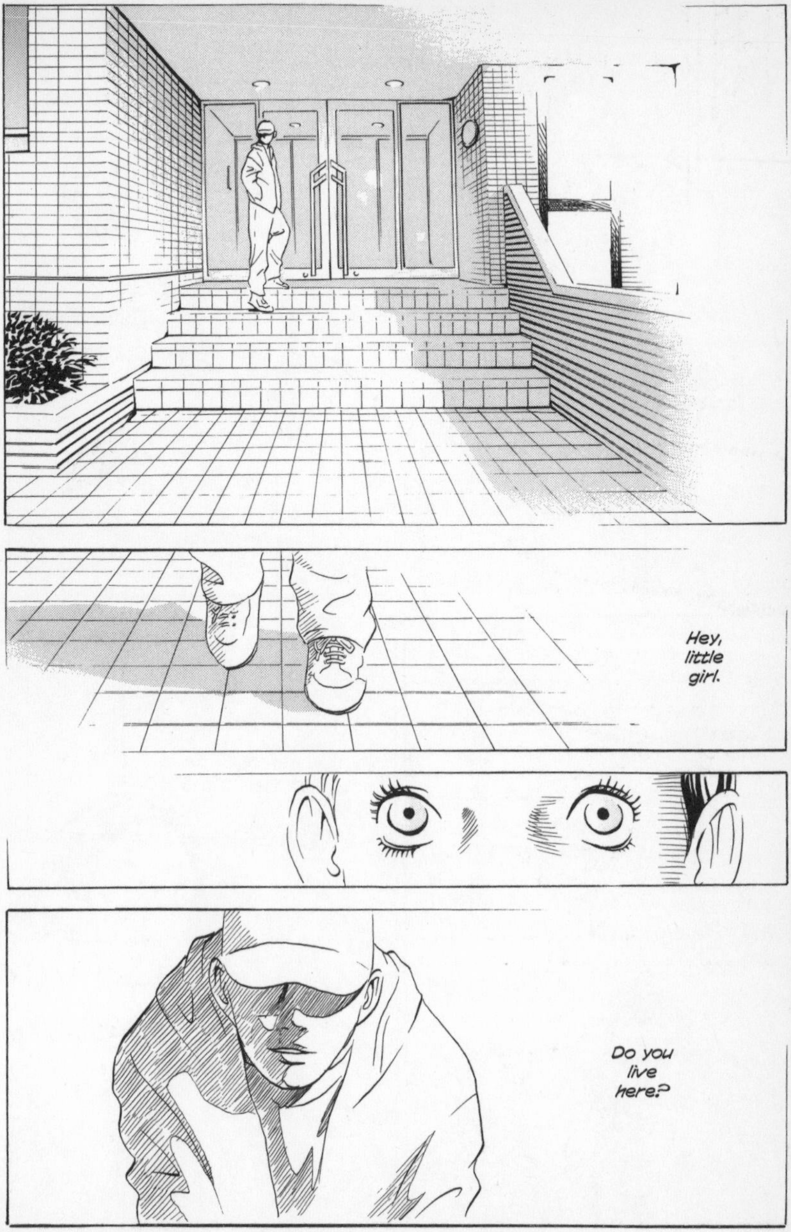
Hey, little girl.
Do you live here?

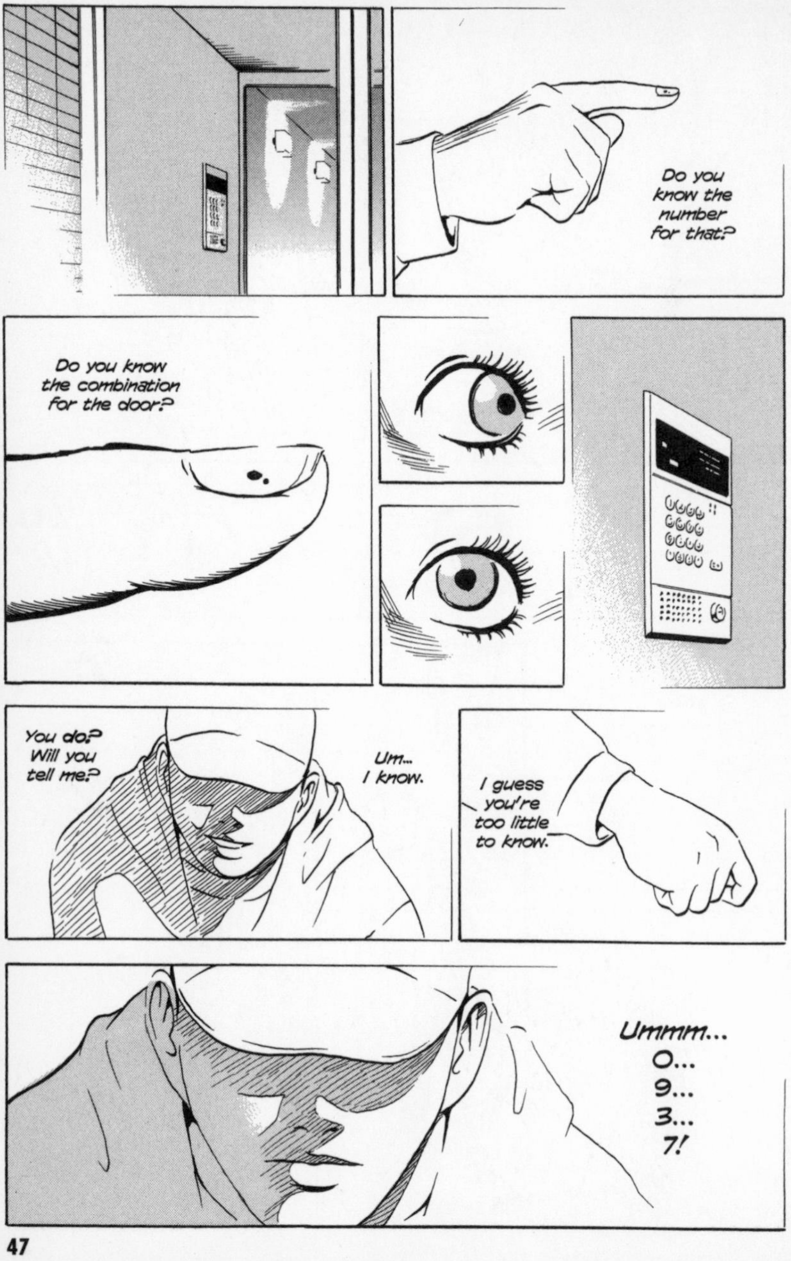
Do you know the number for that?
Do you know the combination for the door?
I guess you're too little to know.
Um... I know.
You do? Will you tell me?
Ummmm... 0... 9... 3... 7!

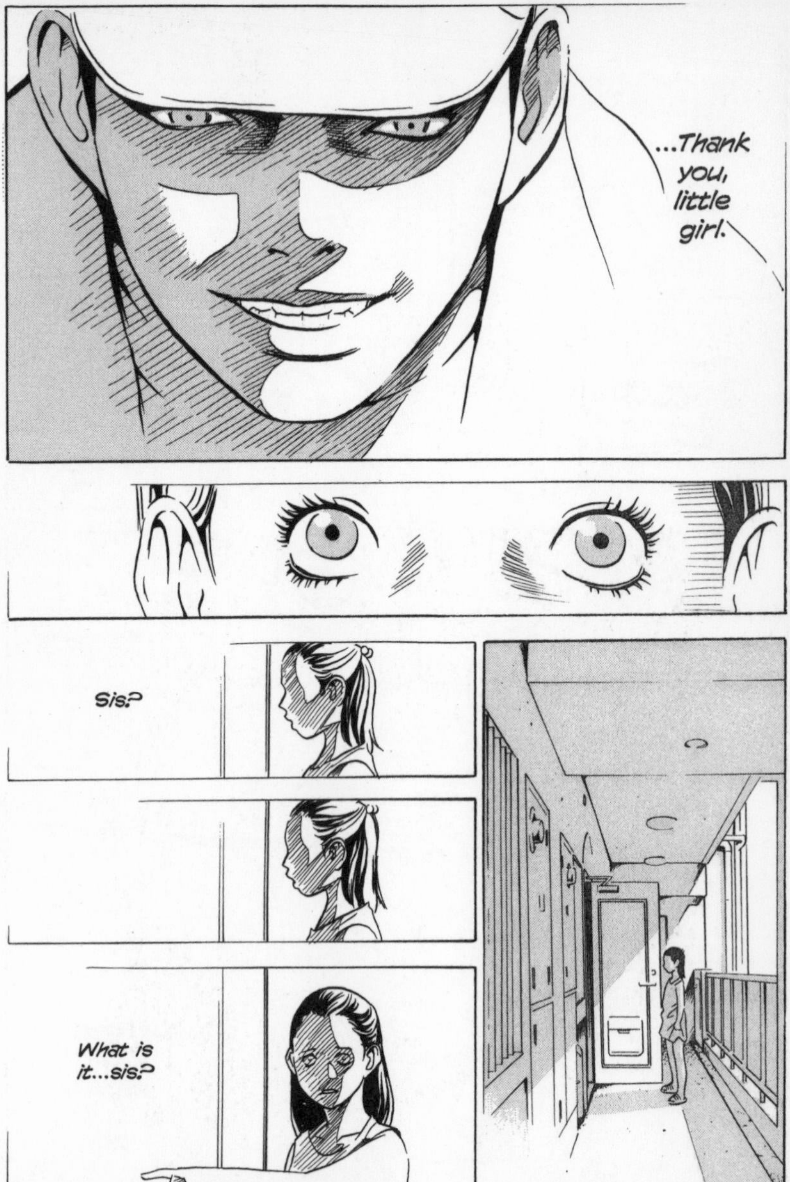
...Thank you, little girl.
Sis?
What is it...sis?

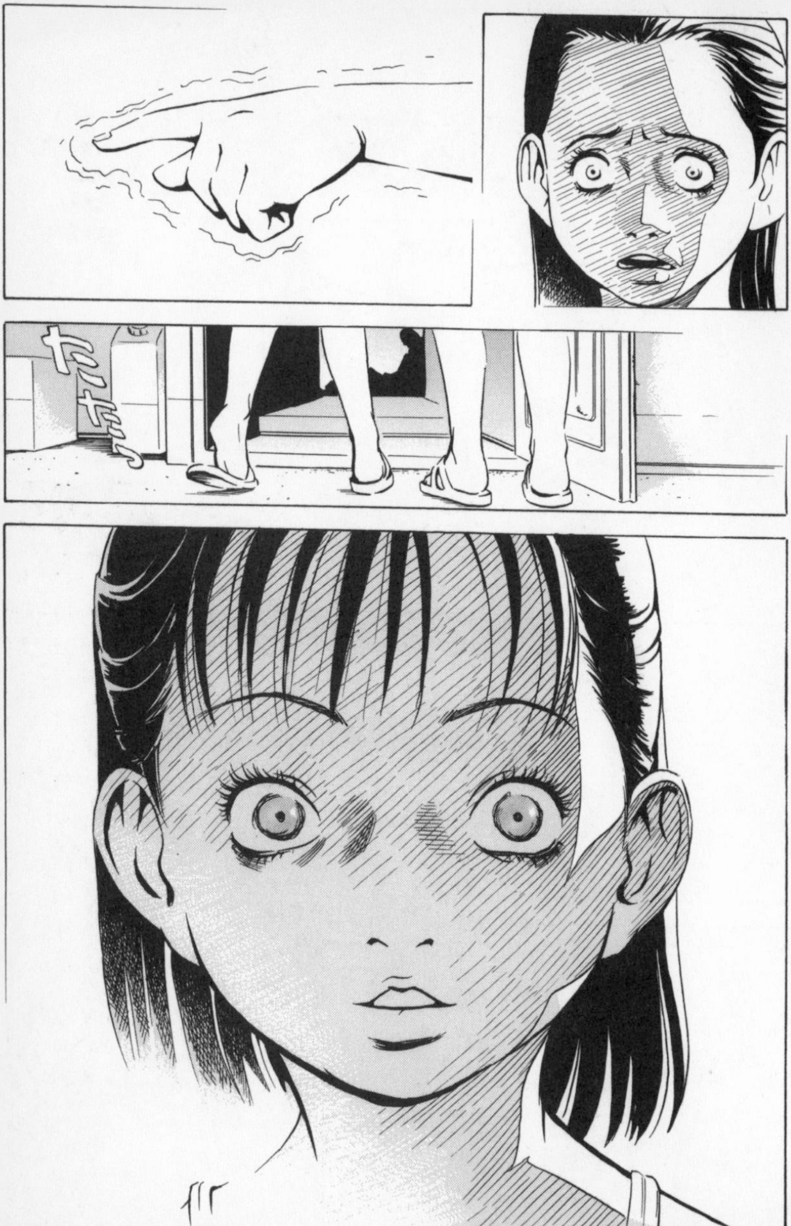
タッタッ

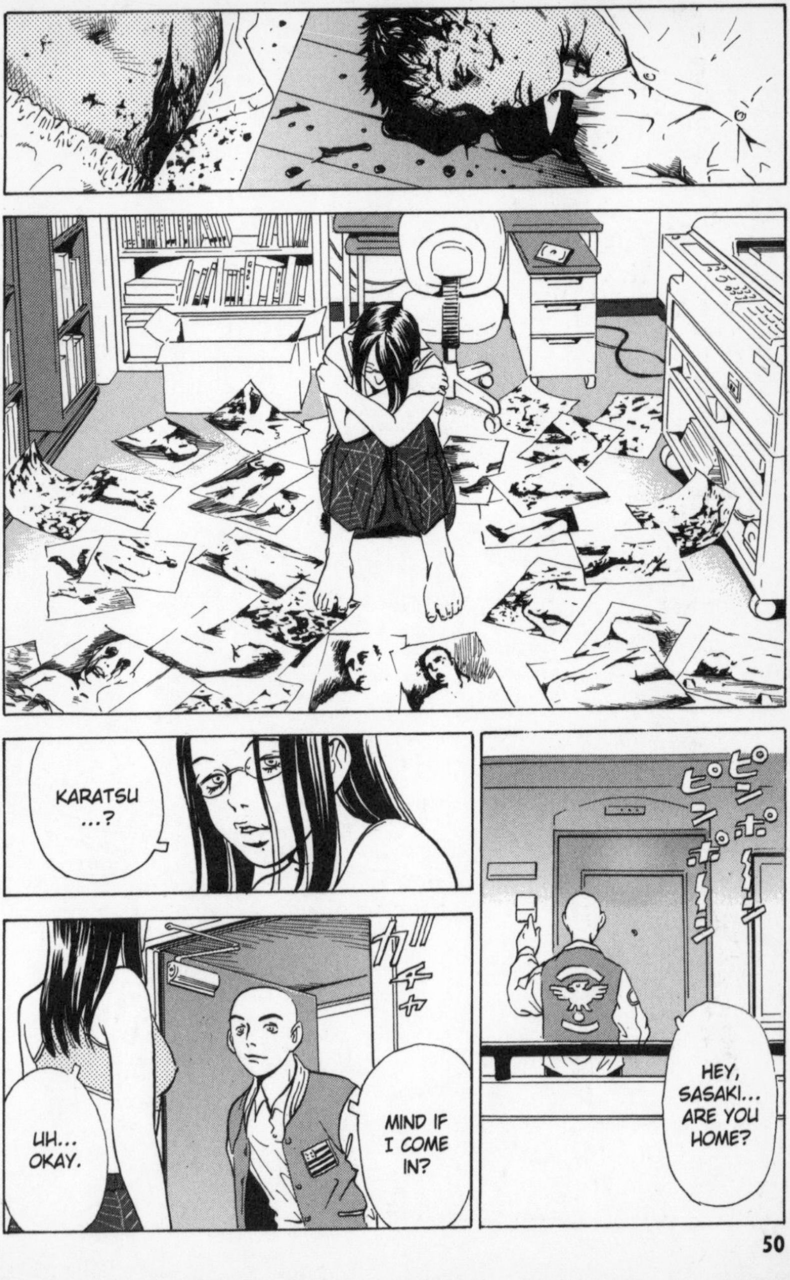
ピンポ～ン
ピンポ～ン
HEY, SASAKI... ARE YOU HOME?
KARATSU ...?
カチャ
MIND IF I COME IN?
UH... OKAY.

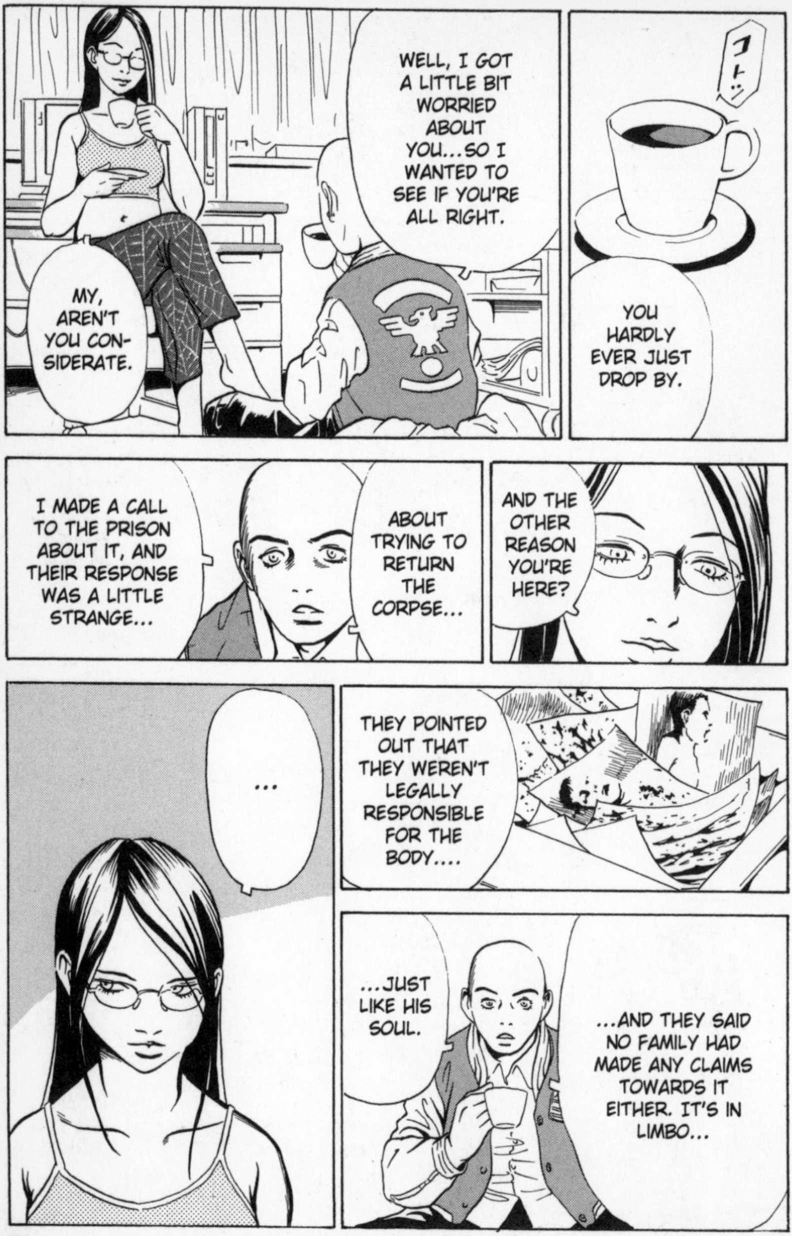
コト…
YOU HARDLY EVER JUST DROP BY.
WELL, I GOT A LITTLE BIT WORRIED ABOUT YOU...SO I WANTED TO SEE IF YOU'RE ALL RIGHT.
MY, AREN'T YOU CONSIDERATE.
AND THE OTHER REASON YOU'RE HERE?
ABOUT TRYING TO RETURN THE CORPSE...
I MADE A CALL TO THE PRISON ABOUT IT, AND THEIR RESPONSE WAS A LITTLE STRANGE...
THEY POINTED OUT THAT THEY WEREN'T LEGALLY RESPONSIBLE FOR THE BODY....
...AND THEY SAID NO FAMILY HAD MADE ANY CLAIMS TOWARDS IT EITHER. IT'S IN LIMBO...
...JUST LIKE HIS SOUL.
...

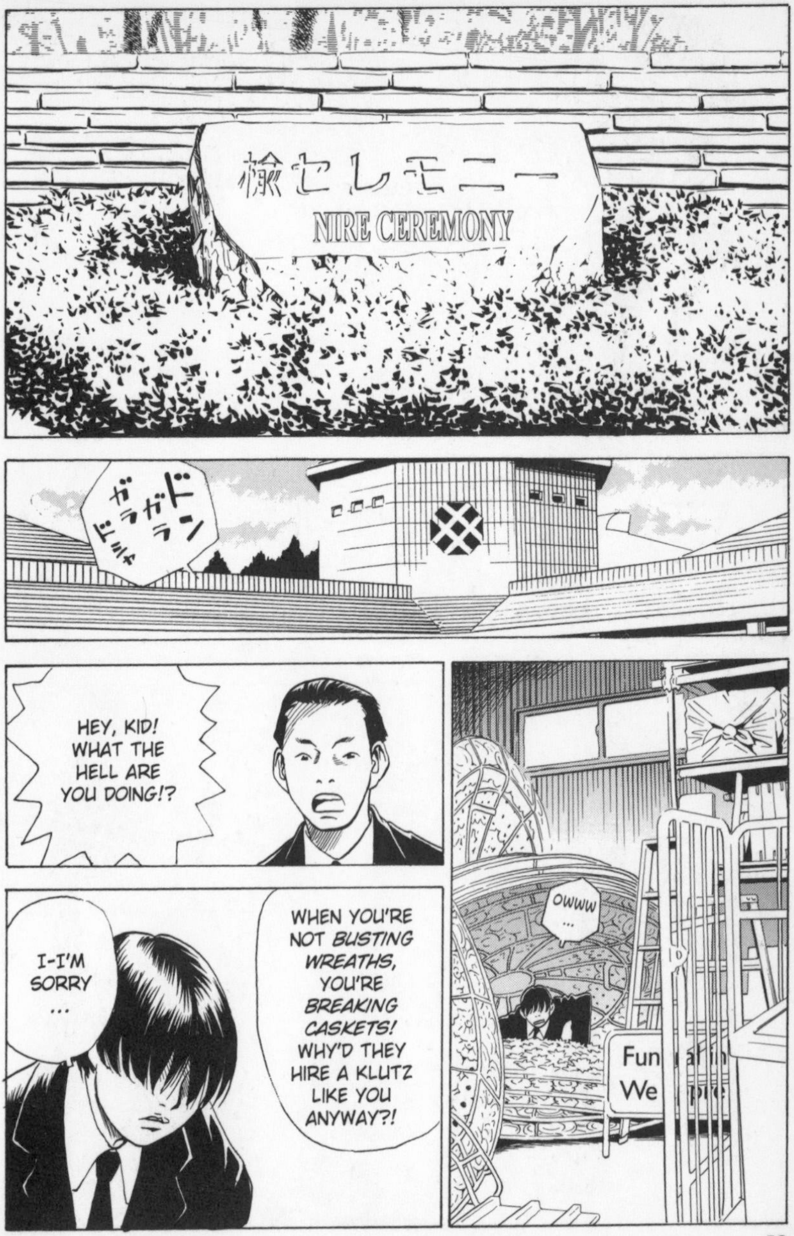

楡セレモニー
NIRE CEREMONY
ガラガドラン ドシャ
OWWW ...
HEY, KID! WHAT THE HELL ARE YOU DOING!?
WHEN YOU'RE NOT *BUSTING WREATHS,* YOU'RE *BREAKING CASKETS!* WHY'D THEY HIRE A KLUTZ LIKE YOU ANYWAY?!
I-I'M SORRY ...

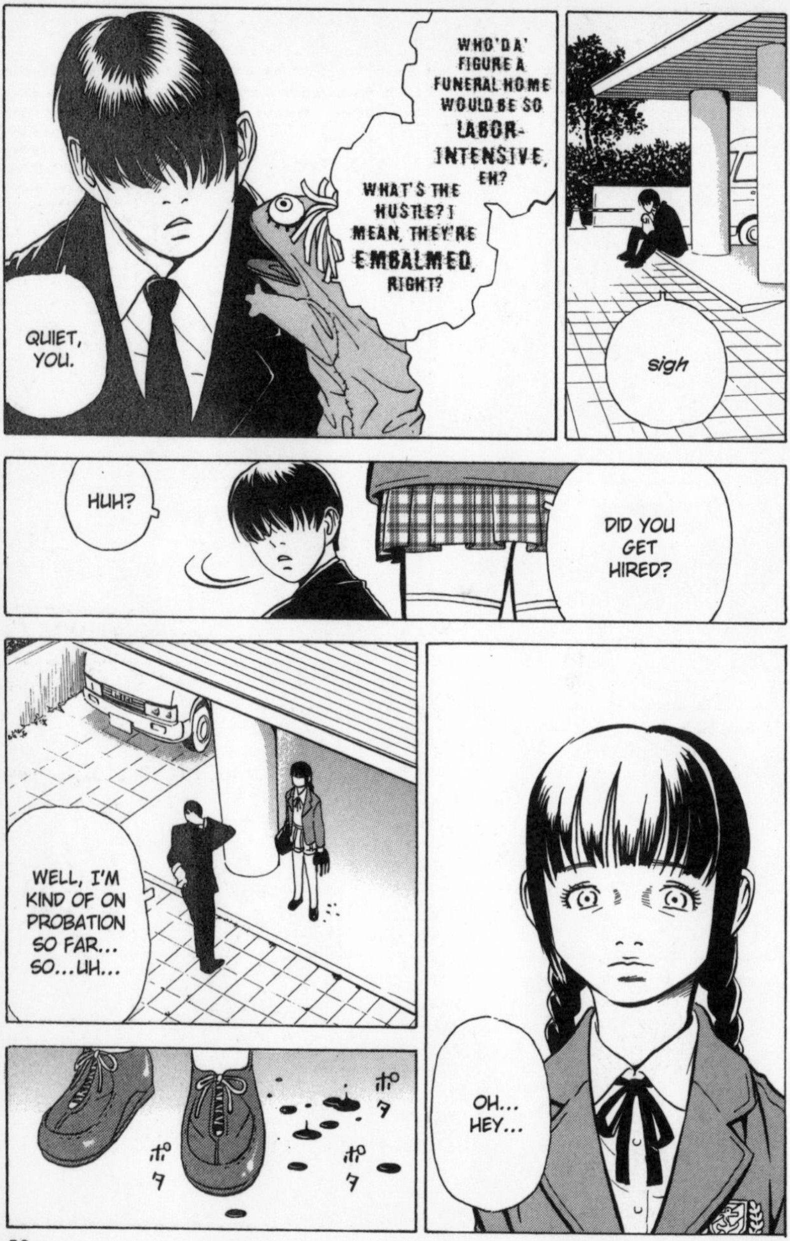
sigh
WHO'DA' FIGURE A FUNERAL HOME WOULD BE SO LABOR-INTENSIVE, EH?
WHAT'S THE HUSTLE? I MEAN, THEY'RE EMBALMED, RIGHT?
QUIET, YOU.
DID YOU GET HIRED?
HUH?
OH... HEY...
WELL, I'M KIND OF ON PROBATION SO FAR... SO...UH...
ポタ
ポタ
ポタ

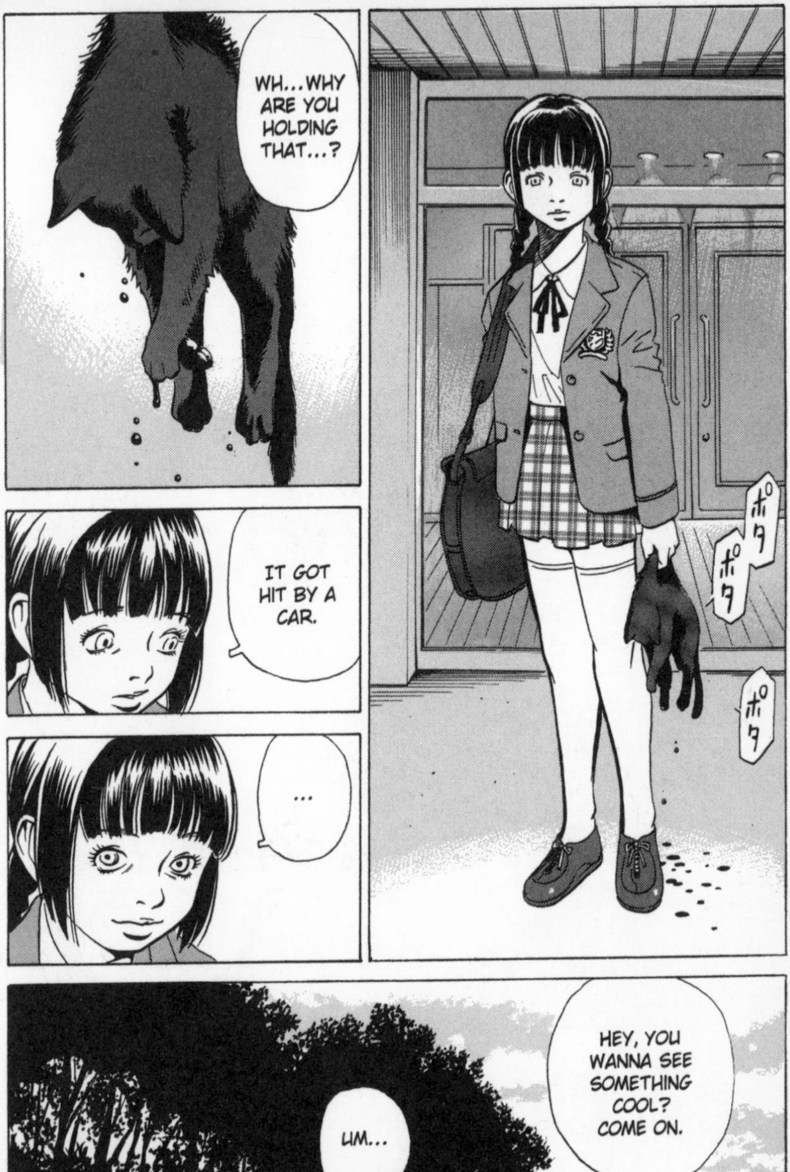
ポタ
ポタ
ポタ
WH...WHY ARE YOU HOLDING THAT...?
IT GOT HIT BY A CAR.
...
HEY, YOU WANNA SEE SOMETHING COOL? COME ON.
UM...

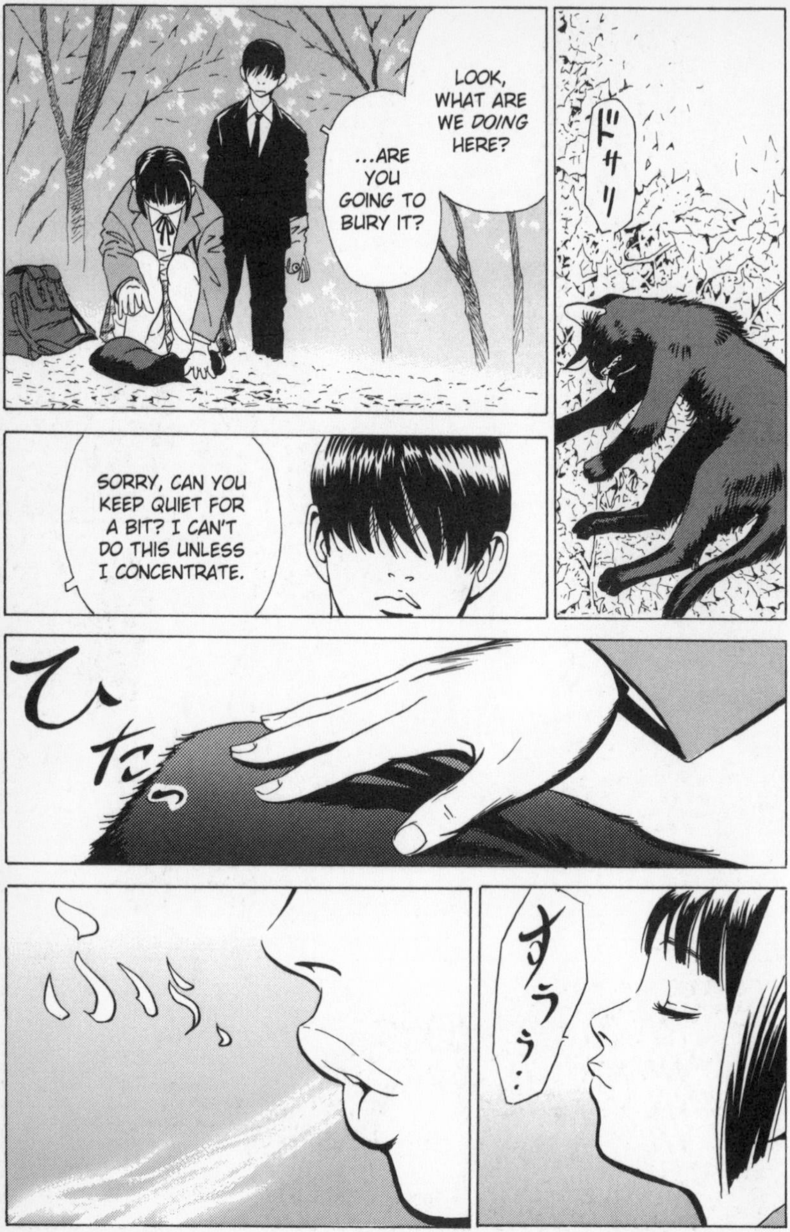
ドサリ
LOOK, WHAT ARE WE *DOING* HERE?
...ARE YOU GOING TO BURY IT?
SORRY, CAN YOU KEEP QUIET FOR A BIT? I CAN'T DO THIS UNLESS I CONCENTRATE.
ひたっ
すうぅ‥
ふぅぅ

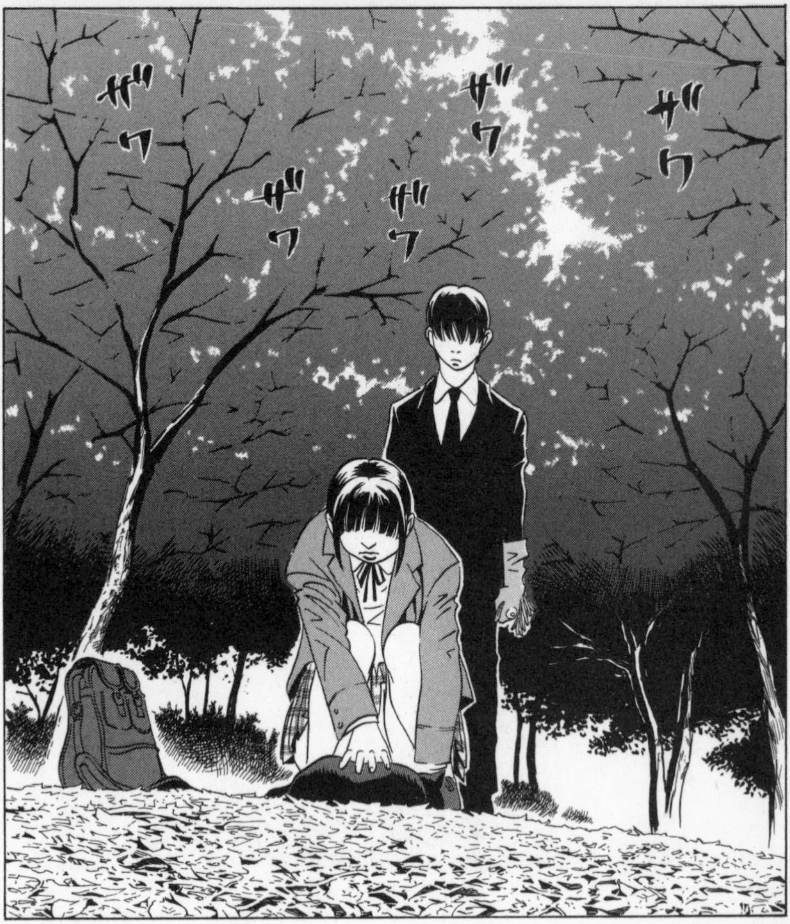
ザワ
ザワ
ザワ
ザワ
ザワ

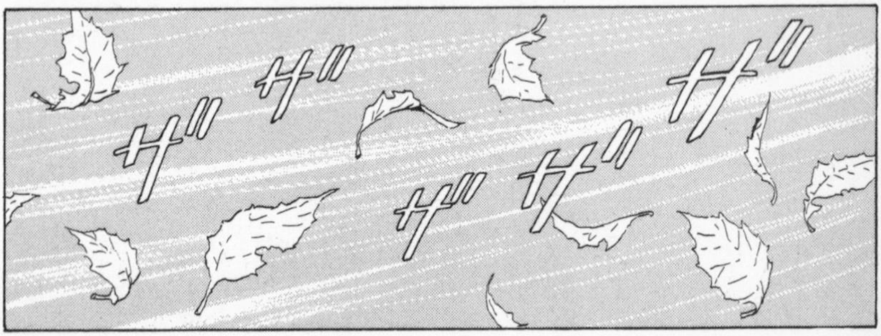
ザ
ザ
ザ
ザ
ザ

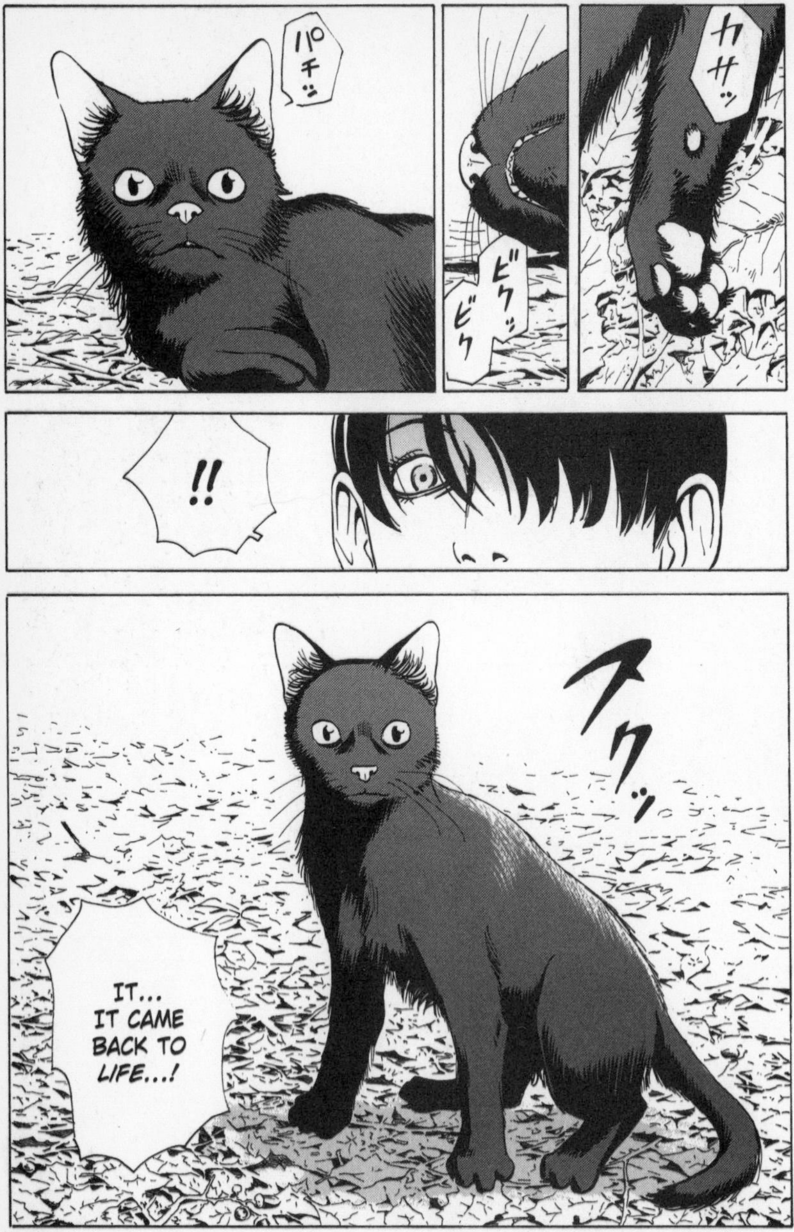
カサッ
ビクッ ビク
パチッ
!!
スクッ
IT... IT CAME BACK TO LIFE...!

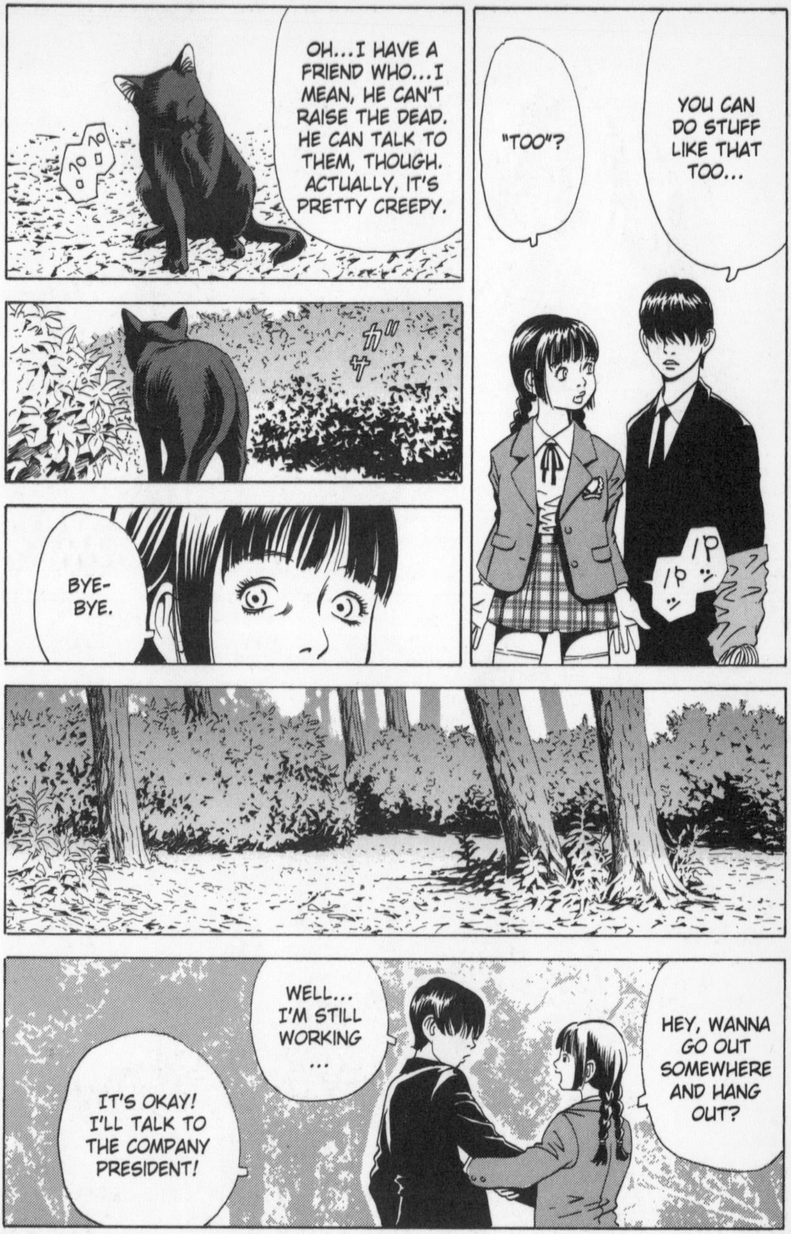
YOU CAN DO STUFF LIKE THAT TOO...
"TOO"?
OH...I HAVE A FRIEND WHO...I MEAN, HE CAN'T RAISE THE DEAD. HE CAN TALK TO THEM, THOUGH. ACTUALLY, IT'S PRETTY CREEPY.
ガサ
BYE-BYE.
HEY, WANNA GO OUT SOMEWHERE AND HANG OUT?
WELL... I'M STILL WORKING ...
IT'S OKAY! I'LL TALK TO THE COMPANY PRESIDENT!

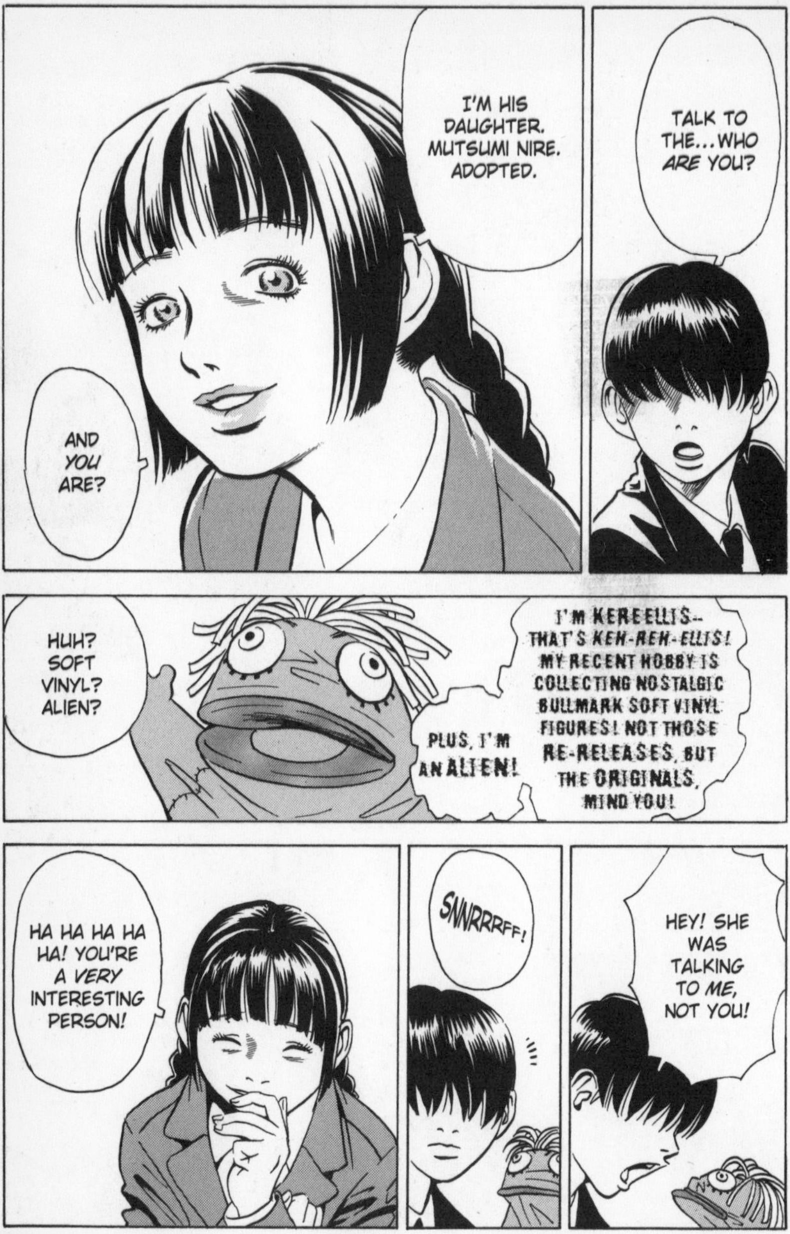
TALK TO THE...WHO ARE YOU?
I'M HIS DAUGHTER. MUTSUMI NIRE. ADOPTED.
AND YOU ARE?
I'M KEREELLIS--THAT'S KEH-REH-ELLIS! MY RECENT HOBBY IS COLLECTING NOSTALGIC BULLMARK SOFT VINYL FIGURES! NOT THOSE RE-RELEASES, BUT THE ORIGINALS, MIND YOU!
PLUS, I'M AN ALIEN!
HUH? SOFT VINYL? ALIEN?
HEY! SHE WAS TALKING TO ME, NOT YOU!
SNNRRRFF!
HA HA HA HA HA! YOU'RE A VERY INTERESTING PERSON!

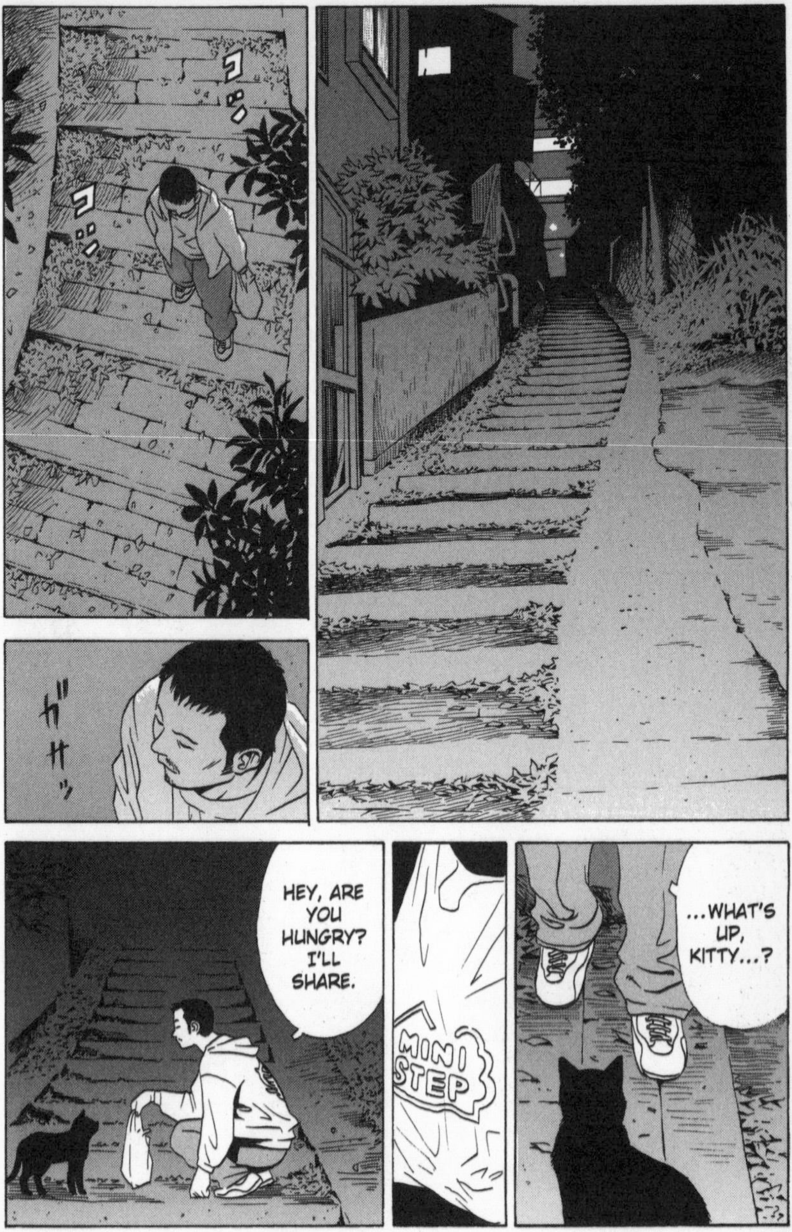
ガサッ
...WHAT'S UP, KITTY...?
MINI STEP
HEY, ARE YOU HUNGRY? I'LL SHARE.

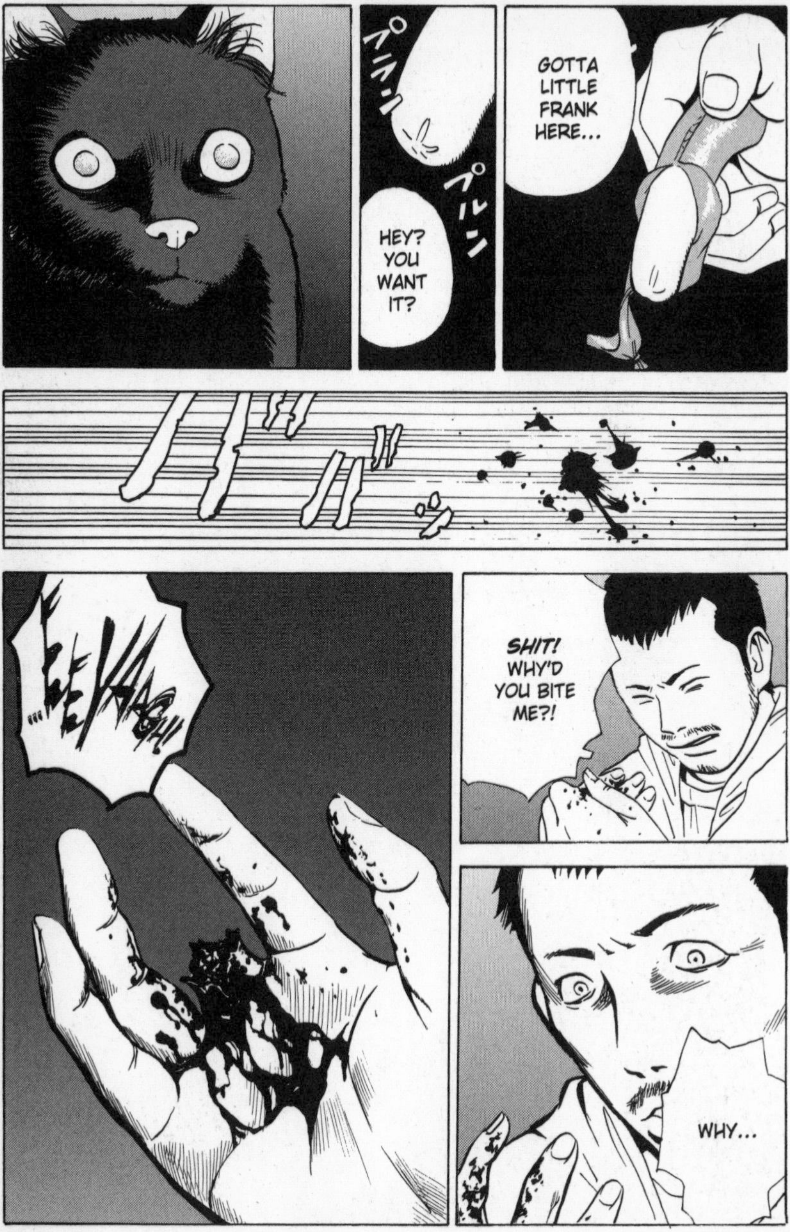
GOTTA LITTLE FRANK HERE...
プラン
プルン
HEY? YOU WANT IT?
SHIT! WHY'D YOU BITE ME?!
WHY...
...EEEYAAGH!!

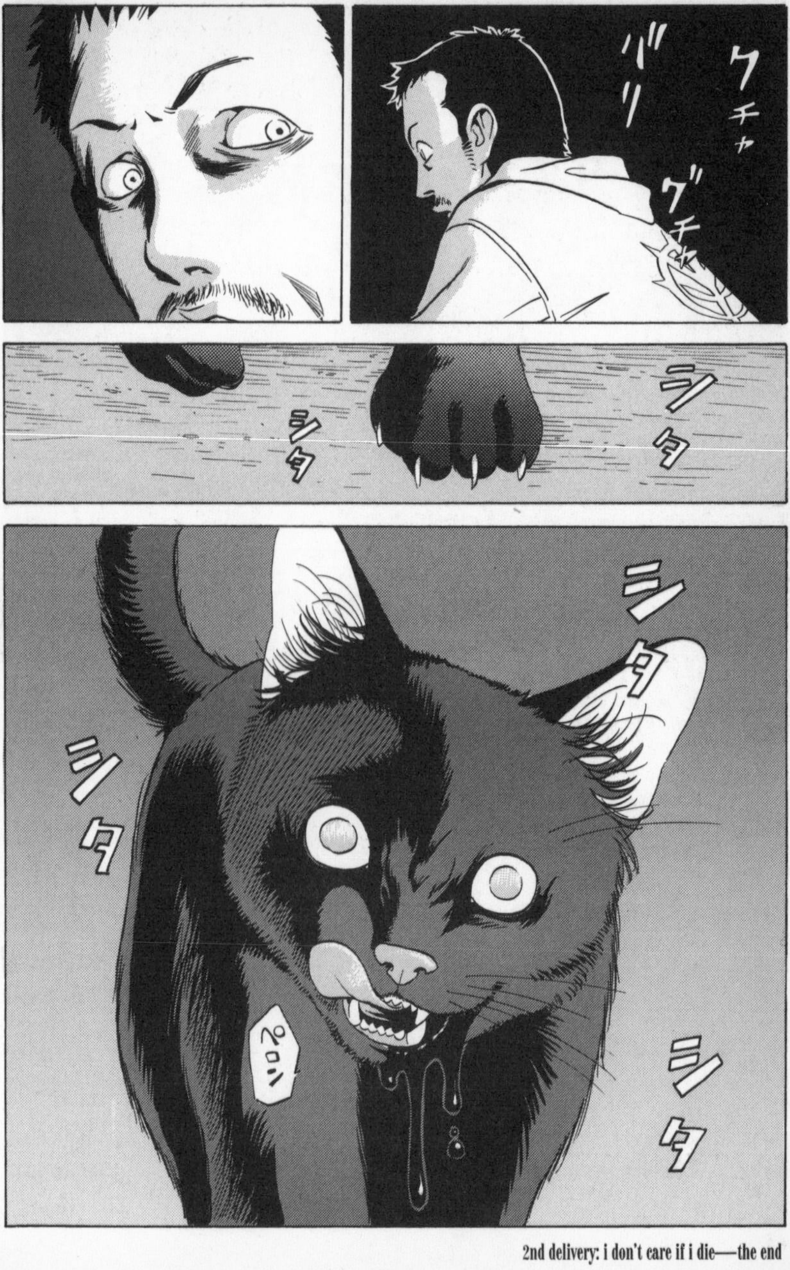
クチャ
バリ
グチャ
シタ
シタ
シタ
シタ
ペロン
シタ

2nd delivery: i don't care if i die—the end

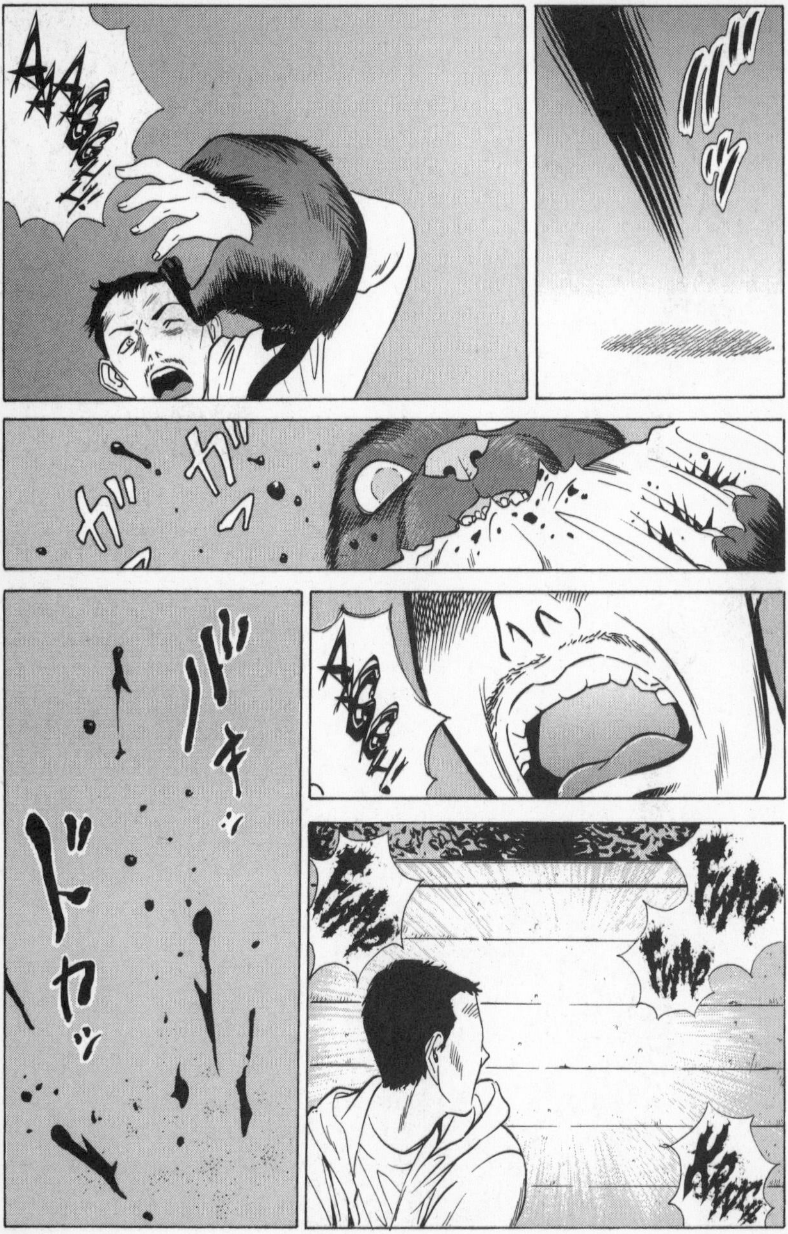
AAAGGHH!!
がっ がっ
AGGH!!
バキッ
ドカッ

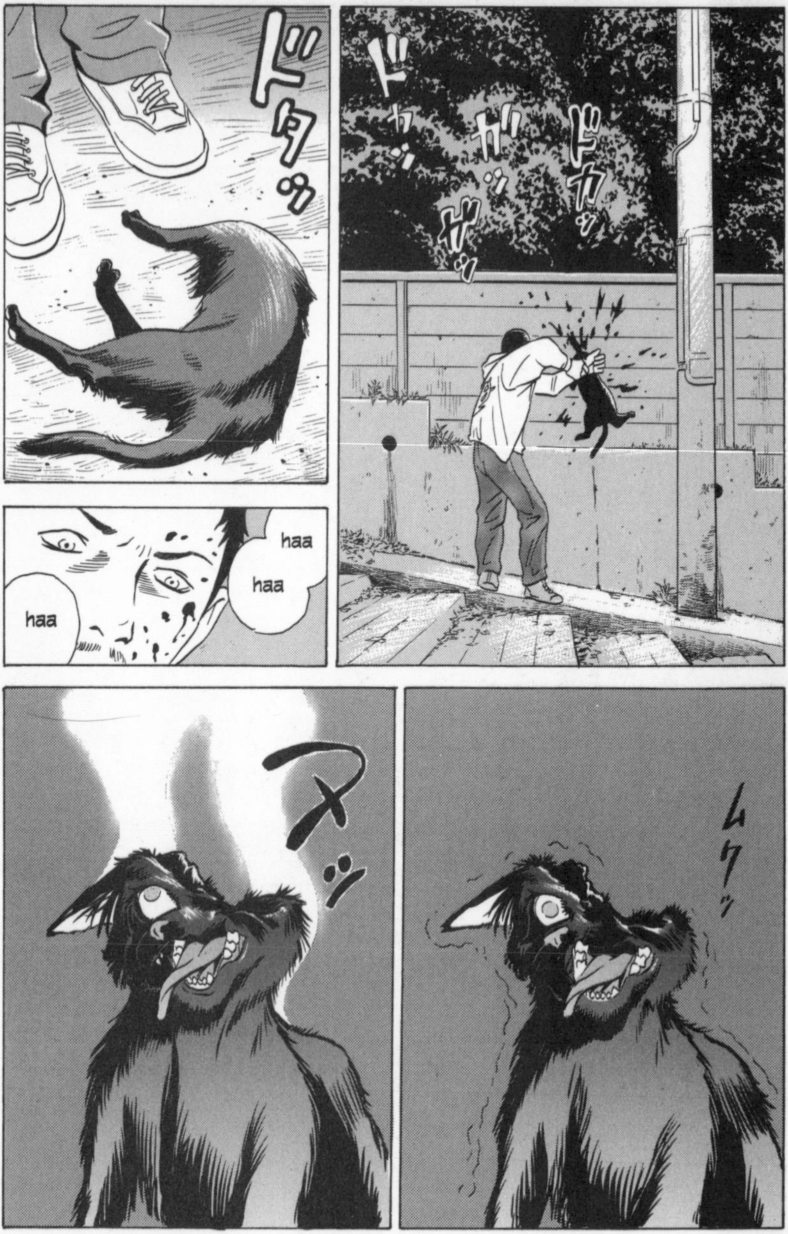

ドカッ
ガッ
ドカッ
ザッ
ドタッ
haa
haa
haa
ムクッ
ヌッ

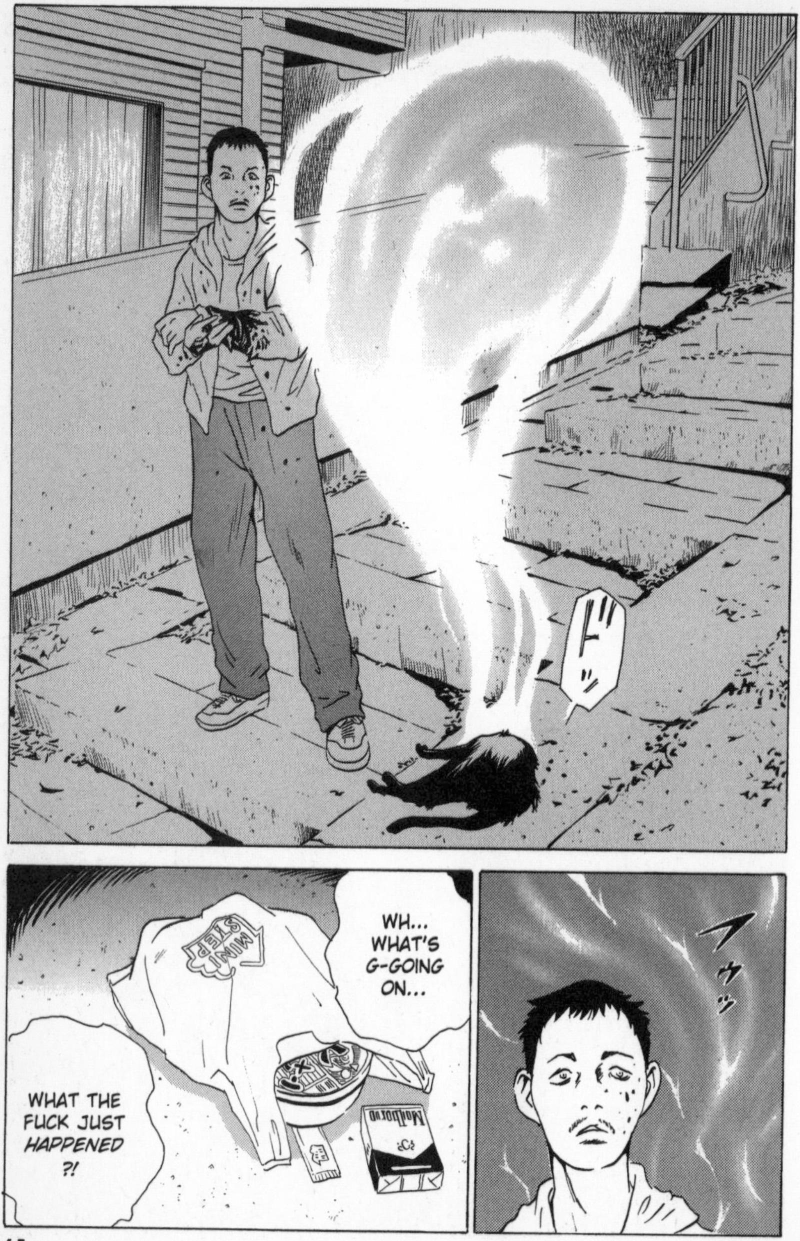
ドッ
WH... WHAT'S G-GOING ON...
WHAT THE FUCK JUST HAPPENED ?!

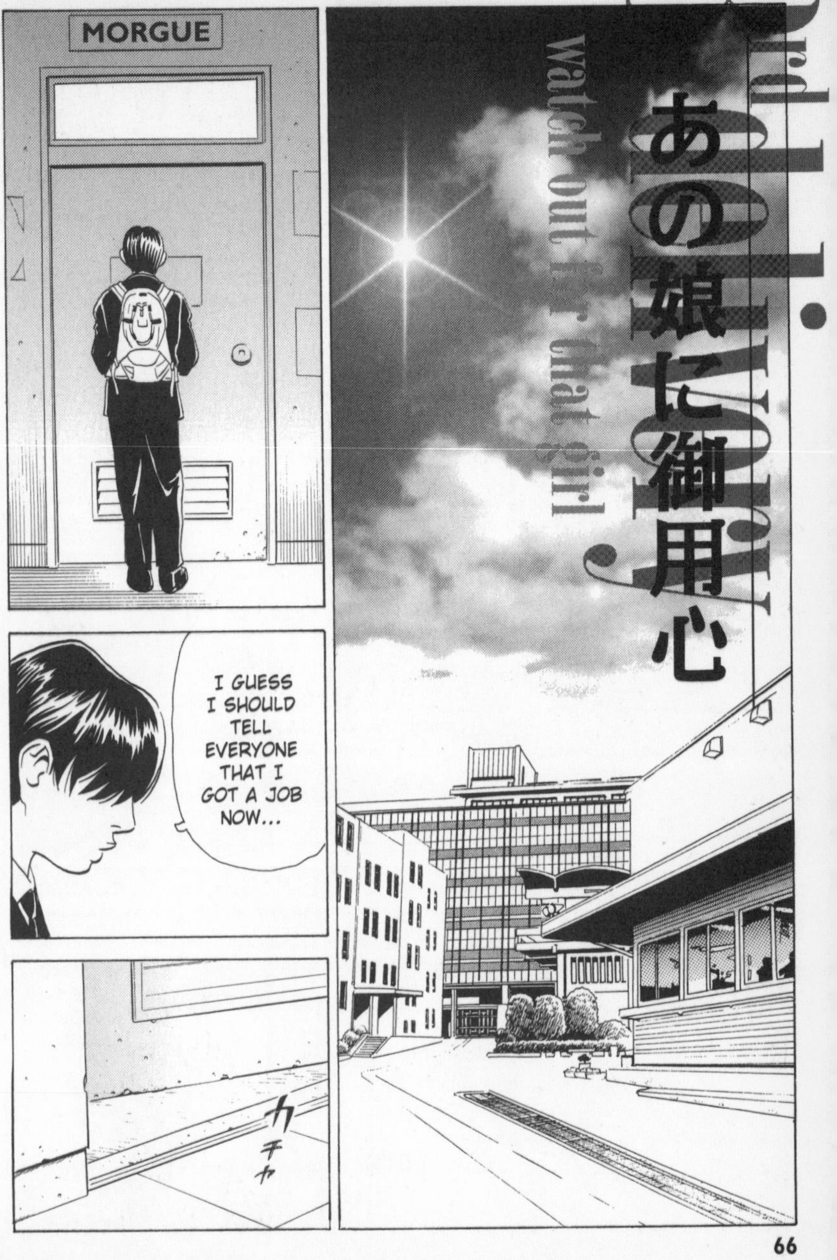

3rd BODY:
あの娘に御用心
Watch out for that girl
MORGUE
I GUESS I SHOULD TELL EVERYONE THAT I GOT A JOB NOW...
カチャ

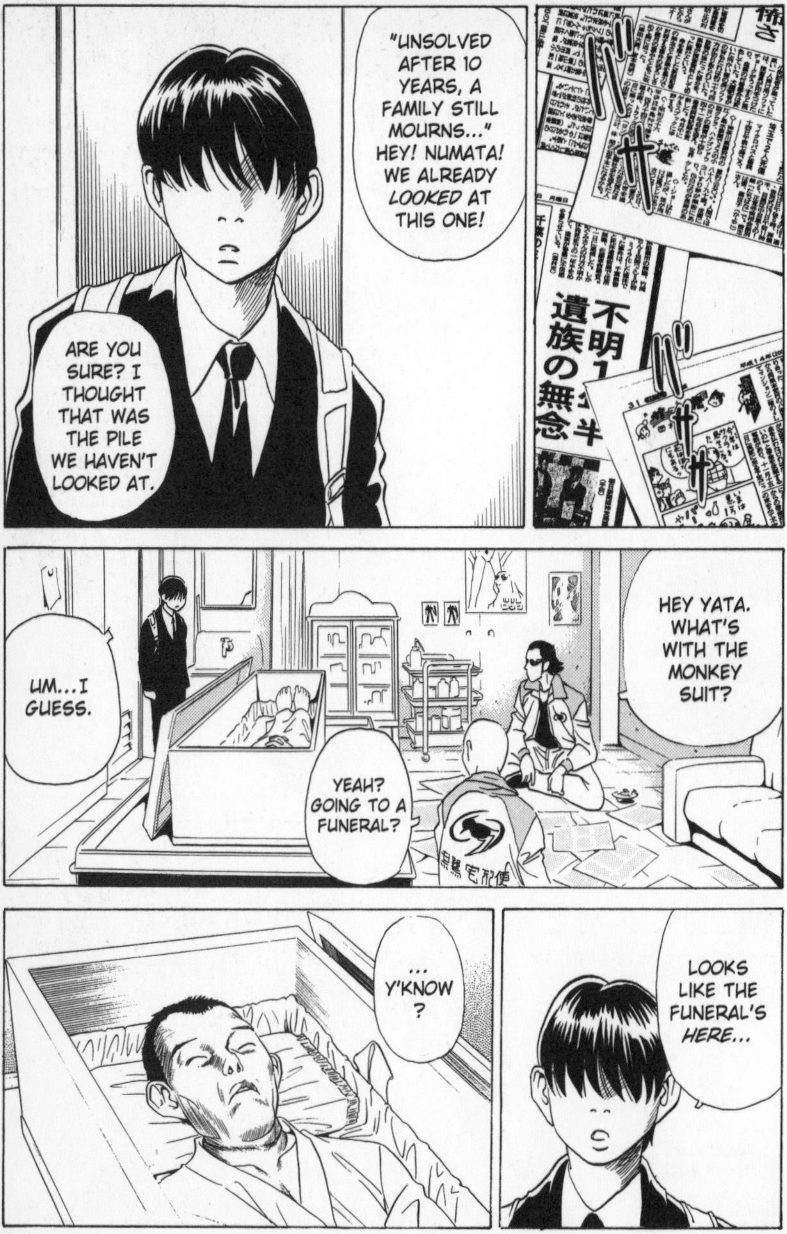
遺族の無念
"UNSOLVED AFTER 10 YEARS, A FAMILY STILL MOURNS..." HEY! NUMATA! WE ALREADY *LOOKED* AT THIS ONE!
ARE YOU SURE? I THOUGHT THAT WAS THE PILE WE HAVEN'T LOOKED AT.
HEY YATA. WHAT'S WITH THE MONKEY SUIT?
YEAH? GOING TO A FUNERAL?
UM...I GUESS.
LOOKS LIKE THE FUNERAL'S *HERE*...
... Y'KNOW ?

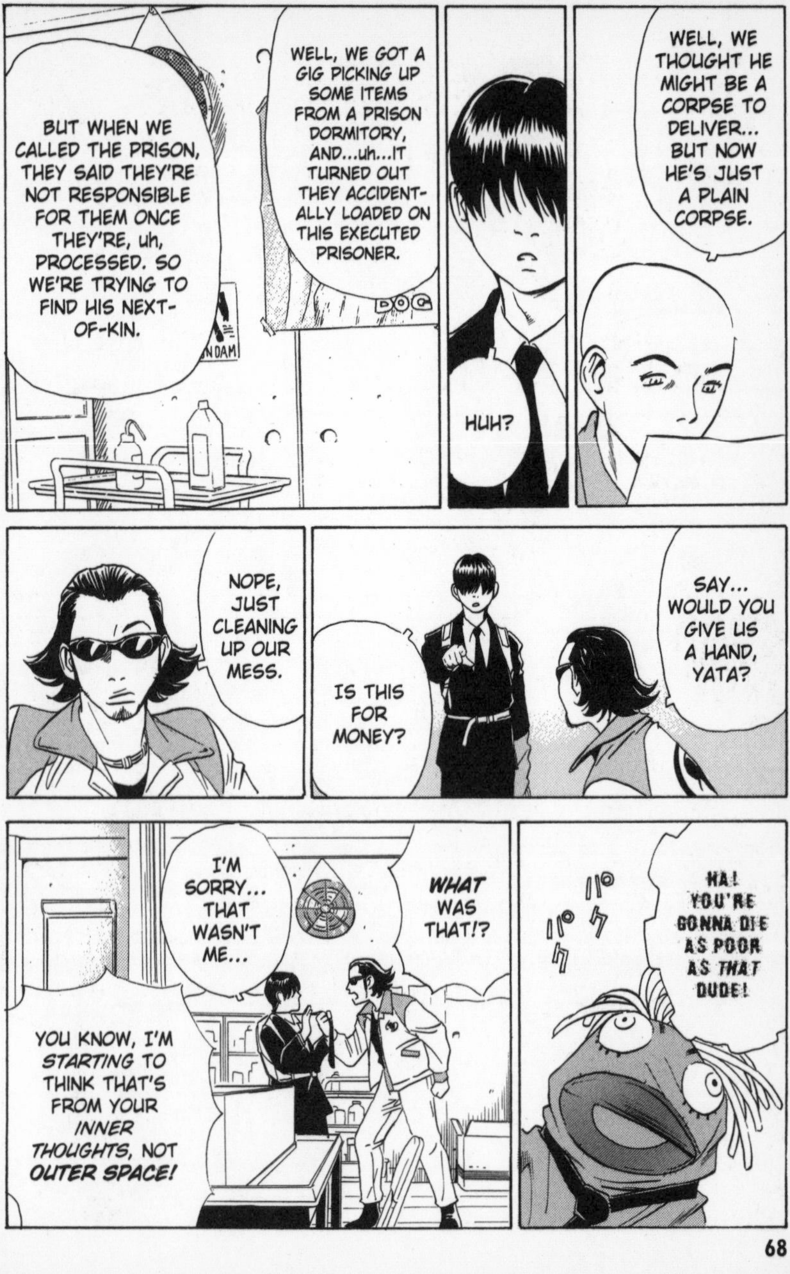
WELL, WE THOUGHT HE MIGHT BE A CORPSE TO DELIVER... BUT NOW HE'S JUST A PLAIN CORPSE.
HUH?
WELL, WE GOT A GIG PICKING UP SOME ITEMS FROM A PRISON DORMITORY, AND...uh...IT TURNED OUT THEY ACCIDENTALLY LOADED ON THIS EXECUTED PRISONER.
BUT WHEN WE CALLED THE PRISON, THEY SAID THEY'RE NOT RESPONSIBLE FOR THEM ONCE THEY'RE, uh, PROCESSED. SO WE'RE TRYING TO FIND HIS NEXT-OF-KIN.
SAY... WOULD YOU GIVE US A HAND, YATA?
IS THIS FOR MONEY?
NOPE, JUST CLEANING UP OUR MESS.
パク
パク
HA! YOU'RE GONNA DIE AS POOR AS *THAT* DUDE!
WHAT WAS THAT!?
I'M SORRY... THAT WASN'T ME...
YOU KNOW, I'M *STARTING* TO THINK THAT'S FROM YOUR *INNER THOUGHTS*, NOT **OUTER SPACE!**

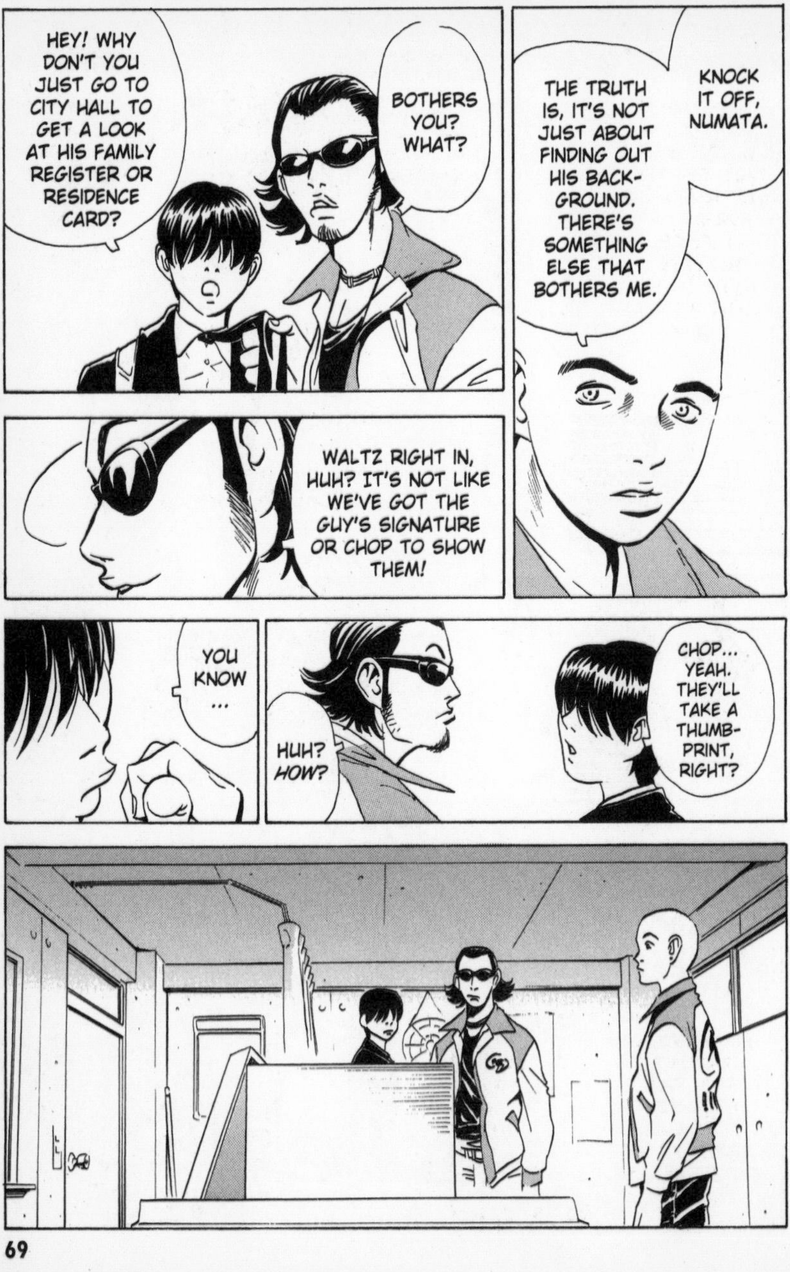
KNOCK IT OFF, NUMATA.
THE TRUTH IS, IT'S NOT JUST ABOUT FINDING OUT HIS BACK-GROUND. THERE'S SOMETHING ELSE THAT BOTHERS ME.
BOTHERS YOU? WHAT?
HEY! WHY DON'T YOU JUST GO TO CITY HALL TO GET A LOOK AT HIS FAMILY REGISTER OR RESIDENCE CARD?
WALTZ RIGHT IN, HUH? IT'S NOT LIKE WE'VE GOT THE GUY'S SIGNATURE OR CHOP TO SHOW THEM!
CHOP... YEAH. THEY'LL TAKE A THUMB-PRINT, RIGHT?
HUH? *HOW?*
YOU KNOW ...

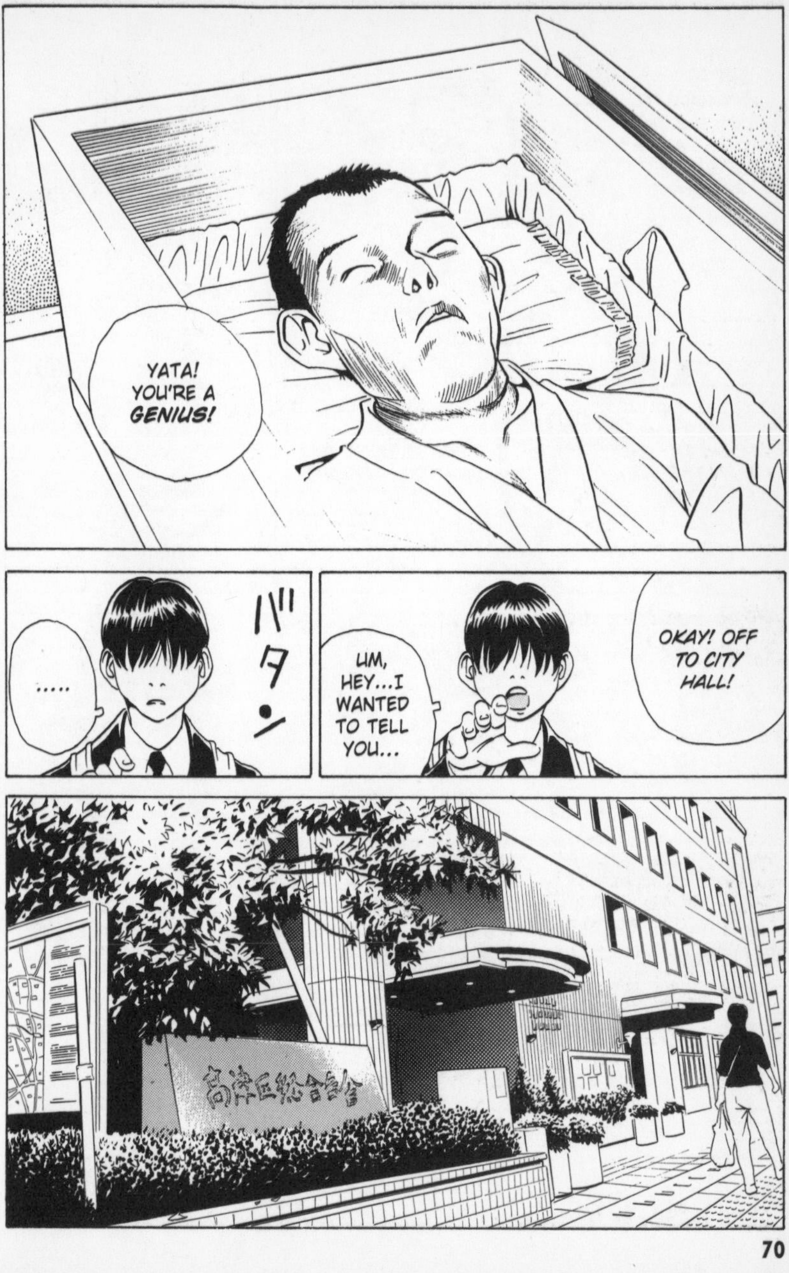
YATA! YOU'RE A GENIUS!
OKAY! OFF TO CITY HALL!
UM, HEY...I WANTED TO TELL YOU...
バタン
.....

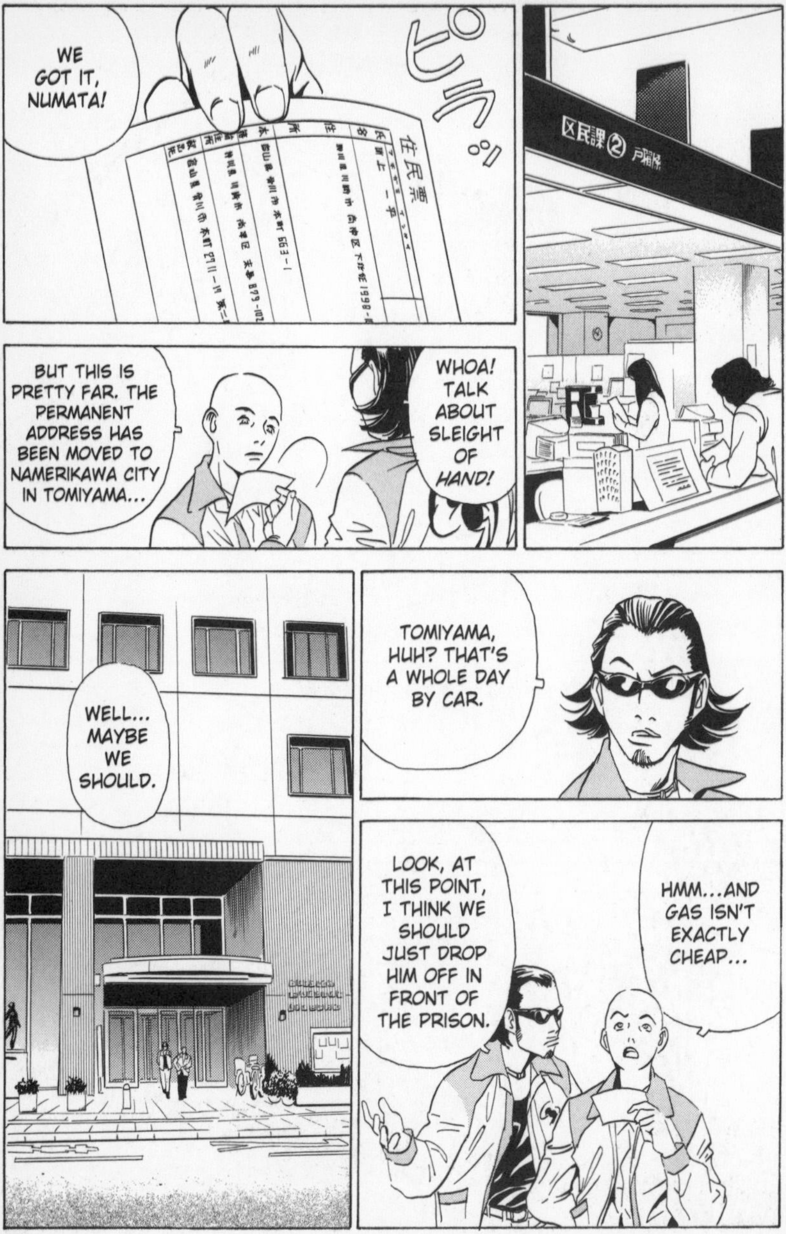
区民課② 戸籍係
ピラッ
住民票
WE GOT IT, NUMATA!
WHOA! TALK ABOUT SLEIGHT OF HAND!
BUT THIS IS PRETTY FAR. THE PERMANENT ADDRESS HAS BEEN MOVED TO NAMERIKAWA CITY IN TOMIYAMA...
TOMIYAMA, HUH? THAT'S A WHOLE DAY BY CAR.
HMM...AND GAS ISN'T EXACTLY CHEAP...
LOOK, AT THIS POINT, I THINK WE SHOULD JUST DROP HIM OFF IN FRONT OF THE PRISON.
WELL... MAYBE WE SHOULD.

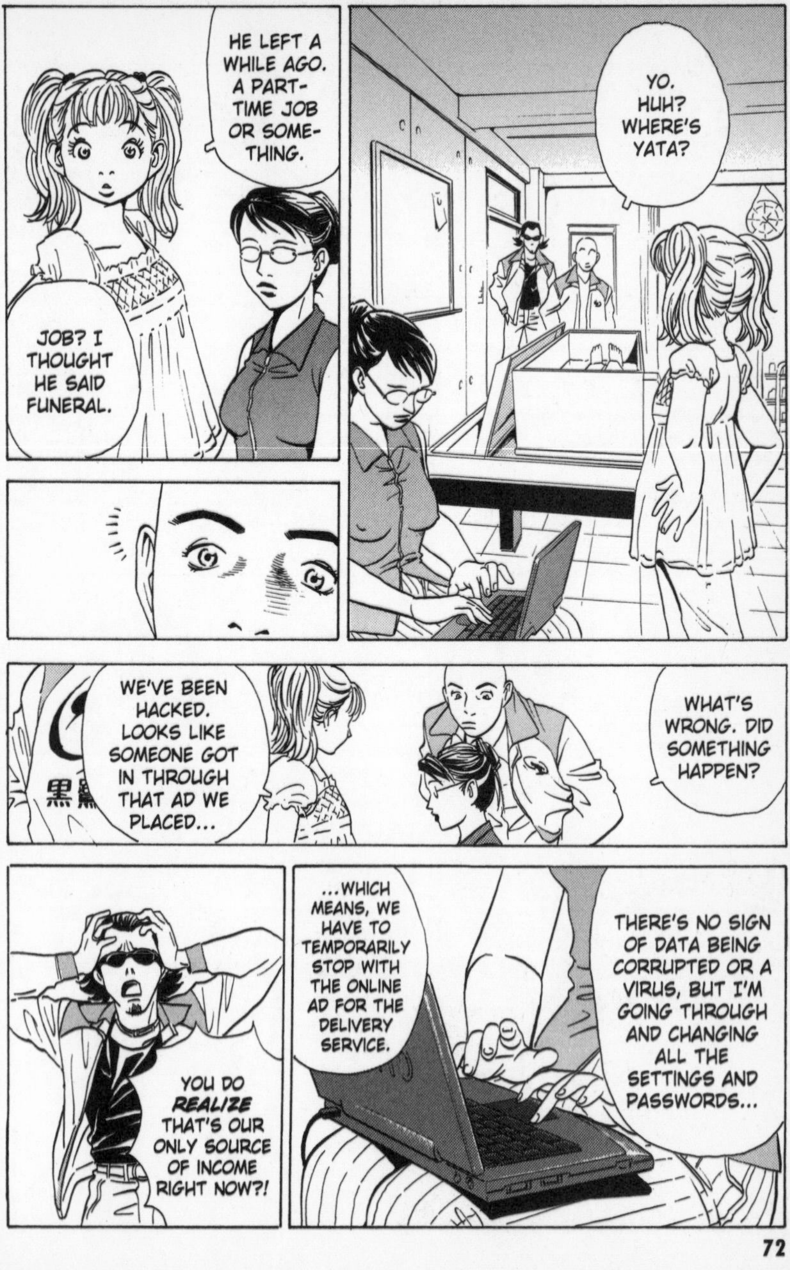
YO. HUH? WHERE'S YATA?
HE LEFT A WHILE AGO. A PART-TIME JOB OR SOME-THING.
JOB? I THOUGHT HE SAID FUNERAL.
WHAT'S WRONG. DID SOMETHING HAPPEN?
WE'VE BEEN HACKED. LOOKS LIKE SOMEONE GOT IN THROUGH THAT AD WE PLACED...
黒
THERE'S NO SIGN OF DATA BEING CORRUPTED OR A VIRUS, BUT I'M GOING THROUGH AND CHANGING ALL THE SETTINGS AND PASSWORDS...
...WHICH MEANS, WE HAVE TO TEMPORARILY STOP WITH THE ONLINE AD FOR THE DELIVERY SERVICE.
YOU DO ***REALIZE*** THAT'S OUR ONLY SOURCE OF INCOME RIGHT NOW?!

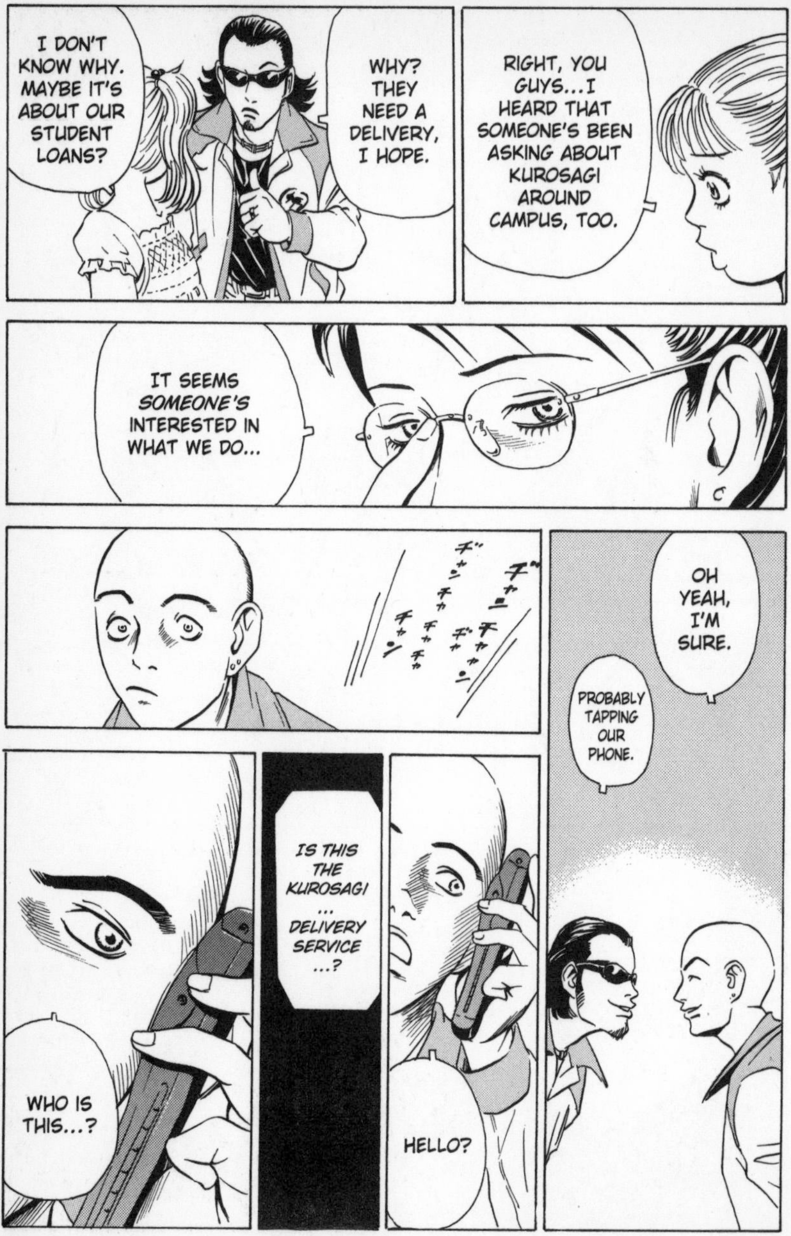
RIGHT, YOU GUYS...I HEARD THAT SOMEONE'S BEEN ASKING ABOUT KUROSAGI AROUND CAMPUS, TOO.
WHY? THEY NEED A DELIVERY, I HOPE.
I DON'T KNOW WHY. MAYBE IT'S ABOUT OUR STUDENT LOANS?
IT SEEMS *SOMEONE'S* INTERESTED IN WHAT WE DO...
OH YEAH, I'M SURE.
PROBABLY TAPPING OUR PHONE.
HELLO?
IS THIS THE KUROSAGI ... DELIVERY SERVICE ...?
WHO IS THIS...?

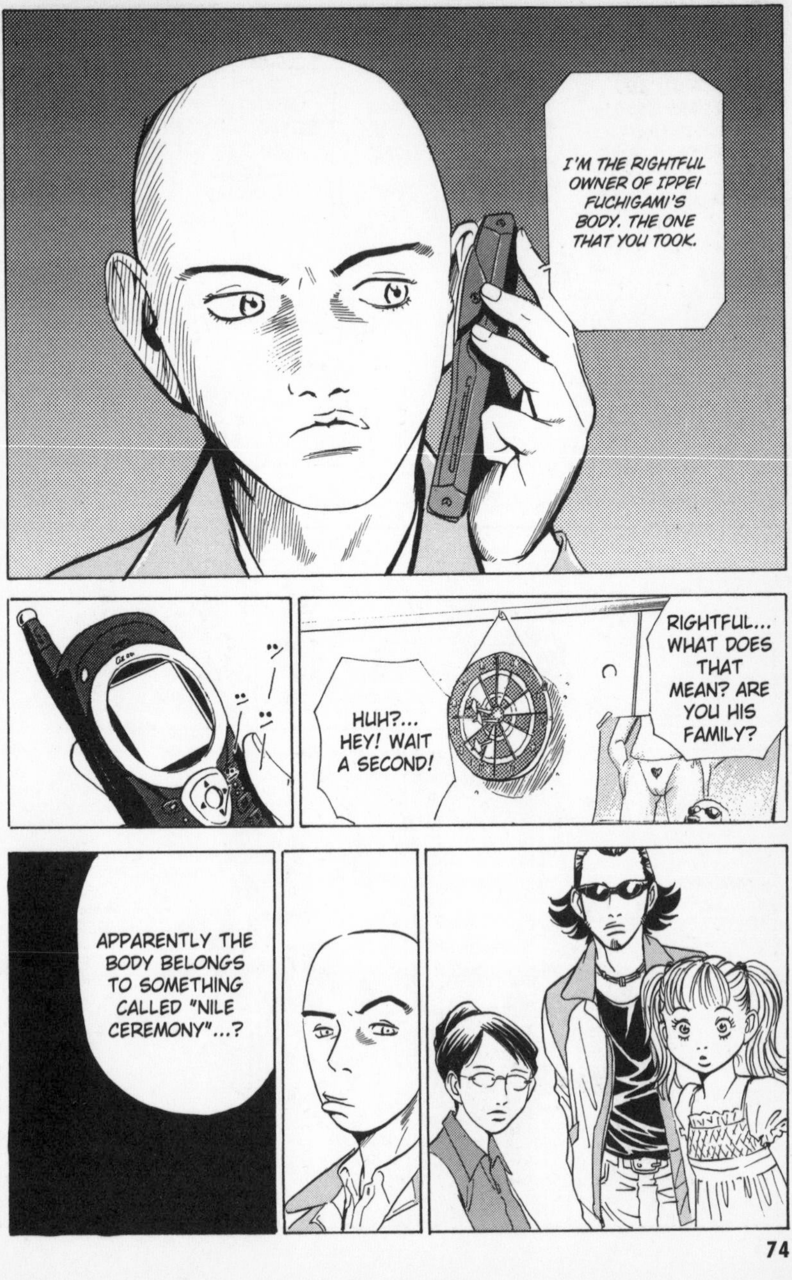
I'M THE RIGHTFUL OWNER OF IPPEI FUCHIGAMI'S BODY. THE ONE THAT YOU TOOK.
RIGHTFUL... WHAT DOES THAT MEAN? ARE YOU HIS FAMILY?
HUH?... HEY! WAIT A SECOND!
APPARENTLY THE BODY BELONGS TO SOMETHING CALLED "NILE CEREMONY"...?

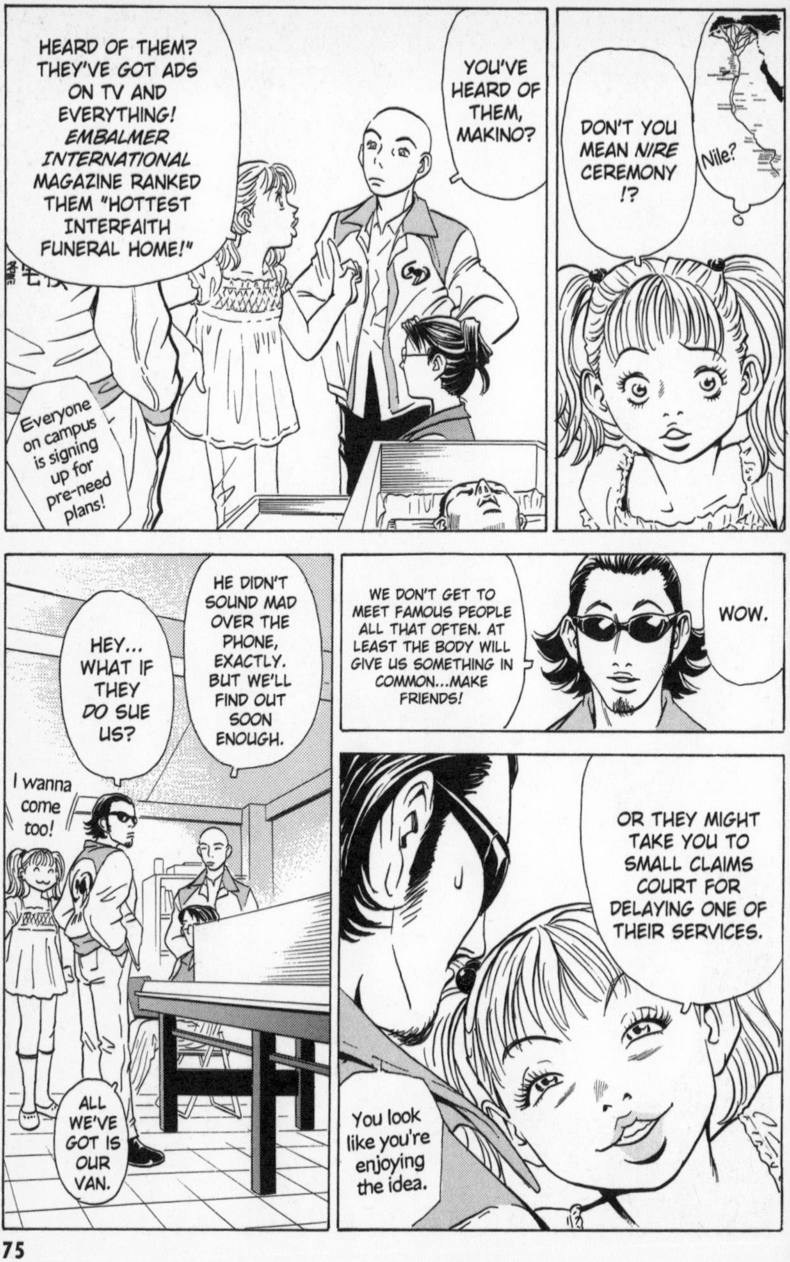
DON'T YOU MEAN *NIRE* CEREMONY !?
Nile?
YOU'VE HEARD OF THEM, MAKINO?
HEARD OF THEM? THEY'VE GOT ADS ON TV AND EVERYTHING! *EMBALMER INTERNATIONAL* MAGAZINE RANKED THEM "HOTTEST INTERFAITH FUNERAL HOME!"
Everyone on campus is signing up for pre-need plans!
WOW.
WE DON'T GET TO MEET FAMOUS PEOPLE ALL THAT OFTEN. AT LEAST THE BODY WILL GIVE US SOMETHING IN COMMON...MAKE FRIENDS!
OR THEY MIGHT TAKE YOU TO SMALL CLAIMS COURT FOR DELAYING ONE OF THEIR SERVICES.
You look like you're enjoying the idea.
HE DIDN'T SOUND MAD OVER THE PHONE, EXACTLY. BUT WE'LL FIND OUT SOON ENOUGH.
HEY... WHAT IF THEY *DO* SUE US?
I wanna come too!
ALL WE'VE GOT IS OUR VAN.

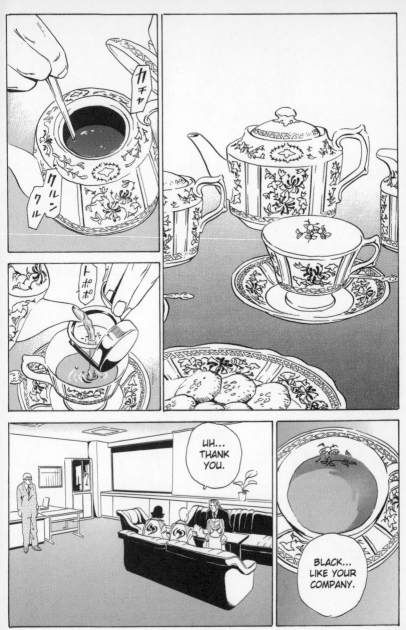

UH... THANK YOU.

BLACK... LIKE YOUR COMPANY.

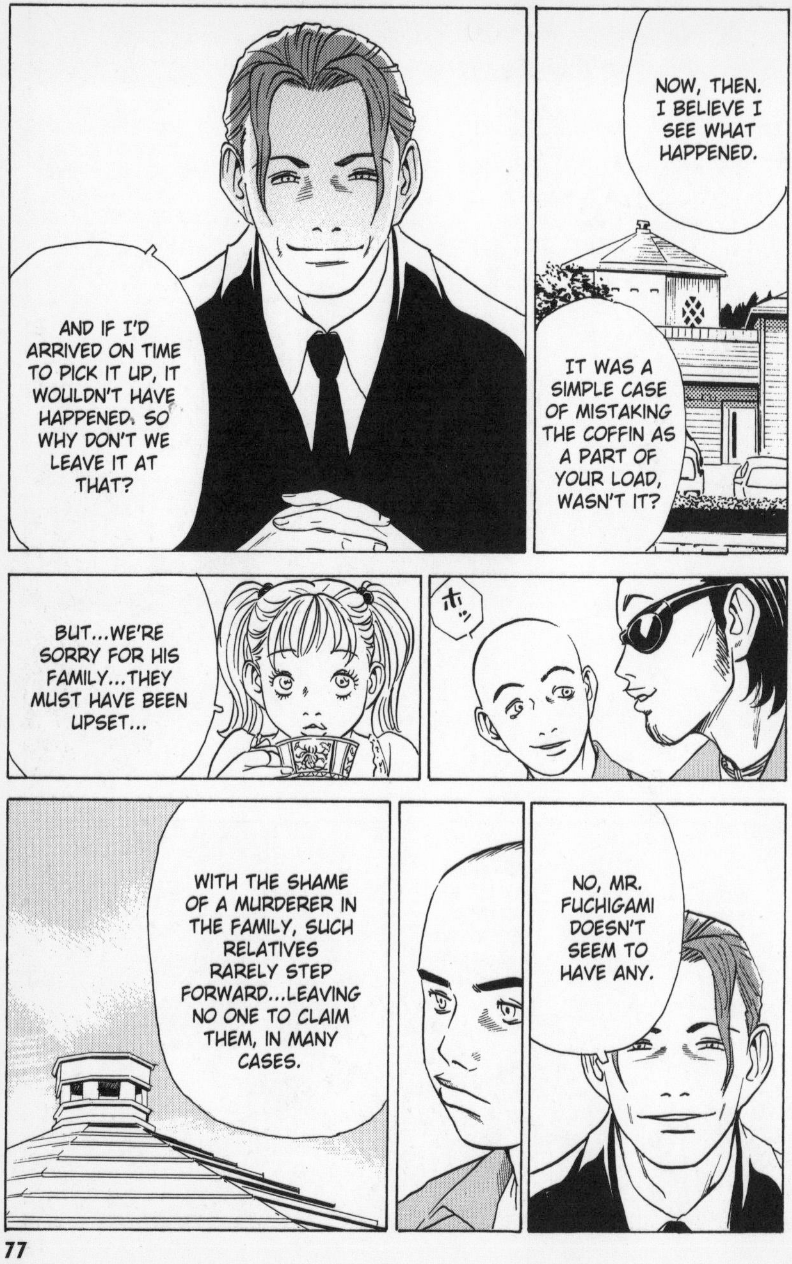
NOW, THEN. I BELIEVE I SEE WHAT HAPPENED.
IT WAS A SIMPLE CASE OF MISTAKING THE COFFIN AS A PART OF YOUR LOAD, WASN'T IT?
AND IF I'D ARRIVED ON TIME TO PICK IT UP, IT WOULDN'T HAVE HAPPENED. SO WHY DON'T WE LEAVE IT AT THAT?
ホッ
BUT...WE'RE SORRY FOR HIS FAMILY...THEY MUST HAVE BEEN UPSET...
NO, MR. FUCHIGAMI DOESN'T SEEM TO HAVE ANY.
WITH THE SHAME OF A MURDERER IN THE FAMILY, SUCH RELATIVES RARELY STEP FORWARD...LEAVING NO ONE TO CLAIM THEM, IN MANY CASES.

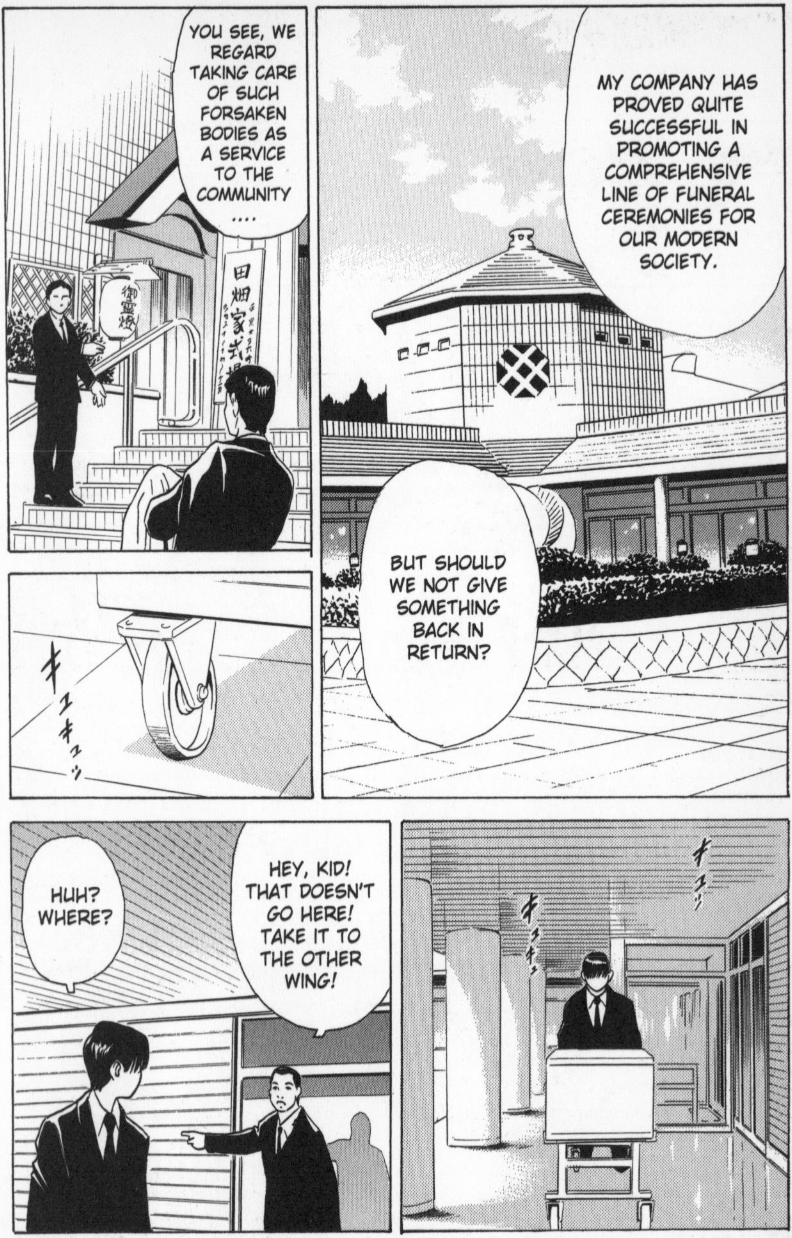
MY COMPANY HAS PROVED QUITE SUCCESSFUL IN PROMOTING A COMPREHENSIVE LINE OF FUNERAL CEREMONIES FOR OUR MODERN SOCIETY.
BUT SHOULD WE NOT GIVE SOMETHING BACK IN RETURN?
YOU SEE, WE REGARD TAKING CARE OF SUCH FORSAKEN BODIES AS A SERVICE TO THE COMMUNITY ....
田畑家式場
キュキュッ
HEY, KID! THAT DOESN'T GO HERE! TAKE IT TO THE OTHER WING!
HUH? WHERE?

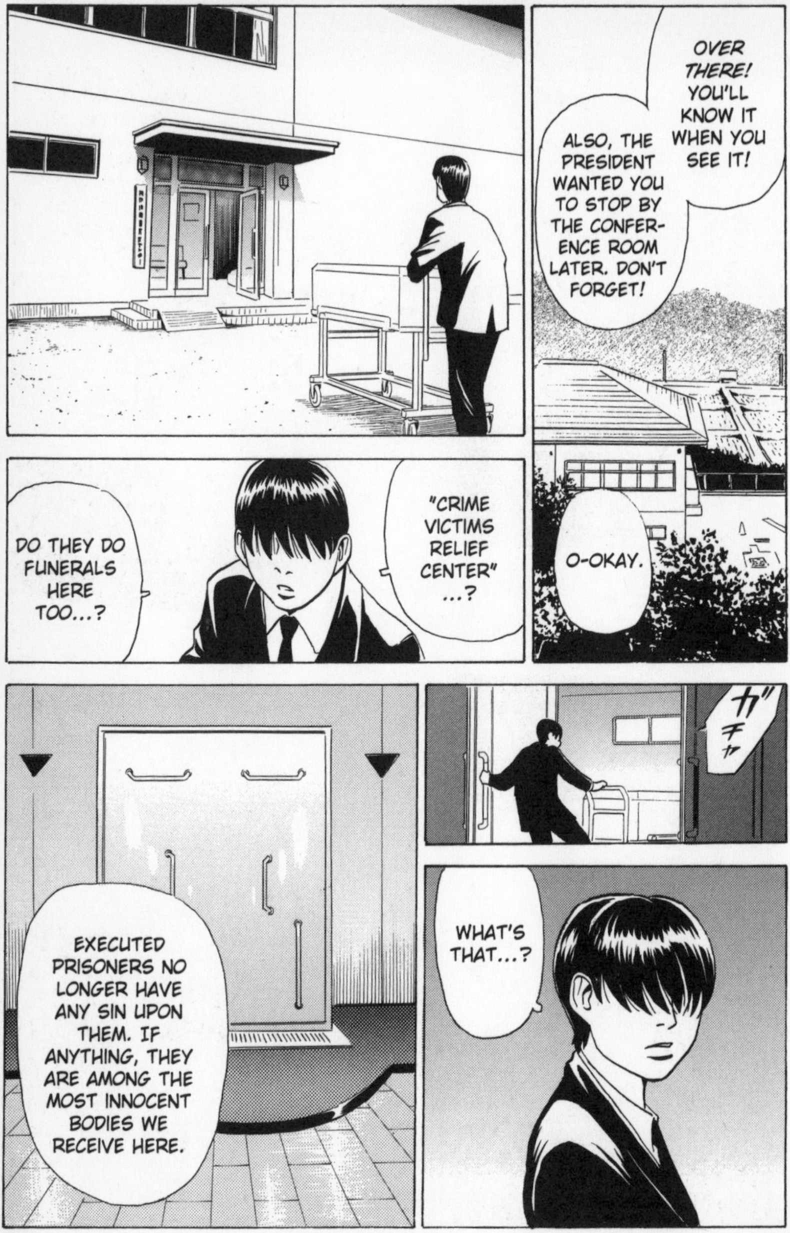
OVER THERE! YOU'LL KNOW IT WHEN YOU SEE IT!
ALSO, THE PRESIDENT WANTED YOU TO STOP BY THE CONFERENCE ROOM LATER. DON'T FORGET!
O-OKAY.
"CRIME VICTIMS RELIEF CENTER" ...?
DO THEY DO FUNERALS HERE TOO...?
ガチャ
WHAT'S THAT...?
EXECUTED PRISONERS NO LONGER HAVE ANY SIN UPON THEM. IF ANYTHING, THEY ARE AMONG THE MOST INNOCENT BODIES WE RECEIVE HERE.

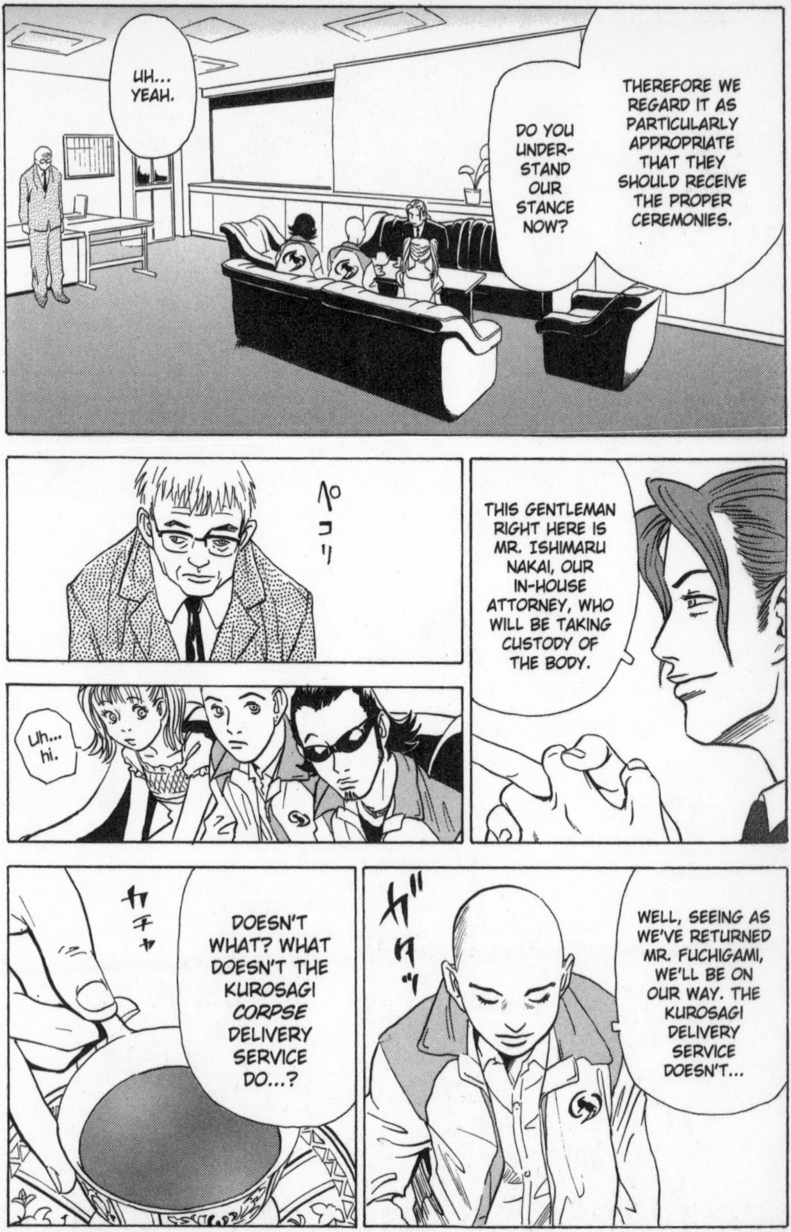
THEREFORE WE REGARD IT AS PARTICULARLY APPROPRIATE THAT THEY SHOULD RECEIVE THE PROPER CEREMONIES.
DO YOU UNDER-STAND OUR STANCE NOW?
UH... YEAH.
THIS GENTLEMAN RIGHT HERE IS MR. ISHIMARU NAKAI, OUR IN-HOUSE ATTORNEY, WHO WILL BE TAKING CUSTODY OF THE BODY.
ペコリ
Uh... hi.
WELL, SEEING AS WE'VE RETURNED MR. FUCHIGAMI, WE'LL BE ON OUR WAY. THE KUROSAGI DELIVERY SERVICE DOESN'T...
ガタッ
DOESN'T WHAT? WHAT DOESN'T THE KUROSAGI *CORPSE* DELIVERY SERVICE DO...?
カチャ

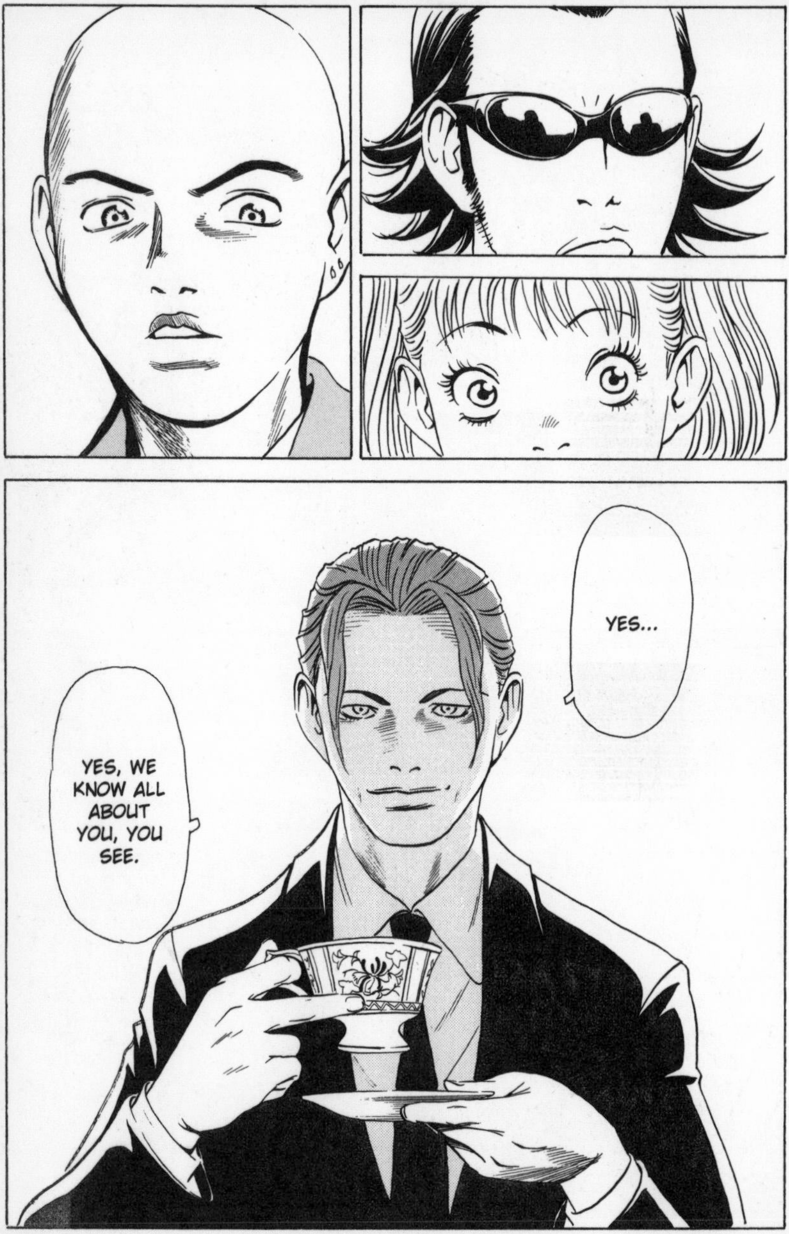
YES...
YES, WE KNOW ALL ABOUT YOU, YOU SEE.

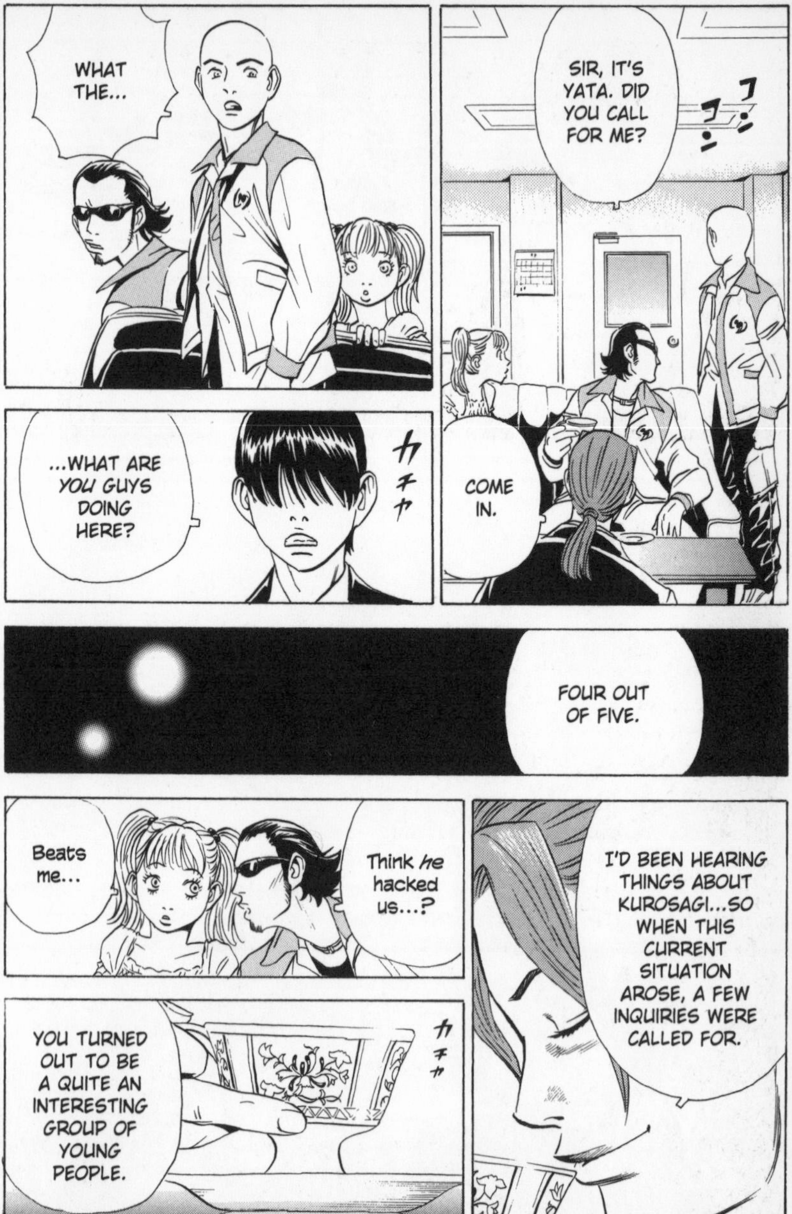
SIR, IT'S YATA. DID YOU CALL FOR ME?
コンコン
COME IN.
WHAT THE...
...WHAT ARE YOU GUYS DOING HERE?
カチャ
FOUR OUT OF FIVE.
I'D BEEN HEARING THINGS ABOUT KUROSAGI...SO WHEN THIS CURRENT SITUATION AROSE, A FEW INQUIRIES WERE CALLED FOR.
Think *he* hacked us...?
Beats me...
YOU TURNED OUT TO BE A QUITE AN INTERESTING GROUP OF YOUNG PEOPLE.
カチャ

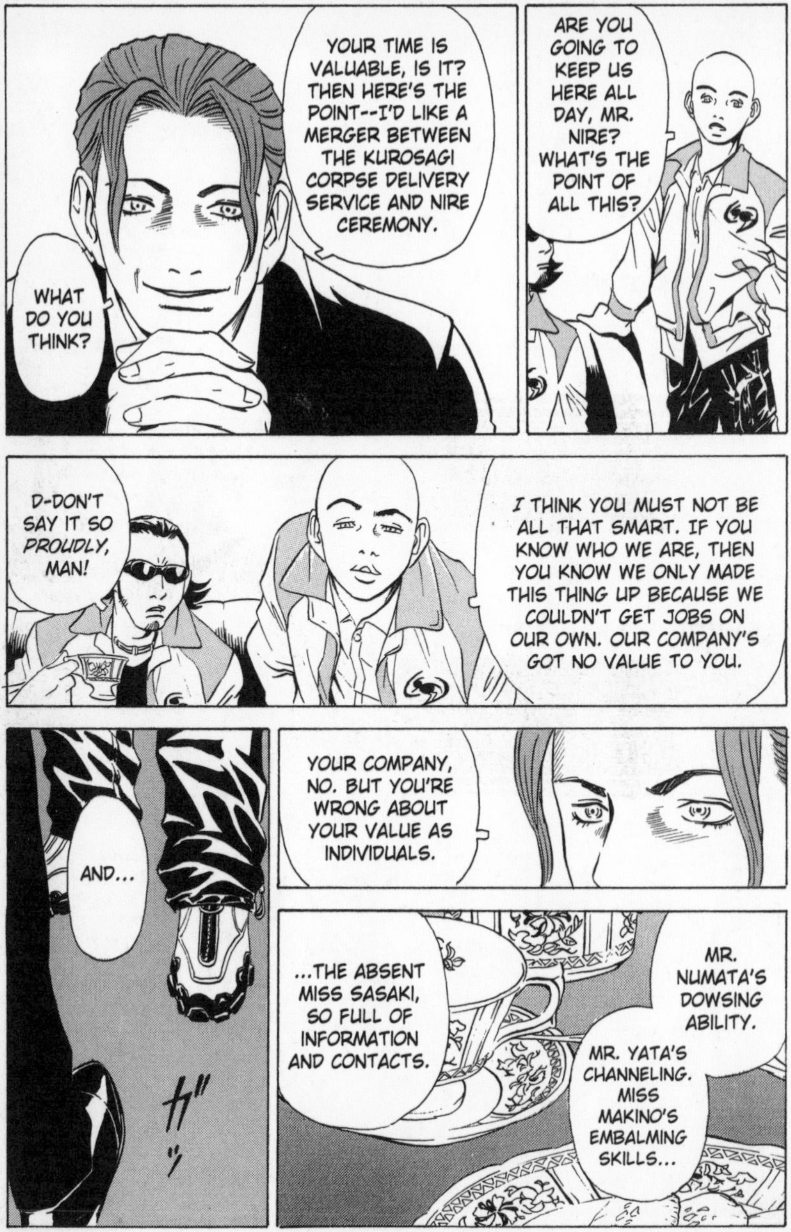
ARE YOU GOING TO KEEP US HERE ALL DAY, MR. NIRE? WHAT'S THE POINT OF ALL THIS?
YOUR TIME IS VALUABLE, IS IT? THEN HERE'S THE POINT--I'D LIKE A MERGER BETWEEN THE KUROSAGI CORPSE DELIVERY SERVICE AND NIRE CEREMONY.
WHAT DO YOU THINK?
I THINK YOU MUST NOT BE ALL THAT SMART. IF YOU KNOW WHO WE ARE, THEN YOU KNOW WE ONLY MADE THIS THING UP BECAUSE WE COULDN'T GET JOBS ON OUR OWN. OUR COMPANY'S GOT NO VALUE TO YOU.
D-DON'T SAY IT SO *PROUDLY*, MAN!
YOUR COMPANY, NO. BUT YOU'RE WRONG ABOUT YOUR VALUE AS INDIVIDUALS.
MR. NUMATA'S DOWSING ABILITY.
MR. YATA'S CHANNELING. MISS MAKINO'S EMBALMING SKILLS...
...THE ABSENT MISS SASAKI, SO FULL OF INFORMATION AND CONTACTS.
AND...
ガッ

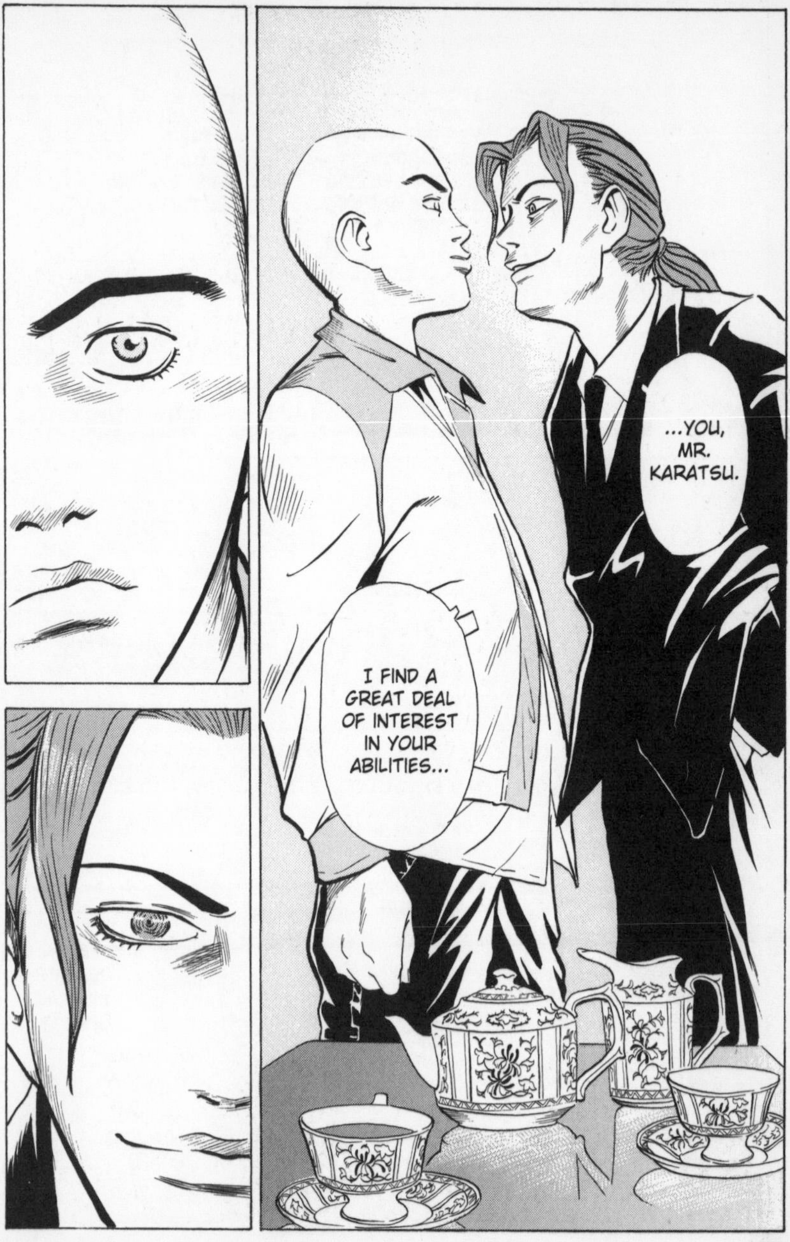
...YOU, MR. KARATSU.
I FIND A GREAT DEAL OF INTEREST IN YOUR ABILITIES...

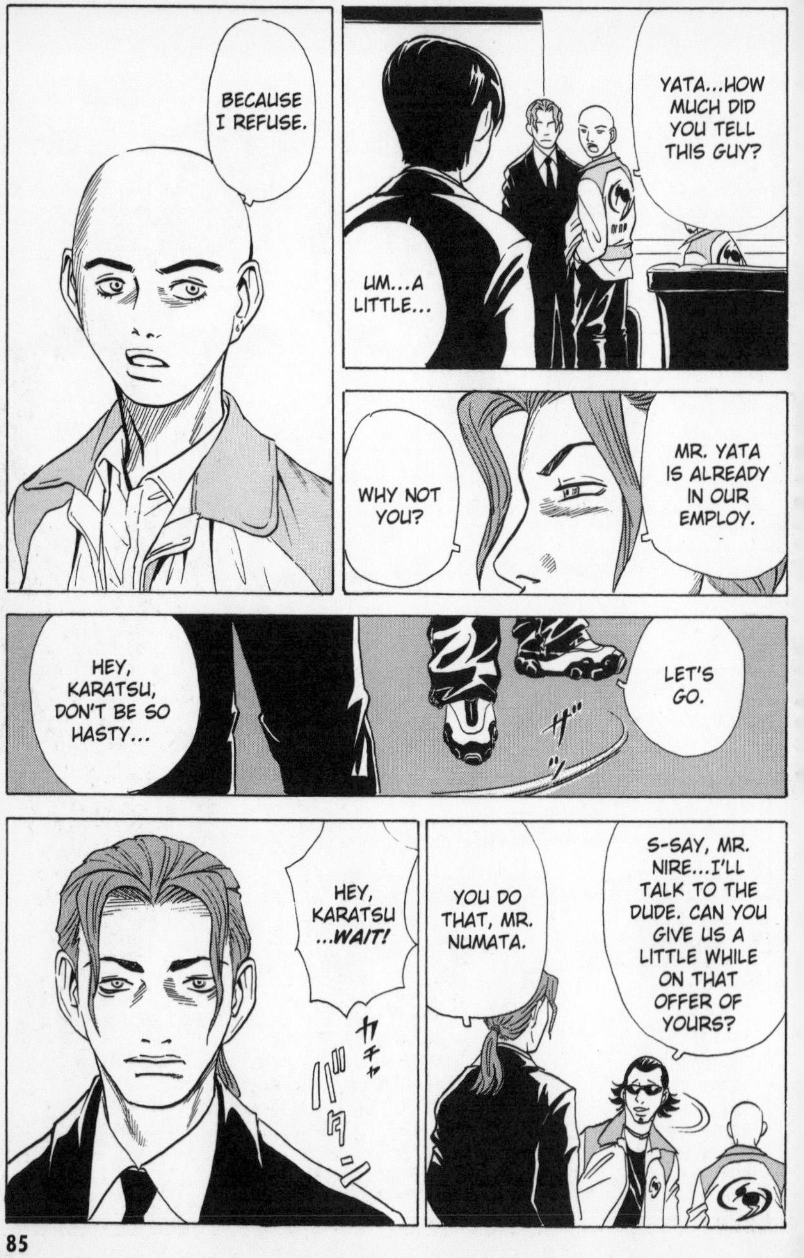
YATA...HOW MUCH DID YOU TELL THIS GUY?
UM...A LITTLE...
MR. YATA IS ALREADY IN OUR EMPLOY.
WHY NOT YOU?
BECAUSE I REFUSE.
LET'S GO.
ザッ
HEY, KARATSU, DON'T BE SO HASTY...
S-SAY, MR. NIRE...I'LL TALK TO THE DUDE. CAN YOU GIVE US A LITTLE WHILE ON THAT OFFER OF YOURS?
YOU DO THAT, MR. NUMATA.
HEY, KARATSU ...*WAIT!*
バタン

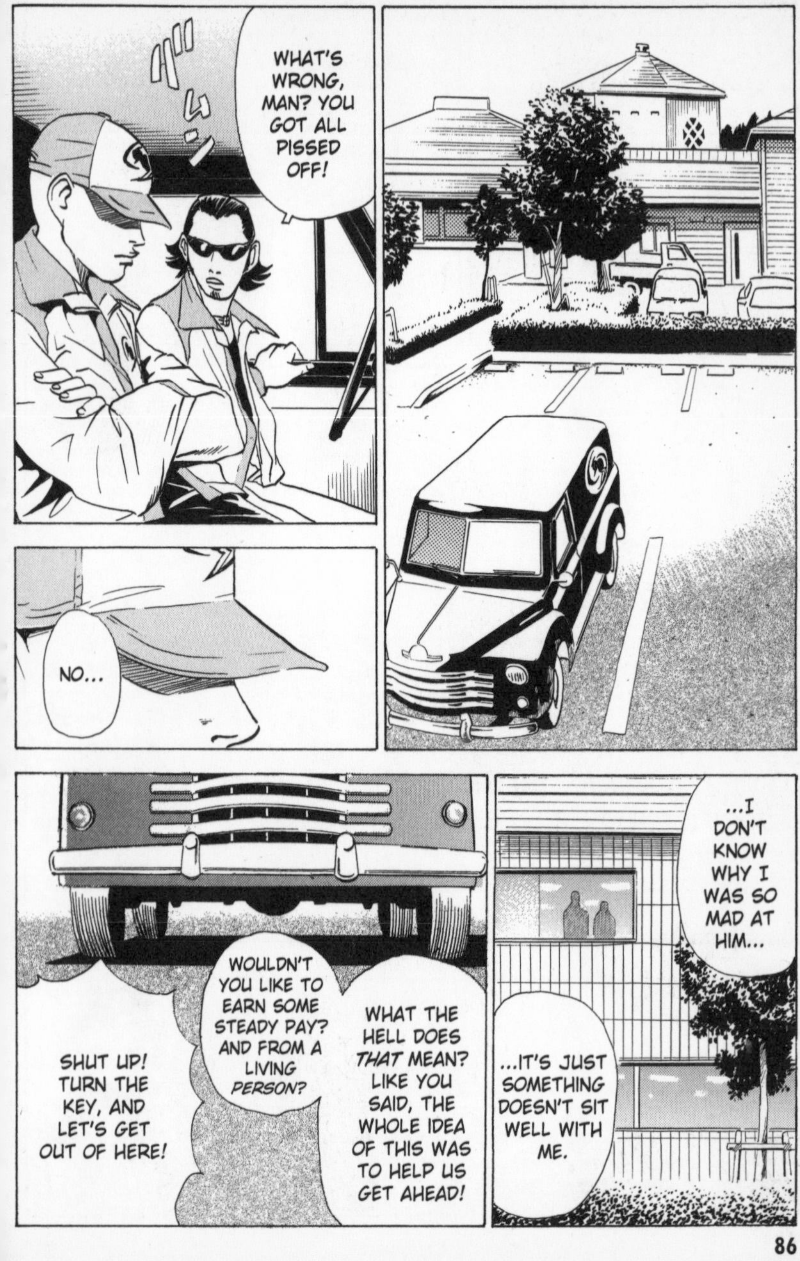
WHAT'S WRONG, MAN? YOU GOT ALL PISSED OFF!
NO...
...I DON'T KNOW WHY I WAS SO MAD AT HIM...
...IT'S JUST SOMETHING DOESN'T SIT WELL WITH ME.
WOULDN'T YOU LIKE TO EARN SOME STEADY PAY? AND FROM A LIVING *PERSON*?
WHAT THE HELL DOES *THAT* MEAN? LIKE YOU SAID, THE WHOLE IDEA OF THIS WAS TO HELP US GET AHEAD!
SHUT UP! TURN THE KEY, AND LET'S GET OUT OF HERE!

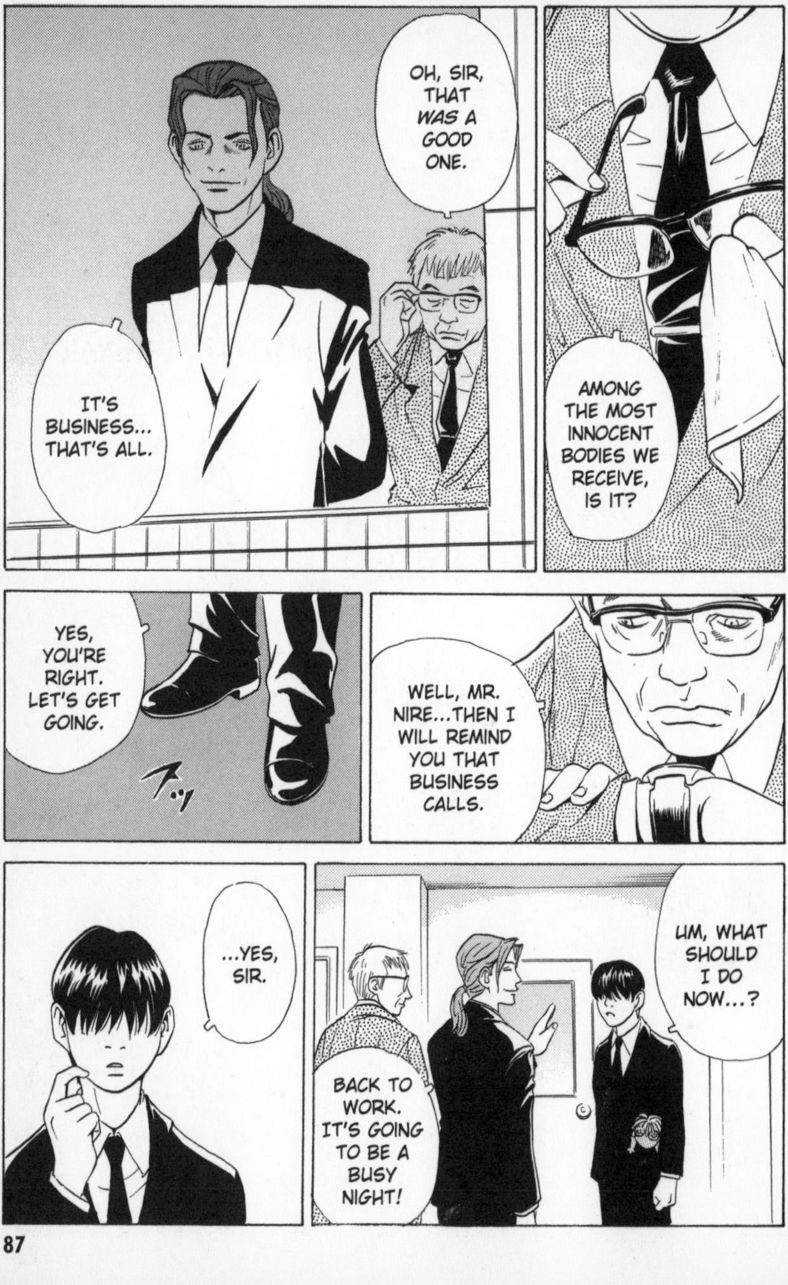
AMONG THE MOST INNOCENT BODIES WE RECEIVE, IS IT?
OH, SIR, THAT *WAS* A GOOD ONE.
IT'S BUSINESS... THAT'S ALL.
WELL, MR. NIRE...THEN I WILL REMIND YOU THAT BUSINESS CALLS.
YES, YOU'RE RIGHT. LET'S GET GOING.
UM, WHAT SHOULD I DO NOW...?
BACK TO WORK. IT'S GOING TO BE A BUSY NIGHT!
...YES, SIR.

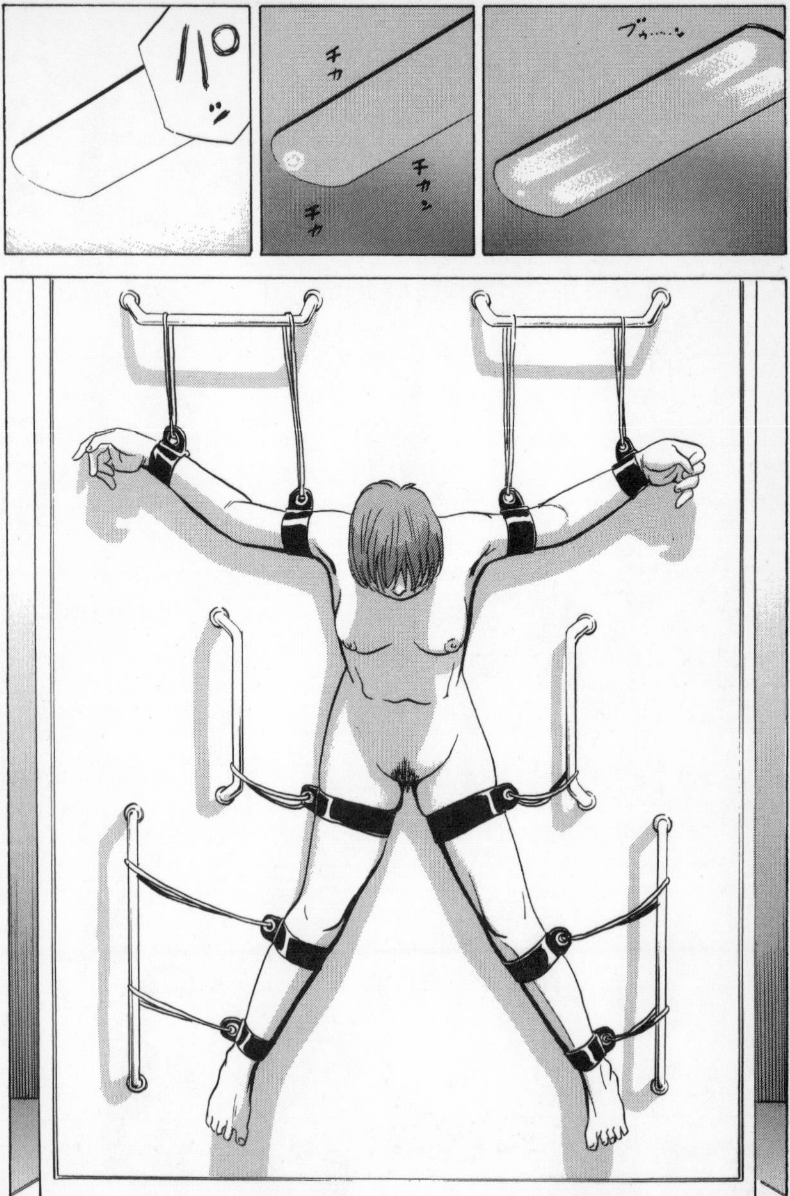
ブゥ…ン
チカ
チカン
チカ
パッ

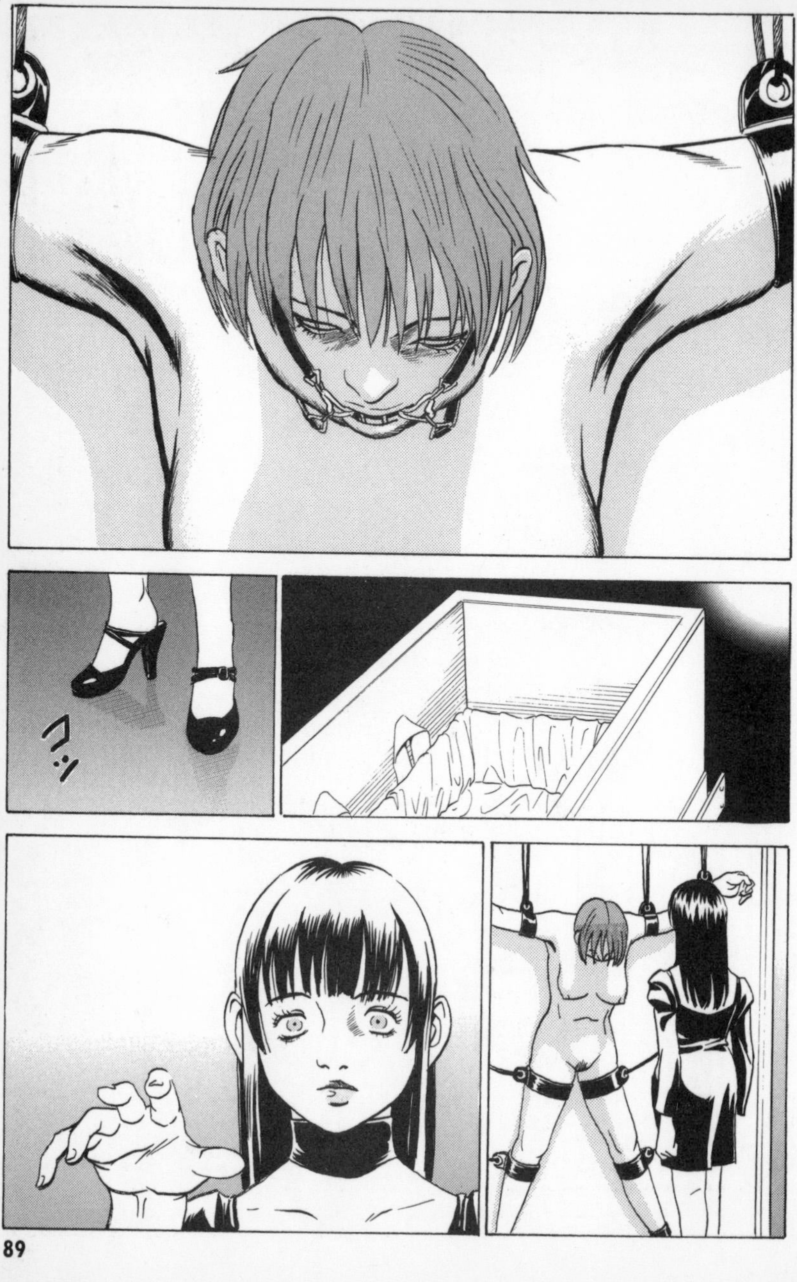
コッ

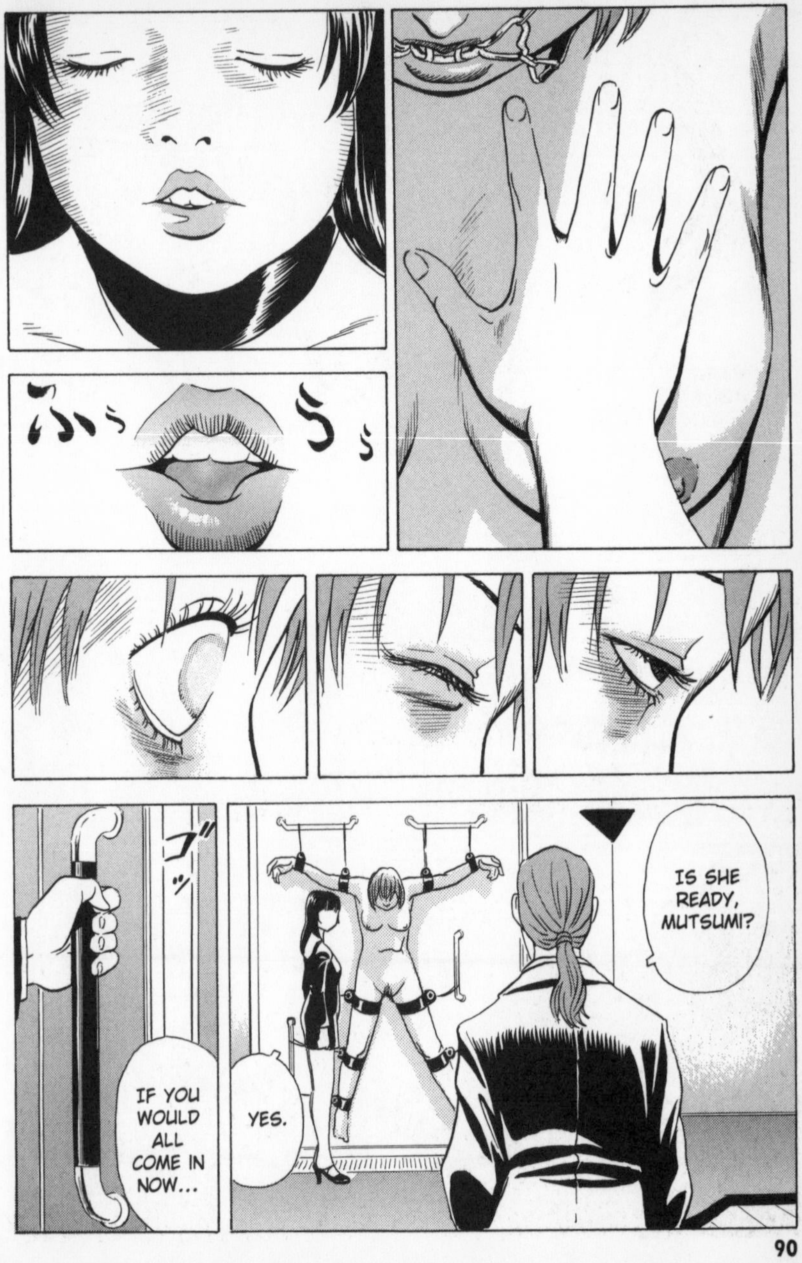
ふぅうぅ
IS SHE READY, MUTSUMI?
YES.
ゴッ
IF YOU WOULD ALL COME IN NOW...

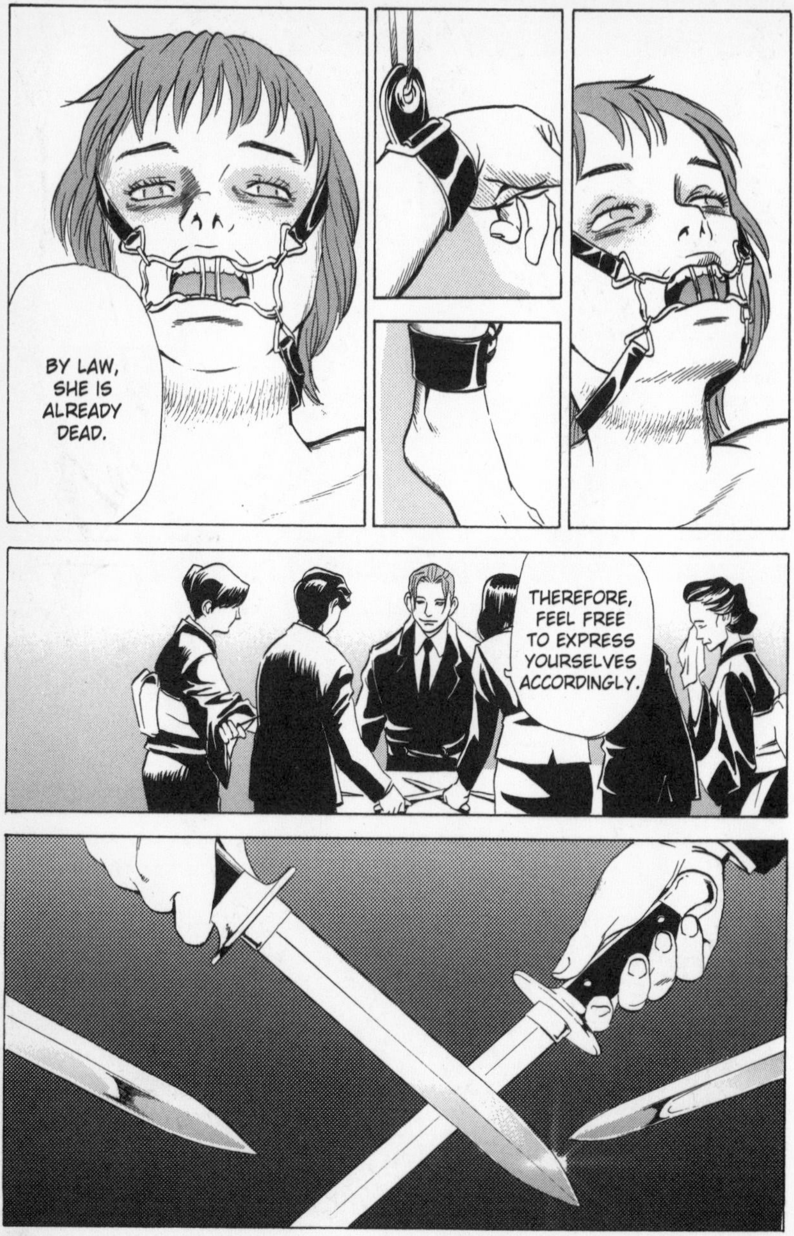
BY LAW, SHE IS ALREADY DEAD.
THEREFORE, FEEL FREE TO EXPRESS YOURSELVES ACCORDINGLY.

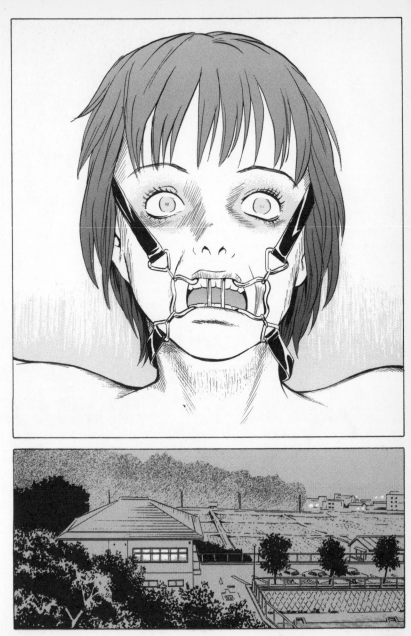

3rd delivery: watch out for that girl——the end

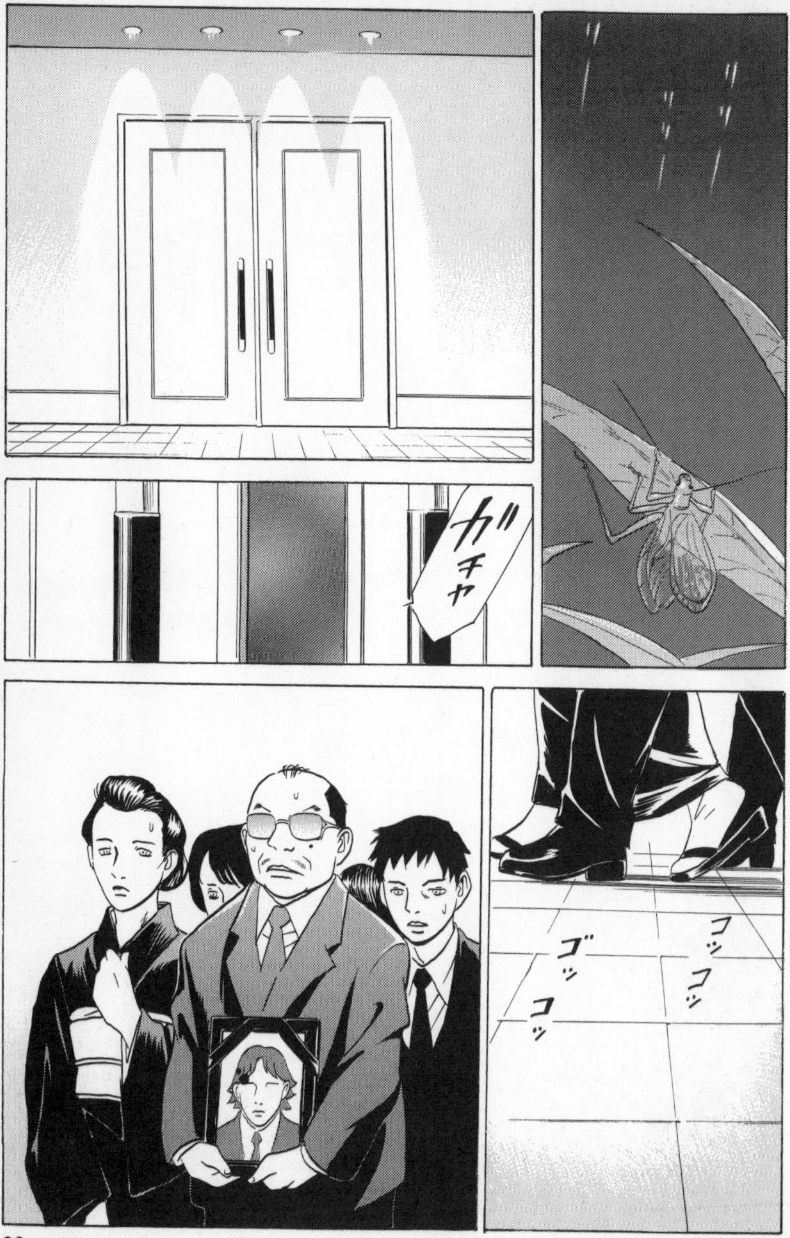
ガチャ
コッ
コッ
ゴッ
コッ

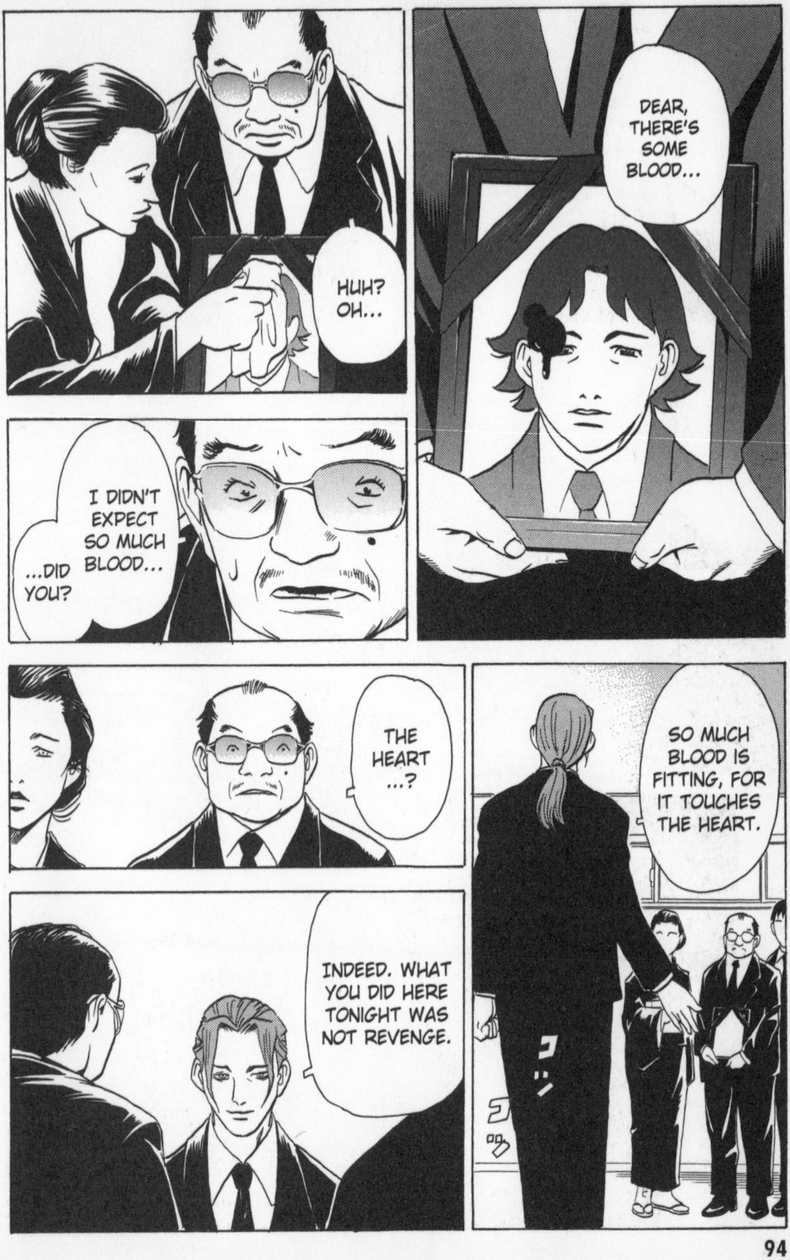
DEAR, THERE'S SOME BLOOD...
HUH? OH...
I DIDN'T EXPECT SO MUCH BLOOD...
...DID YOU?
SO MUCH BLOOD IS FITTING, FOR IT TOUCHES THE HEART.
THE HEART ...?
INDEED. WHAT YOU DID HERE TONIGHT WAS NOT REVENGE.

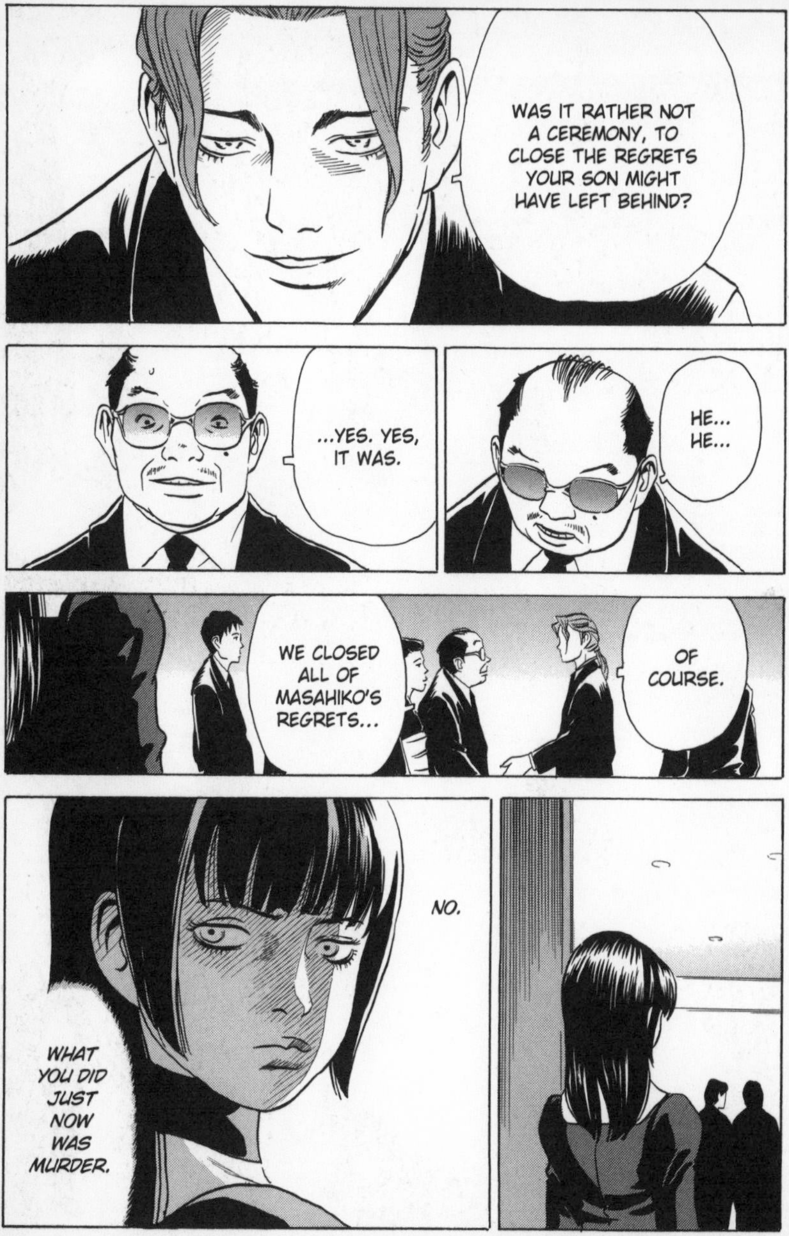
WAS IT RATHER NOT A CEREMONY, TO CLOSE THE REGRETS YOUR SON MIGHT HAVE LEFT BEHIND?
HE... HE...
...YES. YES, IT WAS.
OF COURSE.
WE CLOSED ALL OF MASAHIKO'S REGRETS...
NO.
WHAT YOU DID JUST NOW WAS MURDER.

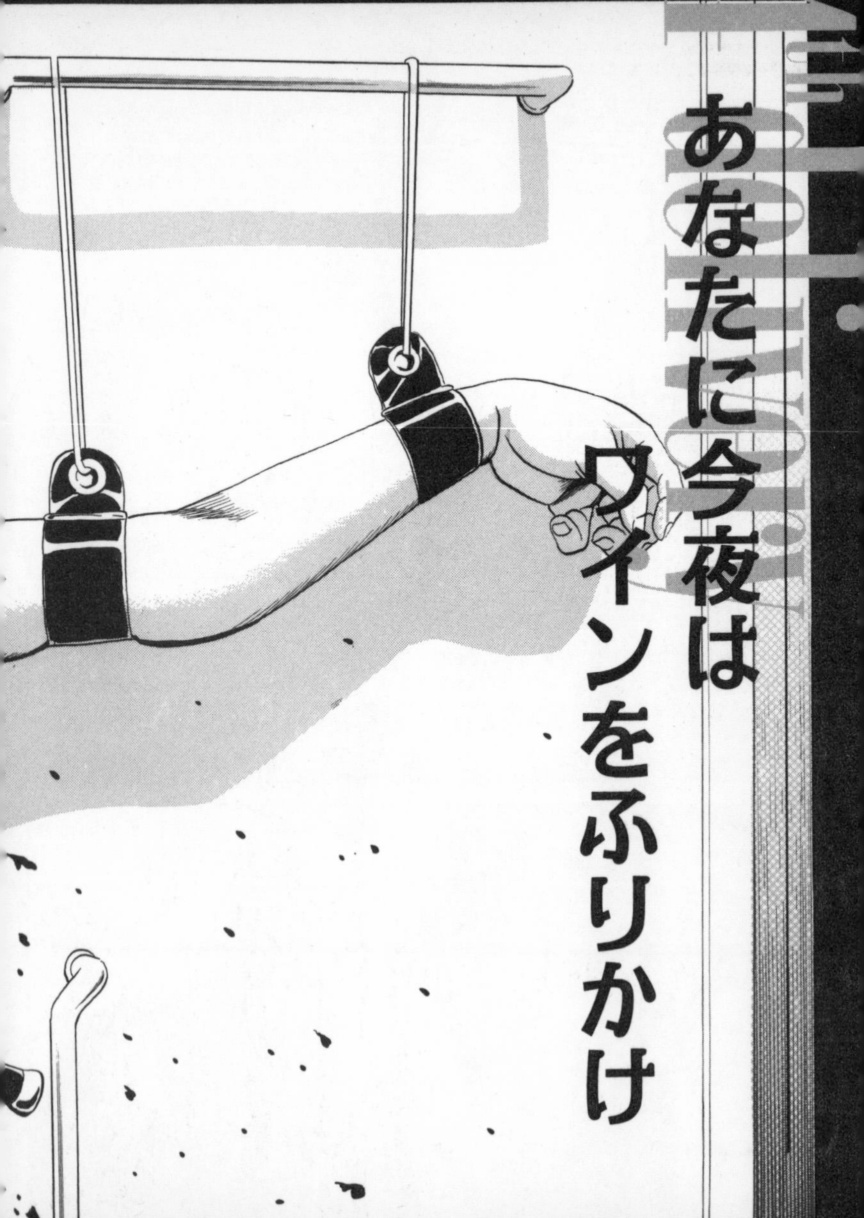
あなたに今夜は
ワインをふりかけ

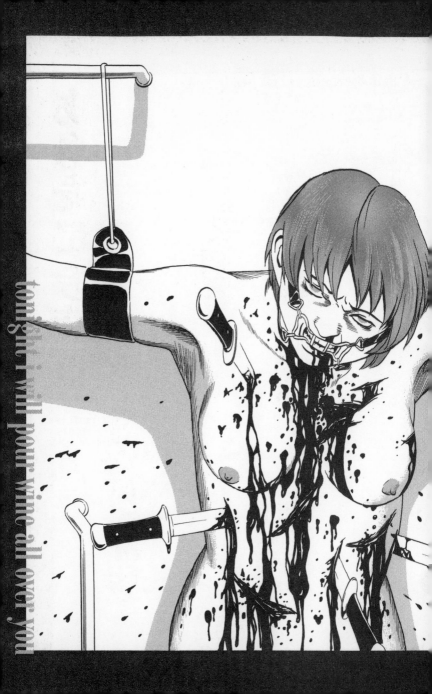

tonight i will pour wine all over you

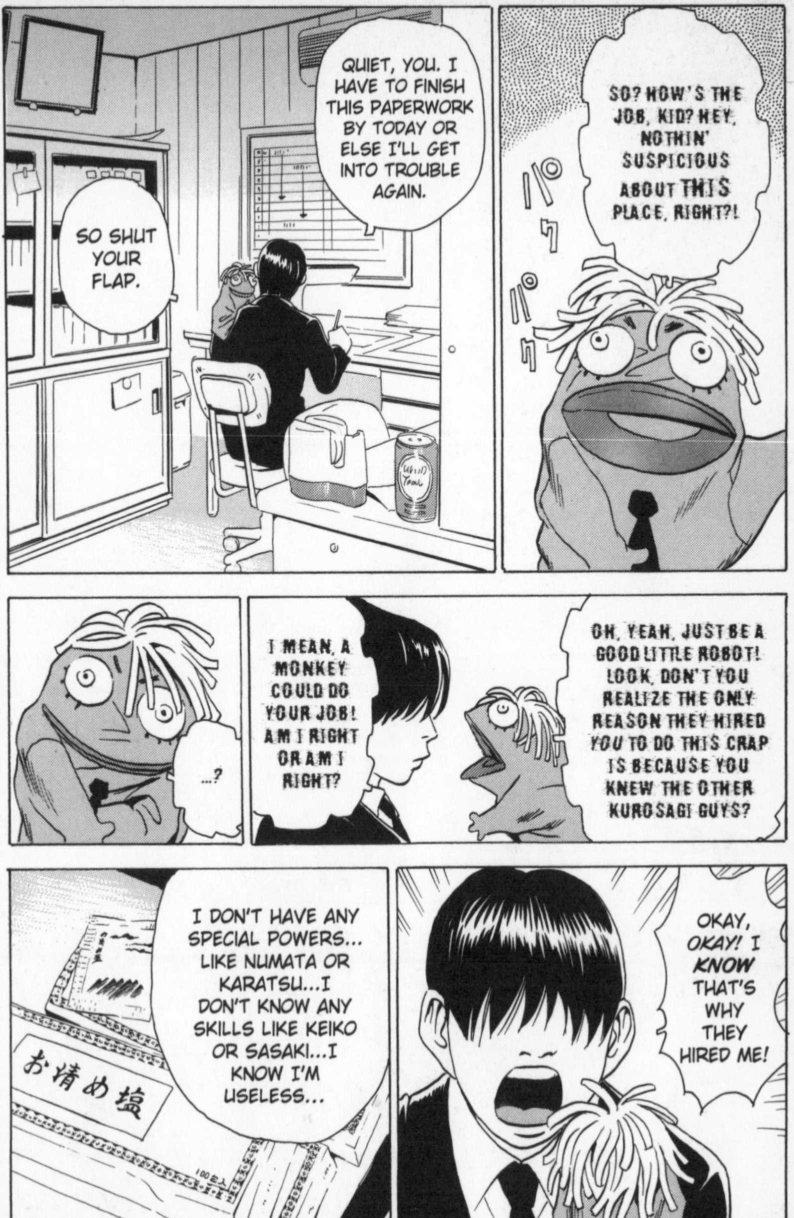
SO? HOW'S THE JOB, KID? HEY, NOTHIN' SUSPICIOUS ABOUT THIS PLACE, RIGHT?!
パク パク
QUIET, YOU. I HAVE TO FINISH THIS PAPERWORK BY TODAY OR ELSE I'LL GET INTO TROUBLE AGAIN.
SO SHUT YOUR FLAP.
OH, YEAH, JUST BE A GOOD LITTLE ROBOT! LOOK, DON'T YOU REALIZE THE ONLY REASON THEY HIRED *YOU* TO DO THIS CRAP IS BECAUSE YOU KNEW THE OTHER KUROSAGI GUYS?
I MEAN, A MONKEY COULD DO YOUR JOB! AM I RIGHT OR AM I RIGHT?
...?
OKAY, *OKAY!* I ***KNOW*** THAT'S WHY THEY HIRED ME!
I DON'T HAVE ANY SPECIAL POWERS... LIKE NUMATA OR KARATSU...I DON'T KNOW ANY SKILLS LIKE KEIKO OR SASAKI...I KNOW I'M USELESS...
お清め塩

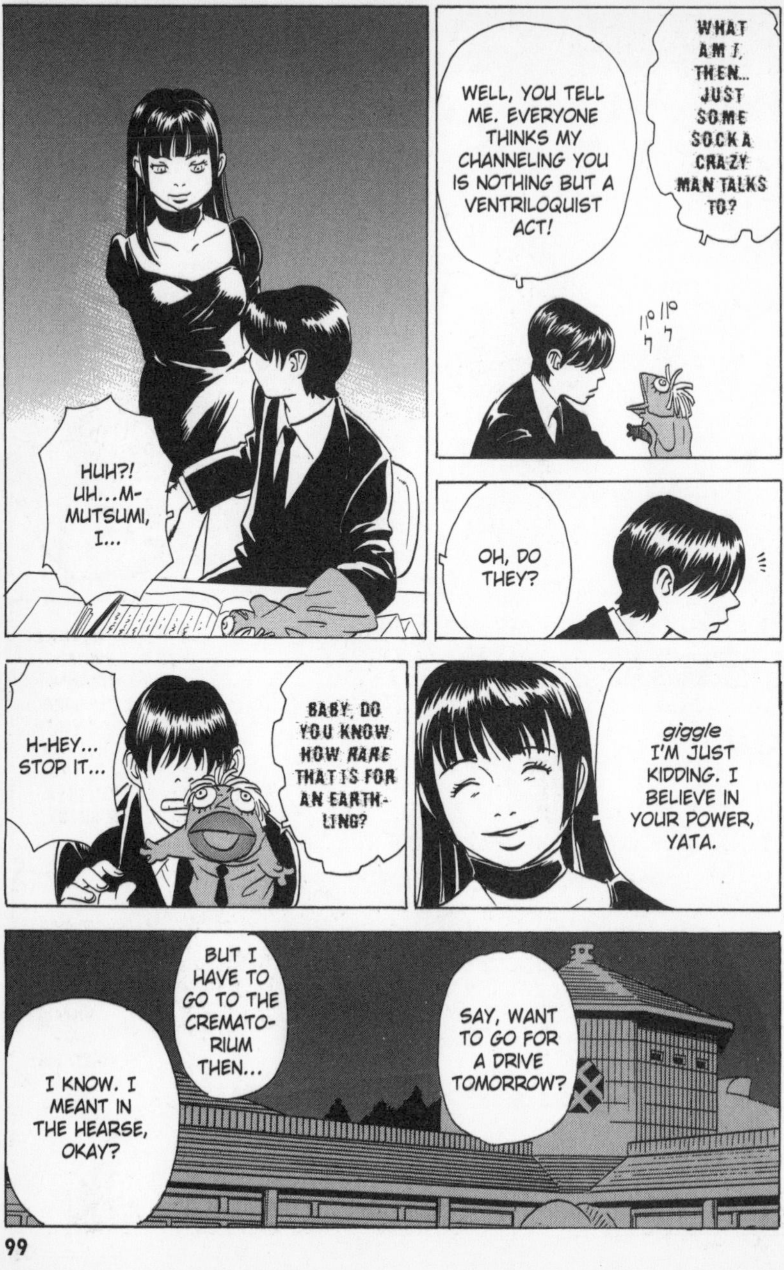
WHAT AM I, THEN.. JUST SOME SOCK A CRAZY MAN TALKS TO?
WELL, YOU TELL ME. EVERYONE THINKS MY CHANNELING YOU IS NOTHING BUT A VENTRILOQUIST ACT!
OH, DO THEY?
HUH?! UH...M-MUTSUMI, I...
giggle I'M JUST KIDDING. I BELIEVE IN YOUR POWER, YATA.
BABY, DO YOU KNOW HOW *RARE* THAT IS FOR AN EARTH-LING?
H-HEY... STOP IT...
SAY, WANT TO GO FOR A DRIVE TOMORROW?
BUT I HAVE TO GO TO THE CREMATO-RIUM THEN...
I KNOW. I MEANT IN THE HEARSE, OKAY?

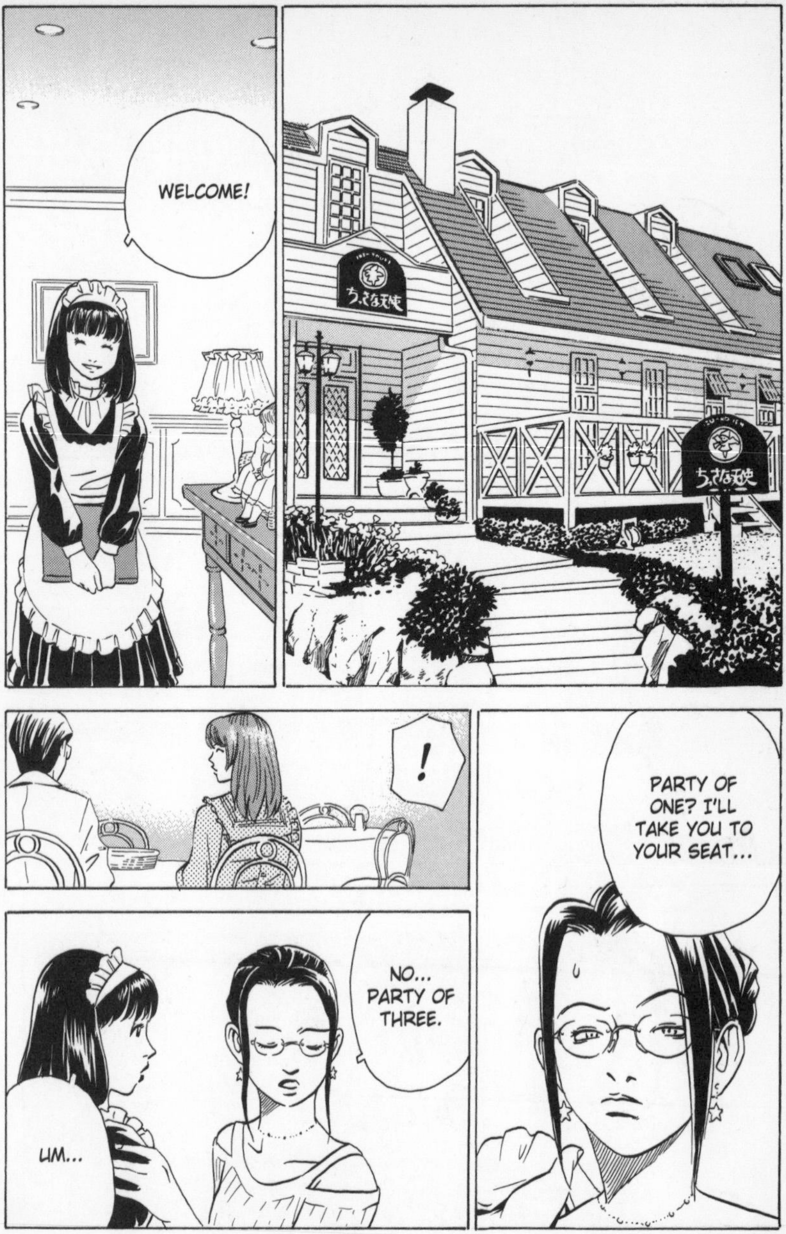
WELCOME!
PARTY OF ONE? I'LL TAKE YOU TO YOUR SEAT...
!
NO... PARTY OF THREE.
UM...

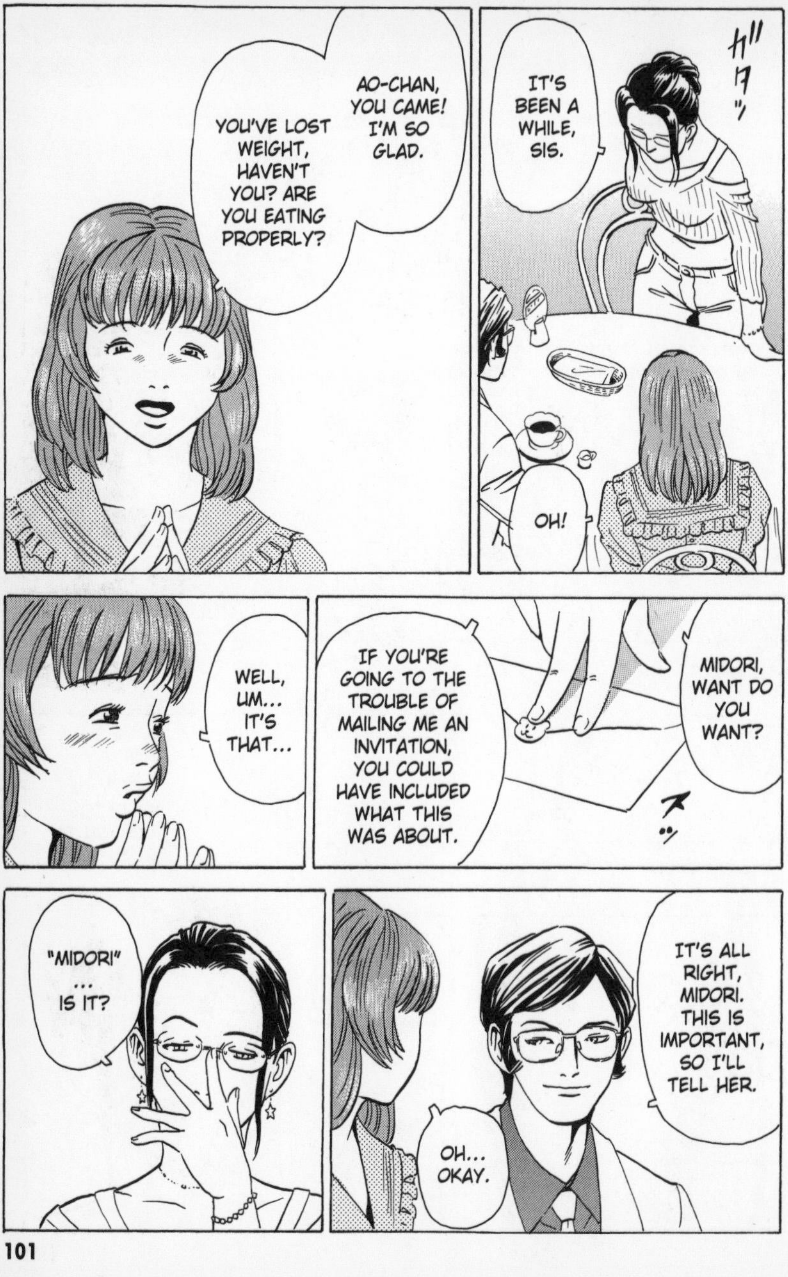

IT'S BEEN A WHILE, SIS.
ガタッ
OH!
AO-CHAN, YOU CAME! I'M SO GLAD.
YOU'VE LOST WEIGHT, HAVEN'T YOU? ARE YOU EATING PROPERLY?
MIDORI, WANT DO YOU WANT?
スッ
IF YOU'RE GOING TO THE TROUBLE OF MAILING ME AN INVITATION, YOU COULD HAVE INCLUDED WHAT THIS WAS ABOUT.
WELL, UM... IT'S THAT...
IT'S ALL RIGHT, MIDORI. THIS IS IMPORTANT, SO I'LL TELL HER.
OH... OKAY.
"MIDORI" ... IS IT?

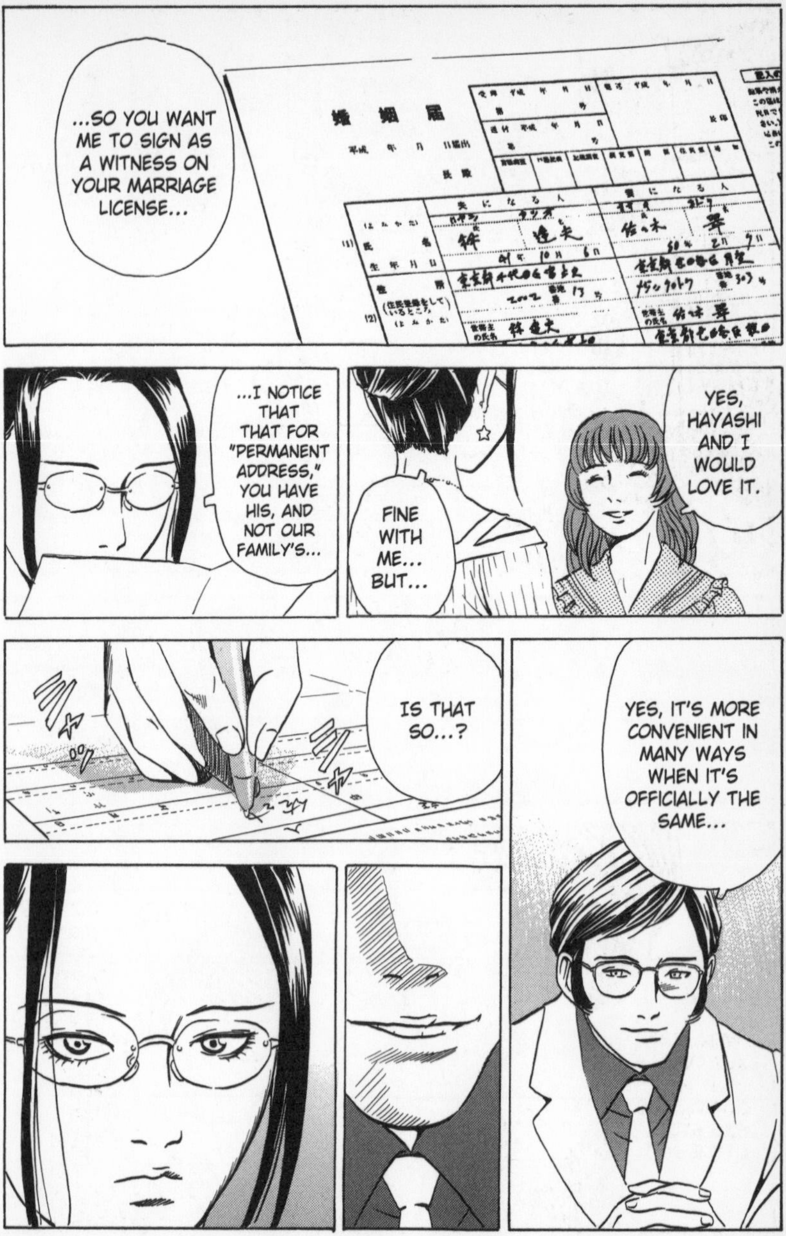
...SO YOU WANT ME TO SIGN AS A WITNESS ON YOUR MARRIAGE LICENSE...
婚姻届
YES, HAYASHI AND I WOULD LOVE IT.
FINE WITH ME... BUT...
...I NOTICE THAT THAT FOR "PERMANENT ADDRESS," YOU HAVE HIS, AND NOT OUR FAMILY'S...
YES, IT'S MORE CONVENIENT IN MANY WAYS WHEN IT'S OFFICIALLY THE SAME...
IS THAT SO...?

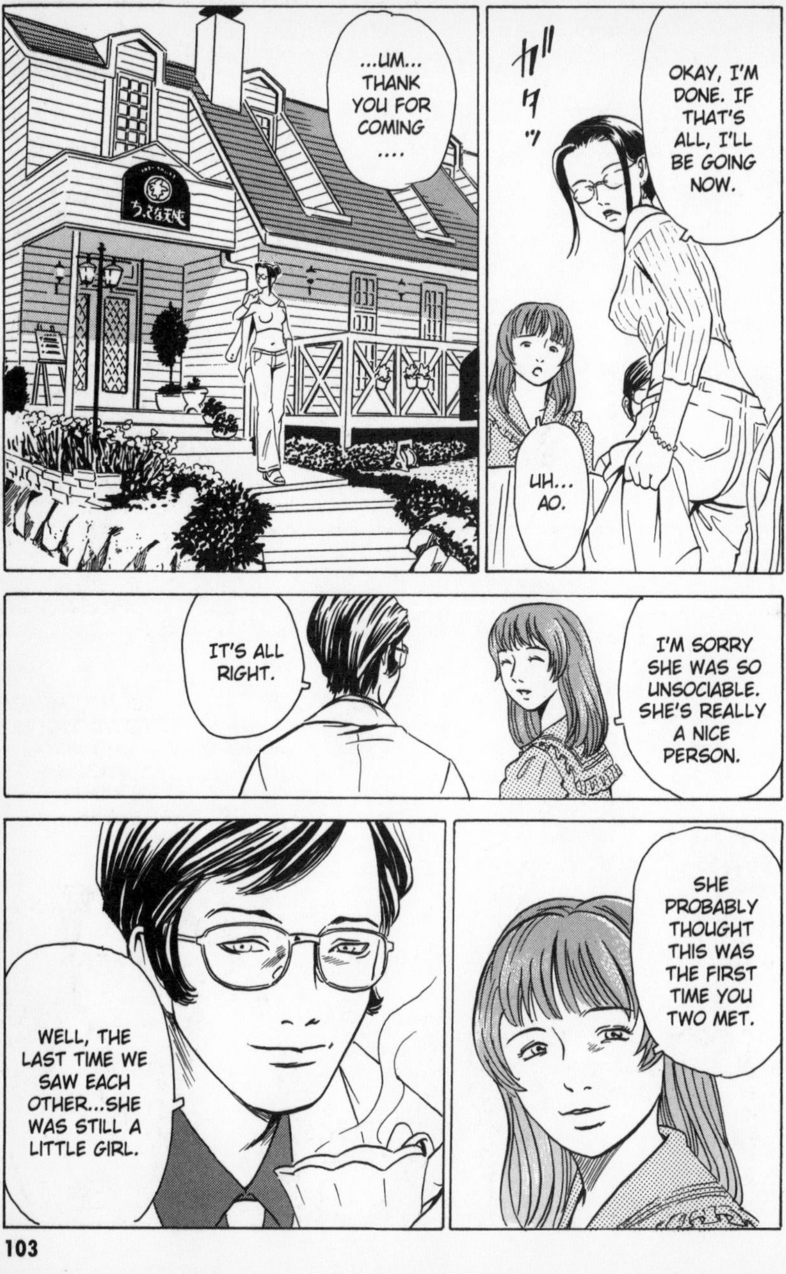
ガタッ
OKAY, I'M DONE. IF THAT'S ALL, I'LL BE GOING NOW.
UH... AO.
...UM... THANK YOU FOR COMING ....
I'M SORRY SHE WAS SO UNSOCIABLE. SHE'S REALLY A NICE PERSON.
IT'S ALL RIGHT.
SHE PROBABLY THOUGHT THIS WAS THE FIRST TIME YOU TWO MET.
WELL, THE LAST TIME WE SAW EACH OTHER...SHE WAS STILL A LITTLE GIRL.

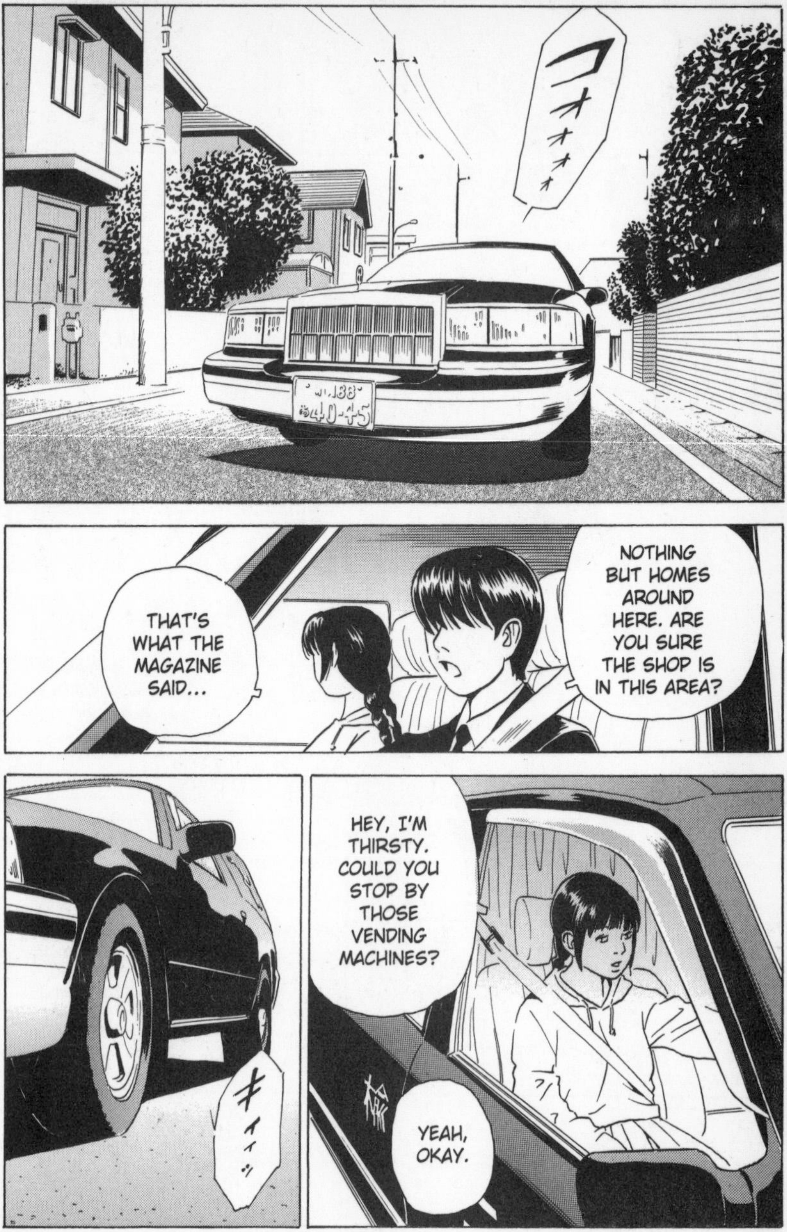
コォォォォ
NOTHING BUT HOMES AROUND HERE. ARE YOU SURE THE SHOP IS IN THIS AREA?
THAT'S WHAT THE MAGAZINE SAID...
HEY, I'M THIRSTY. COULD YOU STOP BY THOSE VENDING MACHINES?
YEAH, OKAY.
キィィッ

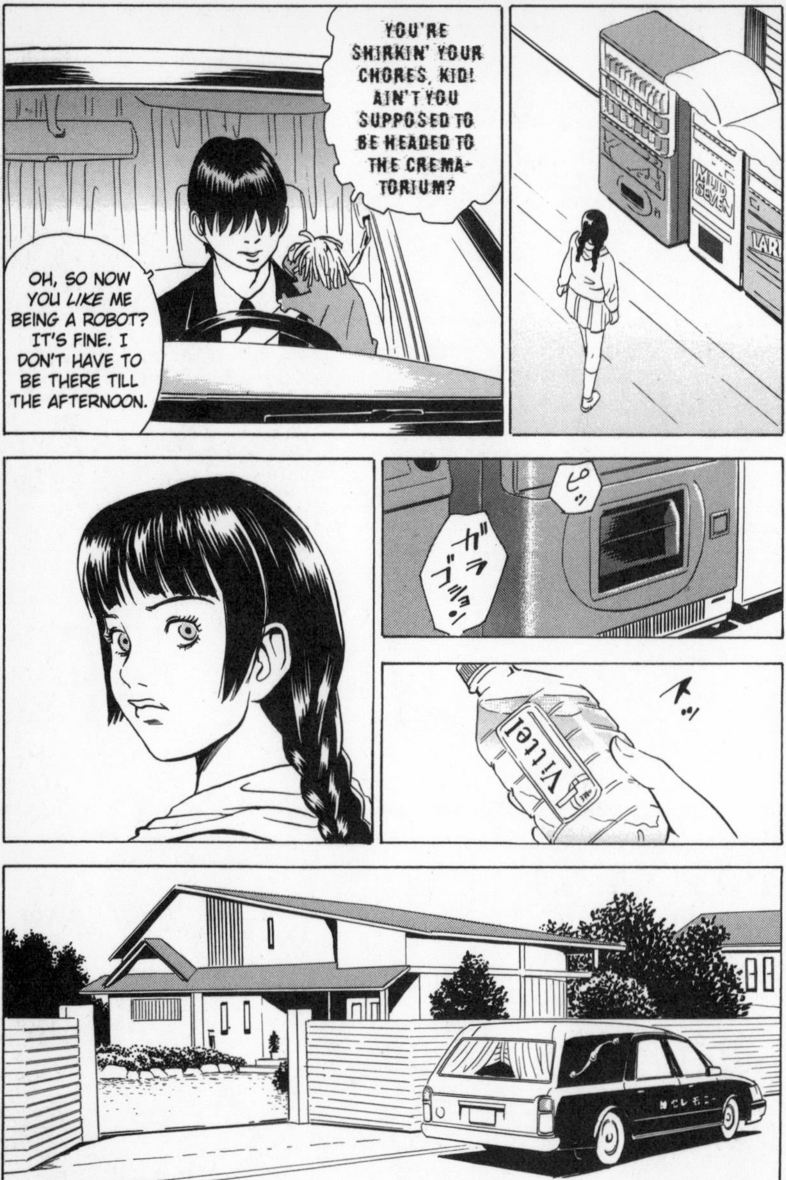
MILD SEVEN
YOU'RE SHIRKIN' YOUR CHORES, KID! AIN'T YOU SUPPOSED TO BE HEADED TO THE CREMA-TORIUM?
OH, SO NOW YOU *LIKE* ME BEING A ROBOT? IT'S FINE. I DON'T HAVE TO BE THERE TILL THE AFTERNOON.
ピッ
ガラゴション
Vittel

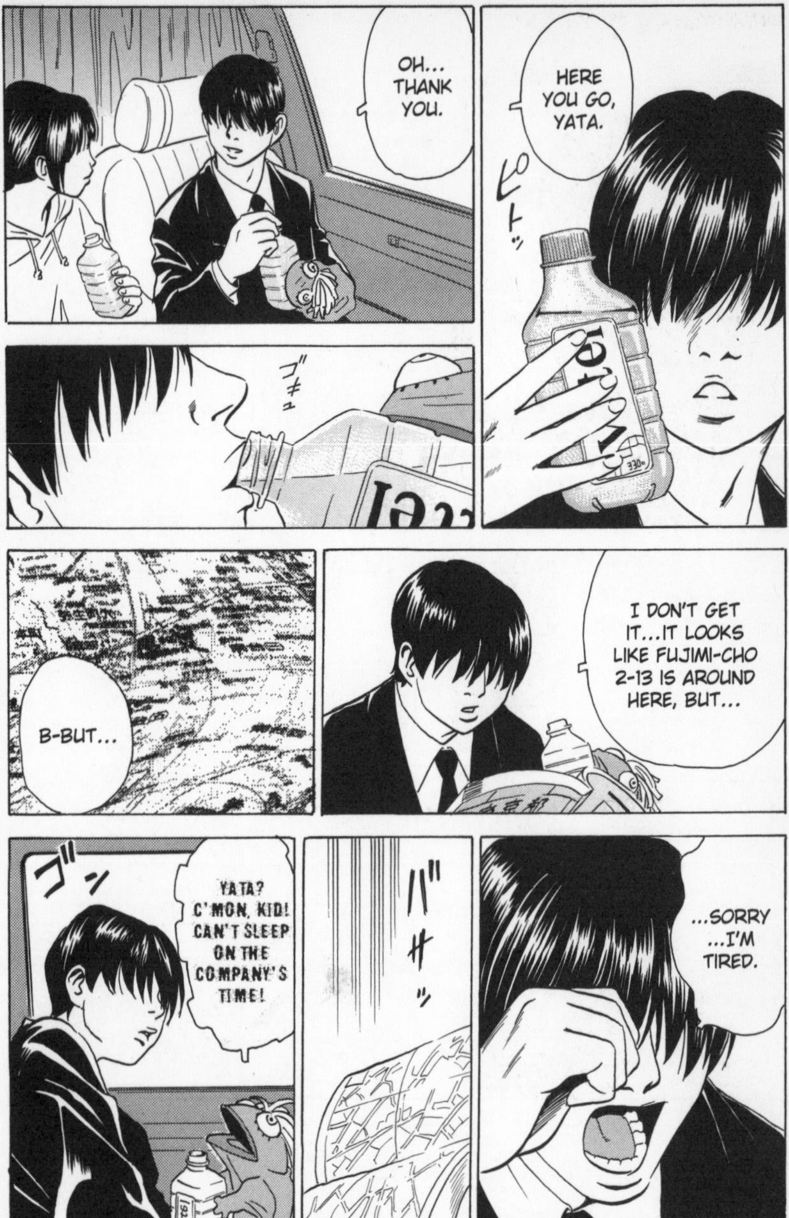
HERE YOU GO, YATA.
ピトッ
OH... THANK YOU.
ゴキュ
I DON'T GET IT...IT LOOKS LIKE FUJIMI-CHO 2-13 IS AROUND HERE, BUT...
B-BUT...
...SORRY ...I'M TIRED.
バサッ
ゴン
YATA? C'MON, KID! CAN'T SLEEP ON THE COMPANY'S TIME!

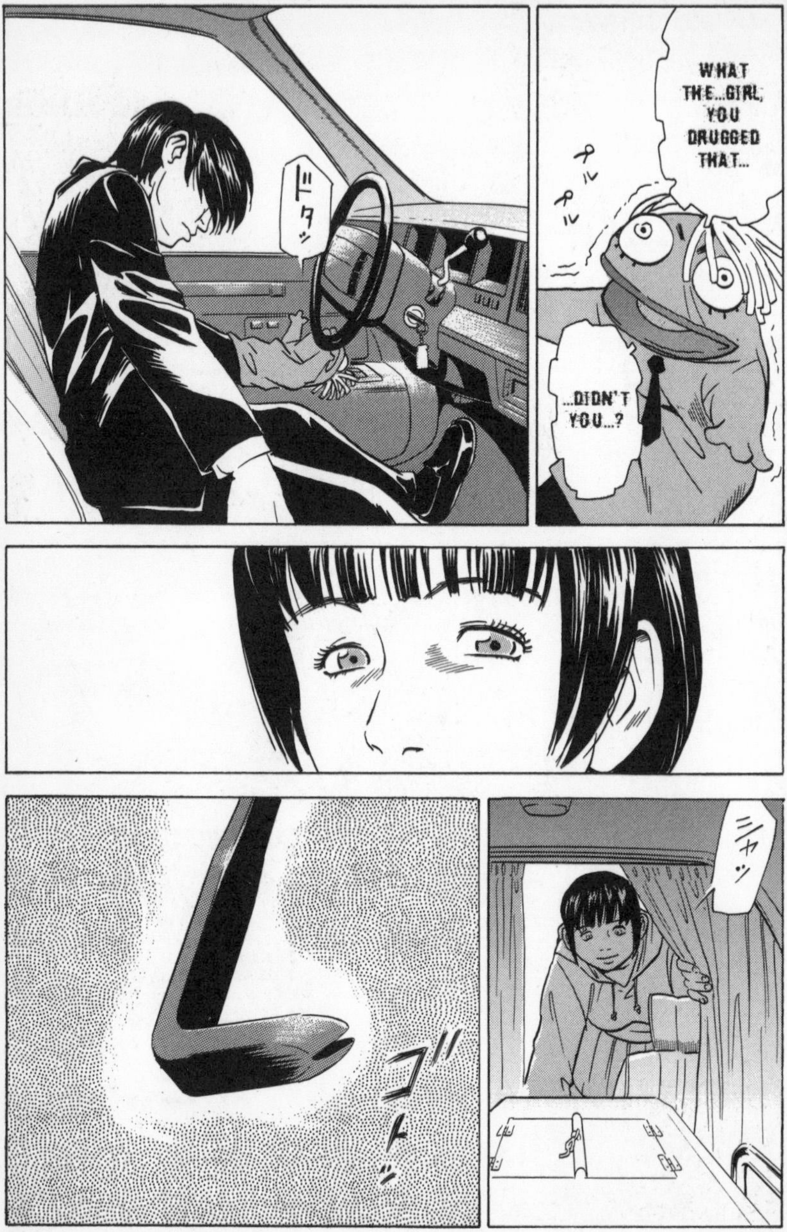
WHAT THE...GIRL, YOU DRUGGED THAT...
プルプル
...DIDN'T YOU...?
ドタッ
シャッ
ゴトッ

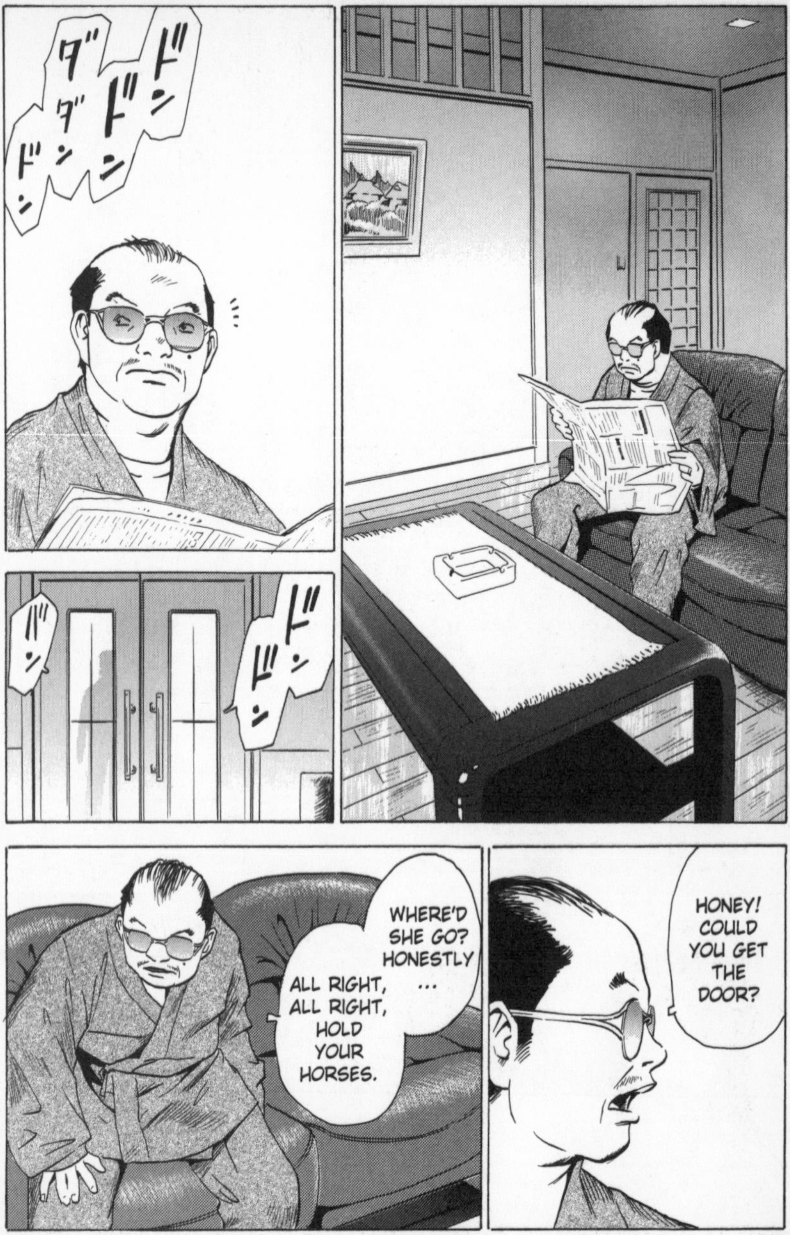
ドンドン
ダダンドン
ドンドン
バン
HONEY! COULD YOU GET THE DOOR?
WHERE'D SHE GO? HONESTLY ...
ALL RIGHT, ALL RIGHT, HOLD YOUR HORSES.

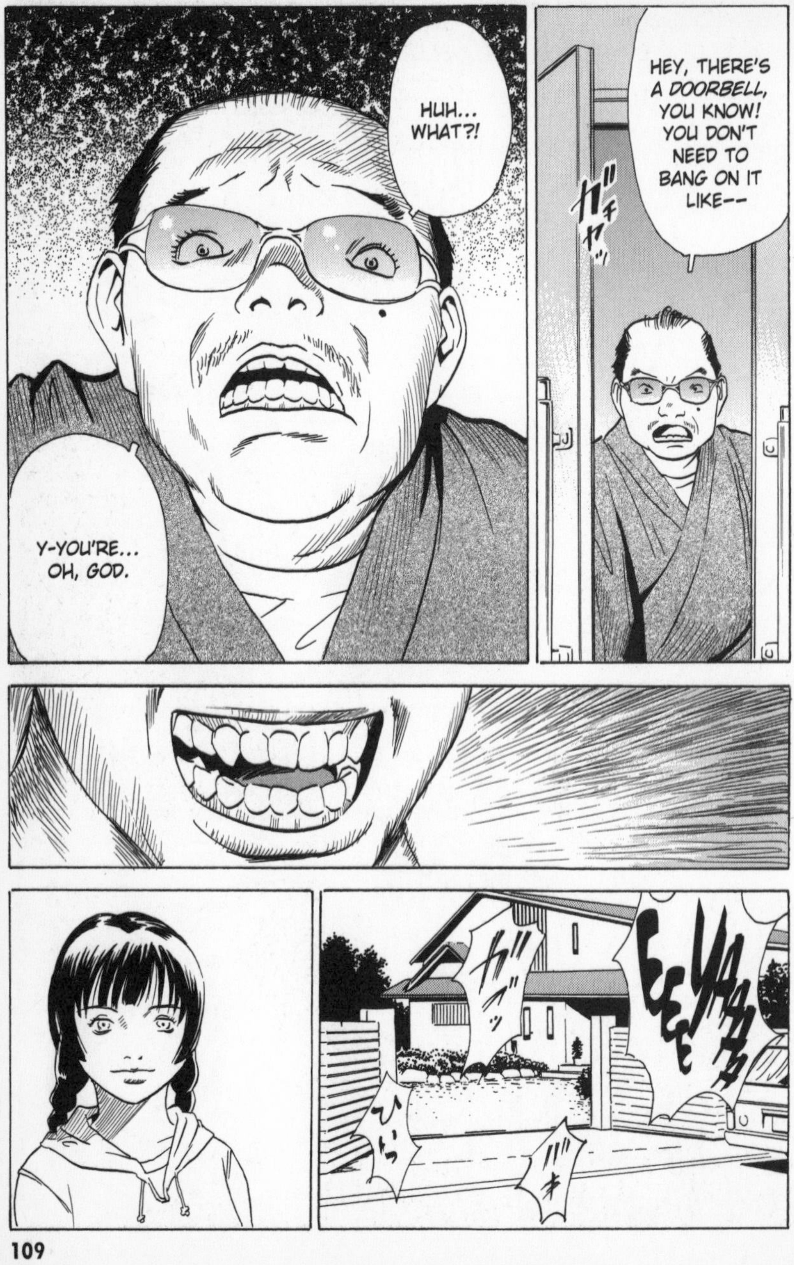
HEY, THERE'S A *DOORBELL*, YOU KNOW! YOU DON'T NEED TO BANG ON IT LIKE--
ガチャッ
HUH... WHAT?!
Y-YOU'RE... OH, GOD.
ガブッ

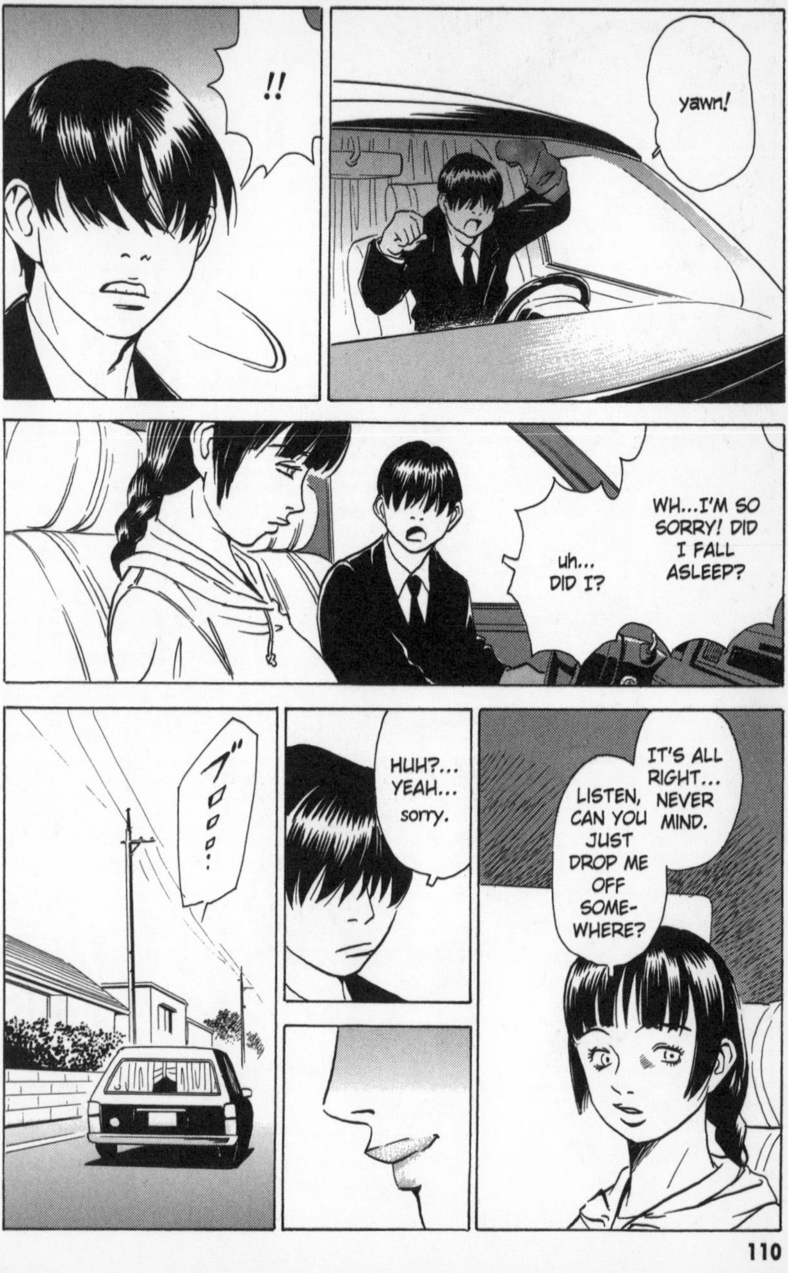
yawn!
!!
WH...I'M SO SORRY! DID I FALL ASLEEP?
uh... DID I?
IT'S ALL RIGHT... NEVER MIND.
LISTEN, CAN YOU JUST DROP ME OFF SOME-WHERE?
HUH?... YEAH... sorry.
ブロロロ…

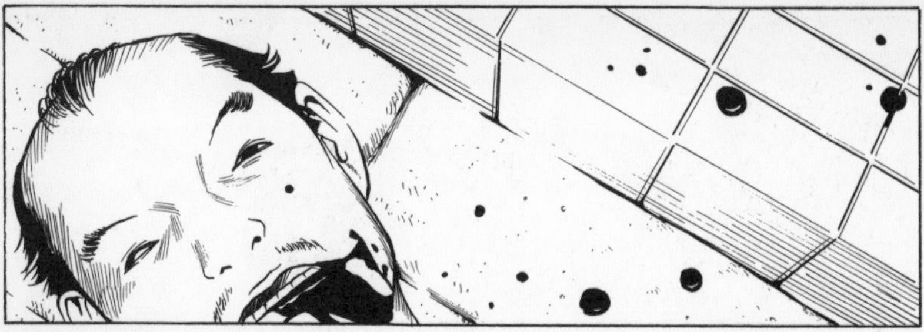
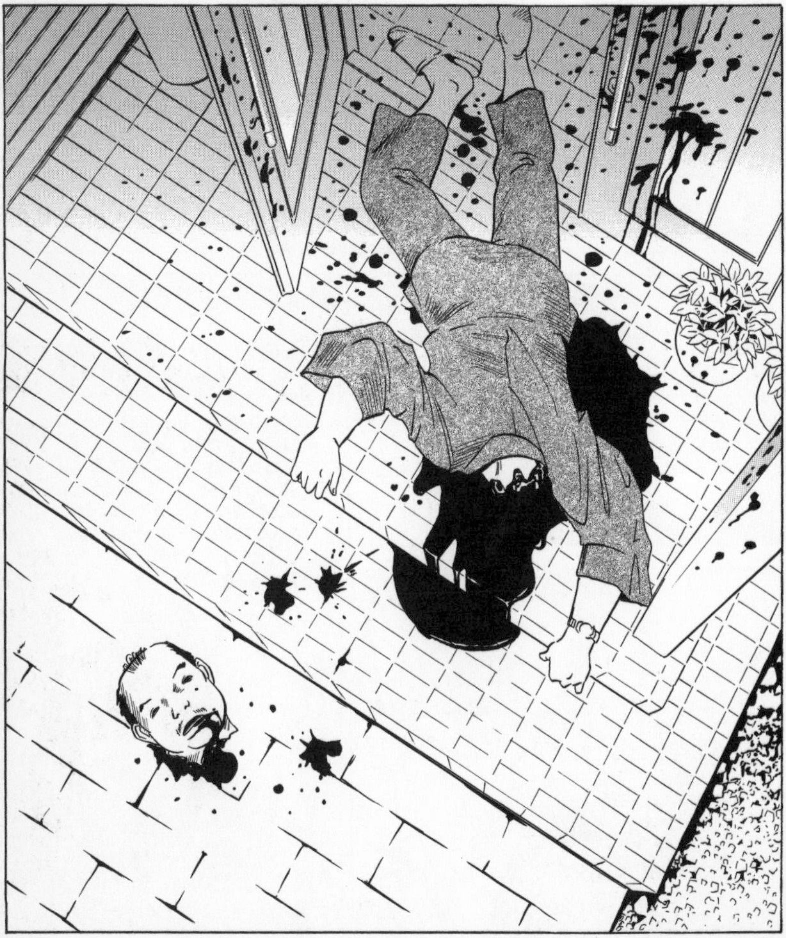

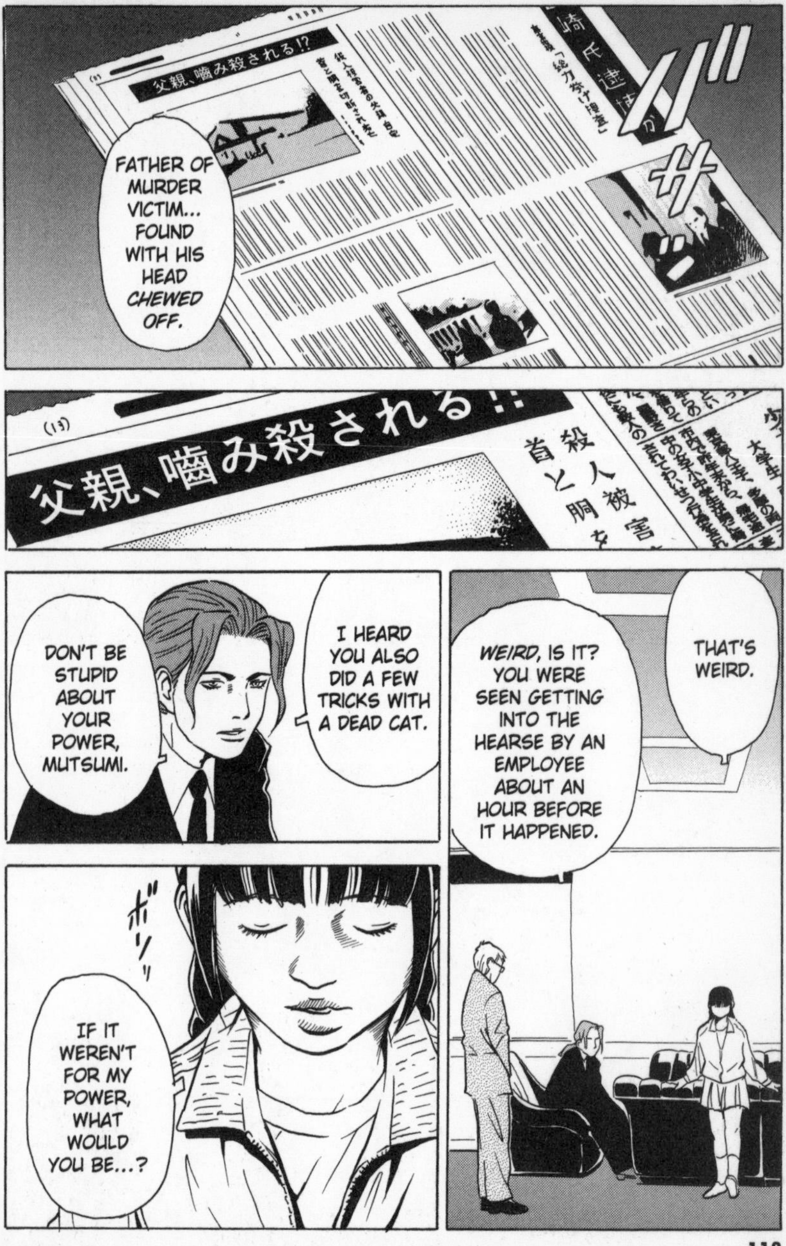
父親、噛み殺される!?
FATHER OF MURDER VICTIM... FOUND WITH HIS HEAD CHEWED OFF.
父親、噛み殺される!!
THAT'S WEIRD.
WEIRD, IS IT? YOU WERE SEEN GETTING INTO THE HEARSE BY AN EMPLOYEE ABOUT AN HOUR BEFORE IT HAPPENED.
I HEARD YOU ALSO DID A FEW TRICKS WITH A DEAD CAT.
DON'T BE STUPID ABOUT YOUR POWER, MUTSUMI.
IF IT WEREN'T FOR MY POWER, WHAT WOULD YOU BE...?

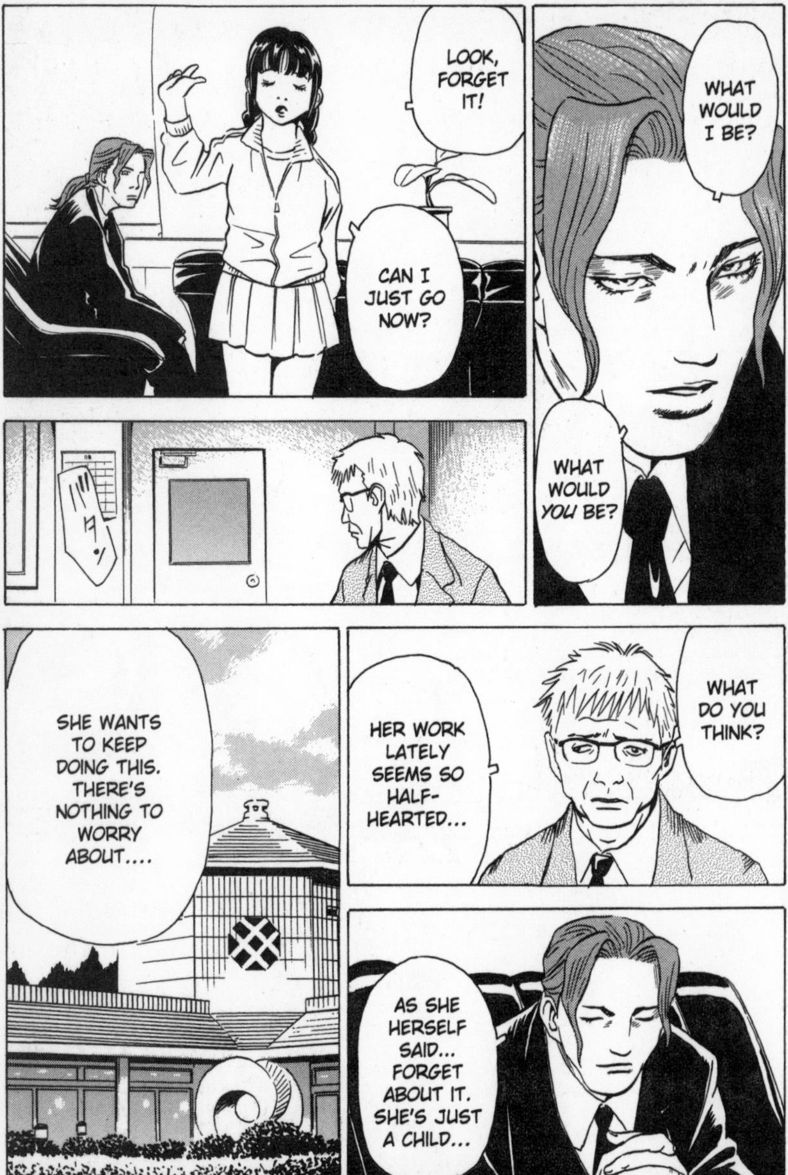
WHAT WOULD I BE?
WHAT WOULD YOU BE?
LOOK, FORGET IT!
CAN I JUST GO NOW?
WHAT DO YOU THINK?
HER WORK LATELY SEEMS SO HALF-HEARTED...
AS SHE HERSELF SAID... FORGET ABOUT IT. SHE'S JUST A CHILD...
SHE WANTS TO KEEP DOING THIS. THERE'S NOTHING TO WORRY ABOUT....

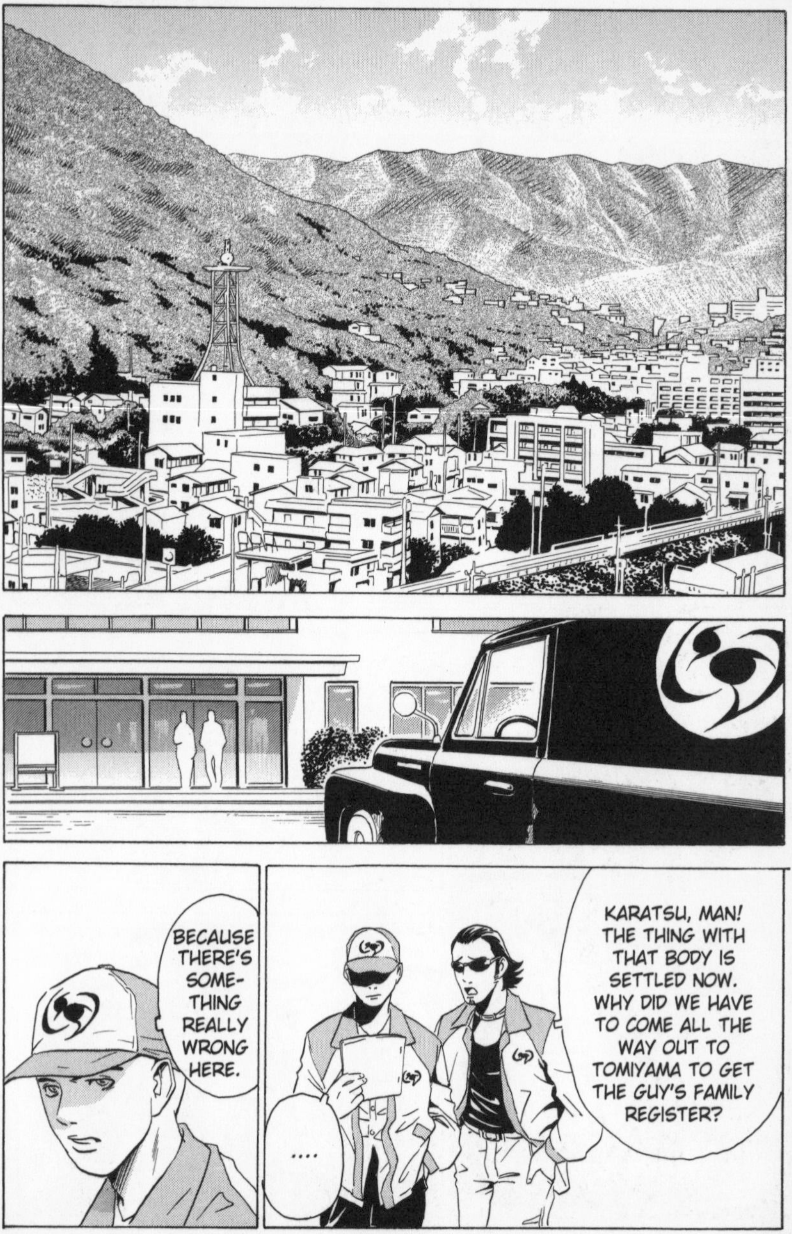
KARATSU, MAN! THE THING WITH THAT BODY IS SETTLED NOW. WHY DID WE HAVE TO COME ALL THE WAY OUT TO TOMIYAMA TO GET THE GUY'S FAMILY REGISTER?
....
BECAUSE THERE'S SOME-THING REALLY WRONG HERE.

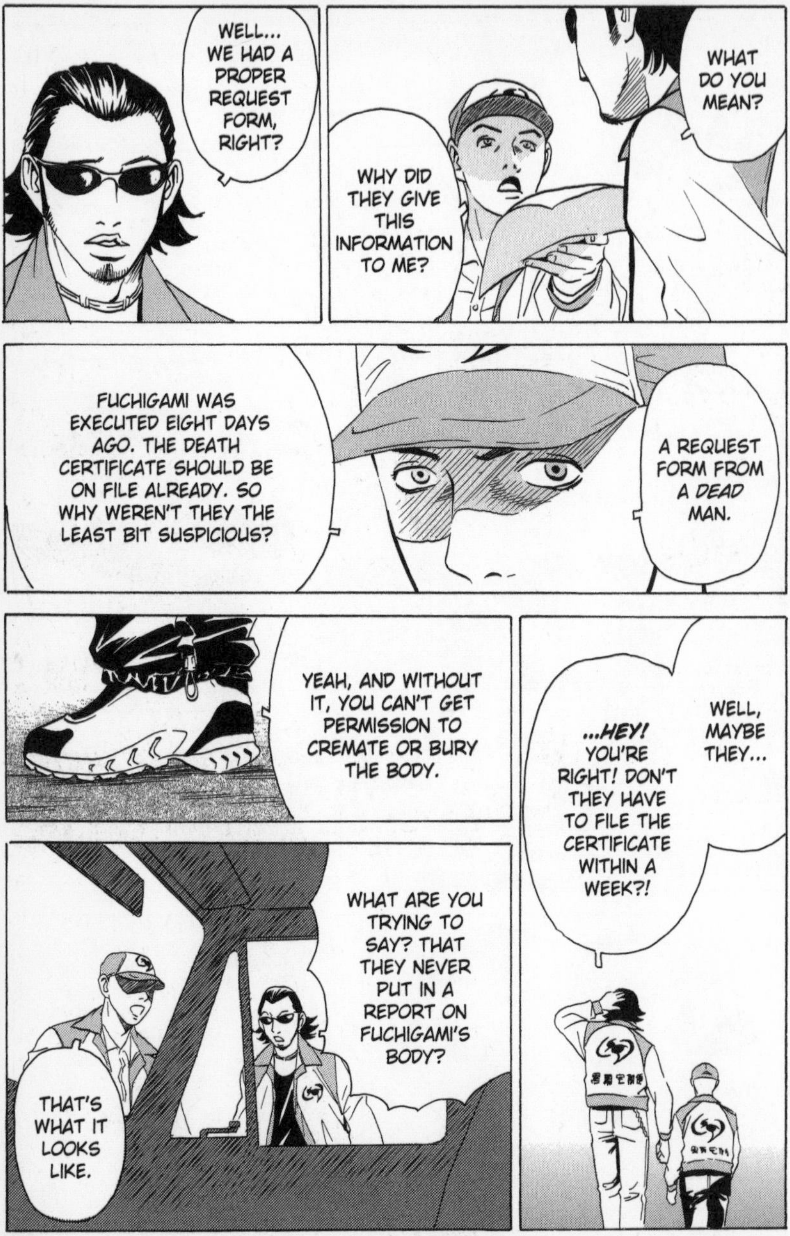
WHAT DO YOU MEAN?
WHY DID THEY GIVE THIS INFORMATION TO ME?
WELL... WE HAD A PROPER REQUEST FORM, RIGHT?
A REQUEST FORM FROM A *DEAD* MAN.
FUCHIGAMI WAS EXECUTED EIGHT DAYS AGO. THE DEATH CERTIFICATE SHOULD BE ON FILE ALREADY. SO WHY WEREN'T THEY THE LEAST BIT SUSPICIOUS?
WELL, MAYBE THEY...
...HEY! YOU'RE RIGHT! DON'T THEY HAVE TO FILE THE CERTIFICATE WITHIN A WEEK?!
YEAH, AND WITHOUT IT, YOU CAN'T GET PERMISSION TO CREMATE OR BURY THE BODY.
WHAT ARE YOU TRYING TO SAY? THAT THEY NEVER PUT IN A REPORT ON FUCHIGAMI'S BODY?
THAT'S WHAT IT LOOKS LIKE.

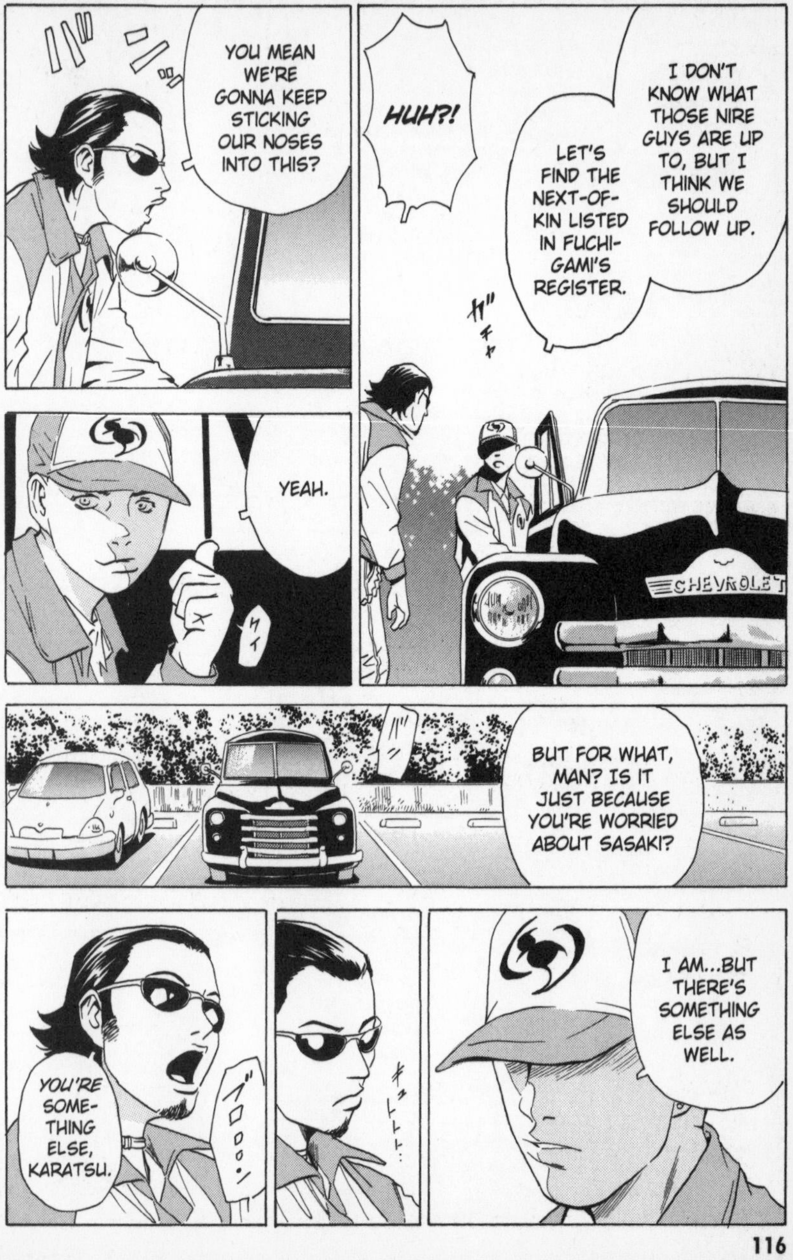
I DON'T KNOW WHAT THOSE NIRE GUYS ARE UP TO, BUT I THINK WE SHOULD FOLLOW UP.
HUH?!
LET'S FIND THE NEXT-OF-KIN LISTED IN FUCHIGAMI'S REGISTER.
CHEVROLET
YOU MEAN WE'RE GONNA KEEP STICKING OUR NOSES INTO THIS?
YEAH.
BUT FOR WHAT, MAN? IS IT JUST BECAUSE YOU'RE WORRIED ABOUT SASAKI?
I AM...BUT THERE'S SOMETHING ELSE AS WELL.
YOU'RE SOMETHING ELSE, KARATSU.

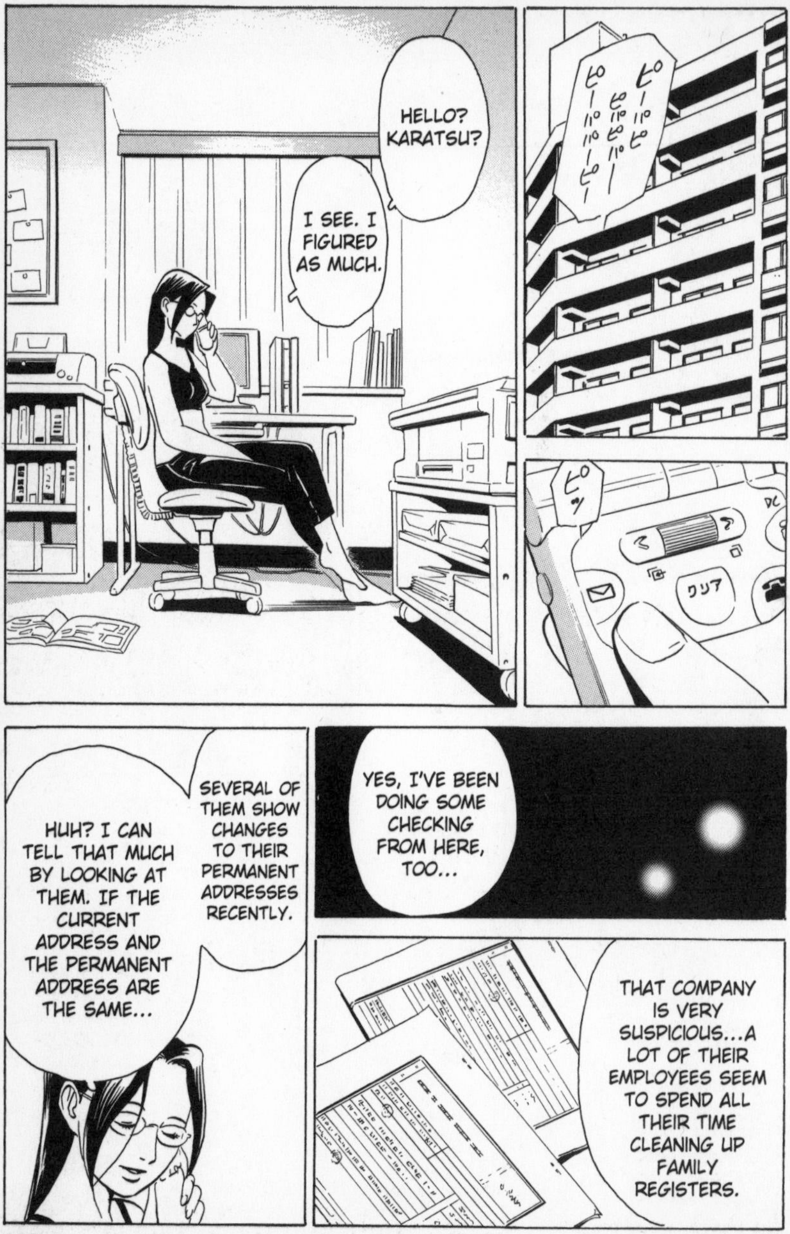

ピーパピ
ピパピパー
ピーパパーピー
ピッ
DC
クリア
HELLO? KARATSU?
I SEE. I FIGURED AS MUCH.
YES, I'VE BEEN DOING SOME CHECKING FROM HERE, TOO...
THAT COMPANY IS VERY SUSPICIOUS...A LOT OF THEIR EMPLOYEES SEEM TO SPEND ALL THEIR TIME CLEANING UP FAMILY REGISTERS.
SEVERAL OF THEM SHOW CHANGES TO THEIR PERMANENT ADDRESSES RECENTLY.
HUH? I CAN TELL THAT MUCH BY LOOKING AT THEM. IF THE CURRENT ADDRESS AND THE PERMANENT ADDRESS ARE THE SAME...

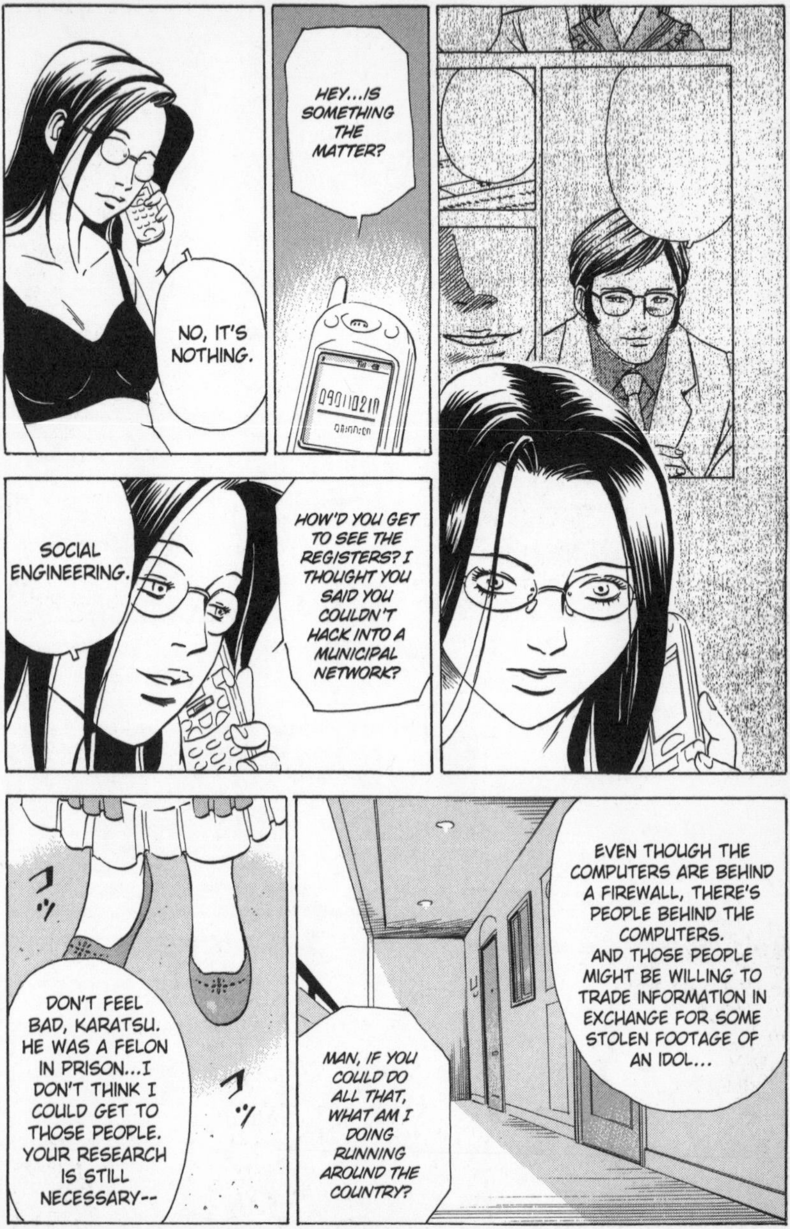
HEY...IS SOMETHING THE MATTER?
NO, IT'S NOTHING.
HOW'D YOU GET TO SEE THE REGISTERS? I THOUGHT YOU SAID YOU COULDN'T HACK INTO A MUNICIPAL NETWORK?
SOCIAL ENGINEERING.
EVEN THOUGH THE COMPUTERS ARE BEHIND A FIREWALL, THERE'S PEOPLE BEHIND THE COMPUTERS.
AND THOSE PEOPLE MIGHT BE WILLING TO TRADE INFORMATION IN EXCHANGE FOR SOME STOLEN FOOTAGE OF AN IDOL...
MAN, IF YOU COULD DO ALL THAT, WHAT AM I DOING RUNNING AROUND THE COUNTRY?
DON'T FEEL BAD, KARATSU. HE WAS A FELON IN PRISON...I DON'T THINK I COULD GET TO THOSE PEOPLE. YOUR RESEARCH IS STILL NECESSARY--

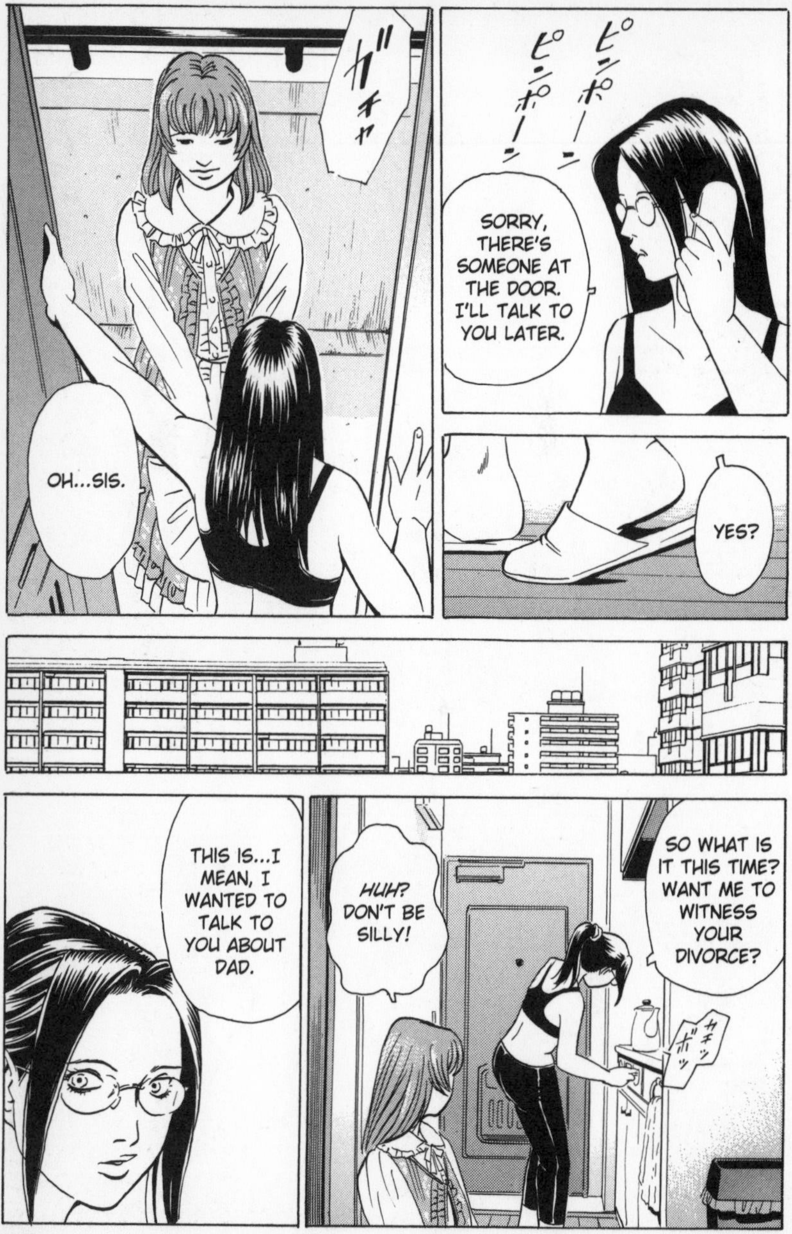
ピンポーン
ピンポーン
SORRY, THERE'S SOMEONE AT THE DOOR. I'LL TALK TO YOU LATER.
YES?
ガチャ
OH...SIS.
SO WHAT IS IT THIS TIME? WANT ME TO WITNESS YOUR DIVORCE?
HUH? DON'T BE SILLY!
カチッ
ボッ
THIS IS...I MEAN, I WANTED TO TALK TO YOU ABOUT DAD.

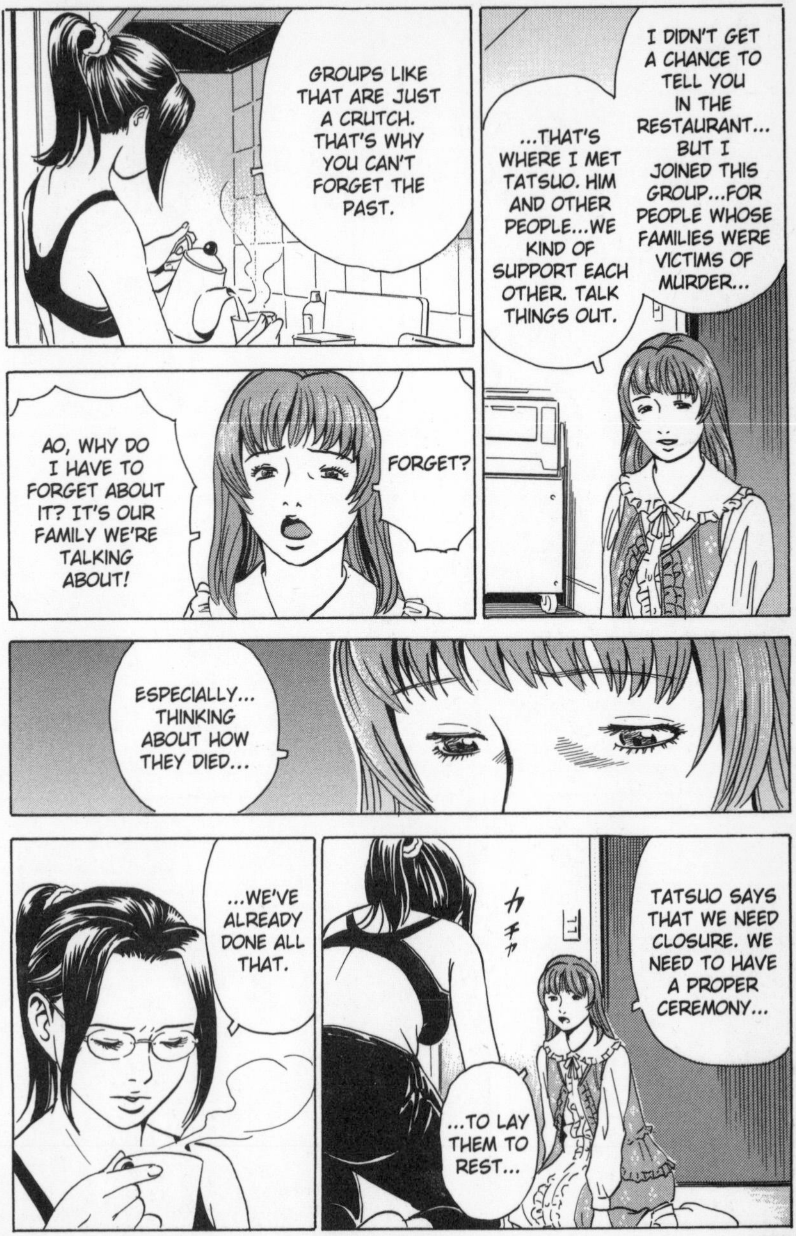
I DIDN'T GET A CHANCE TO TELL YOU IN THE RESTAURANT... BUT I JOINED THIS GROUP...FOR PEOPLE WHOSE FAMILIES WERE VICTIMS OF MURDER...
...THAT'S WHERE I MET TATSUO. HIM AND OTHER PEOPLE...WE KIND OF SUPPORT EACH OTHER. TALK THINGS OUT.
GROUPS LIKE THAT ARE JUST A CRUTCH. THAT'S WHY YOU CAN'T FORGET THE PAST.
FORGET?
AO, WHY DO I HAVE TO FORGET ABOUT IT? IT'S OUR FAMILY WE'RE TALKING ABOUT!
ESPECIALLY... THINKING ABOUT HOW THEY DIED...
TATSUO SAYS THAT WE NEED CLOSURE. WE NEED TO HAVE A PROPER CEREMONY...
カチャ
...TO LAY THEM TO REST...
...WE'VE ALREADY DONE ALL THAT.

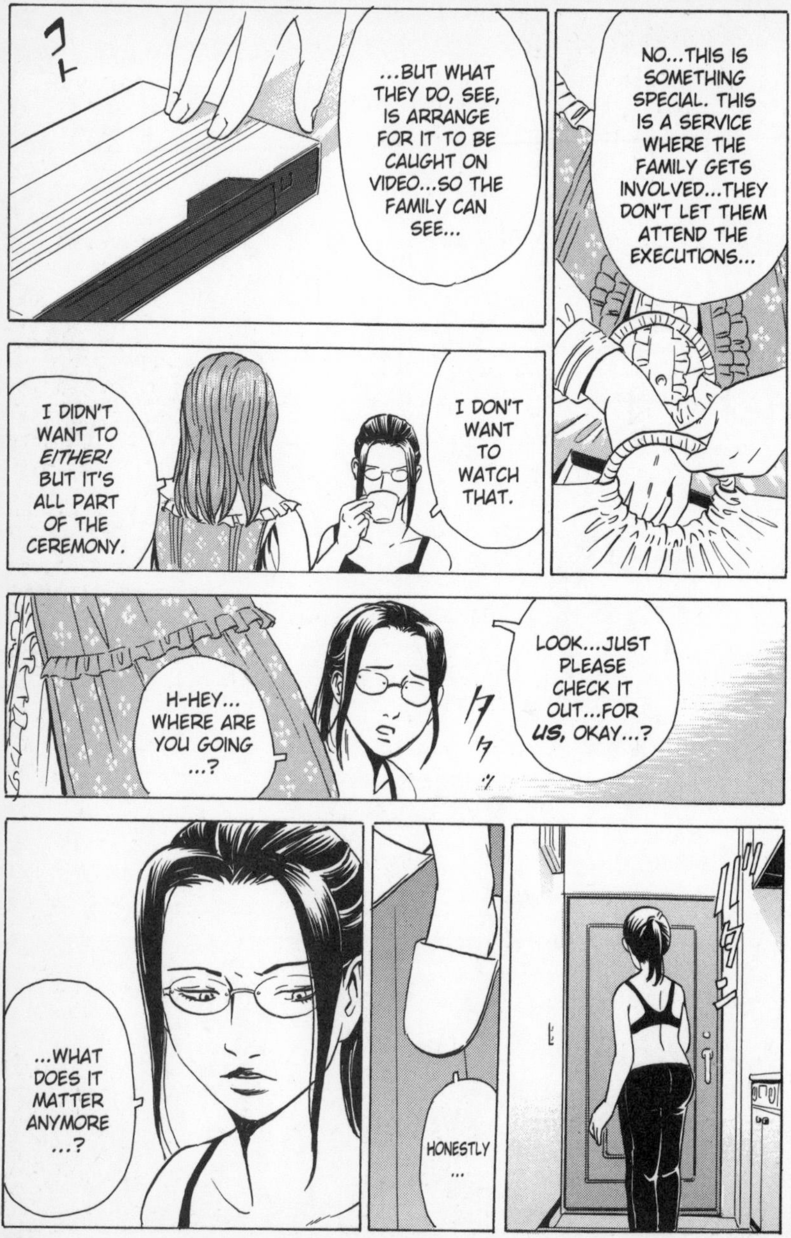
NO...THIS IS SOMETHING SPECIAL. THIS IS A SERVICE WHERE THE FAMILY GETS INVOLVED...THEY DON'T LET THEM ATTEND THE EXECUTIONS...
...BUT WHAT THEY DO, SEE, IS ARRANGE FOR IT TO BE CAUGHT ON VIDEO...SO THE FAMILY CAN SEE...
I DON'T WANT TO WATCH THAT.
I DIDN'T WANT TO *EITHER!* BUT IT'S ALL PART OF THE CEREMONY.
LOOK...JUST PLEASE CHECK IT OUT...FOR ***US***, OKAY...?
H-HEY... WHERE ARE YOU GOING ...?
HONESTLY ...
...WHAT DOES IT MATTER ANYMORE ...?

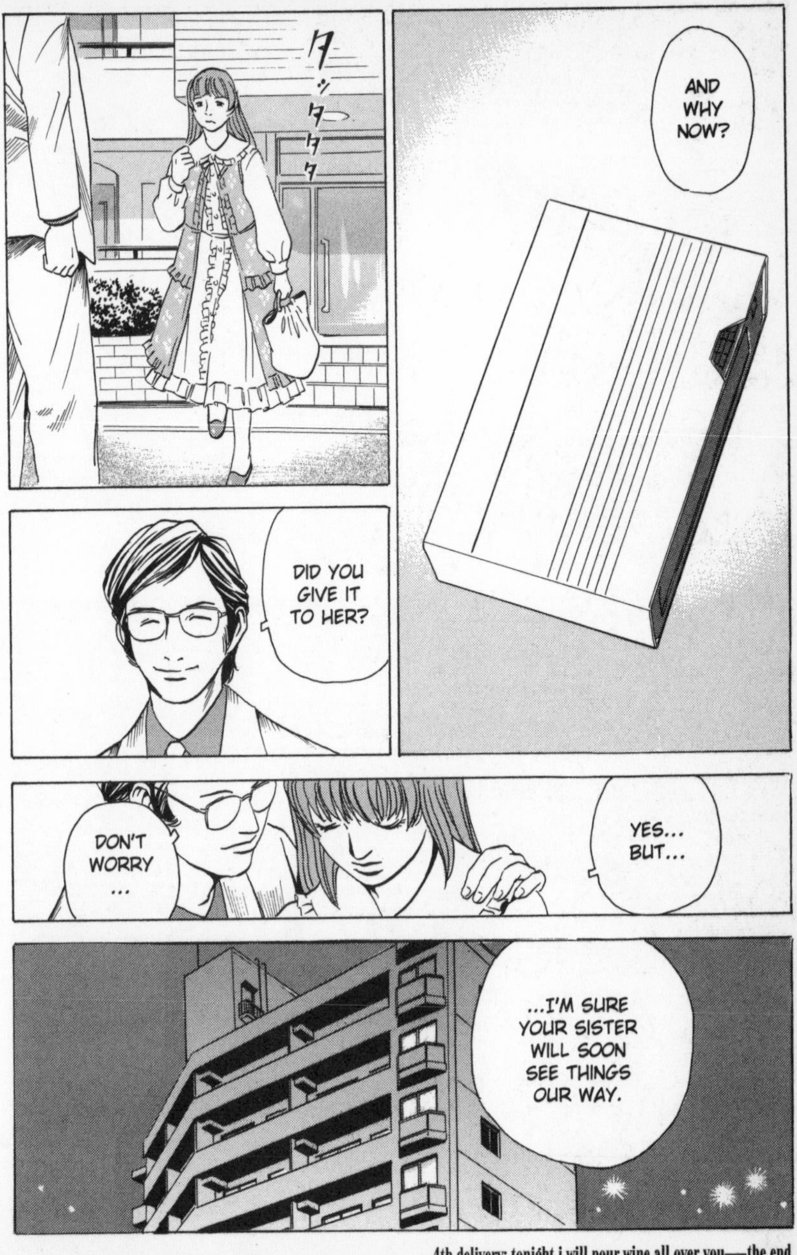
AND WHY NOW?
DID YOU GIVE IT TO HER?
YES... BUT...
DON'T WORRY ...
...I'M SURE YOUR SISTER WILL SOON SEE THINGS OUR WAY.

4th delivery: tonight i will pour wine all over you—the end

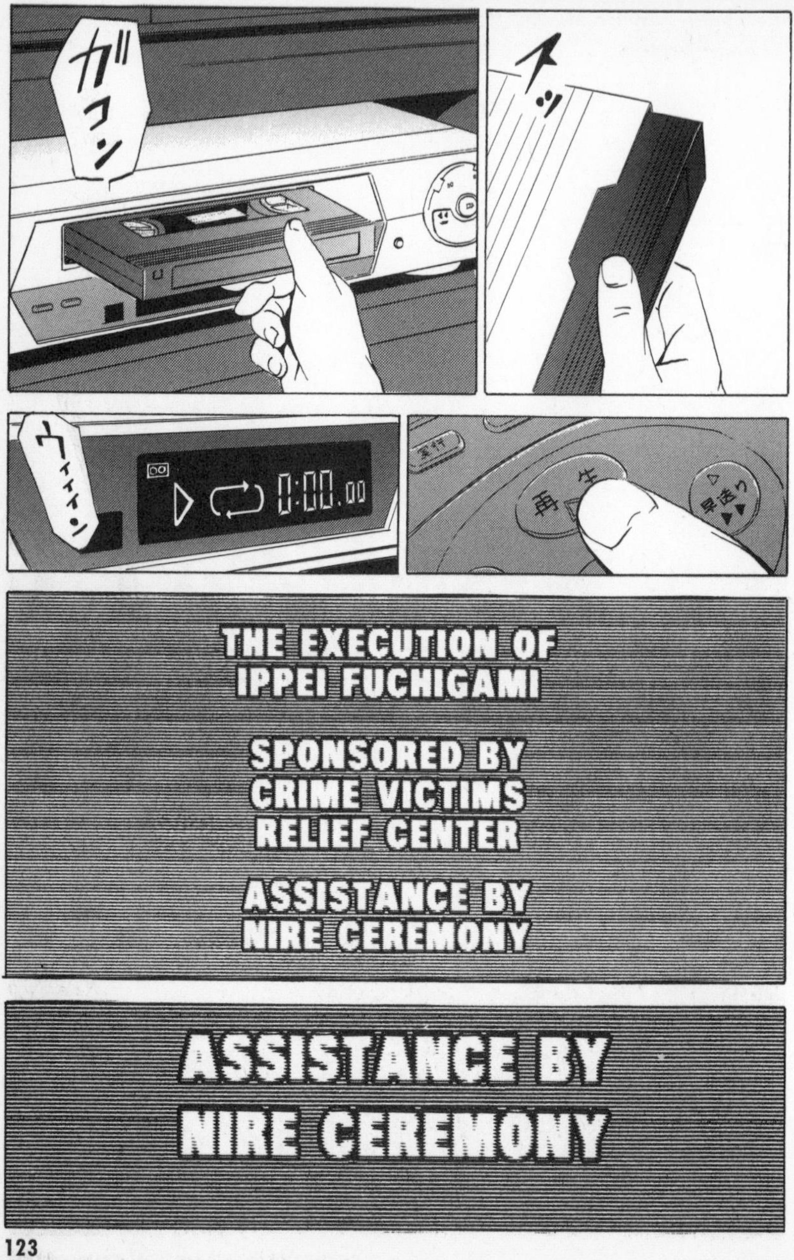
スッ
ガコン
再生
早送り
ウィイイン
0:00.00
THE EXECUTION OF IPPEI FUCHIGAMI
SPONSORED BY CRIME VICTIMS RELIEF CENTER
ASSISTANCE BY NIRE CEREMONY
ASSISTANCE BY NIRE CEREMONY

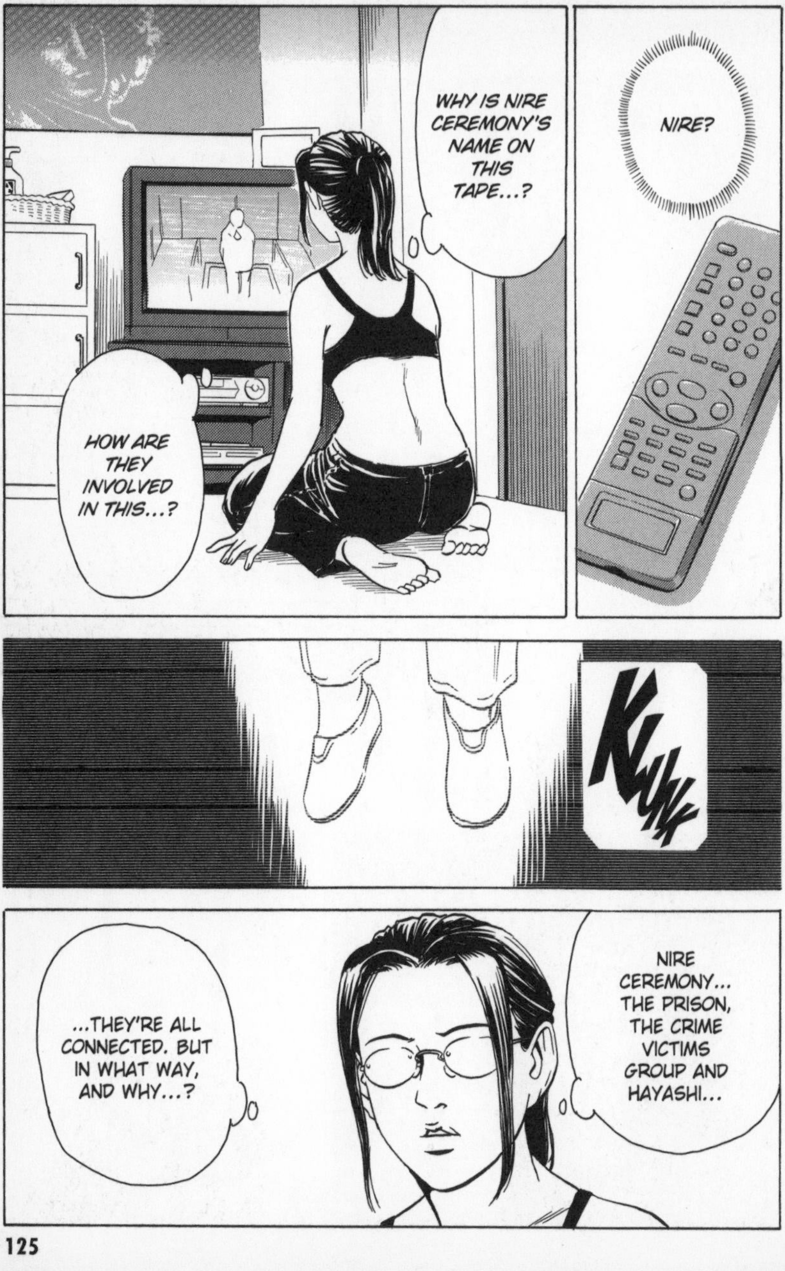
NIRE?
WHY IS NIRE CEREMONY'S NAME ON THIS TAPE...?
HOW ARE THEY INVOLVED IN THIS...?
KLUNK
NIRE CEREMONY... THE PRISON, THE CRIME VICTIMS GROUP AND HAYASHI...
...THEY'RE ALL CONNECTED. BUT IN WHAT WAY, AND WHY...?

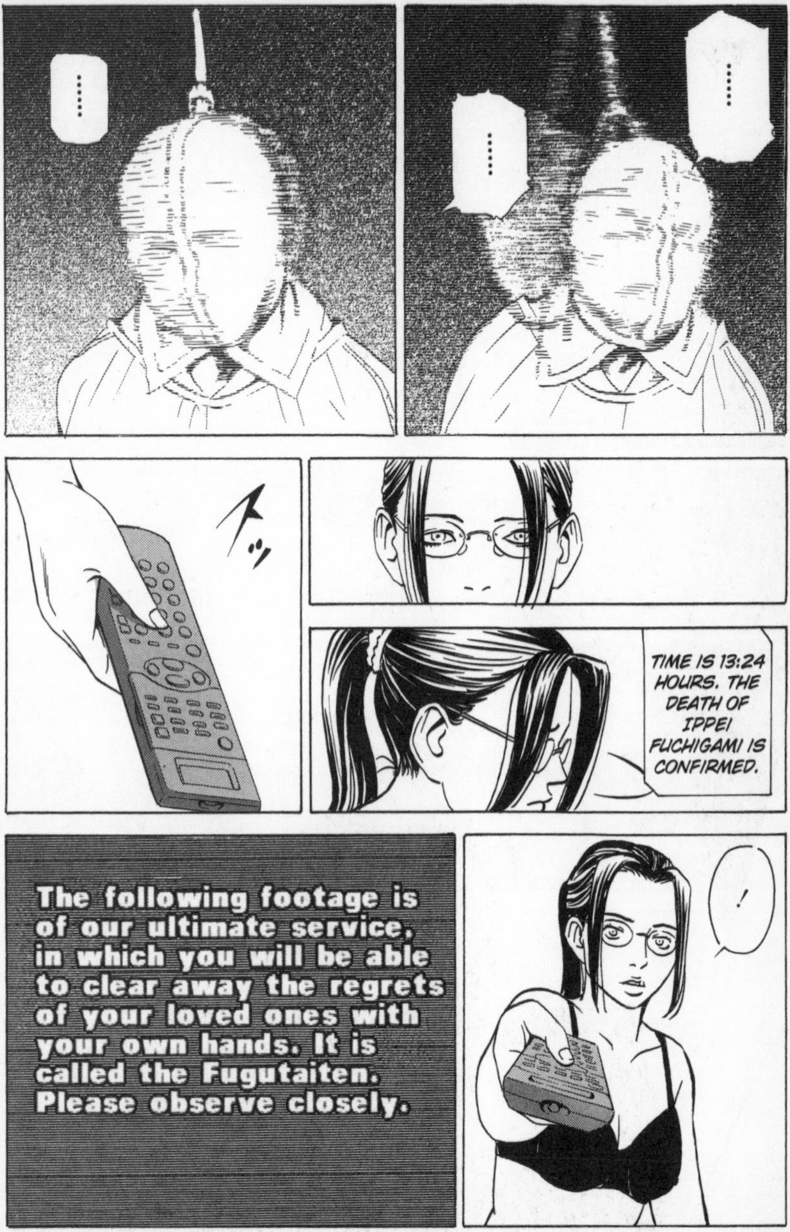

......
......
......
TIME IS 13:24 HOURS. THE DEATH OF IPPEI FUCHIGAMI IS CONFIRMED.
!
The following footage is of our ultimate service, in which you will be able to clear away the regrets of your loved ones with your own hands. It is called the Fugutaiten. Please observe closely.

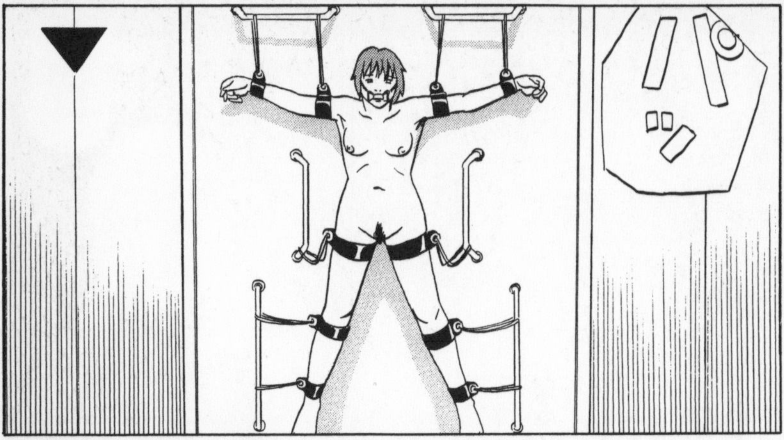

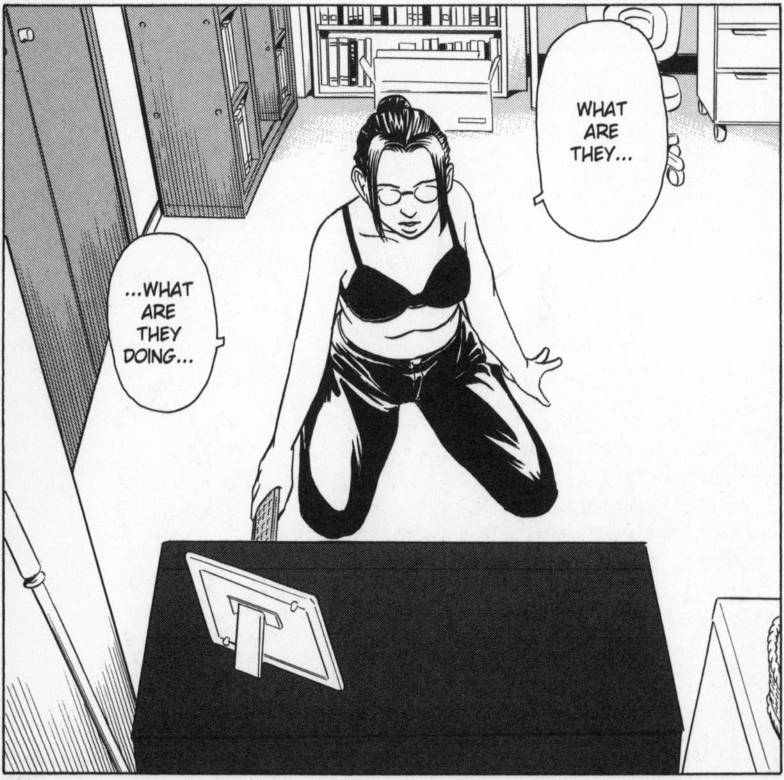
WHAT ARE THEY...
...WHAT ARE THEY DOING...

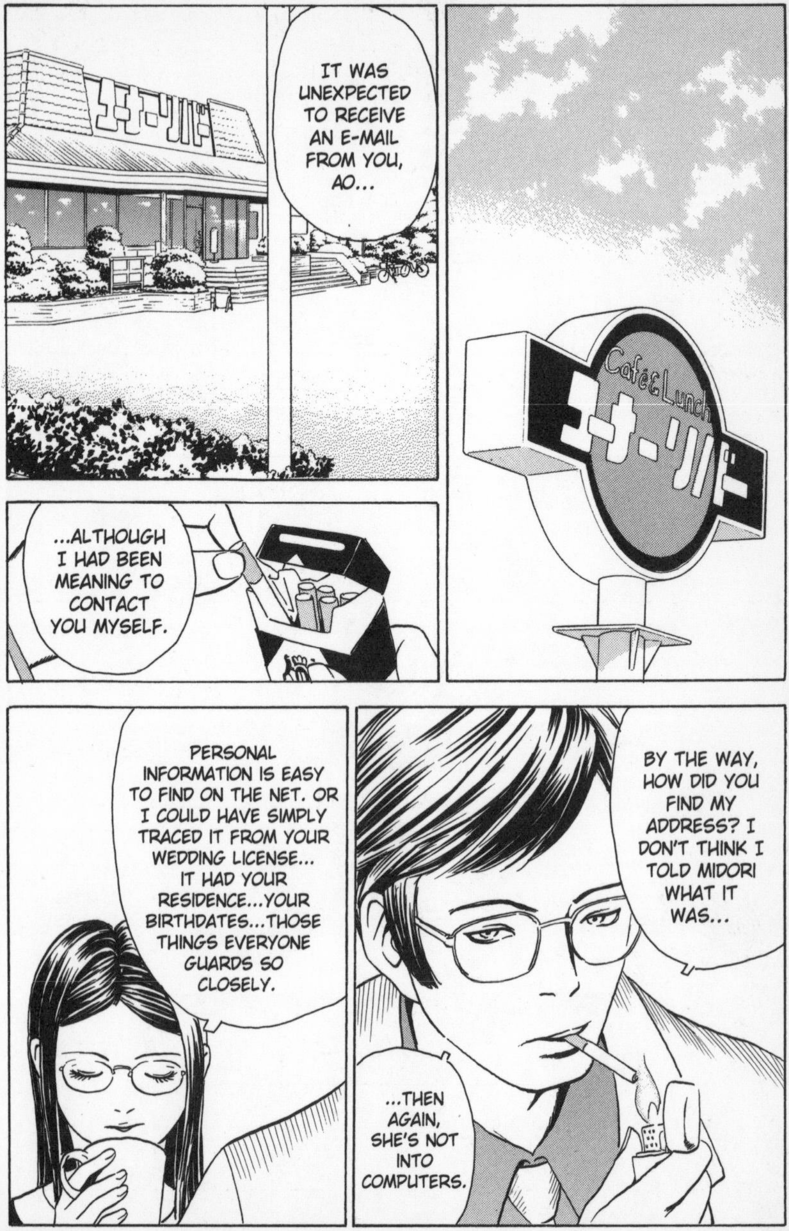
Café&Lunch
IT WAS UNEXPECTED TO RECEIVE AN E-MAIL FROM YOU, AO...
...ALTHOUGH I HAD BEEN MEANING TO CONTACT YOU MYSELF.
BY THE WAY, HOW DID YOU FIND MY ADDRESS? I DON'T THINK I TOLD MIDORI WHAT IT WAS...
...THEN AGAIN, SHE'S NOT INTO COMPUTERS.
PERSONAL INFORMATION IS EASY TO FIND ON THE NET. OR I COULD HAVE SIMPLY TRACED IT FROM YOUR WEDDING LICENSE... IT HAD YOUR RESIDENCE...YOUR BIRTHDATES...THOSE THINGS EVERYONE GUARDS SO CLOSELY.

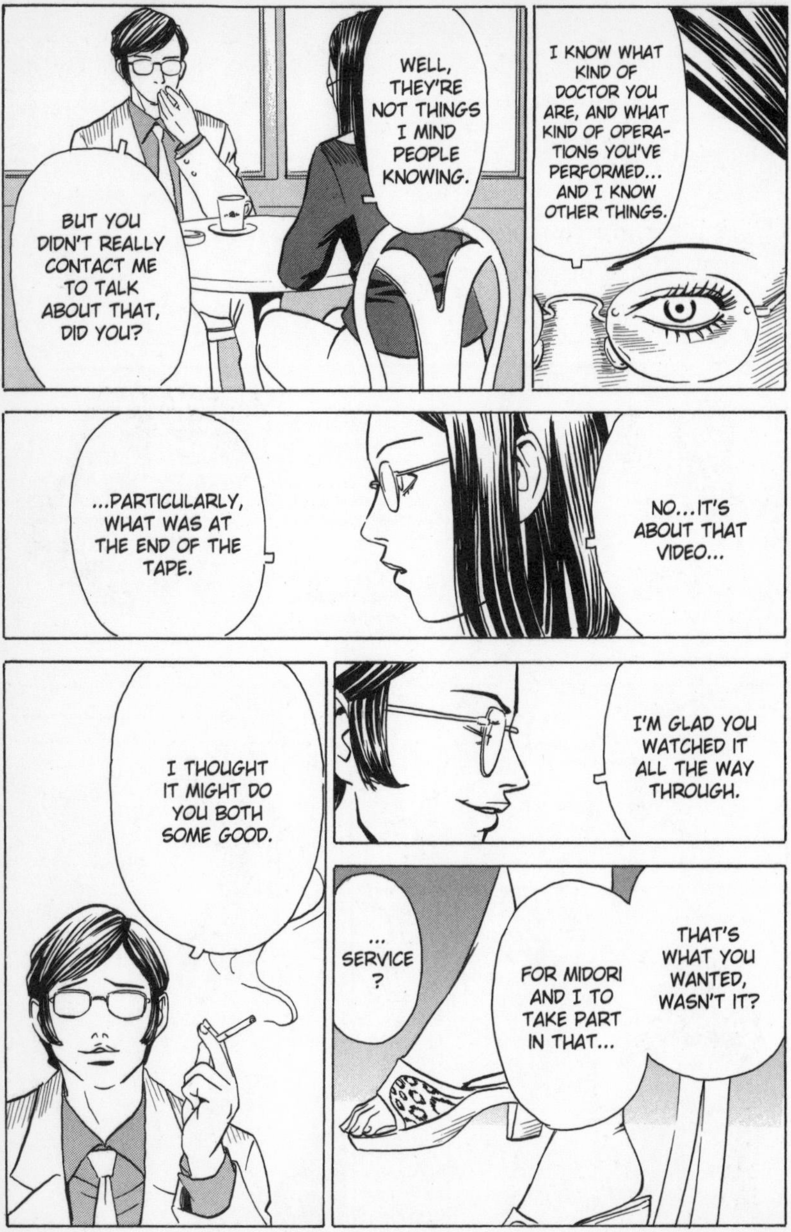
I KNOW WHAT KIND OF DOCTOR YOU ARE, AND WHAT KIND OF OPERATIONS YOU'VE PERFORMED... AND I KNOW OTHER THINGS.
WELL, THEY'RE NOT THINGS I MIND PEOPLE KNOWING.
BUT YOU DIDN'T REALLY CONTACT ME TO TALK ABOUT THAT, DID YOU?
NO...IT'S ABOUT THAT VIDEO...
...PARTICULARLY, WHAT WAS AT THE END OF THE TAPE.
I'M GLAD YOU WATCHED IT ALL THE WAY THROUGH.
THAT'S WHAT YOU WANTED, WASN'T IT?
FOR MIDORI AND I TO TAKE PART IN THAT...
... SERVICE ?
I THOUGHT IT MIGHT DO YOU BOTH SOME GOOD.

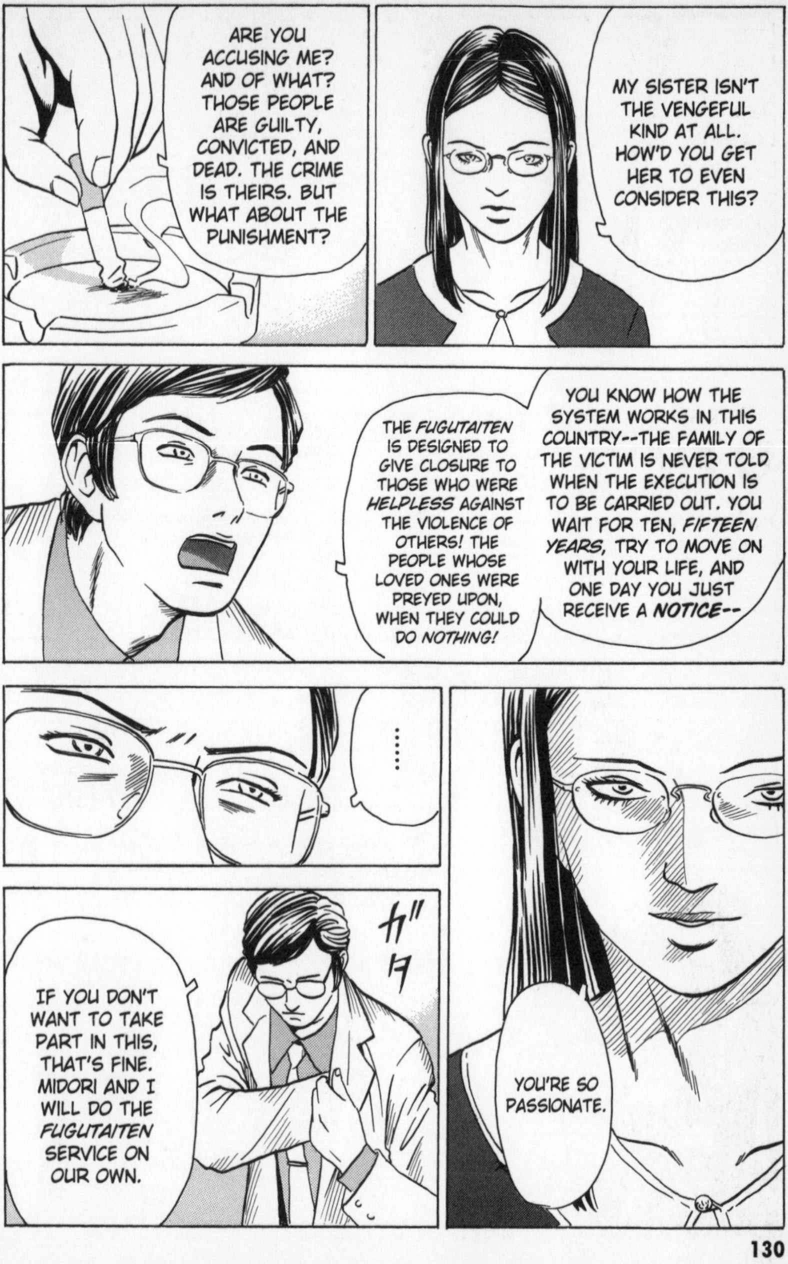
MY SISTER ISN'T THE VENGEFUL KIND AT ALL. HOW'D YOU GET HER TO EVEN CONSIDER THIS?
ARE YOU ACCUSING ME? AND OF WHAT? THOSE PEOPLE ARE GUILTY, CONVICTED, AND DEAD. THE CRIME IS THEIRS. BUT WHAT ABOUT THE PUNISHMENT?
YOU KNOW HOW THE SYSTEM WORKS IN THIS COUNTRY--THE FAMILY OF THE VICTIM IS NEVER TOLD WHEN THE EXECUTION IS TO BE CARRIED OUT. YOU WAIT FOR TEN, *FIFTEEN YEARS*, TRY TO MOVE ON WITH YOUR LIFE, AND ONE DAY YOU JUST RECEIVE A ***NOTICE***--
THE *FUGUTAITEN* IS DESIGNED TO GIVE CLOSURE TO THOSE WHO WERE *HELPLESS* AGAINST THE VIOLENCE OF OTHERS! THE PEOPLE WHOSE LOVED ONES WERE PREYED UPON, WHEN THEY COULD DO *NOTHING!*
YOU'RE SO PASSIONATE.
......
ガタ
IF YOU DON'T WANT TO TAKE PART IN THIS, THAT'S FINE. MIDORI AND I WILL DO THE *FUGUTAITEN* SERVICE ON OUR OWN.

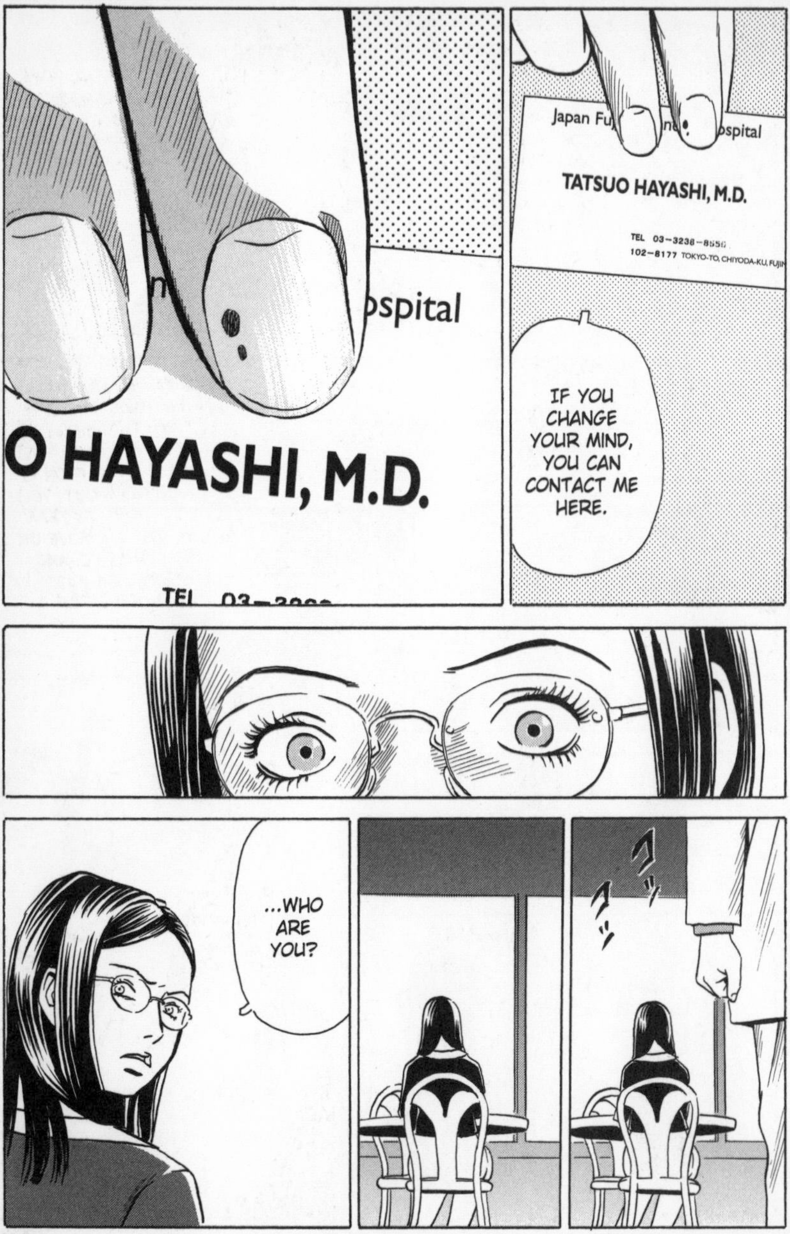
TATSUO HAYASHI, M.D.
TEL 03-3238-8556
IF YOU CHANGE YOUR MIND, YOU CAN CONTACT ME HERE.
O HAYASHI, M.D.
コッ
コッ
...WHO ARE YOU?

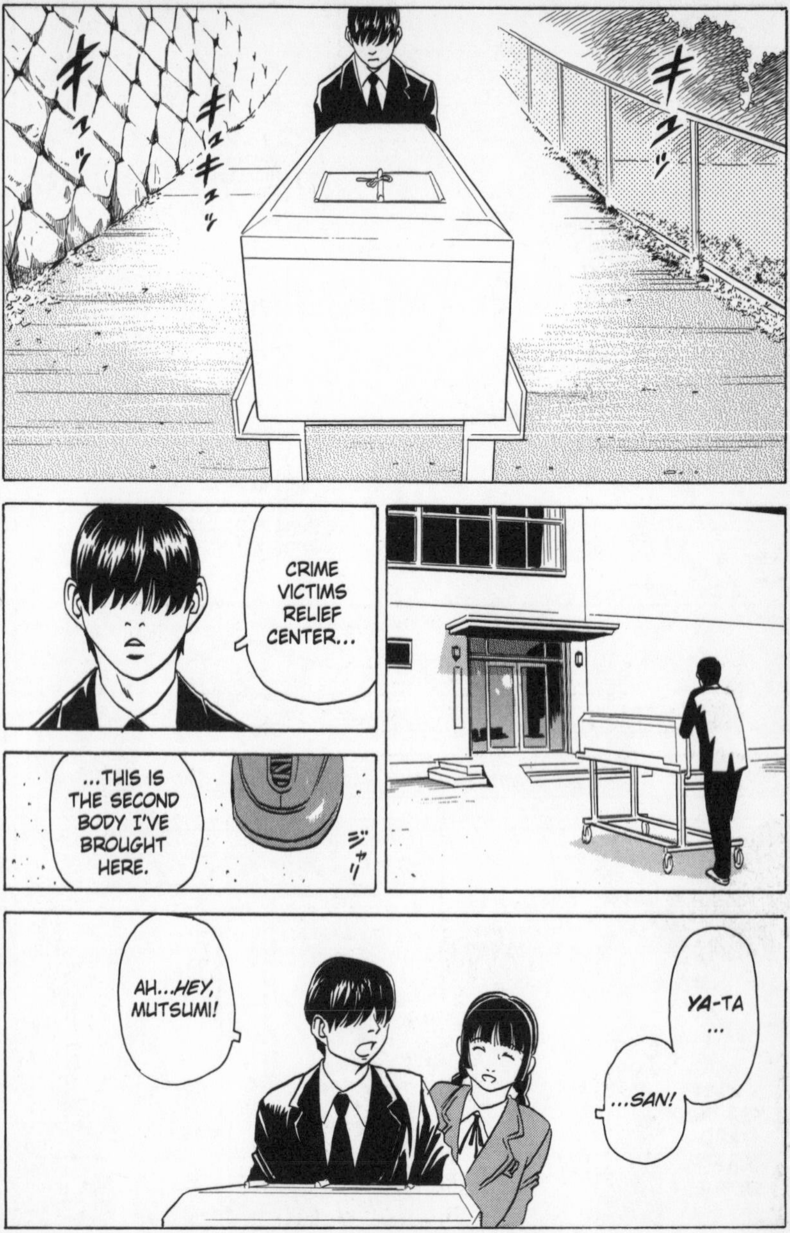
キュッ
キュキュッ
キュッ
CRIME VICTIMS RELIEF CENTER...
...THIS IS THE SECOND BODY I'VE BROUGHT HERE.
ジャリ
YA-TA ...
...SAN!
AH...*HEY*, MUTSUMI!

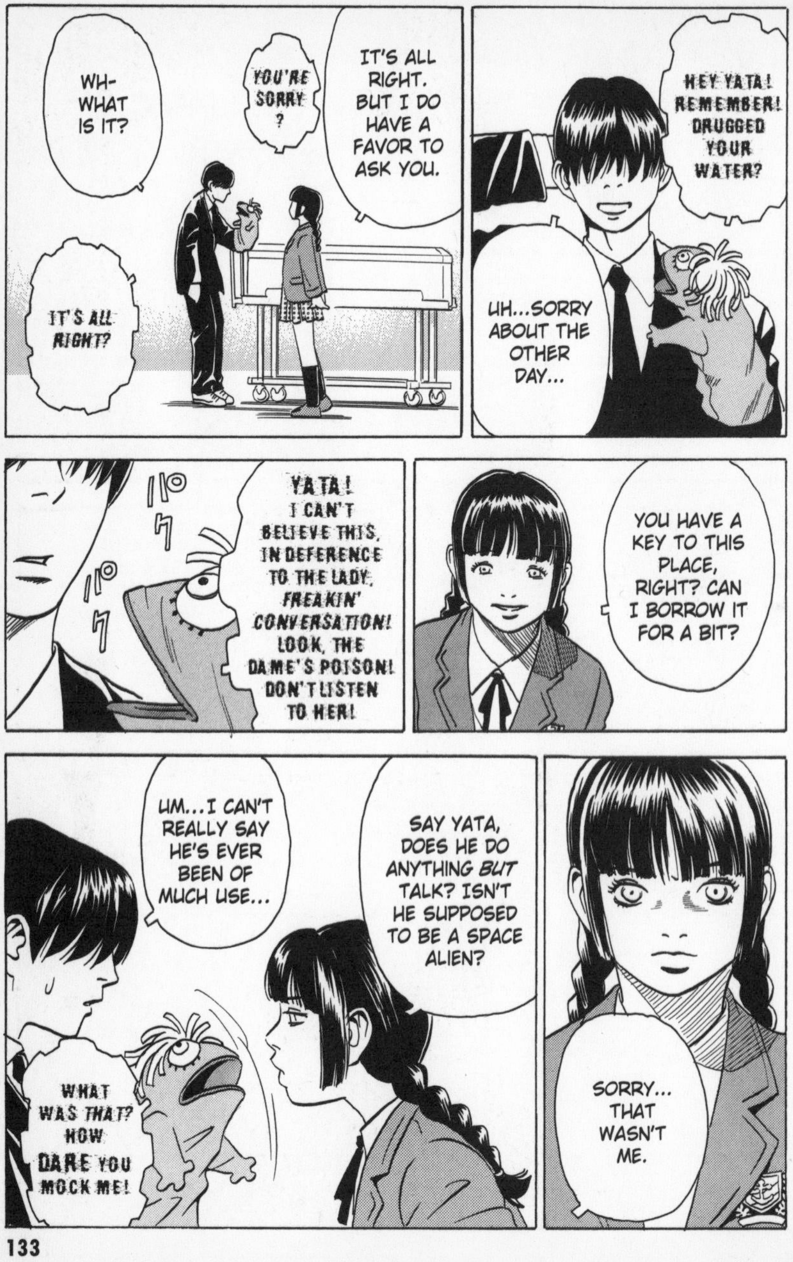
HEY YATA! REMEMBER! DRUGGED YOUR WATER?
UH...SORRY ABOUT THE OTHER DAY...
IT'S ALL RIGHT. BUT I DO HAVE A FAVOR TO ASK YOU.
YOU'RE SORRY?
WH-WHAT IS IT?
IT'S ALL RIGHT?
YOU HAVE A KEY TO THIS PLACE, RIGHT? CAN I BORROW IT FOR A BIT?
YATA! I CAN'T BELIEVE THIS. IN DEFERENCE TO THE LADY. FREAKIN' CONVERSATION! LOOK, THE DAME'S POISON! DON'T LISTEN TO HER!
パク
パク
SORRY... THAT WASN'T ME.
SAY YATA, DOES HE DO ANYTHING *BUT* TALK? ISN'T HE SUPPOSED TO BE A SPACE ALIEN?
UM...I CAN'T REALLY SAY HE'S EVER BEEN OF MUCH USE...
WHAT WAS *THAT*? HOW DARE YOU MOCK ME!

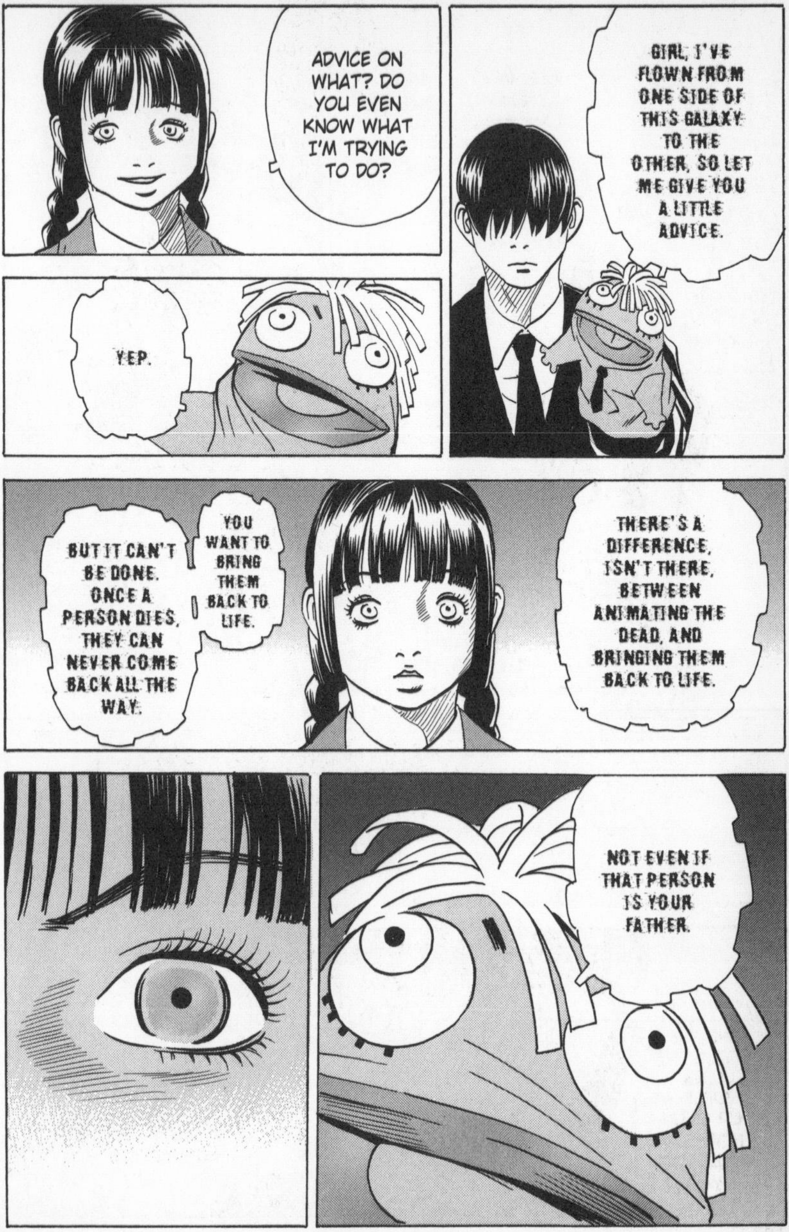
GIRL, I'VE FLOWN FROM ONE SIDE OF THIS GALAXY TO THE OTHER, SO LET ME GIVE YOU A LITTLE ADVICE.
ADVICE ON WHAT? DO YOU EVEN KNOW WHAT I'M TRYING TO DO?
YEP.
THERE'S A DIFFERENCE, ISN'T THERE, BETWEEN ANIMATING THE DEAD, AND BRINGING THEM BACK TO LIFE.
YOU WANT TO BRING THEM BACK TO LIFE.
BUT IT CAN'T BE DONE. ONCE A PERSON DIES, THEY CAN NEVER COME BACK ALL THE WAY.
NOT EVEN IF THAT PERSON IS YOUR FATHER.

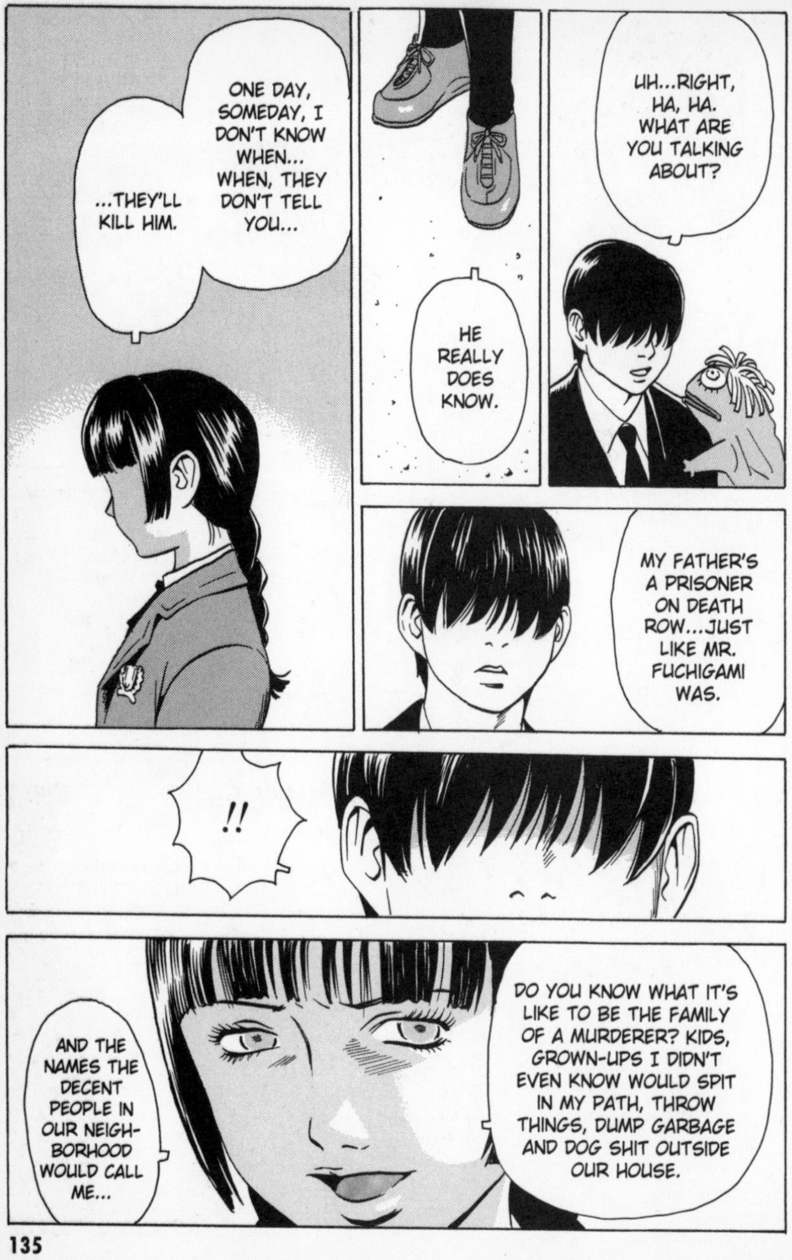
UH...RIGHT, HA, HA. WHAT ARE YOU TALKING ABOUT?
HE REALLY DOES KNOW.
MY FATHER'S A PRISONER ON DEATH ROW...JUST LIKE MR. FUCHIGAMI WAS.
ONE DAY, SOMEDAY, I DON'T KNOW WHEN... WHEN, THEY DON'T TELL YOU...
...THEY'LL KILL HIM.
!!
DO YOU KNOW WHAT IT'S LIKE TO BE THE FAMILY OF A MURDERER? KIDS, GROWN-UPS I DIDN'T EVEN KNOW WOULD SPIT IN MY PATH, THROW THINGS, DUMP GARBAGE AND DOG SHIT OUTSIDE OUR HOUSE.
AND THE NAMES THE DECENT PEOPLE IN OUR NEIGH-BORHOOD WOULD CALL ME...

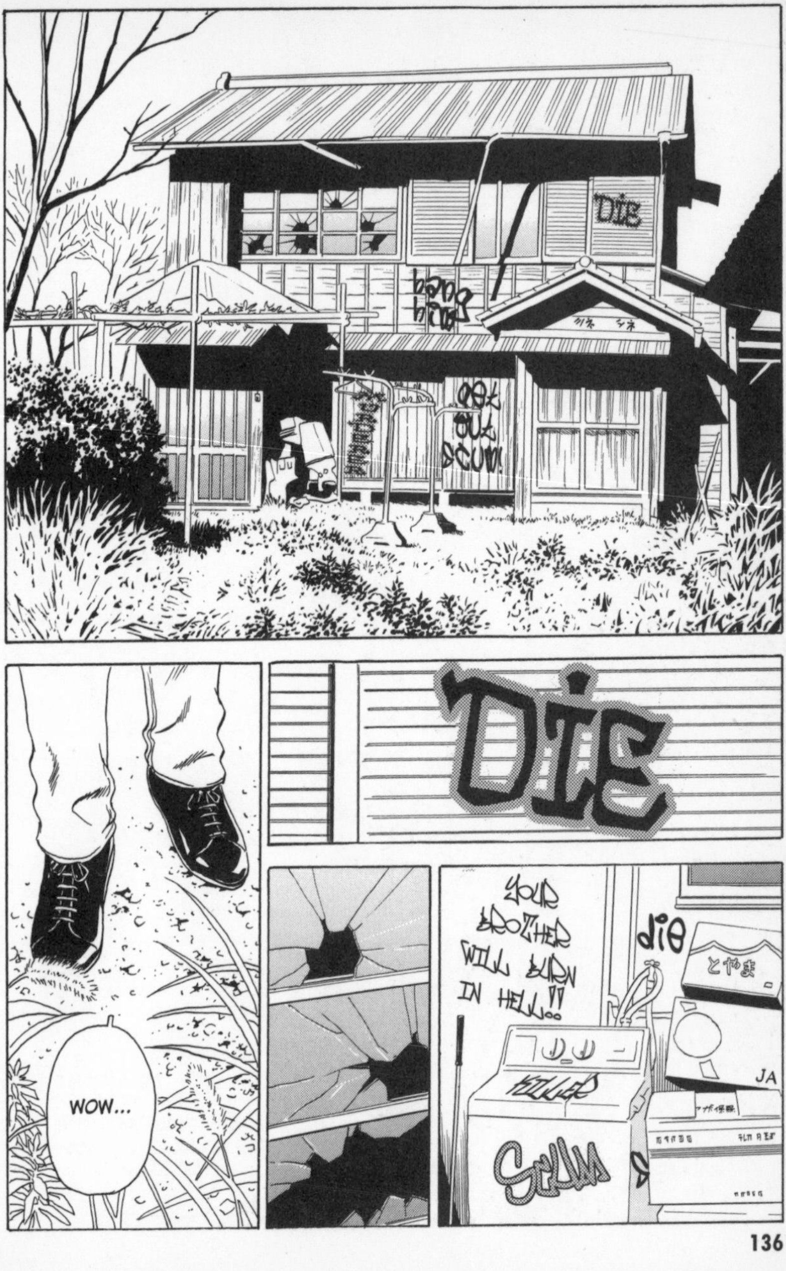
DIE
GET OUT SCUM!
DIE
YOUR BROTHER WILL BURN IN HELL!!
die
KILLER
SCUM
WOW...

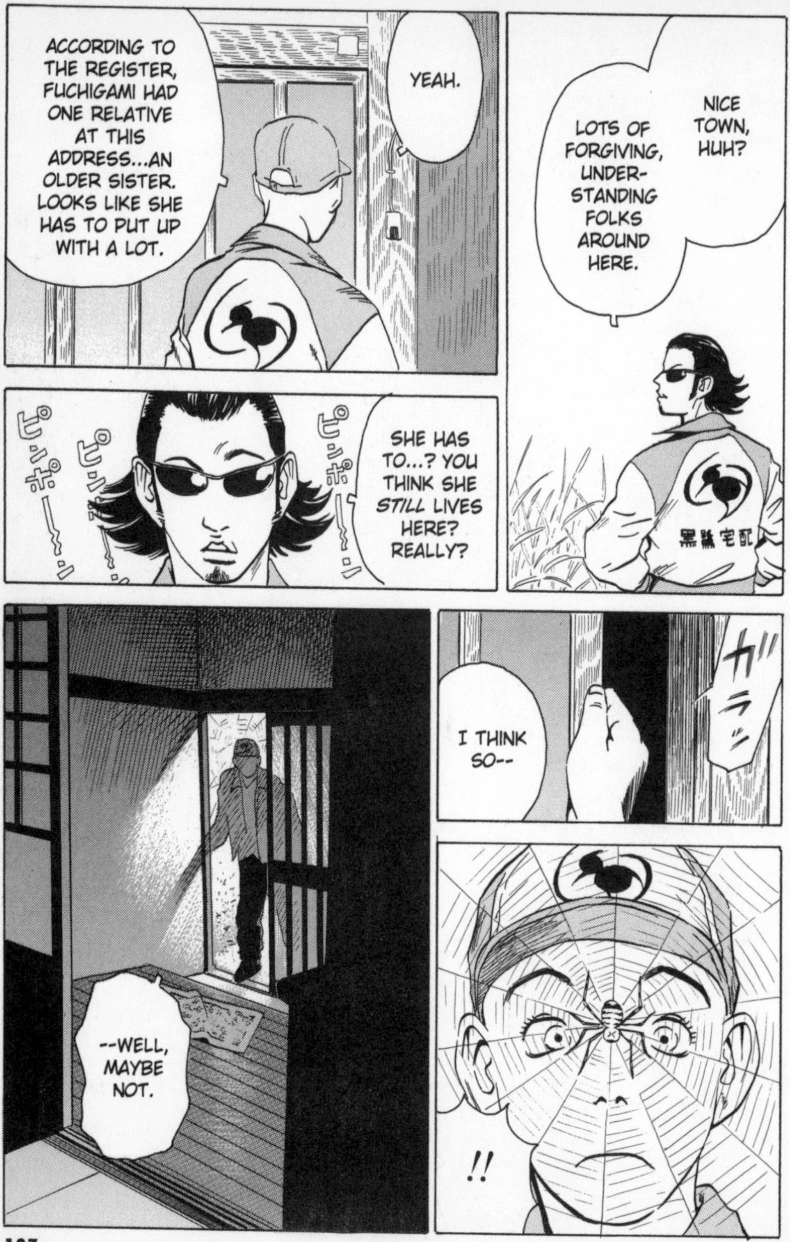
NICE TOWN, HUH?
LOTS OF FORGIVING, UNDER-STANDING FOLKS AROUND HERE.
YEAH.
ACCORDING TO THE REGISTER, FUCHIGAMI HAD ONE RELATIVE AT THIS ADDRESS...AN OLDER SISTER. LOOKS LIKE SHE HAS TO PUT UP WITH A LOT.
SHE HAS TO...? YOU THINK SHE *STILL* LIVES HERE? REALLY?
ガラッ
I THINK SO--
!!
--WELL, MAYBE NOT.

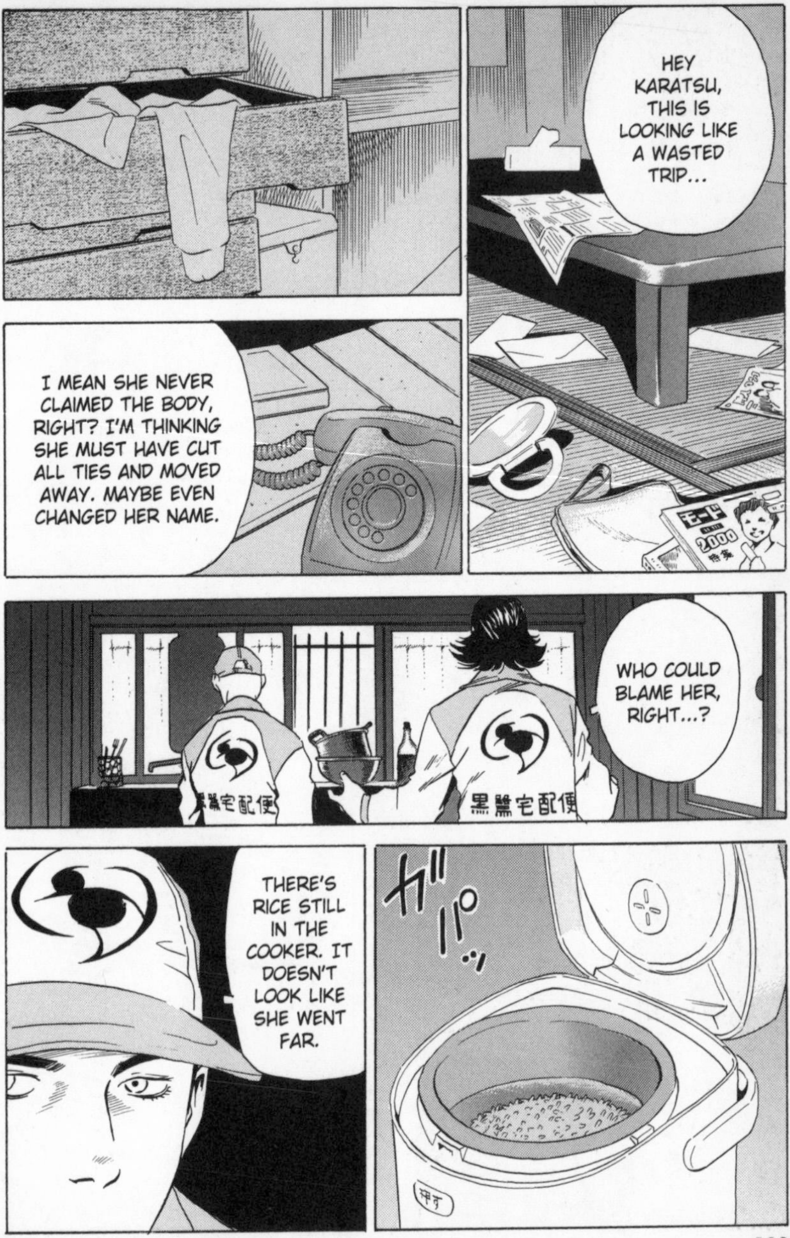
HEY KARATSU, THIS IS LOOKING LIKE A WASTED TRIP...
I MEAN SHE NEVER CLAIMED THE BODY, RIGHT? I'M THINKING SHE MUST HAVE CUT ALL TIES AND MOVED AWAY. MAYBE EVEN CHANGED HER NAME.
WHO COULD BLAME HER, RIGHT...?
黒鷺宅配便
ガパッ
THERE'S RICE STILL IN THE COOKER. IT DOESN'T LOOK LIKE SHE WENT FAR.

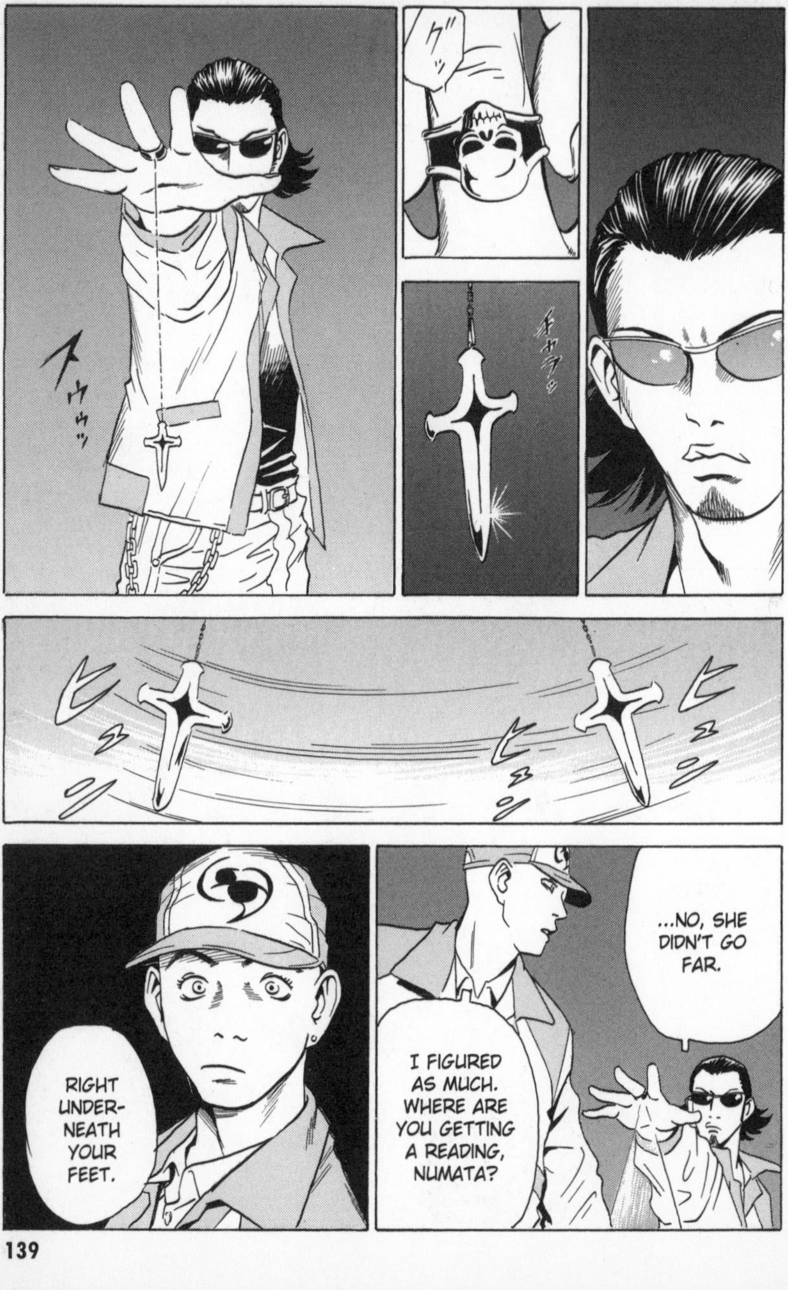
...NO, SHE DIDN'T GO FAR.
I FIGURED AS MUCH. WHERE ARE YOU GETTING A READING, NUMATA?
RIGHT UNDER-NEATH YOUR FEET.

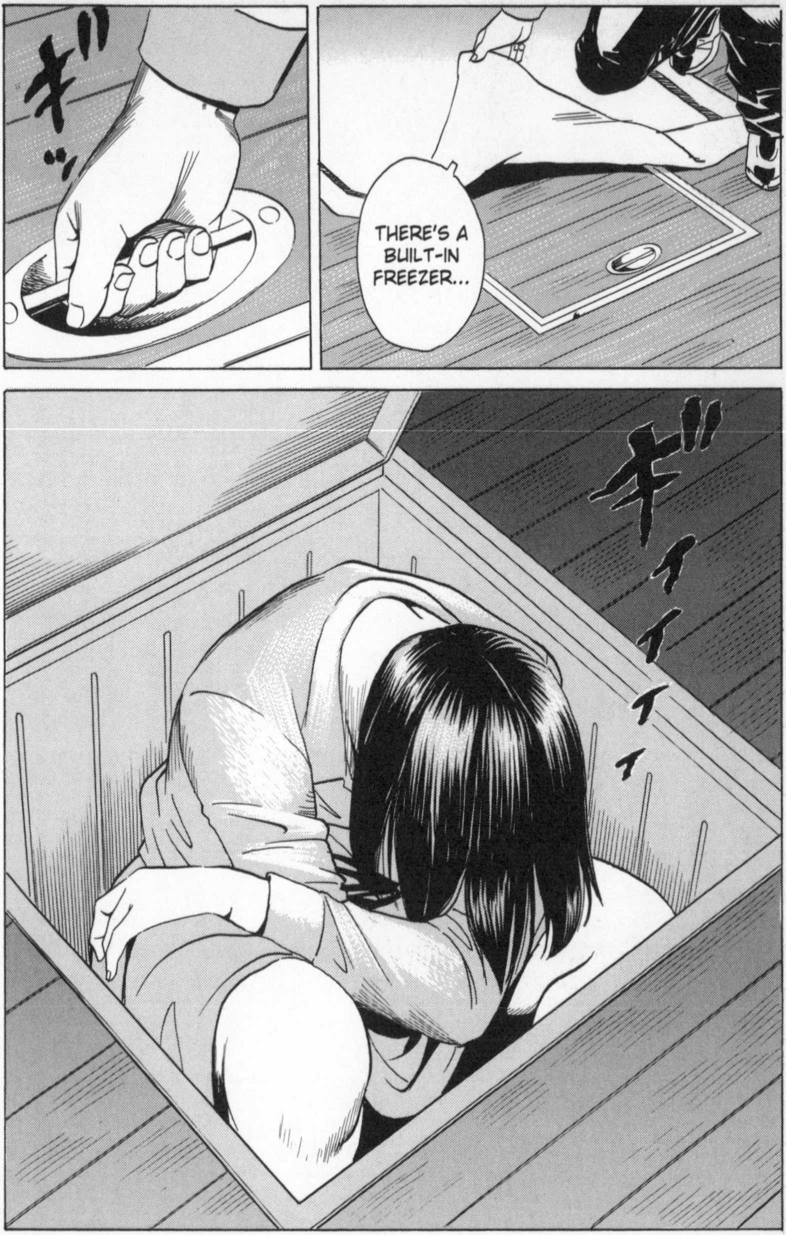
THERE'S A BUILT-IN FREEZER...
ギッ
ギイイイイ

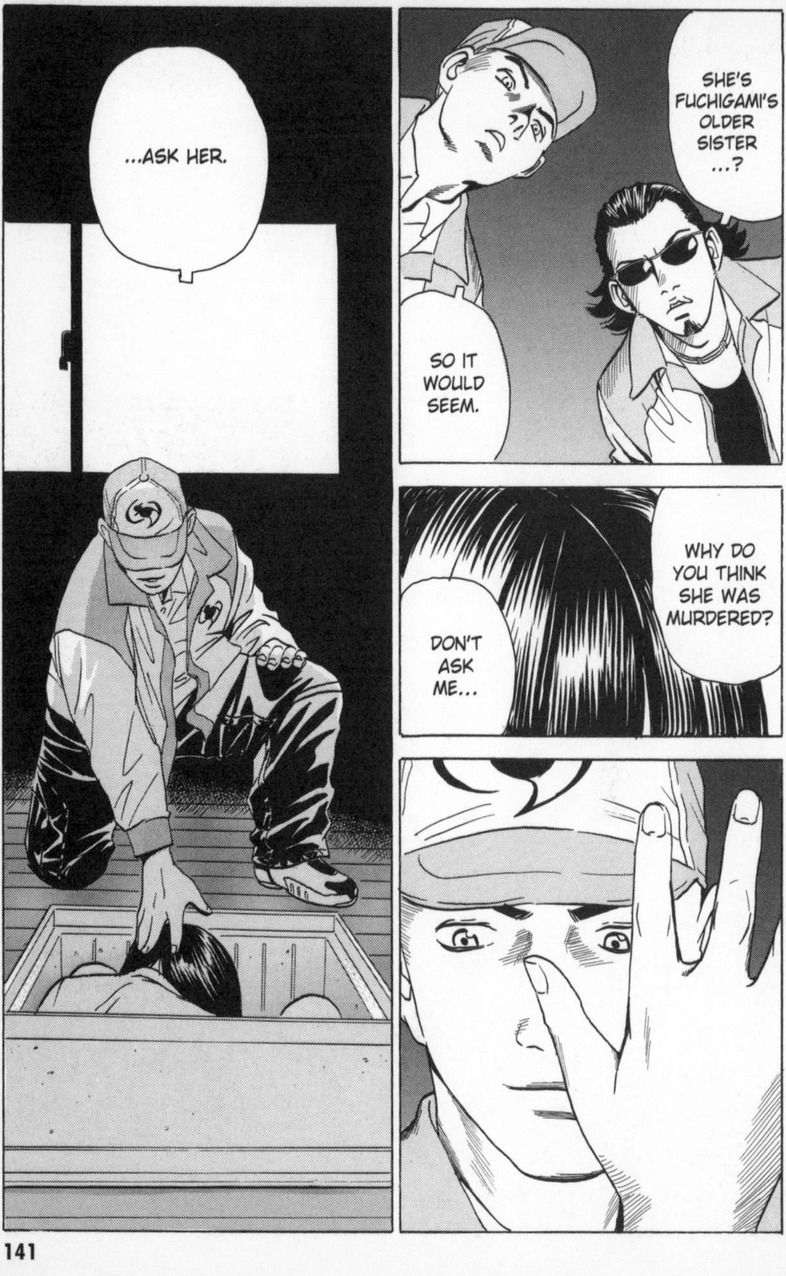
SHE'S FUCHIGAMI'S OLDER SISTER ...?
SO IT WOULD SEEM.
WHY DO YOU THINK SHE WAS MURDERED?
DON'T ASK ME...
...ASK HER.

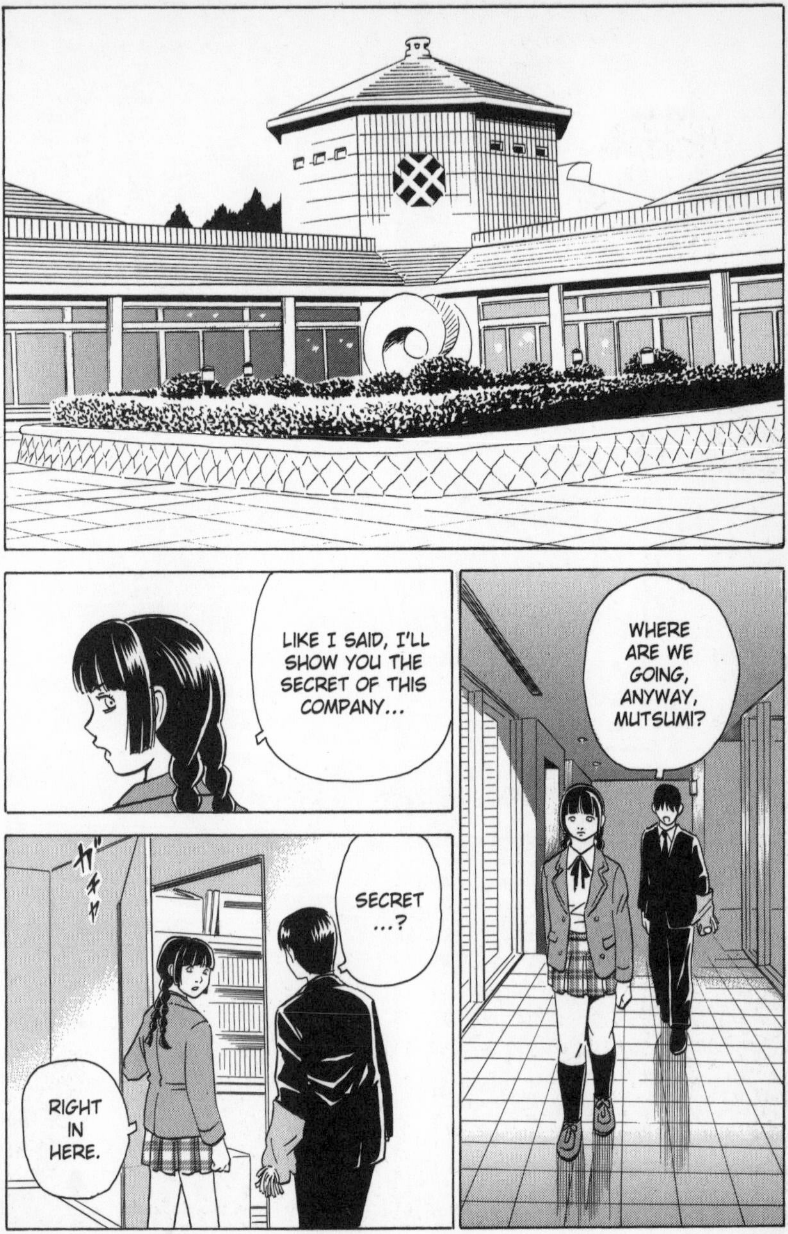
WHERE ARE WE GOING, ANYWAY, MUTSUMI?
LIKE I SAID, I'LL SHOW YOU THE SECRET OF THIS COMPANY...
SECRET ...?
ガチャ
RIGHT IN HERE.

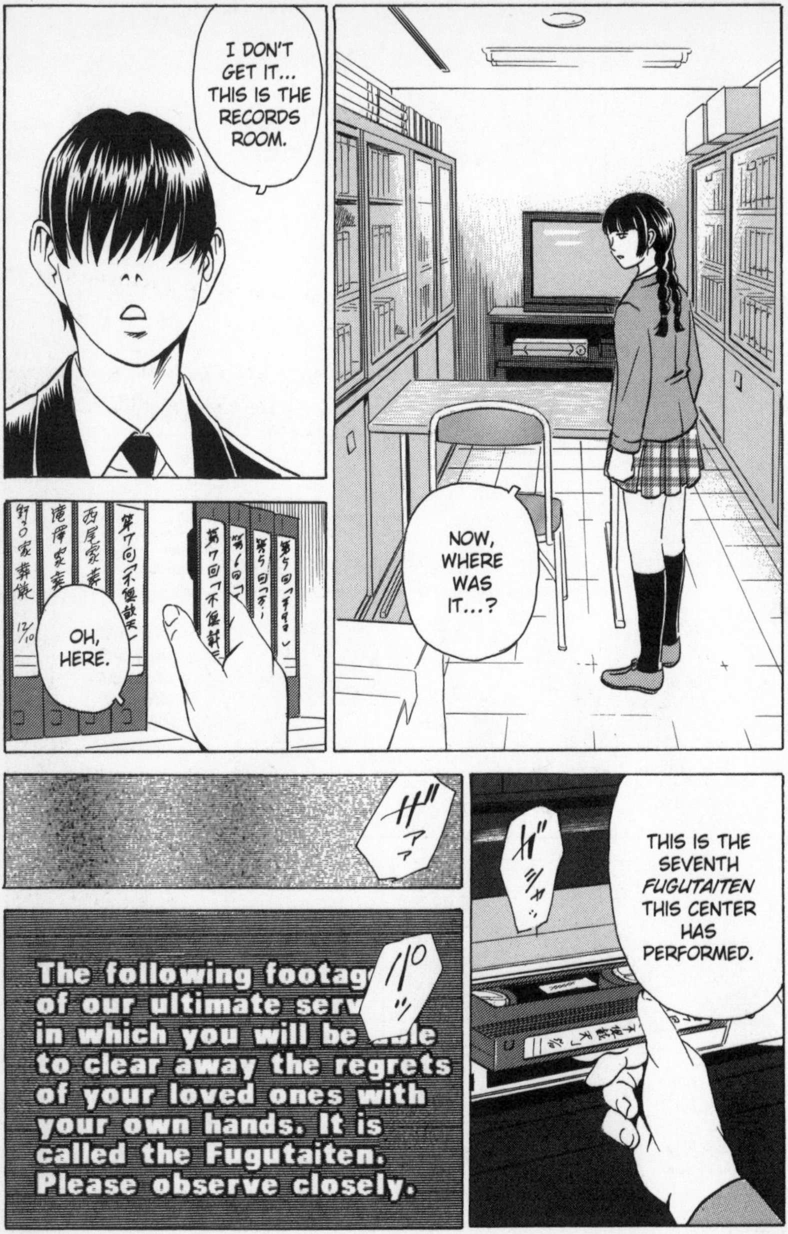

NOW, WHERE WAS IT...?
I DON'T GET IT... THIS IS THE RECORDS ROOM.
OH, HERE.
THIS IS THE SEVENTH *FUGUTAITEN* THIS CENTER HAS PERFORMED.
ガシャ
ザァァ
パッ
The following footag
of our ultimate serv
in which you will be
to clear away the regrets
of your loved ones with
your own hands. It is
called the Fugutaiten.
Please observe closely.

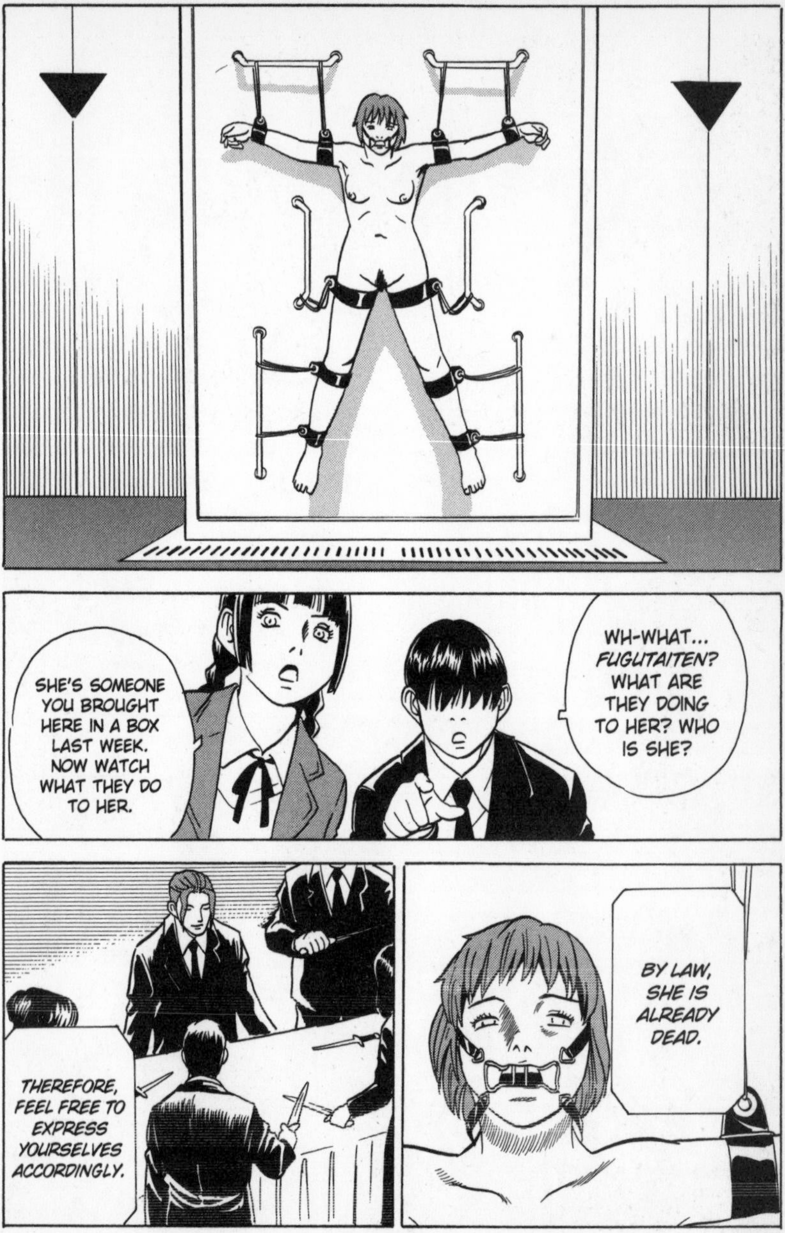
WH-WHAT... FUGUTAITEN? WHAT ARE THEY DOING TO HER? WHO IS SHE?
SHE'S SOMEONE YOU BROUGHT HERE IN A BOX LAST WEEK. NOW WATCH WHAT THEY DO TO HER.
BY LAW, SHE IS ALREADY DEAD.
THEREFORE, FEEL FREE TO EXPRESS YOURSELVES ACCORDINGLY.

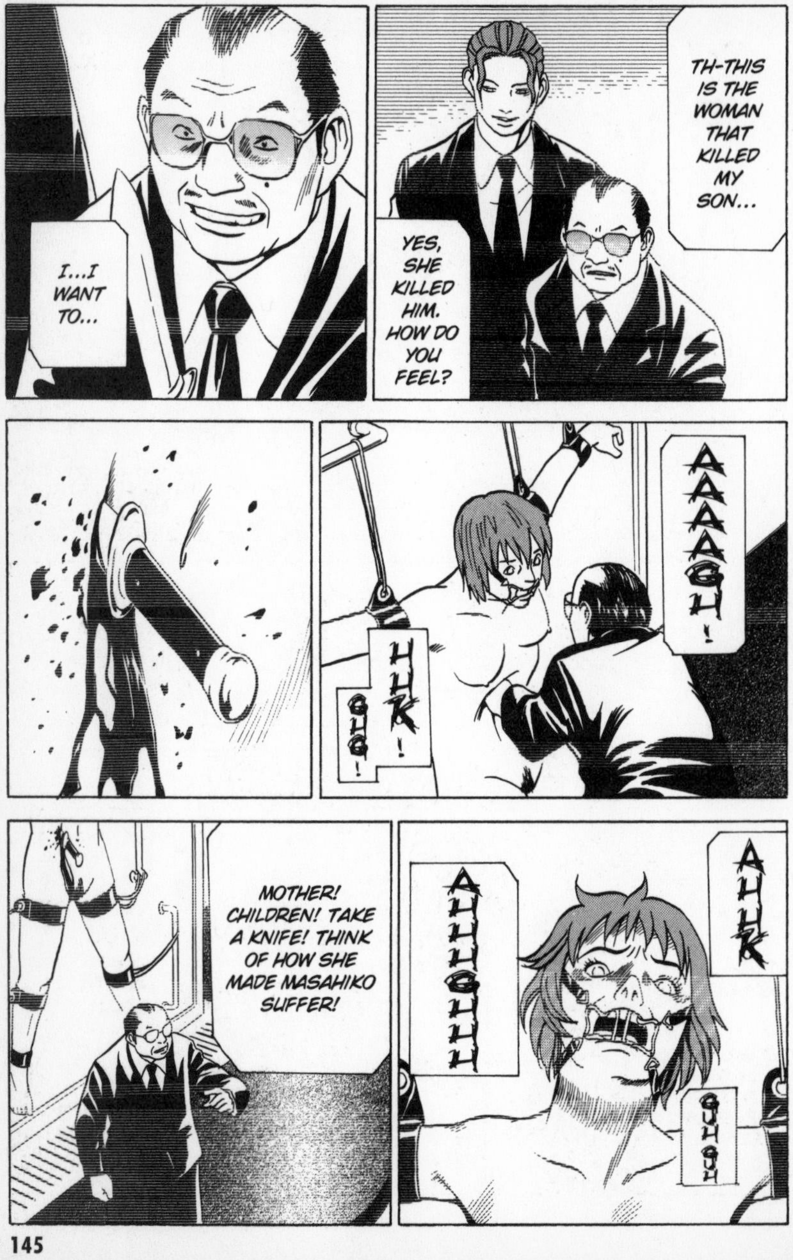
TH-THIS IS THE WOMAN THAT KILLED MY SON...
YES, SHE KILLED HIM. HOW DO YOU FEEL?
I...I WANT TO...
AAAAGH!
HHK!
GHG!
MOTHER! CHILDREN! TAKE A KNIFE! THINK OF HOW SHE MADE MASAHIKO SUFFER!
AHHK
AHHHGHHH
GUHGUH

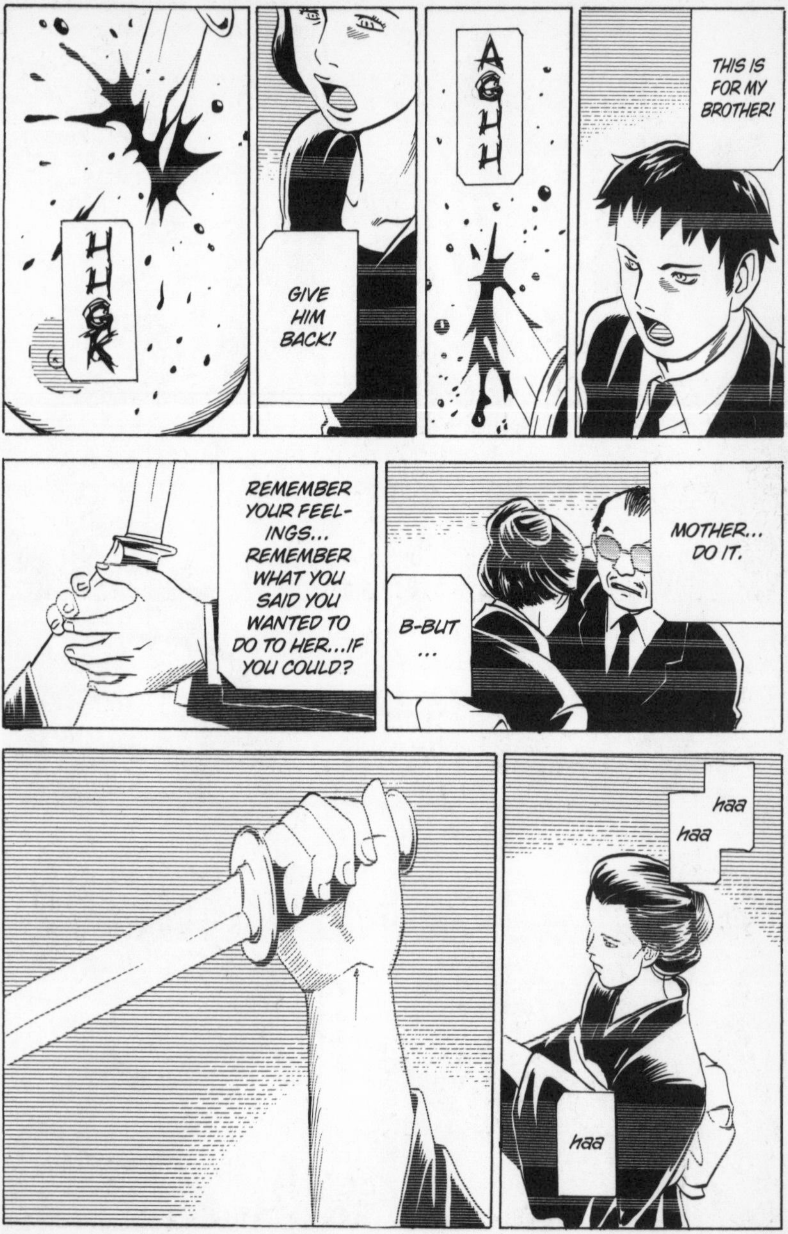
THIS IS FOR MY BROTHER!
AGHH
GIVE HIM BACK!
HHGK
MOTHER... DO IT.
B-BUT ...
REMEMBER YOUR FEEL-INGS... REMEMBER WHAT YOU SAID YOU WANTED TO DO TO HER...IF YOU COULD?
haa haa
haa

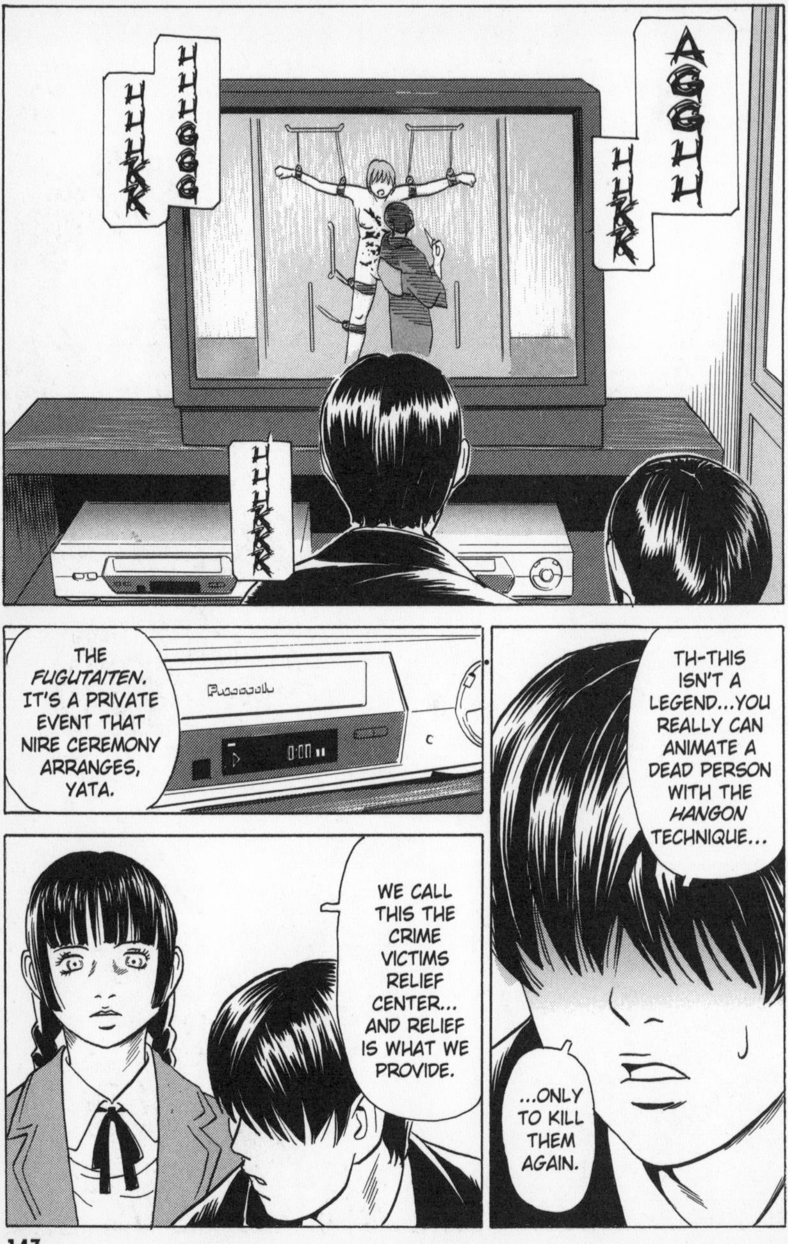
AGGHH
HHKK
HHHGGG
HHHKK
HHHKKK
TH-THIS ISN'T A LEGEND...YOU REALLY CAN ANIMATE A DEAD PERSON WITH THE *HANGON* TECHNIQUE...
...ONLY TO KILL THEM AGAIN.
THE *FUGUTAITEN.* IT'S A PRIVATE EVENT THAT NIRE CEREMONY ARRANGES, YATA.
WE CALL THIS THE CRIME VICTIMS RELIEF CENTER... AND RELIEF IS WHAT WE PROVIDE.

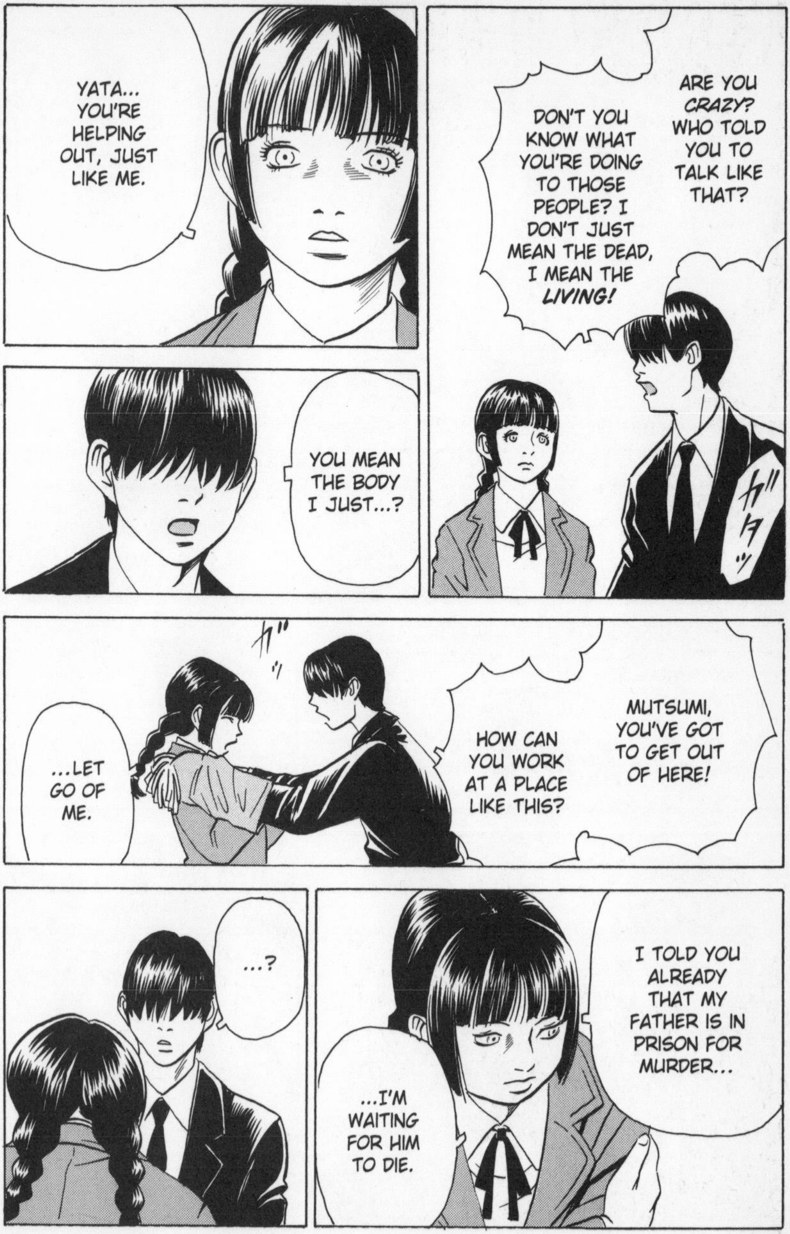
ARE YOU *CRAZY?* WHO TOLD YOU TO TALK LIKE THAT?
DON'T YOU KNOW WHAT YOU'RE DOING TO THOSE PEOPLE? I DON'T JUST MEAN THE DEAD, I MEAN THE ***LIVING!***
ガタッ
YATA... YOU'RE HELPING OUT, JUST LIKE ME.
YOU MEAN THE BODY I JUST...?
MUTSUMI, YOU'VE GOT TO GET OUT OF HERE!
HOW CAN YOU WORK AT A PLACE LIKE THIS?
ガッ
...LET GO OF ME.
I TOLD YOU ALREADY THAT MY FATHER IS IN PRISON FOR MURDER...
...I'M WAITING FOR HIM TO DIE.
...?

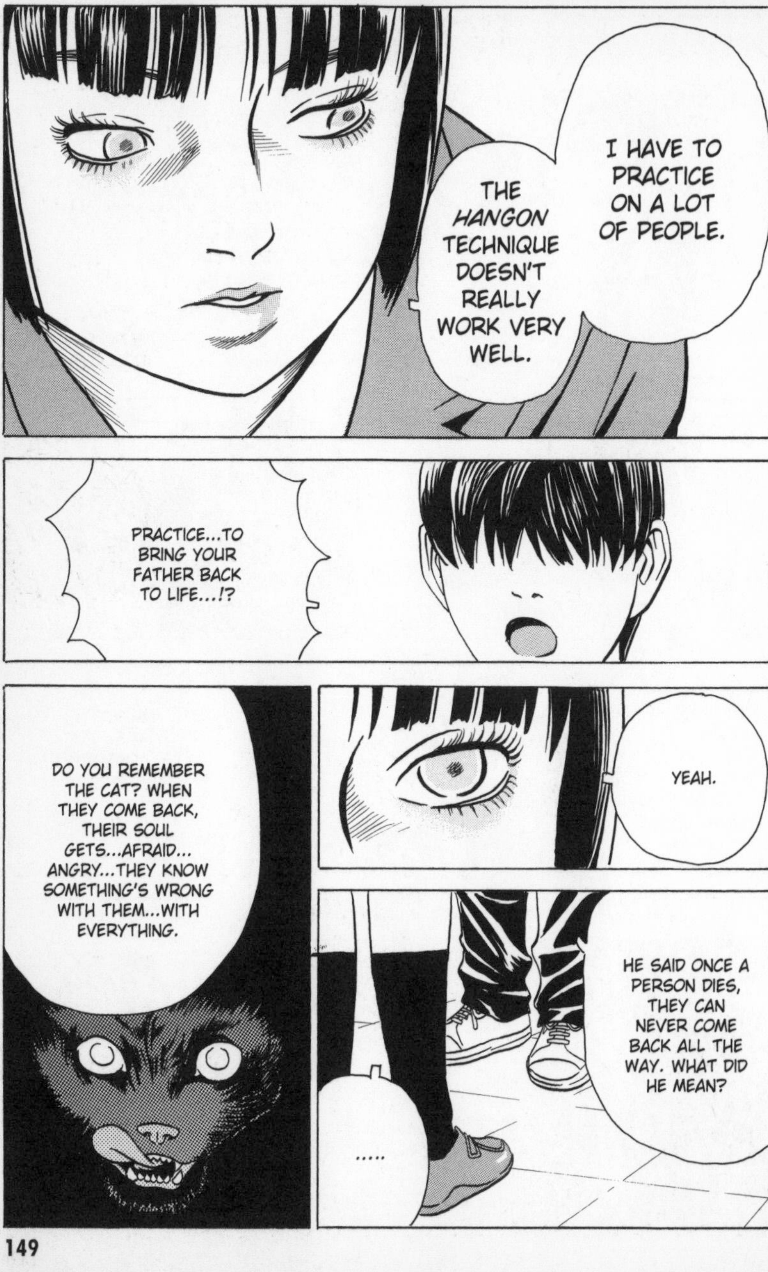
I HAVE TO PRACTICE ON A LOT OF PEOPLE.
THE *HANGON* TECHNIQUE DOESN'T REALLY WORK VERY WELL.
PRACTICE...TO BRING YOUR FATHER BACK TO LIFE...!?
YEAH.
HE SAID ONCE A PERSON DIES, THEY CAN NEVER COME BACK ALL THE WAY. WHAT DID HE MEAN?
.....
DO YOU REMEMBER THE CAT? WHEN THEY COME BACK, THEIR SOUL GETS...AFRAID... ANGRY...THEY KNOW SOMETHING'S WRONG WITH THEM...WITH EVERYTHING.

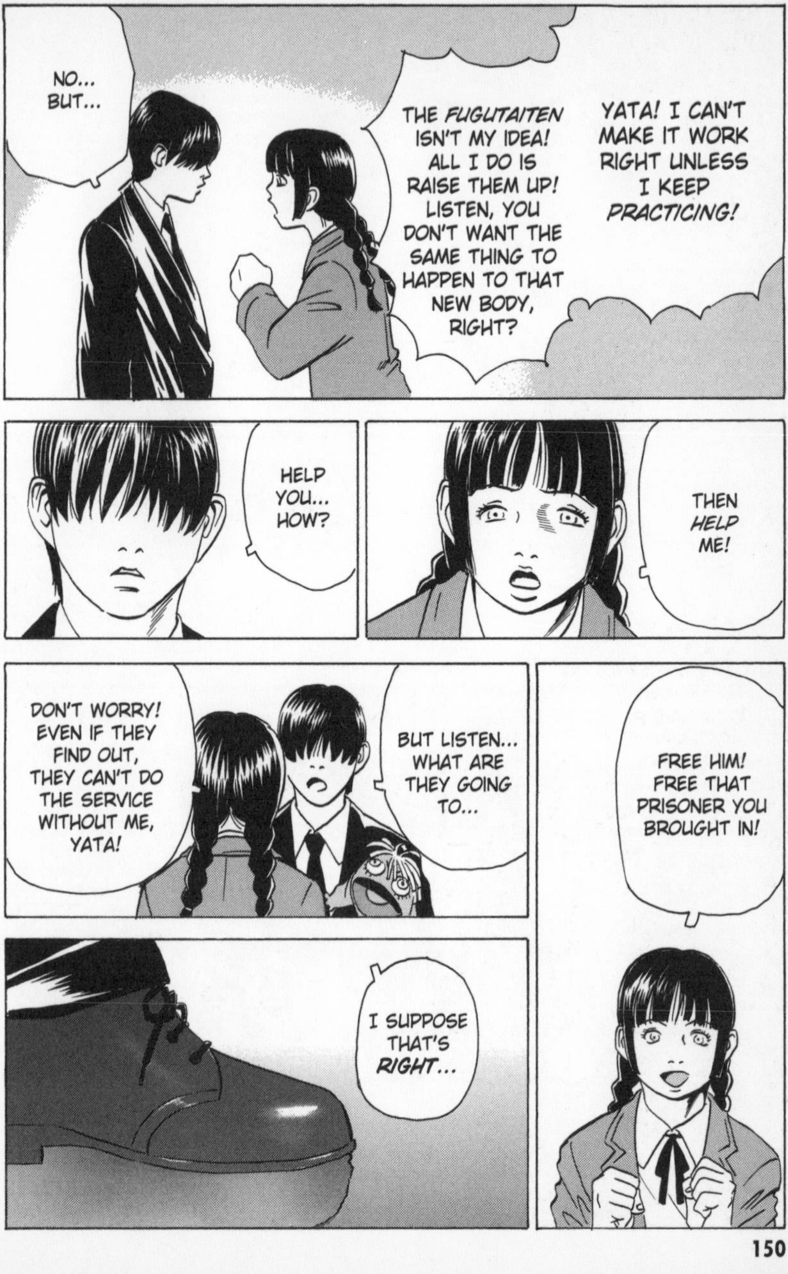
YATA! I CAN'T MAKE IT WORK RIGHT UNLESS I KEEP *PRACTICING!*
THE *FUGUTAITEN* ISN'T MY IDEA! ALL I DO IS RAISE THEM UP! LISTEN, YOU DON'T WANT THE SAME THING TO HAPPEN TO THAT NEW BODY, RIGHT?
NO... BUT...
THEN *HELP* ME!
HELP YOU... HOW?
FREE HIM! FREE THAT PRISONER YOU BROUGHT IN!
BUT LISTEN... WHAT ARE THEY GOING TO...
DON'T WORRY! EVEN IF THEY FIND OUT, THEY CAN'T DO THE SERVICE WITHOUT ME, YATA!
I SUPPOSE THAT'S ***RIGHT***...

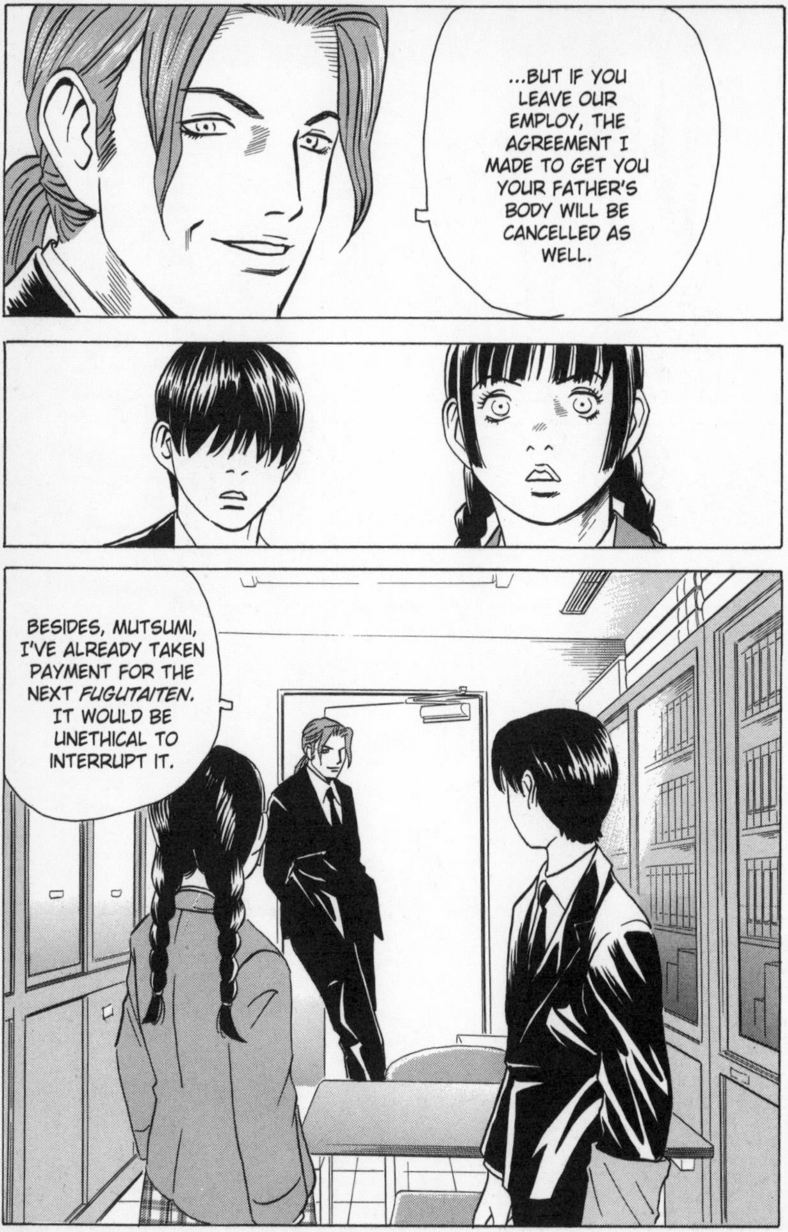
...BUT IF YOU LEAVE OUR EMPLOY, THE AGREEMENT I MADE TO GET YOU YOUR FATHER'S BODY WILL BE CANCELLED AS WELL.
BESIDES, MUTSUMI, I'VE ALREADY TAKEN PAYMENT FOR THE NEXT *FUGUTAITEN*. IT WOULD BE UNETHICAL TO INTERRUPT IT.

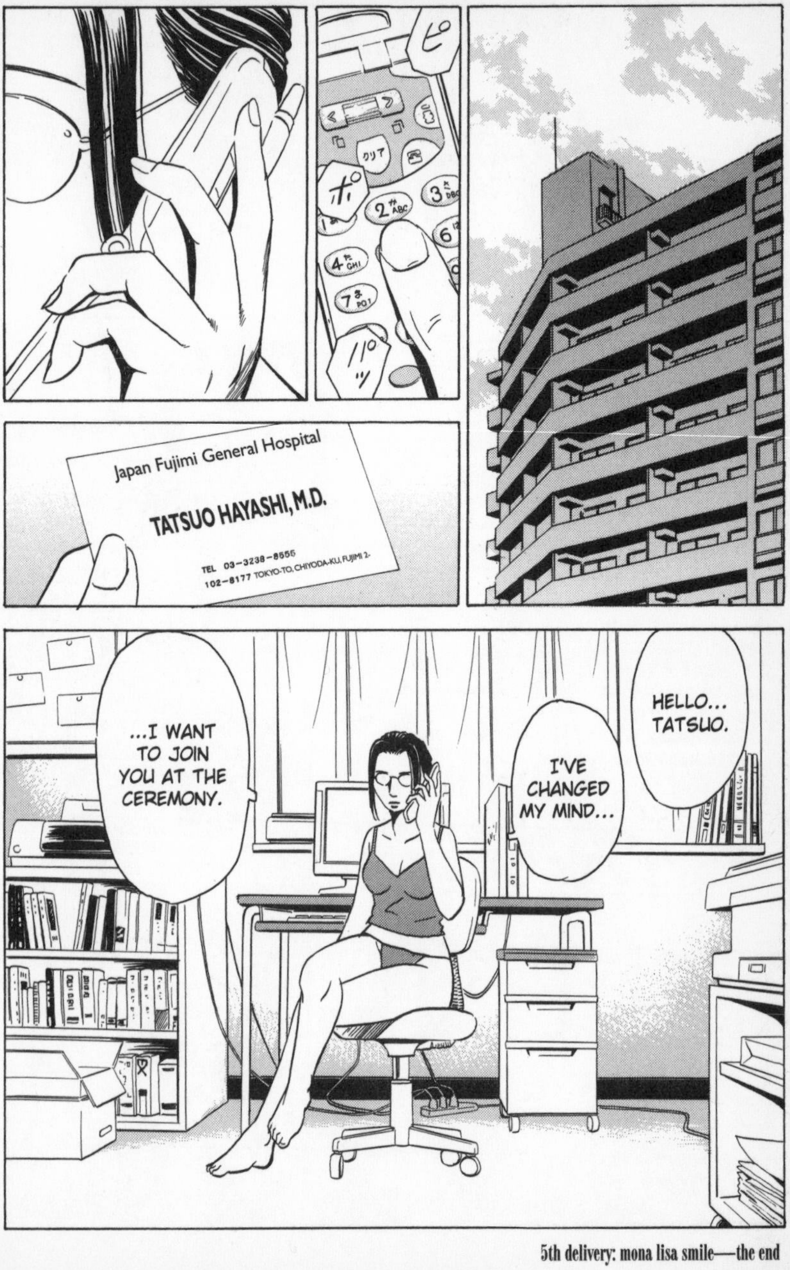
ピ
ポ
Japan Fujimi General Hospital
TATSUO HAYASHI, M.D.
TEL 03-3238-8555
102-8177 TOKYO-TO, CHIYODA-KU, FUJIMI 2-
HELLO... TATSUO.
I'VE CHANGED MY MIND...
...I WANT TO JOIN YOU AT THE CEREMONY.

5th delivery: mona lisa smile—the end

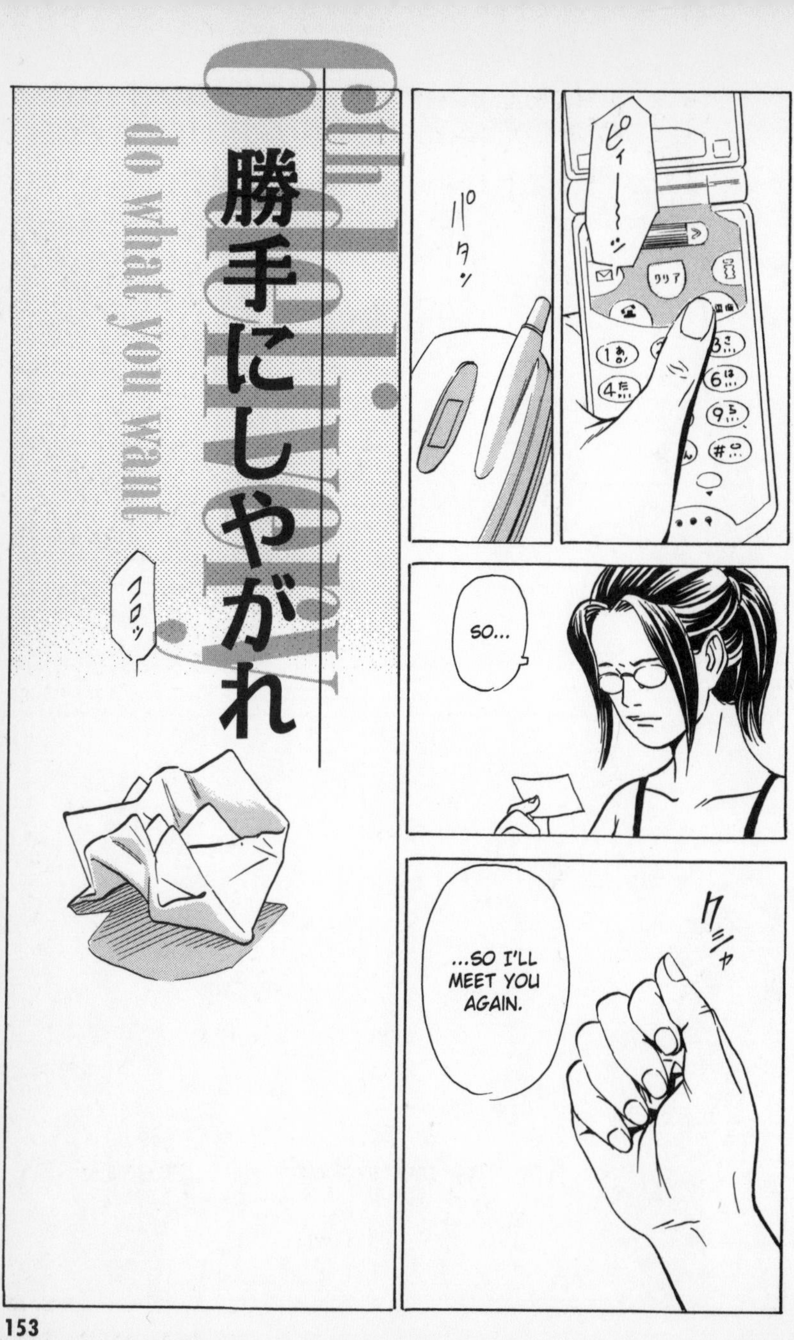
ピィ～ッ
パタン
SO...
クシャ
...SO I'LL MEET YOU AGAIN.
6th story
勝手にしやがれ
do what you want
コロッ

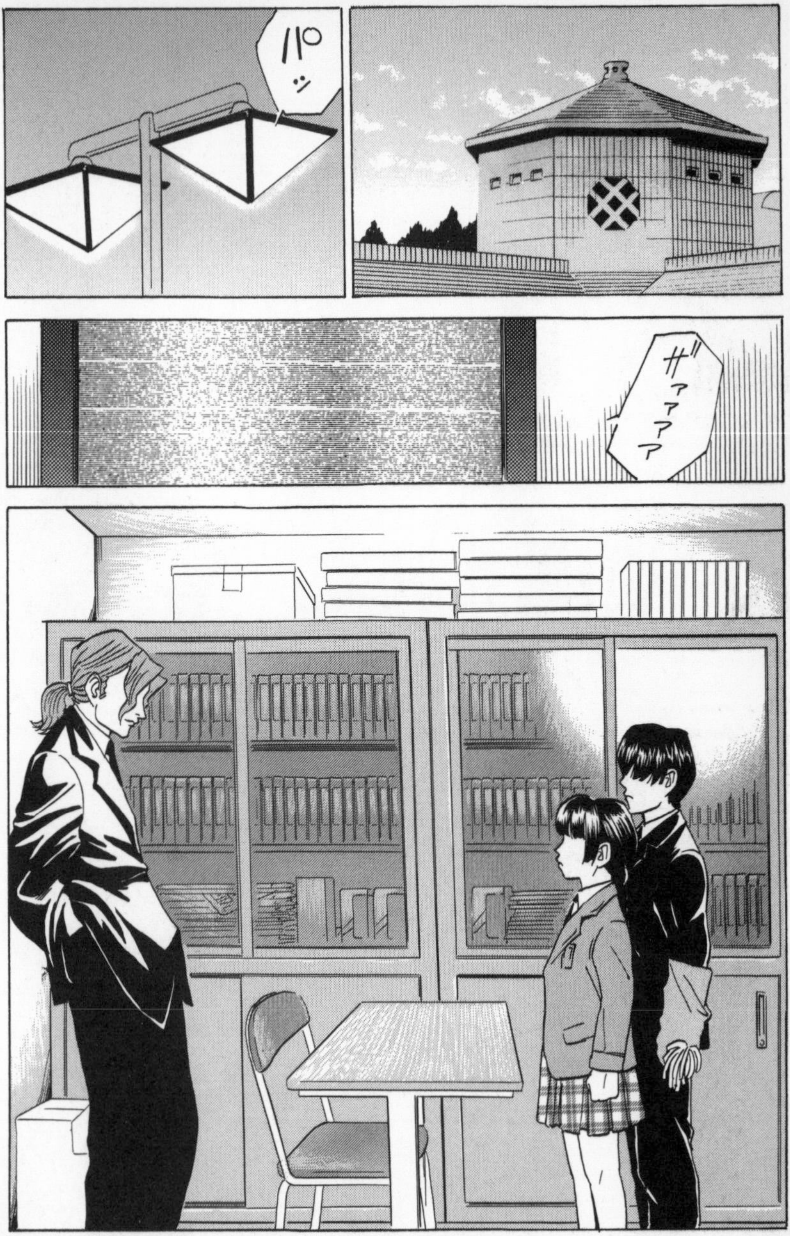
パッ
ザァァァァ

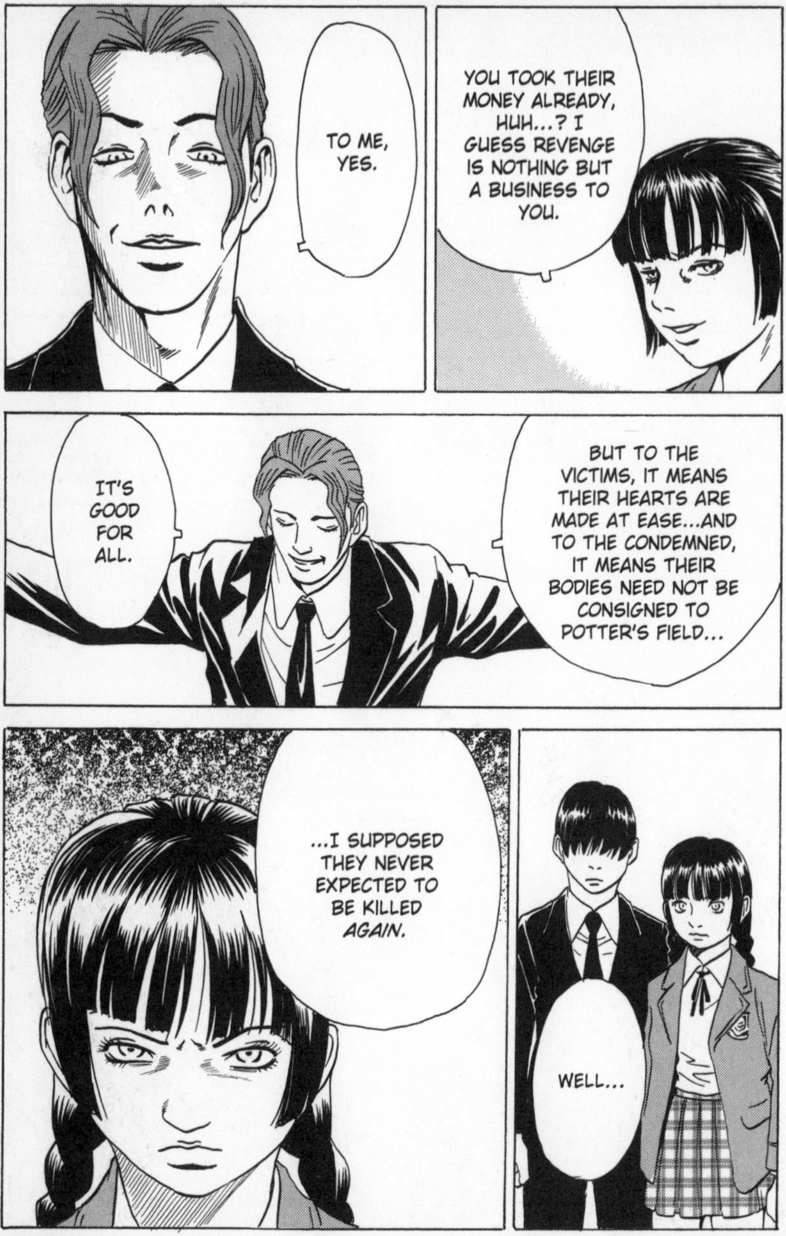
YOU TOOK THEIR MONEY ALREADY, HUH...? I GUESS REVENGE IS NOTHING BUT A BUSINESS TO YOU.
TO ME, YES.
BUT TO THE VICTIMS, IT MEANS THEIR HEARTS ARE MADE AT EASE...AND TO THE CONDEMNED, IT MEANS THEIR BODIES NEED NOT BE CONSIGNED TO POTTER'S FIELD...
IT'S GOOD FOR ALL.
WELL...
...I SUPPOSED THEY NEVER EXPECTED TO BE KILLED *AGAIN*.

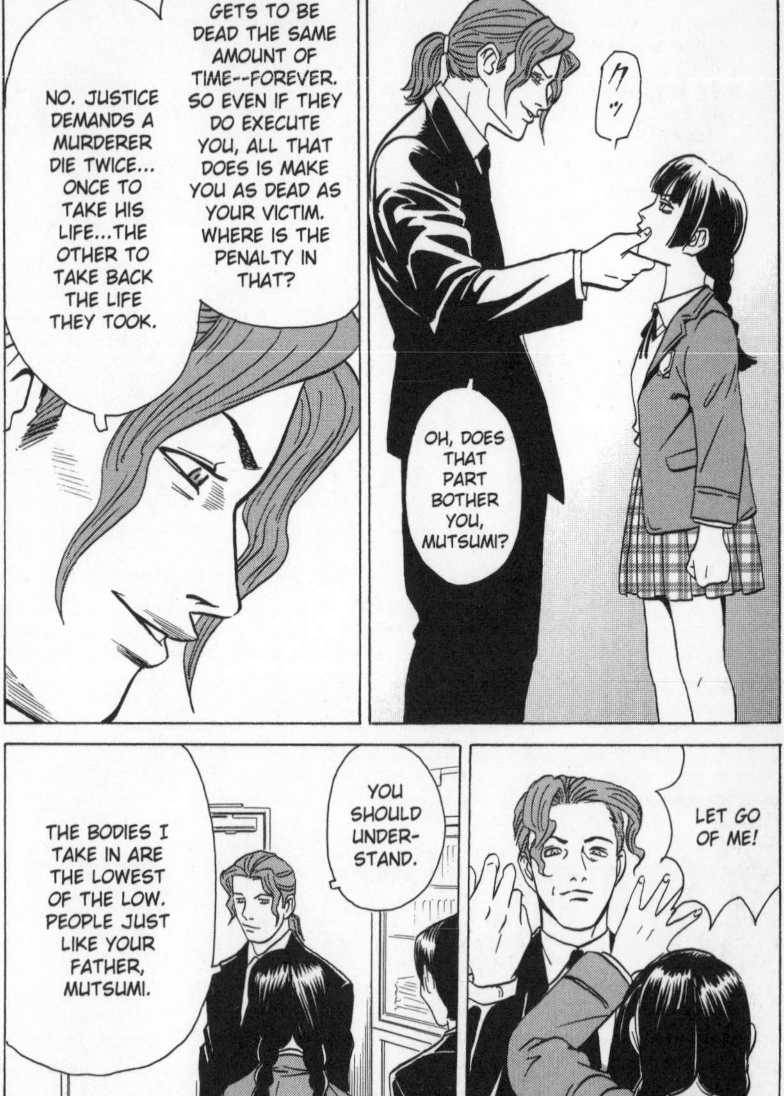
ハッ
OH, DOES THAT PART BOTHER YOU, MUTSUMI?
EVERYBODY GETS TO BE DEAD THE SAME AMOUNT OF TIME--FOREVER. SO EVEN IF THEY DO EXECUTE YOU, ALL THAT DOES IS MAKE YOU AS DEAD AS YOUR VICTIM. WHERE IS THE PENALTY IN THAT?
NO. JUSTICE DEMANDS A MURDERER DIE TWICE... ONCE TO TAKE HIS LIFE...THE OTHER TO TAKE BACK THE LIFE THEY TOOK.
LET GO OF ME!
YOU SHOULD UNDER-STAND.
THE BODIES I TAKE IN ARE THE LOWEST OF THE LOW. PEOPLE JUST LIKE YOUR FATHER, MUTSUMI.

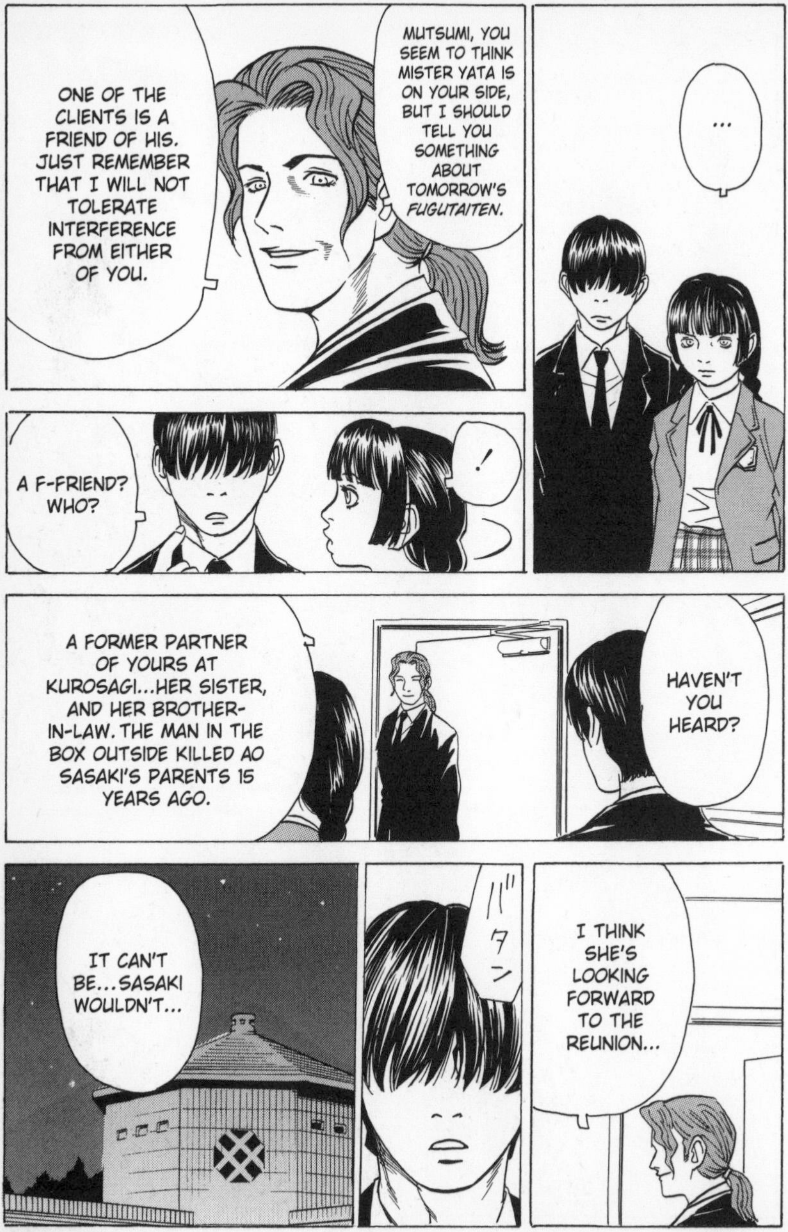
...
MUTSUMI, YOU SEEM TO THINK MISTER YATA IS ON YOUR SIDE, BUT I SHOULD TELL YOU SOMETHING ABOUT TOMORROW'S *FUGUTAITEN.*
ONE OF THE CLIENTS IS A FRIEND OF HIS. JUST REMEMBER THAT I WILL NOT TOLERATE INTERFERENCE FROM EITHER OF YOU.
!
A F-FRIEND? WHO?
HAVEN'T YOU HEARD?
A FORMER PARTNER OF YOURS AT KUROSAGI...HER SISTER, AND HER BROTHER-IN-LAW. THE MAN IN THE BOX OUTSIDE KILLED AO SASAKI'S PARENTS 15 YEARS AGO.
I THINK SHE'S LOOKING FORWARD TO THE REUNION...
バタン
IT CAN'T BE...SASAKI WOULDN'T...

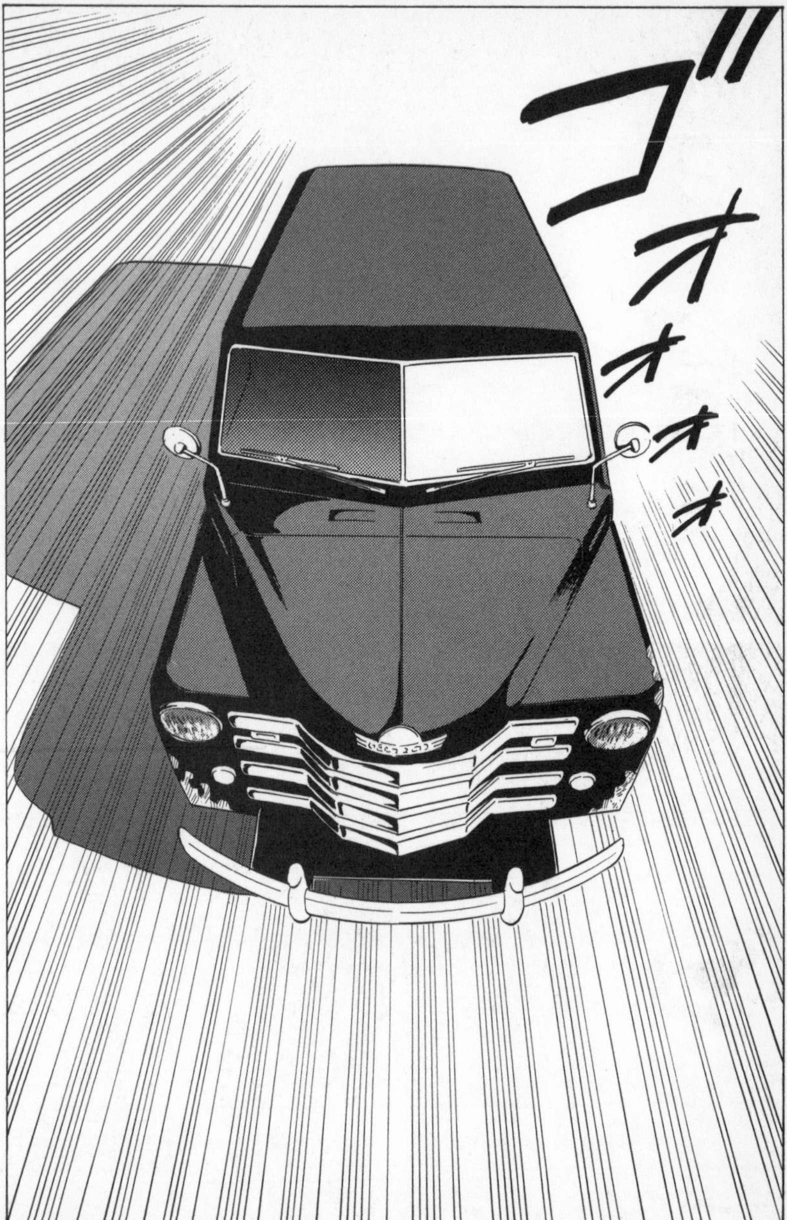
ゴオォォォ

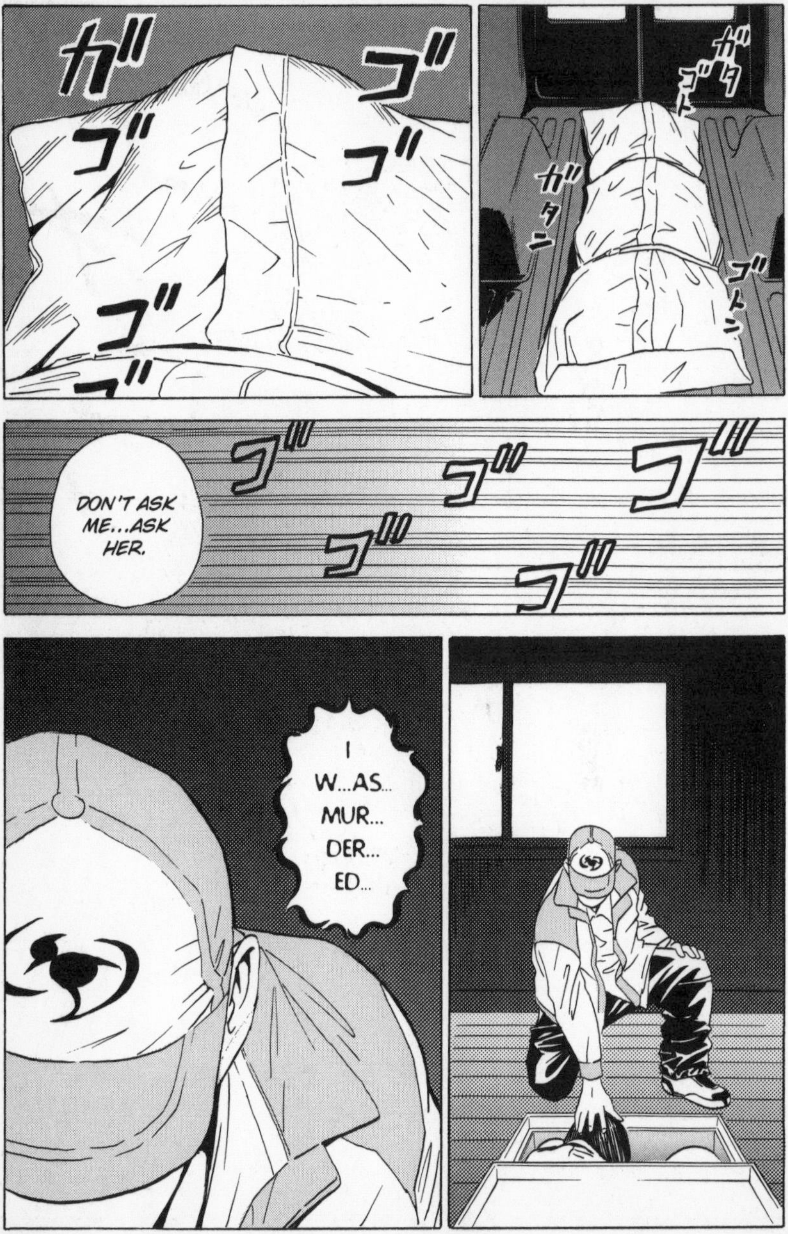
ガタ
ゴト
ガタン
ゴトン
ゴ
ゴ
ガ
ゴ
ゴ
ゴ
ゴ
ゴ
ゴ
ゴ
DON'T ASK ME...ASK HER.
I W...AS... MUR... DER... ED...

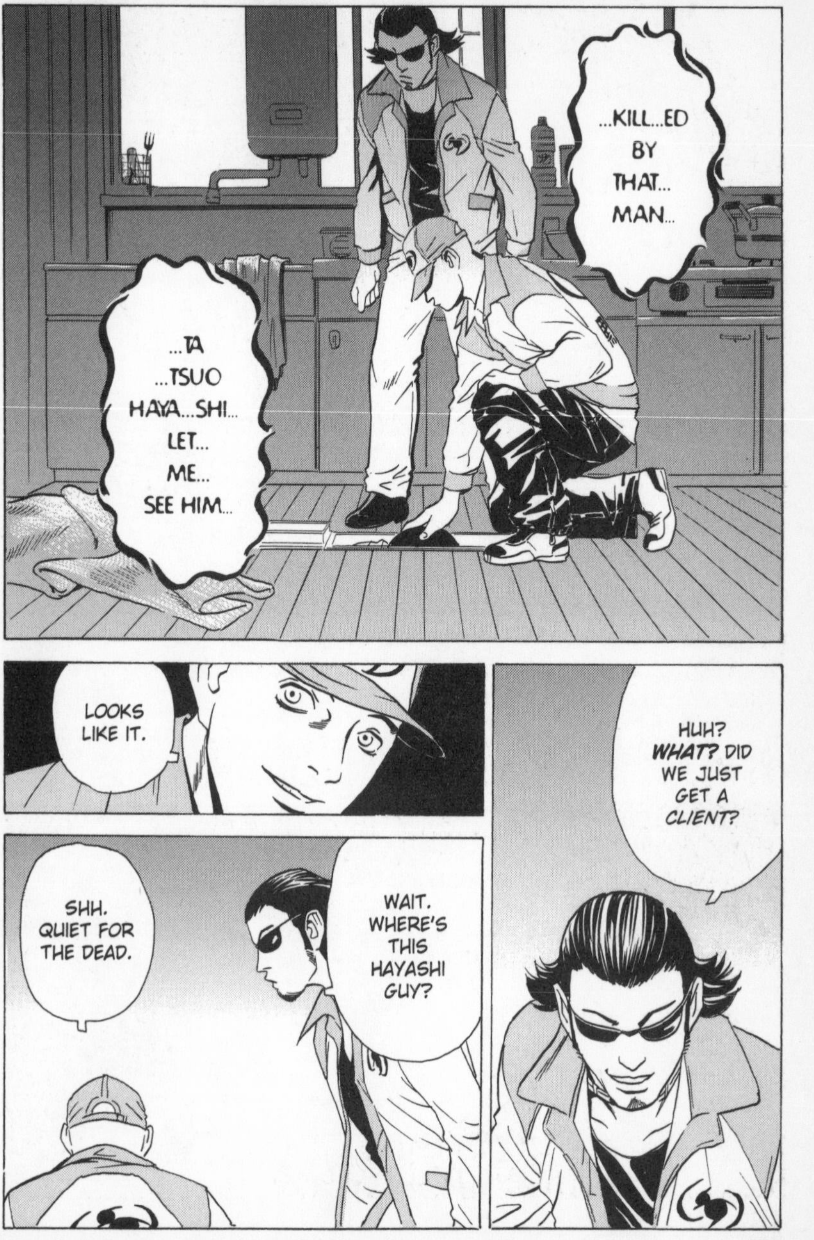
...KILL...ED BY THAT... MAN...
...TA ...TSUO HAYA...SHI... LET... ME... SEE HIM...
HUH? *WHAT?* DID WE JUST GET A *CLIENT?*
LOOKS LIKE IT.
WAIT. WHERE'S THIS HAYASHI GUY?
SHH. QUIET FOR THE DEAD.

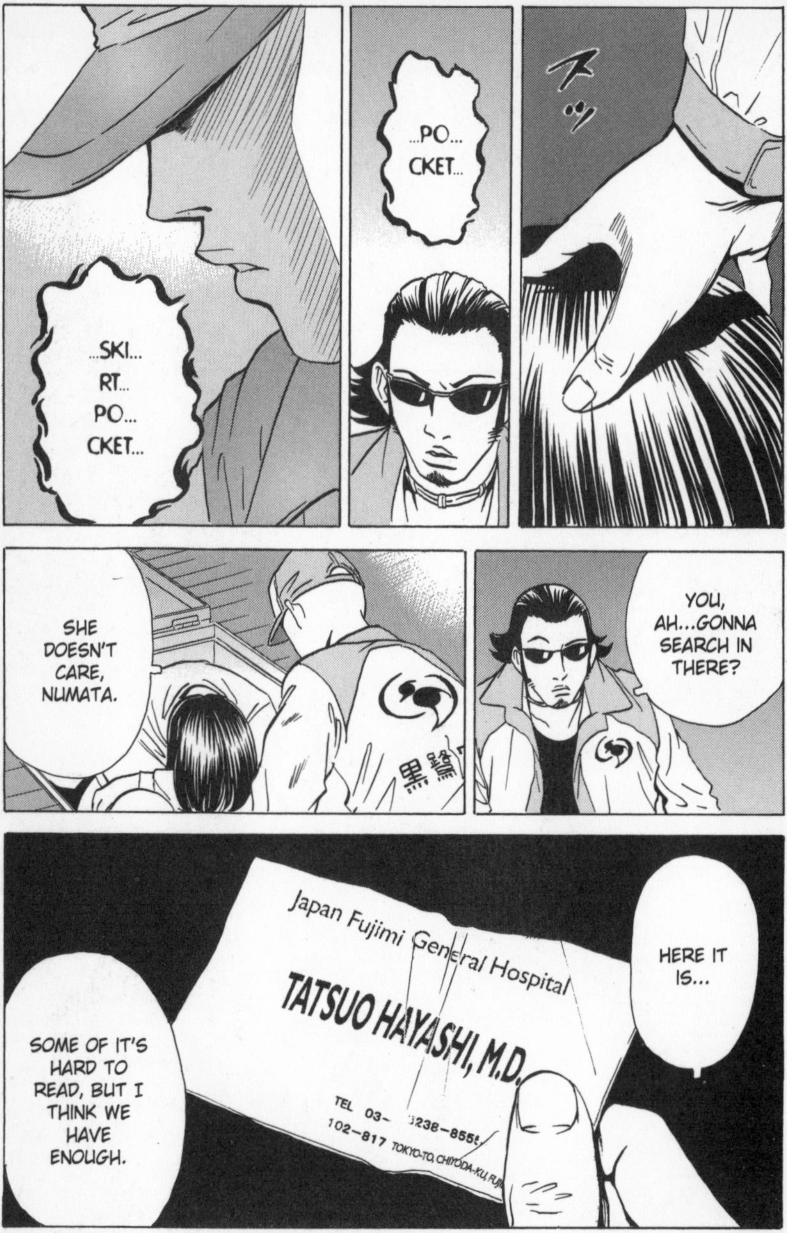

スッ
...PO... CKET...
...SKI... RT... PO... CKET...
YOU, AH...GONNA SEARCH IN THERE?
SHE DOESN'T CARE, NUMATA.
HERE IT IS...
Japan Fujimi General Hospital
TATSUO HAYASHI, M.D.
SOME OF IT'S HARD TO READ, BUT I THINK WE HAVE ENOUGH.

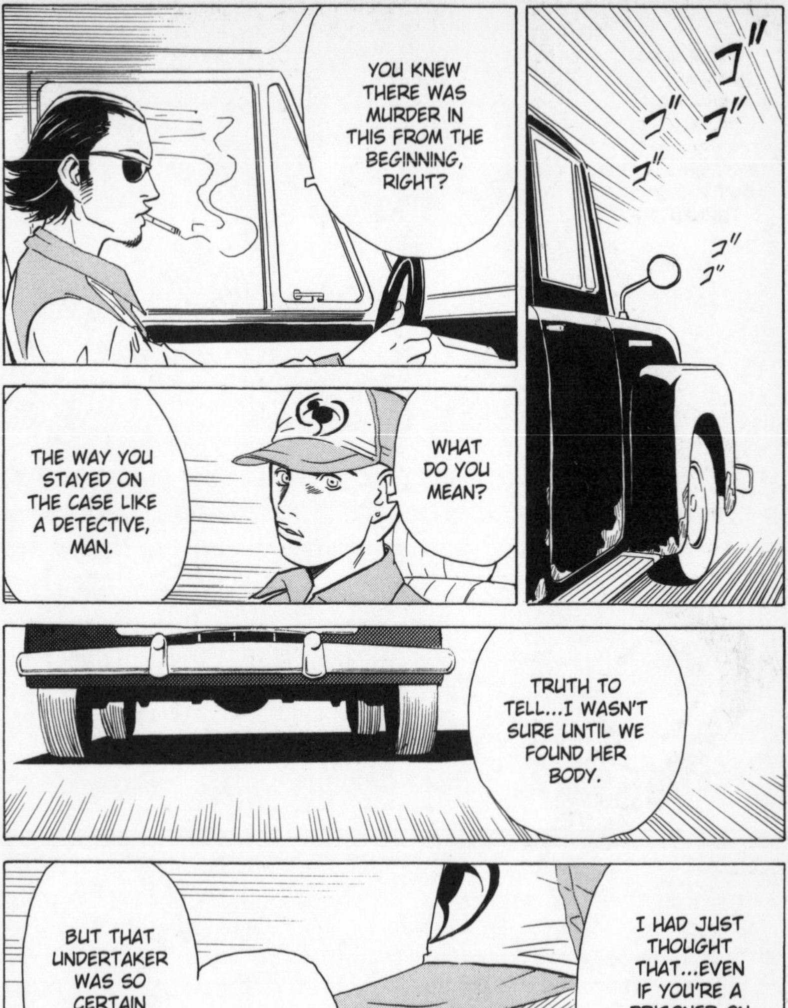
ゴゴゴゴ
ゴゴ
YOU KNEW THERE WAS MURDER IN THIS FROM THE BEGINNING, RIGHT?
WHAT DO YOU MEAN?
THE WAY YOU STAYED ON THE CASE LIKE A DETECTIVE, MAN.
TRUTH TO TELL...I WASN'T SURE UNTIL WE FOUND HER BODY.
I HAD JUST THOUGHT THAT...EVEN IF YOU'RE A PRISONER ON DEATH ROW, THEY OUGHT TO HAVE SOMEONE WHO CARES FOR THEM...
...THAT'S JUST WHAT I THOUGHT, IS ALL.
BUT THAT UNDERTAKER WAS SO CERTAIN THERE WAS NO ONE.

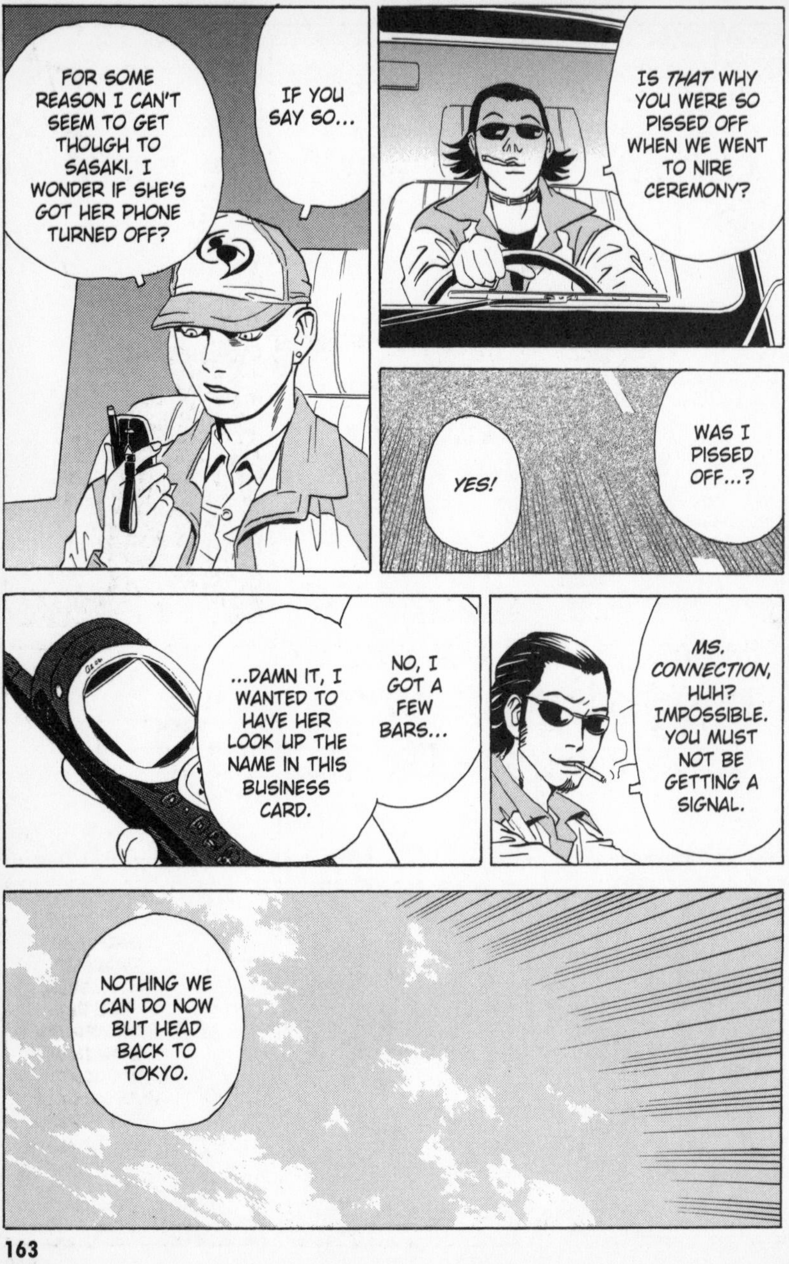
IS *THAT* WHY YOU WERE SO PISSED OFF WHEN WE WENT TO NIRE CEREMONY?
WAS I PISSED OFF...?
YES!
IF YOU SAY SO...
FOR SOME REASON I CAN'T SEEM TO GET THOUGH TO SASAKI. I WONDER IF SHE'S GOT HER PHONE TURNED OFF?
MS. CONNECTION, HUH? IMPOSSIBLE. YOU MUST NOT BE GETTING A SIGNAL.
NO, I GOT A FEW BARS...
...DAMN IT, I WANTED TO HAVE HER LOOK UP THE NAME IN THIS BUSINESS CARD.
NOTHING WE CAN DO NOW BUT HEAD BACK TO TOKYO.

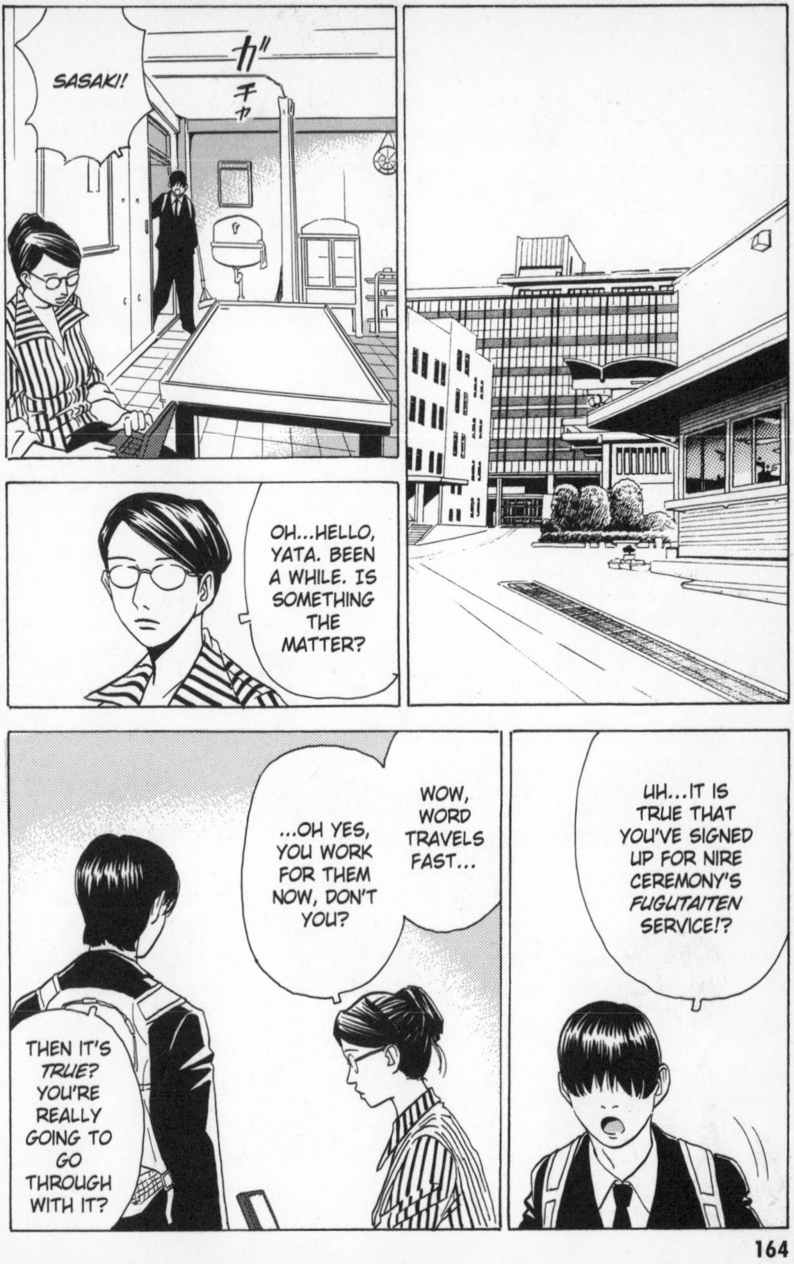
SASAKI!
ガチャ
OH...HELLO, YATA. BEEN A WHILE. IS SOMETHING THE MATTER?
UH...IT IS TRUE THAT YOU'VE SIGNED UP FOR NIRE CEREMONY'S *FUGUTAITEN* SERVICE!?
WOW, WORD TRAVELS FAST...
...OH YES, YOU WORK FOR THEM NOW, DON'T YOU?
THEN IT'S *TRUE?* YOU'RE REALLY GOING TO GO THROUGH WITH IT?

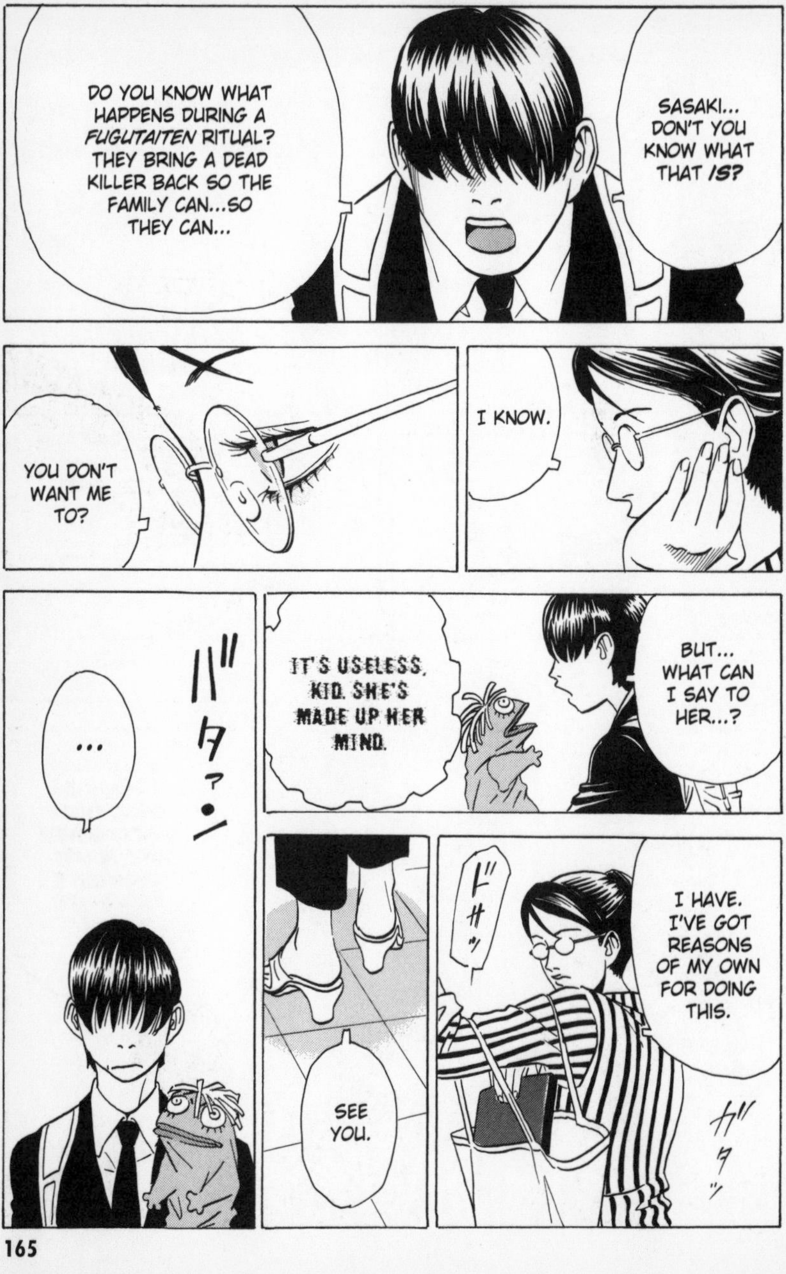
SASAKI... DON'T YOU KNOW WHAT THAT *IS*?
DO YOU KNOW WHAT HAPPENS DURING A *FUGUTAITEN* RITUAL? THEY BRING A DEAD KILLER BACK SO THE FAMILY CAN...SO THEY CAN...
I KNOW.
YOU DON'T WANT ME TO?
BUT... WHAT CAN I SAY TO HER...?
IT'S USELESS, KID. SHE'S MADE UP HER MIND.
I HAVE. I'VE GOT REASONS OF MY OWN FOR DOING THIS.
ガタッ
ドサッ
SEE YOU.
バタッ
...

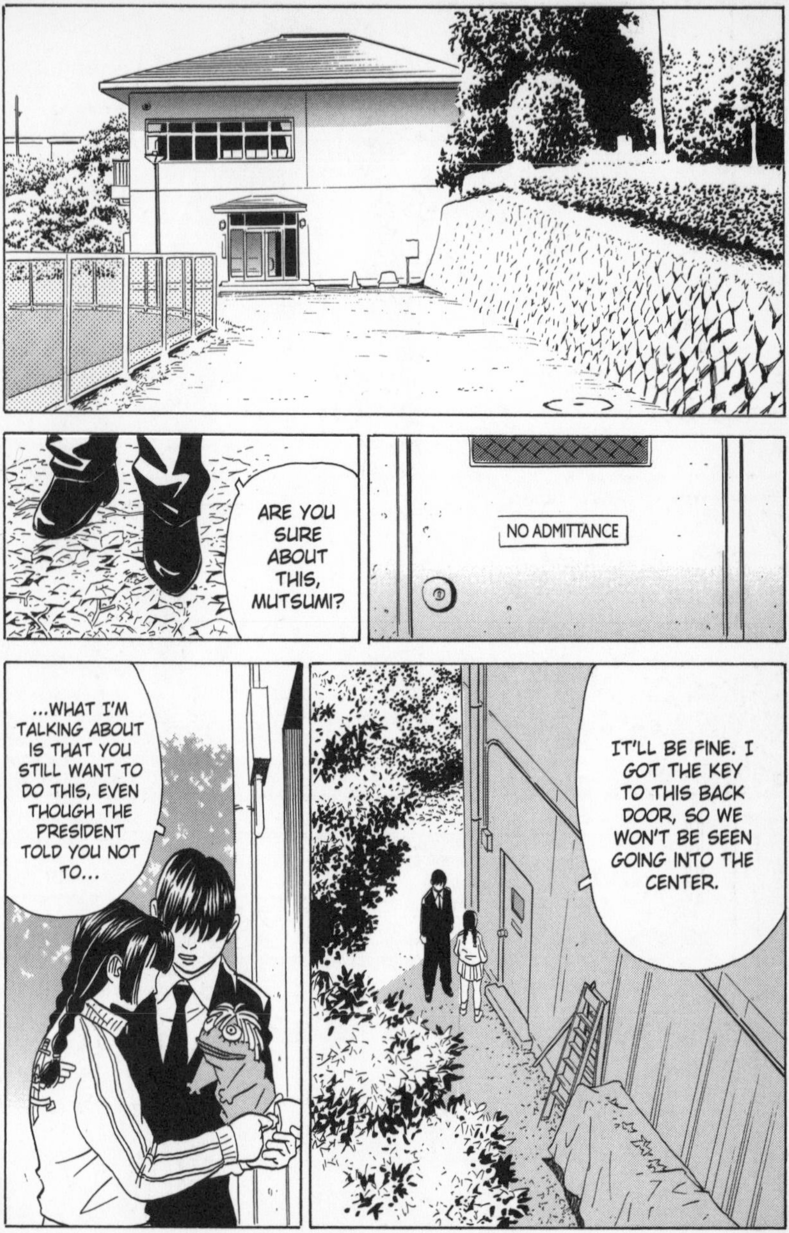
NO ADMITTANCE
ARE YOU SURE ABOUT THIS, MUTSUMI?
IT'LL BE FINE. I GOT THE KEY TO THIS BACK DOOR, SO WE WON'T BE SEEN GOING INTO THE CENTER.
...WHAT I'M TALKING ABOUT IS THAT YOU STILL WANT TO DO THIS, EVEN THOUGH THE PRESIDENT TOLD YOU NOT TO...

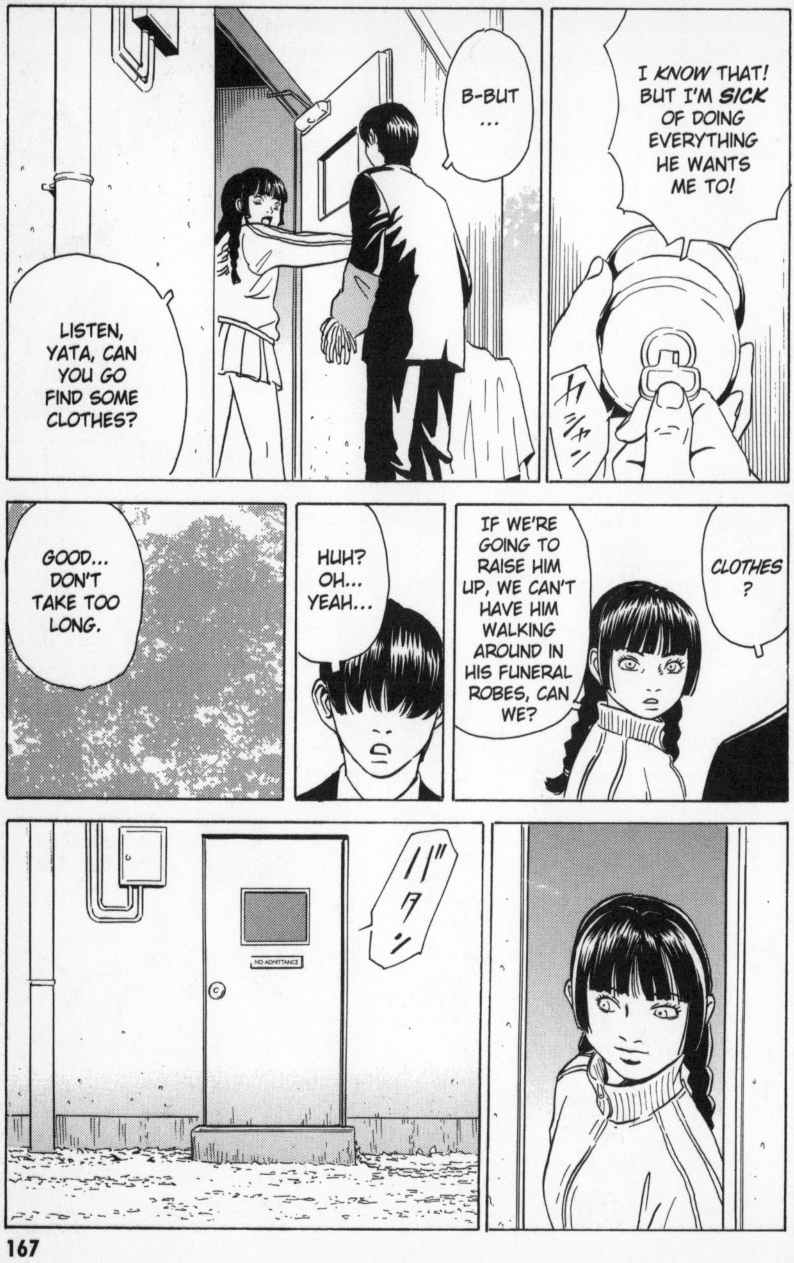
I KNOW THAT! BUT I'M SICK OF DOING EVERYTHING HE WANTS ME TO!
カシャン
B-BUT ...
LISTEN, YATA, CAN YOU GO FIND SOME CLOTHES?
CLOTHES ?
IF WE'RE GOING TO RAISE HIM UP, WE CAN'T HAVE HIM WALKING AROUND IN HIS FUNERAL ROBES, CAN WE?
HUH? OH... YEAH...
GOOD... DON'T TAKE TOO LONG.
バタン
NO ADMITTANCE

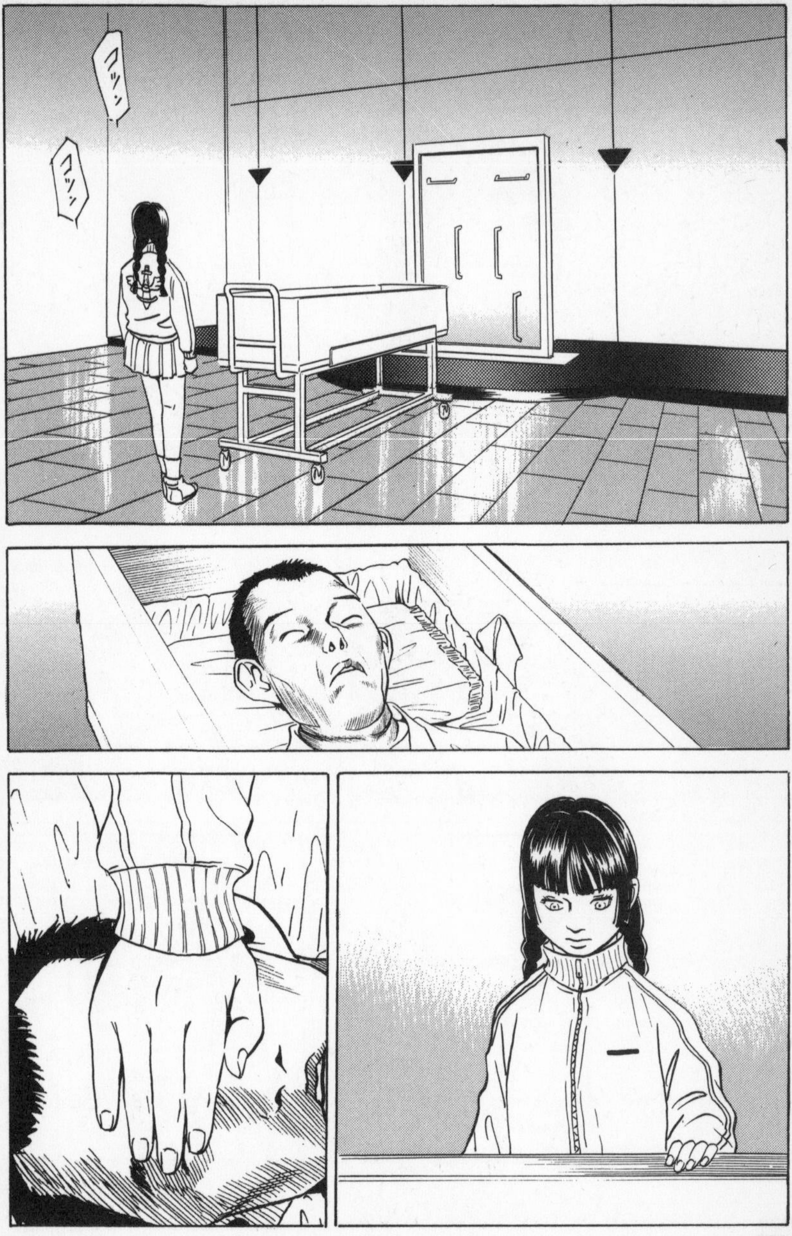
コツン
コツン

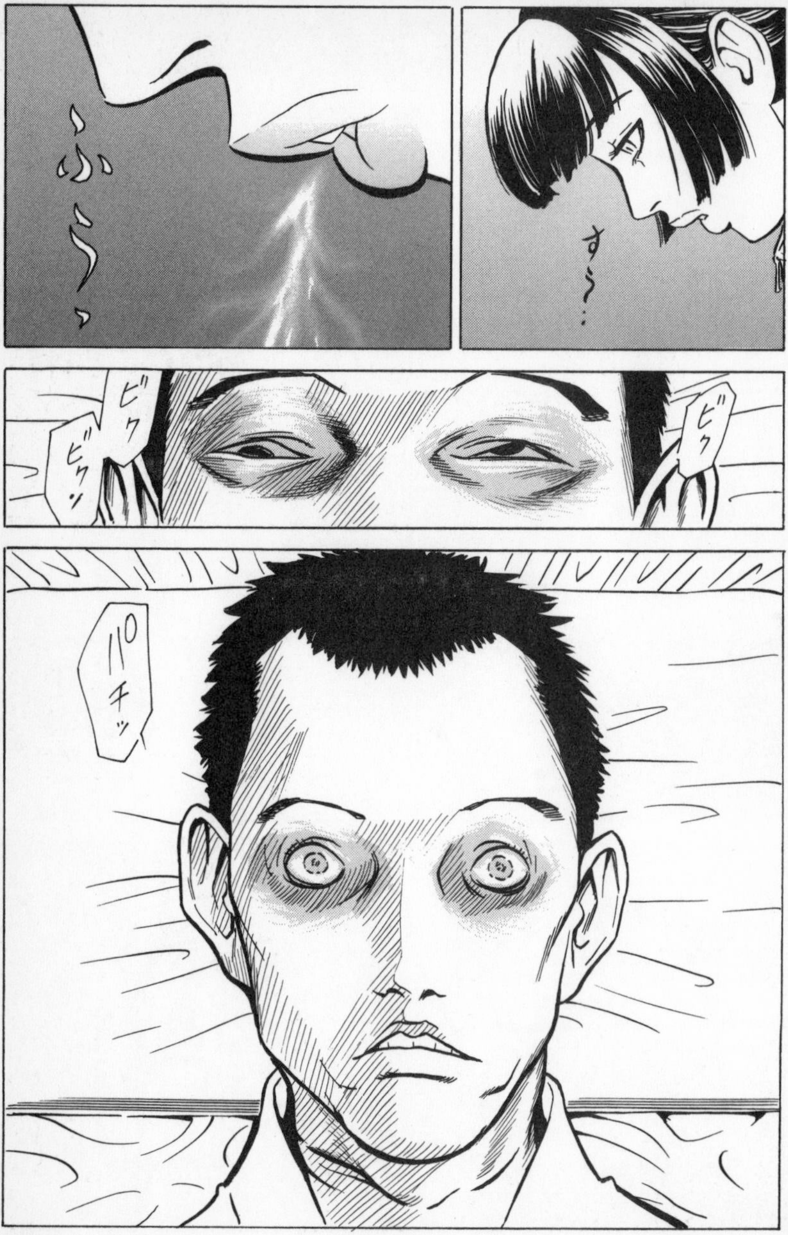
すう～…
ふう～～
ビク
ビク
ビクッ
パチッ

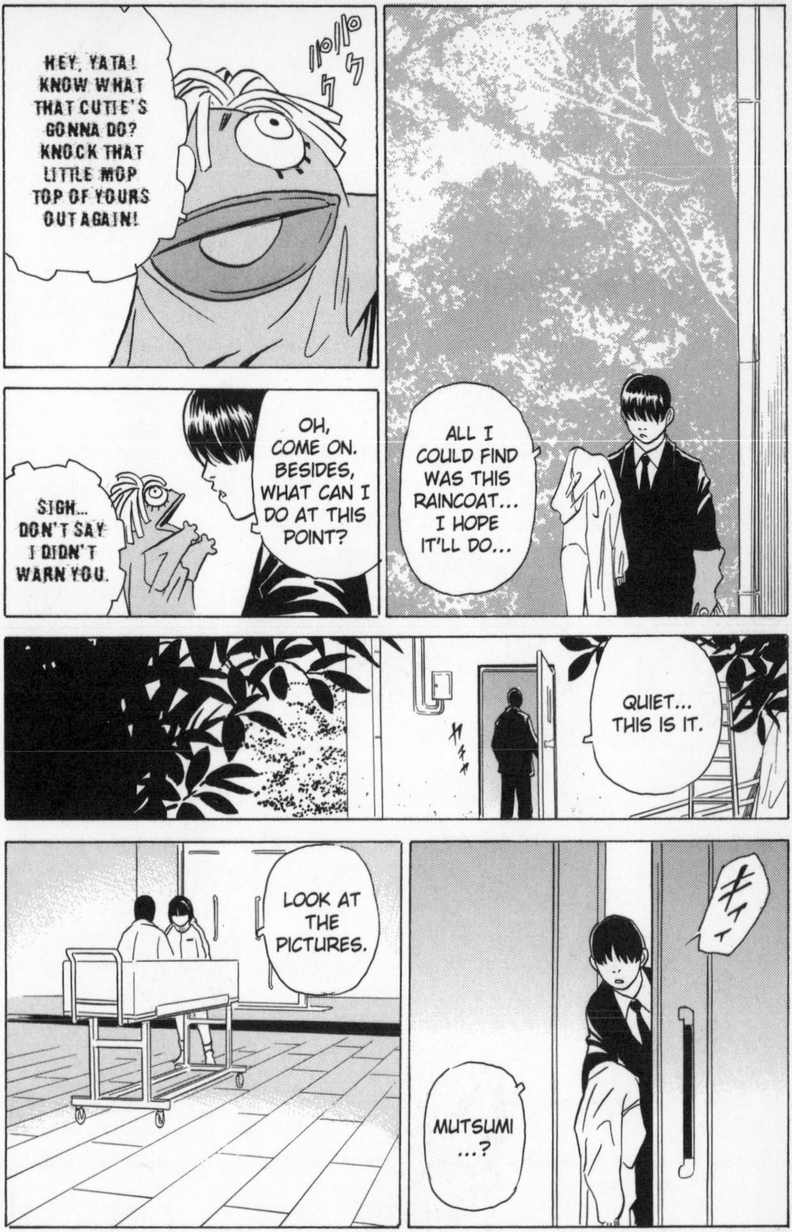
ALL I COULD FIND WAS THIS RAINCOAT... I HOPE IT'LL DO...
パクパク
HEY, YATA! KNOW WHAT THAT CUTIE'S GONNA DO? KNOCK THAT LITTLE MOP TOP OF YOURS OUT AGAIN!
OH, COME ON. BESIDES, WHAT CAN I DO AT THIS POINT?
SIGH... DON'T SAY I DIDN'T WARN YOU.
QUIET... THIS IS IT.
ガチャ
キィ
MUTSUMI ...?
LOOK AT THE PICTURES.

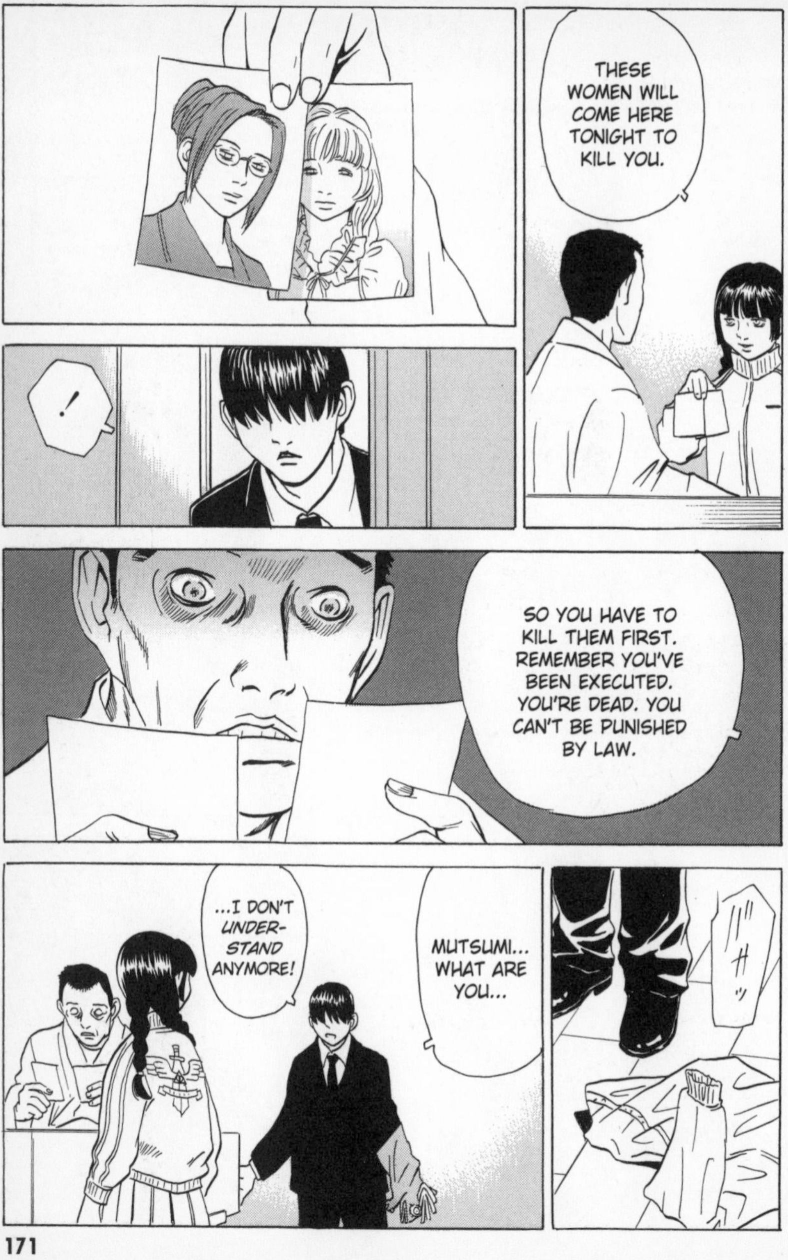
THESE WOMEN WILL COME HERE TONIGHT TO KILL YOU.
!
SO YOU HAVE TO KILL THEM FIRST. REMEMBER YOU'VE BEEN EXECUTED. YOU'RE DEAD. YOU CAN'T BE PUNISHED BY LAW.
バサッ
MUTSUMI... WHAT ARE YOU...
...I DON'T UNDER-STAND ANYMORE!

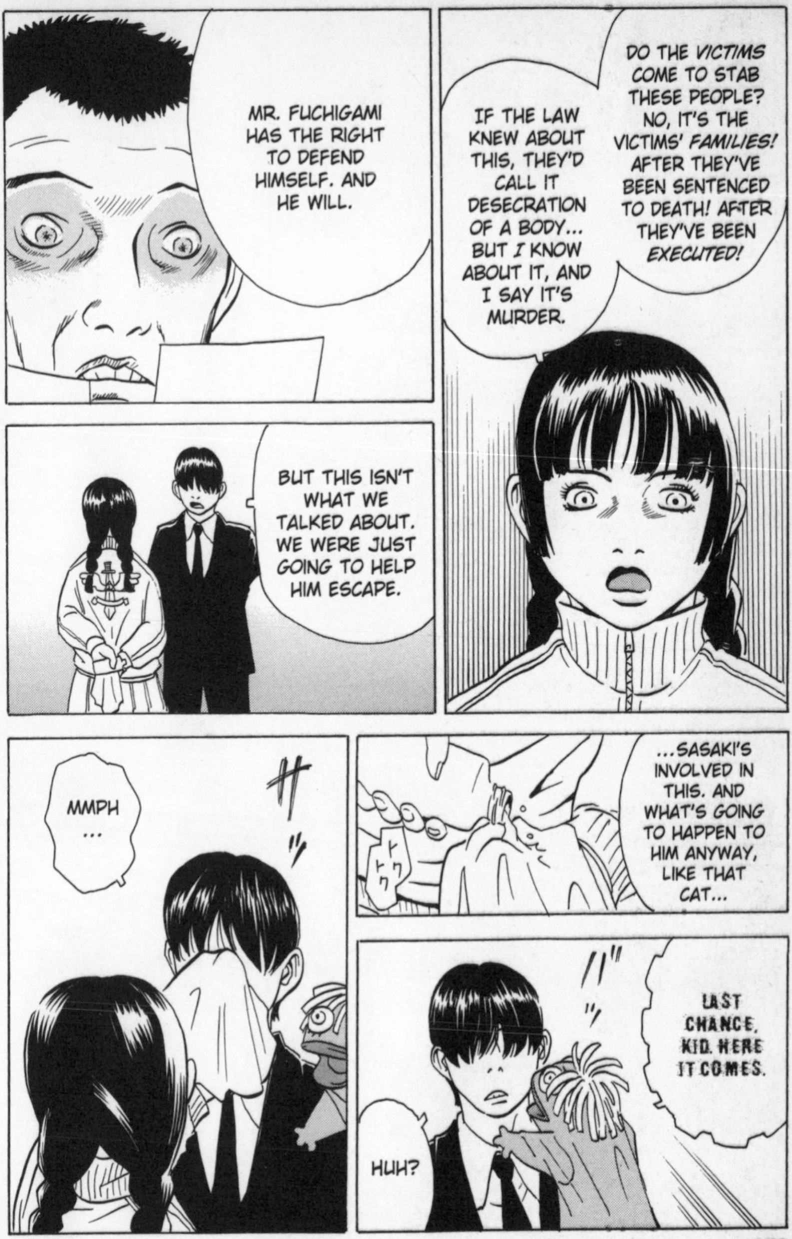
DO THE VICTIMS COME TO STAB THESE PEOPLE? NO, IT'S THE VICTIMS' FAMILIES! AFTER THEY'VE BEEN SENTENCED TO DEATH! AFTER THEY'VE BEEN EXECUTED!
IF THE LAW KNEW ABOUT THIS, THEY'D CALL IT DESECRATION OF A BODY... BUT I KNOW ABOUT IT, AND I SAY IT'S MURDER.
MR. FUCHIGAMI HAS THE RIGHT TO DEFEND HIMSELF. AND HE WILL.
BUT THIS ISN'T WHAT WE TALKED ABOUT. WE WERE JUST GOING TO HELP HIM ESCAPE.
...SASAKI'S INVOLVED IN THIS. AND WHAT'S GOING TO HAPPEN TO HIM ANYWAY, LIKE THAT CAT...
LAST CHANCE, KID. HERE IT COMES.
HUH?
MMPH ...

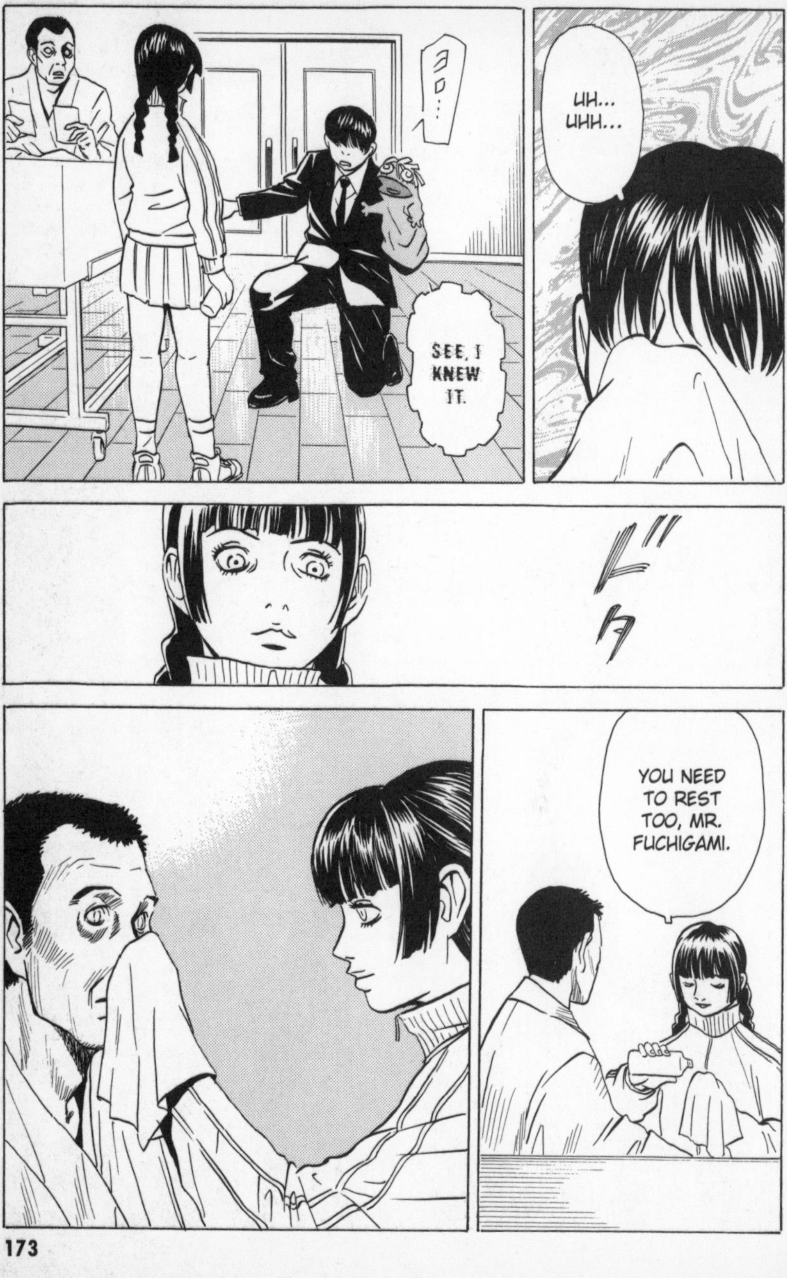
UH...
UHH...
ヨロ...
SEE, I KNEW IT.
ドク
YOU NEED TO REST TOO, MR. FUCHIGAMI.

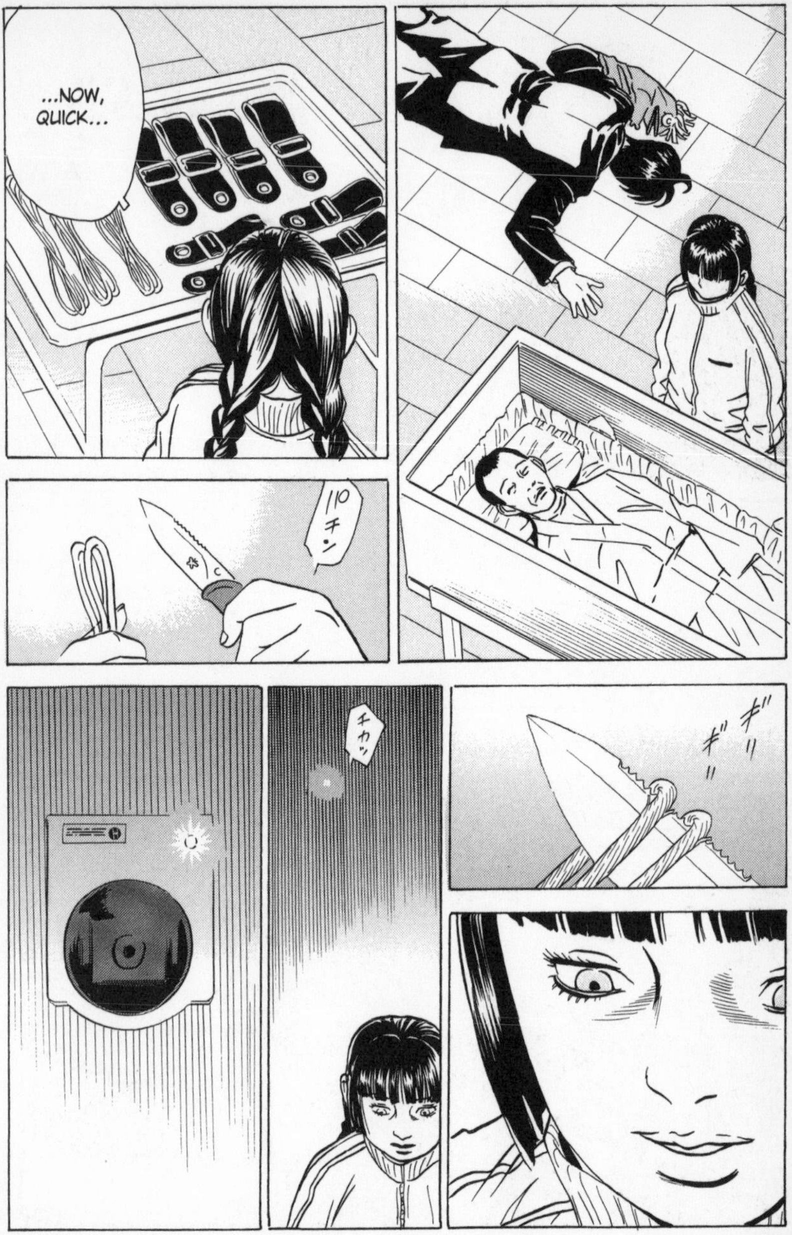

...NOW, QUICK...
パチン
ギリ
ギリ
チカッ

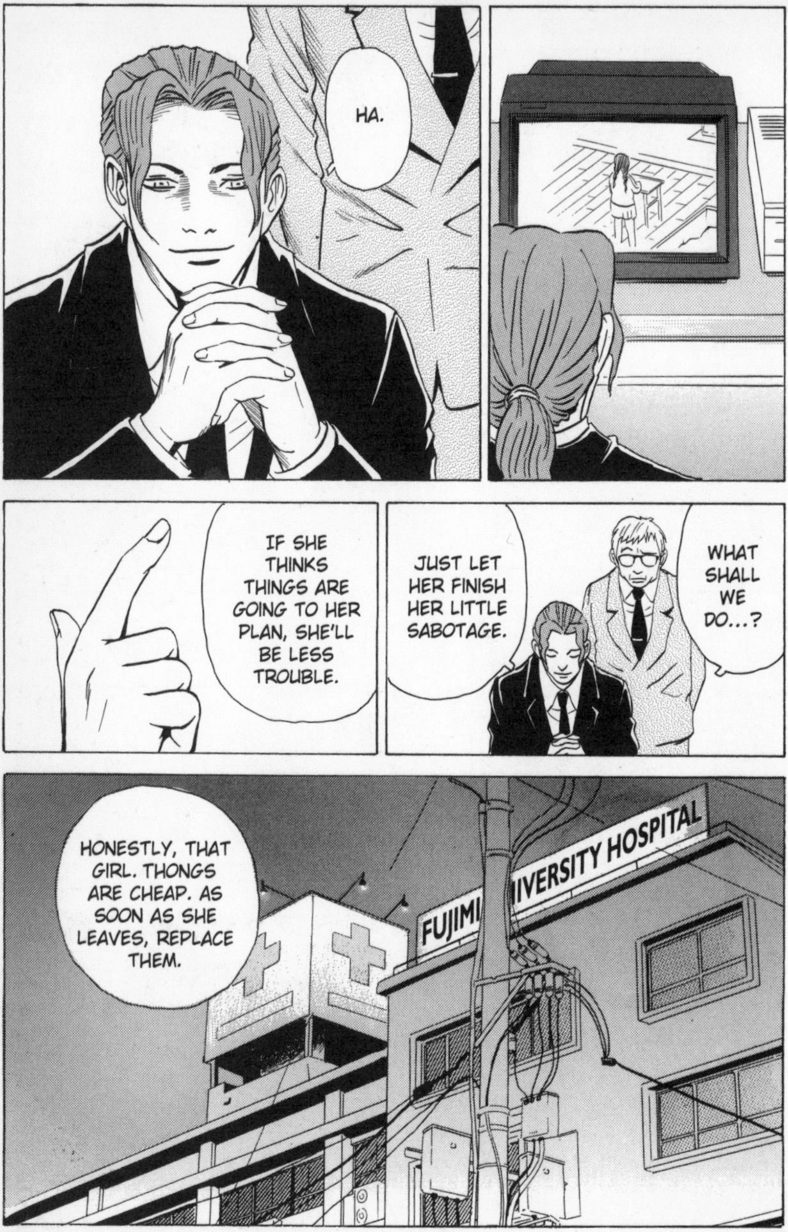
HA.
WHAT SHALL WE DO...?
JUST LET HER FINISH HER LITTLE SABOTAGE.
IF SHE THINKS THINGS ARE GOING TO HER PLAN, SHE'LL BE LESS TROUBLE.
FUJIMI
IVERSITY HOSPITAL
HONESTLY, THAT GIRL. THONGS ARE CHEAP. AS SOON AS SHE LEAVES, REPLACE THEM.

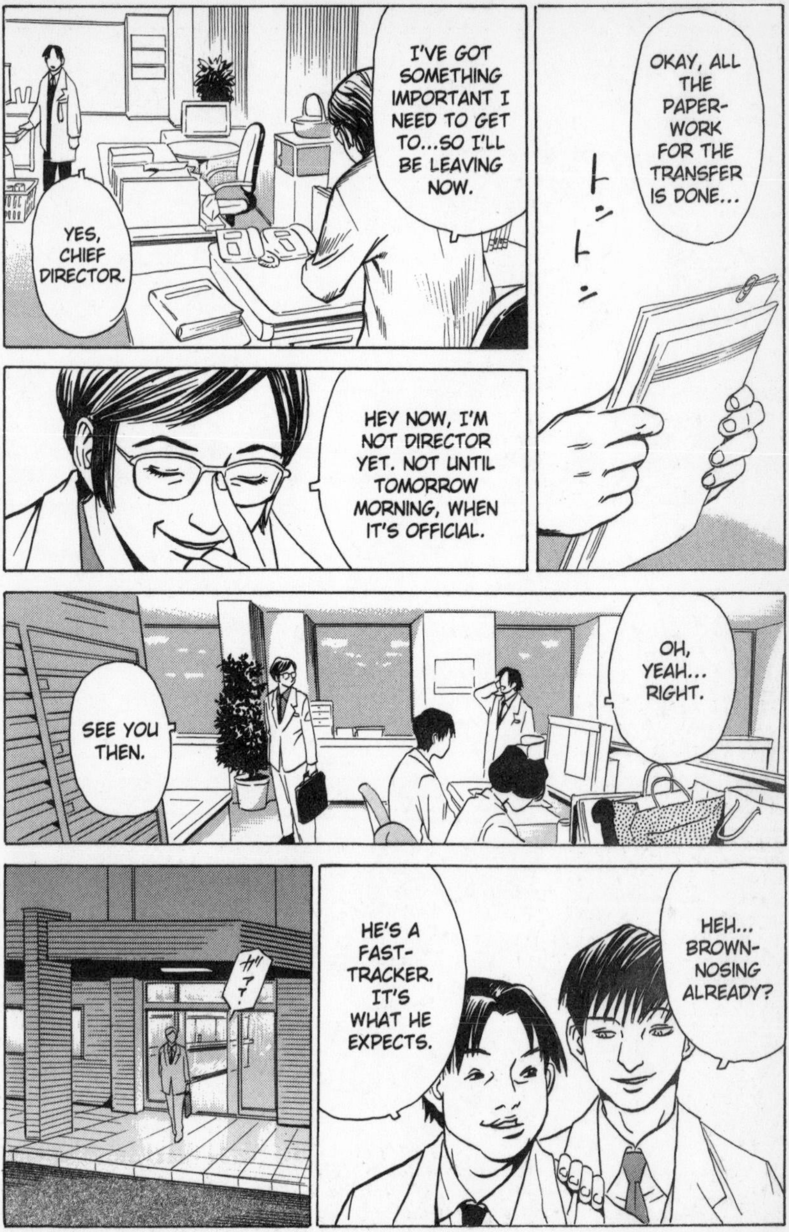
OKAY, ALL THE PAPER-WORK FOR THE TRANSFER IS DONE...
トン トン
I'VE GOT SOMETHING IMPORTANT I NEED TO GET TO...SO I'LL BE LEAVING NOW.
YES, CHIEF DIRECTOR.
HEY NOW, I'M NOT DIRECTOR YET. NOT UNTIL TOMORROW MORNING, WHEN IT'S OFFICIAL.
OH, YEAH... RIGHT.
SEE YOU THEN.
HEH... BROWN-NOSING ALREADY?
HE'S A FAST-TRACKER. IT'S WHAT HE EXPECTS.

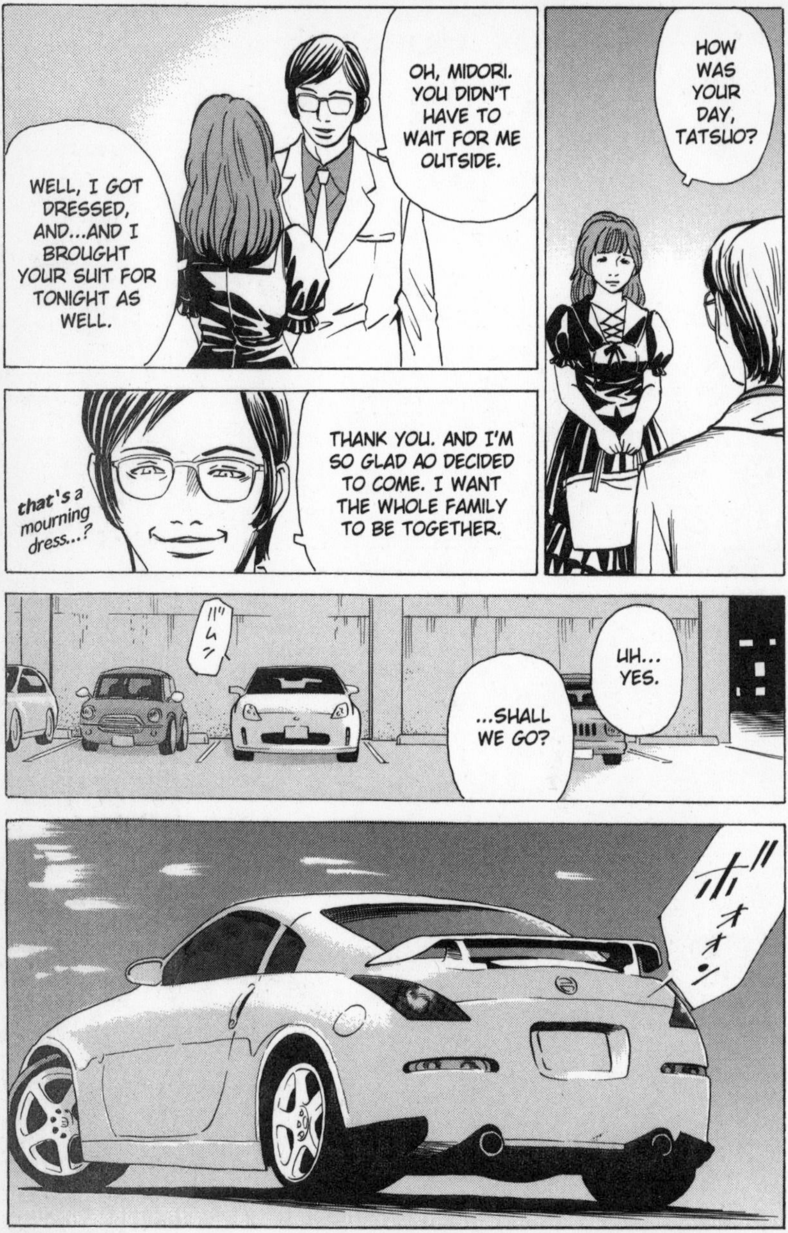
HOW WAS YOUR DAY, TATSUO?
OH, MIDORI. YOU DIDN'T HAVE TO WAIT FOR ME OUTSIDE.
WELL, I GOT DRESSED, AND...AND I BROUGHT YOUR SUIT FOR TONIGHT AS WELL.
THANK YOU. AND I'M SO GLAD AO DECIDED TO COME. I WANT THE WHOLE FAMILY TO BE TOGETHER.
that's a mourning dress...?
バムッ
UH... YES.
...SHALL WE GO?
ボオオン

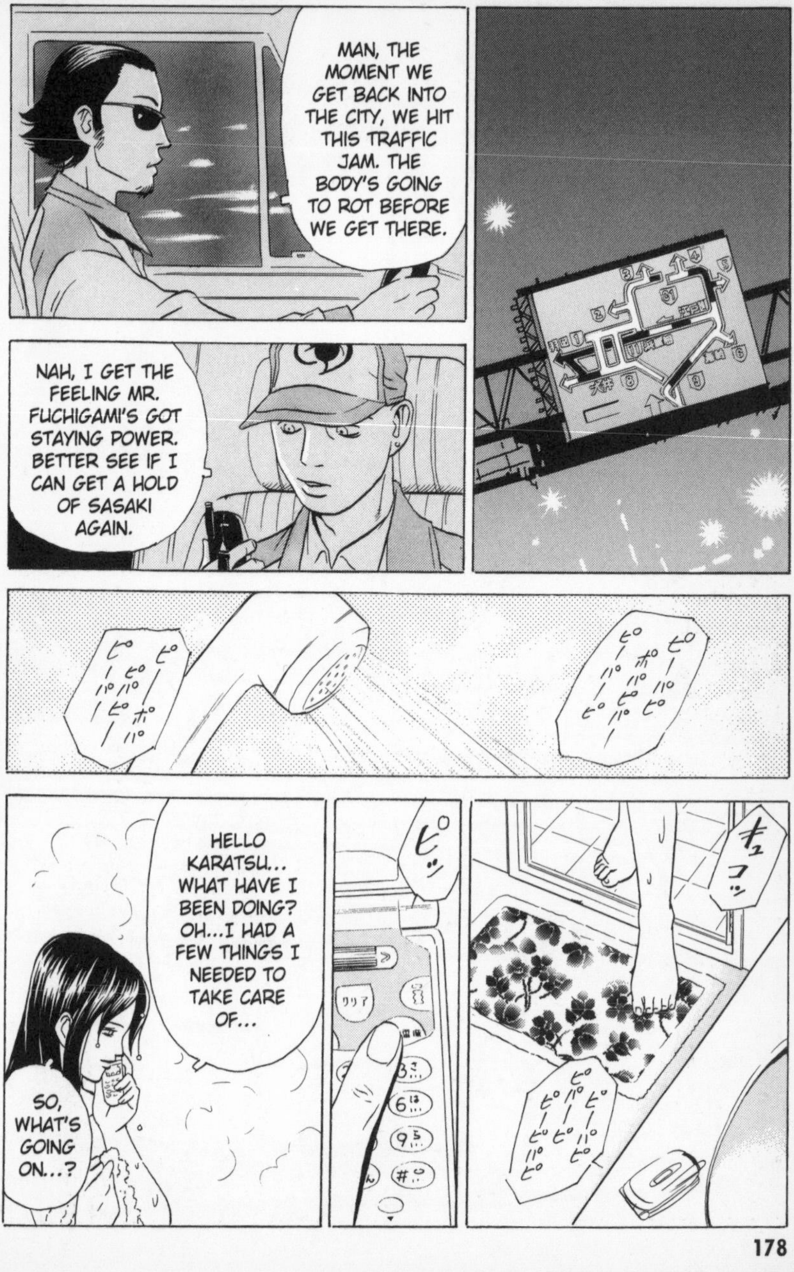
MAN, THE MOMENT WE GET BACK INTO THE CITY, WE HIT THIS TRAFFIC JAM. THE BODY'S GOING TO ROT BEFORE WE GET THERE.
NAH, I GET THE FEELING MR. FUCHIGAMI'S GOT STAYING POWER. BETTER SEE IF I CAN GET A HOLD OF SASAKI AGAIN.
キュコッ
ピッ
HELLO KARATSU... WHAT HAVE I BEEN DOING? OH...I HAD A FEW THINGS I NEEDED TO TAKE CARE OF...
SO, WHAT'S GOING ON...?

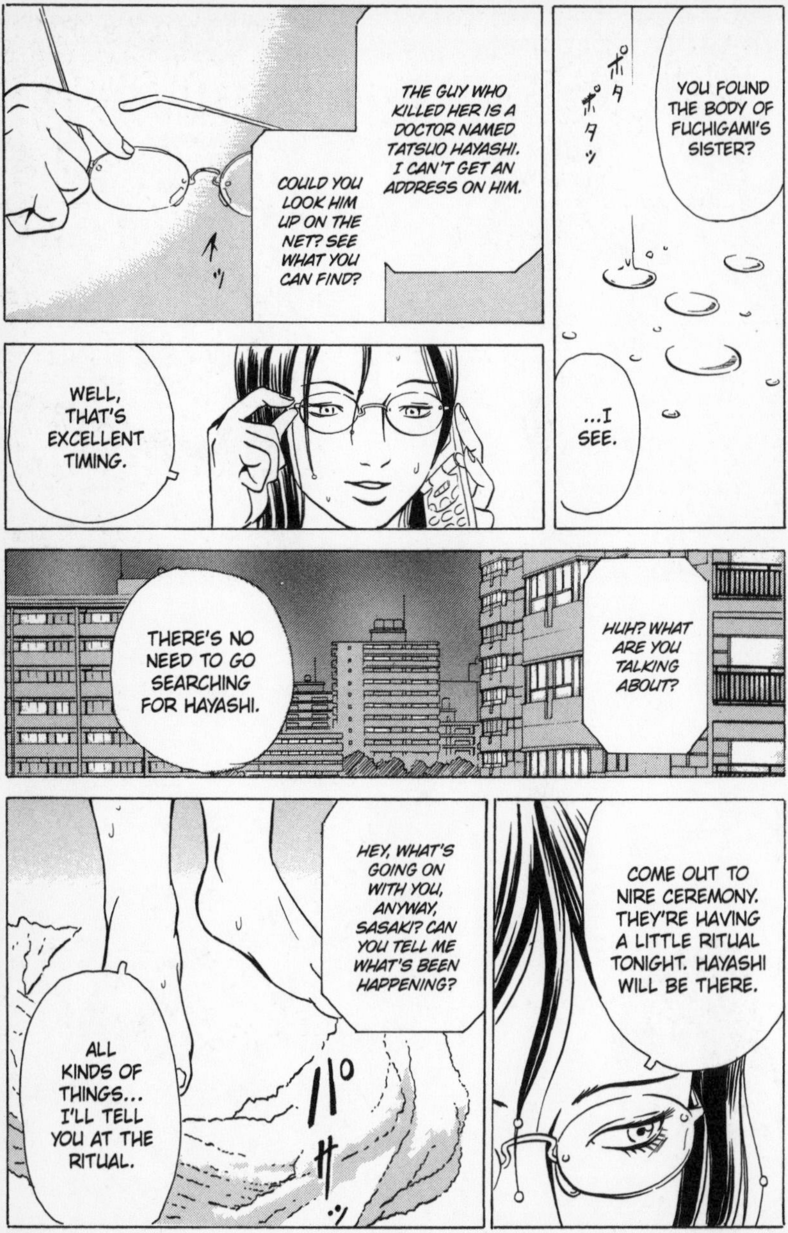
YOU FOUND THE BODY OF FUCHIGAMI'S SISTER?
ポタ
ポタッ
...I SEE.
THE GUY WHO KILLED HER IS A DOCTOR NAMED TATSUO HAYASHI. I CAN'T GET AN ADDRESS ON HIM.
COULD YOU LOOK HIM UP ON THE NET? SEE WHAT YOU CAN FIND?
WELL, THAT'S EXCELLENT TIMING.
HUH? WHAT ARE YOU TALKING ABOUT?
THERE'S NO NEED TO GO SEARCHING FOR HAYASHI.
COME OUT TO NIRE CEREMONY. THEY'RE HAVING A LITTLE RITUAL TONIGHT. HAYASHI WILL BE THERE.
HEY, WHAT'S GOING ON WITH YOU, ANYWAY, SASAKI? CAN YOU TELL ME WHAT'S BEEN HAPPENING?
ALL KINDS OF THINGS... I'LL TELL YOU AT THE RITUAL.

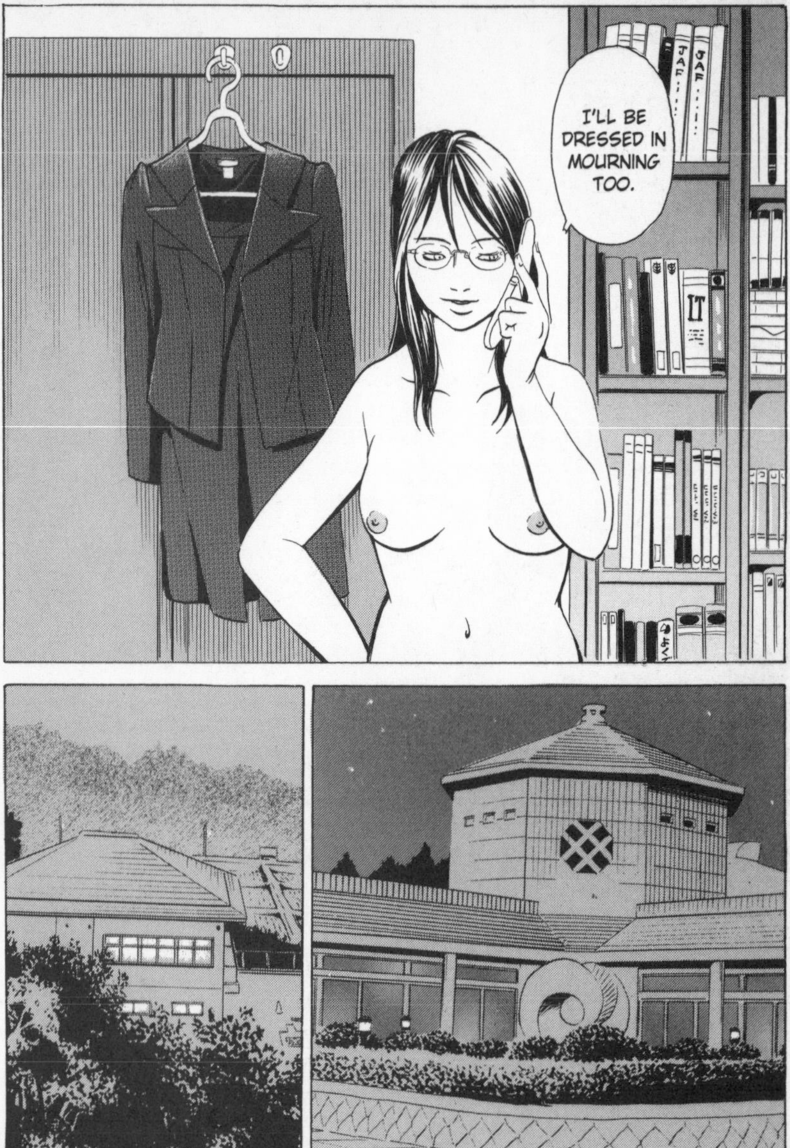
I'LL BE DRESSED IN MOURNING TOO.

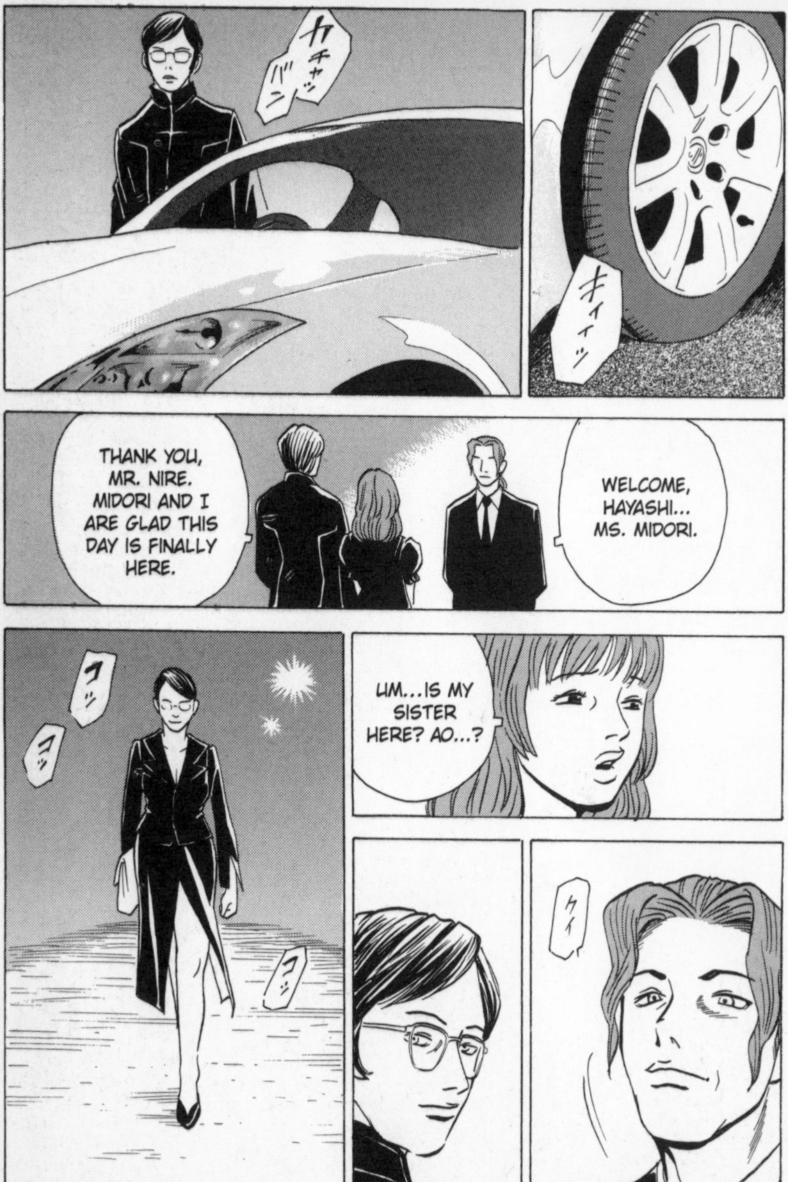
ギイイッ
カチャッ
バン
WELCOME, HAYASHI... MS. MIDORI.
THANK YOU, MR. NIRE. MIDORI AND I ARE GLAD THIS DAY IS FINALLY HERE.
UM...IS MY SISTER HERE? AO...?
クイ
コツ
コツ
コツ

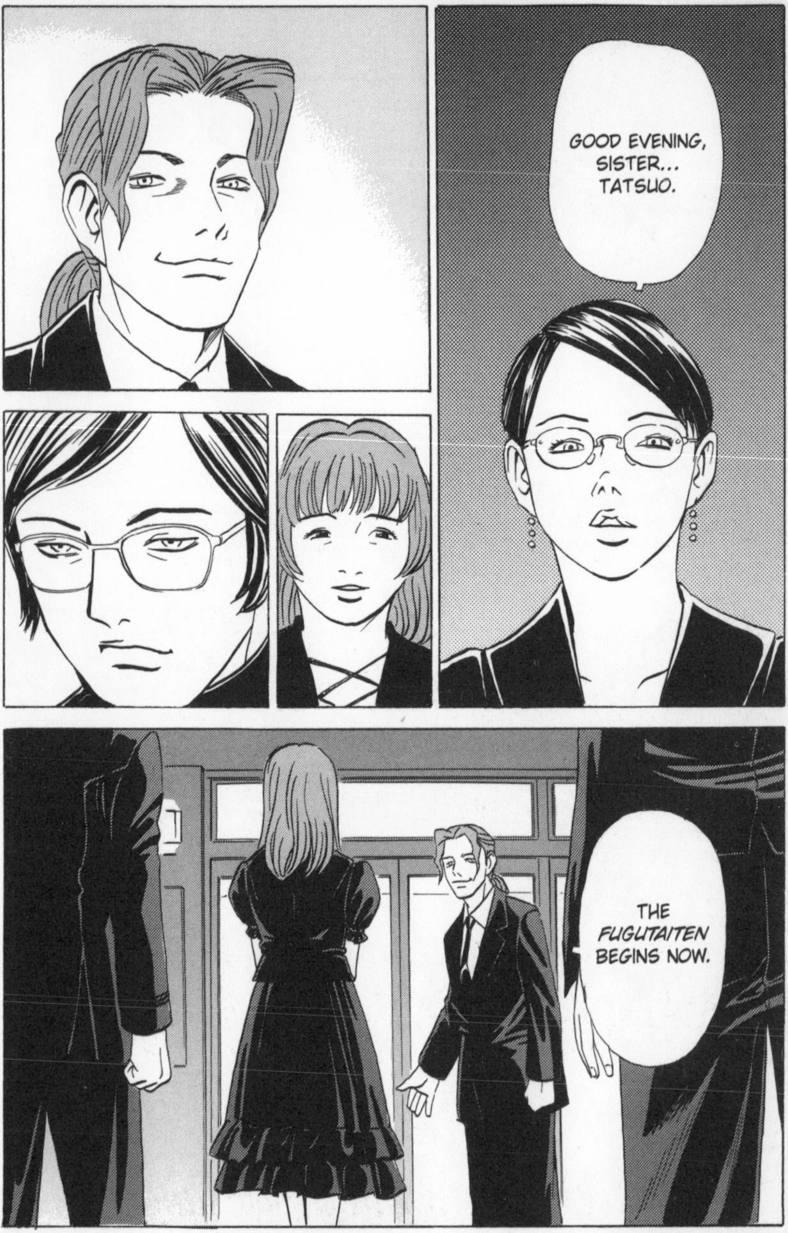
GOOD EVENING, SISTER... TATSUO.
THE *FUGUTAITEN* BEGINS NOW.

6th delivery: do what you want—the end

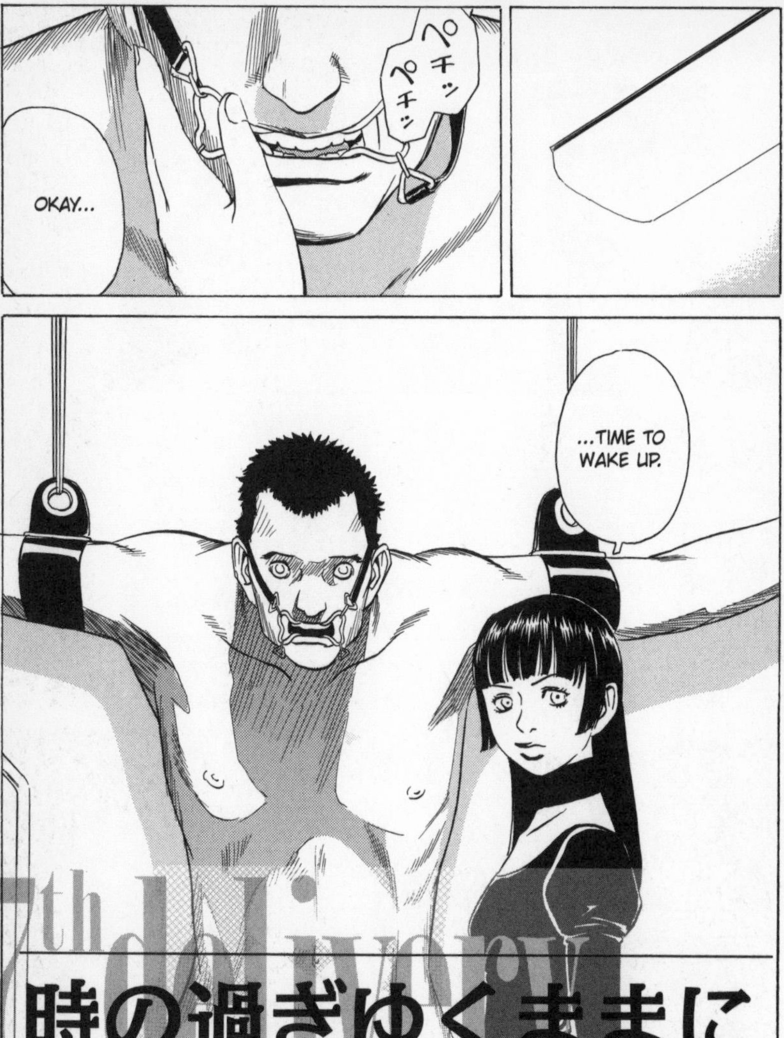
ペチッ ペチッ
OKAY...
...TIME TO WAKE UP.
7th delivery
時の過ぎゆくままに
as time goes by

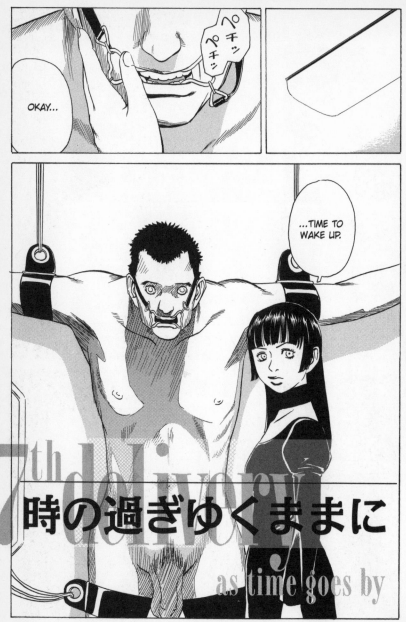

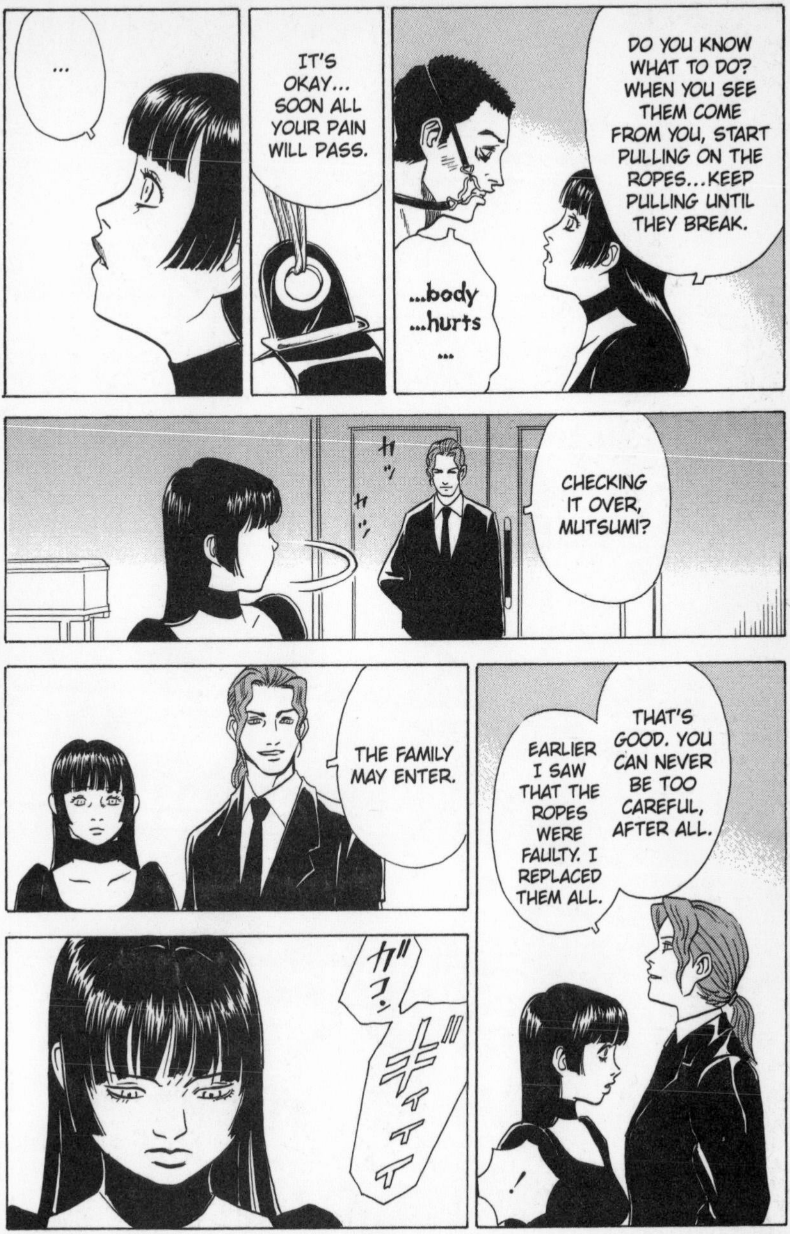

DO YOU KNOW WHAT TO DO? WHEN YOU SEE THEM COME FROM YOU, START PULLING ON THE ROPES...KEEP PULLING UNTIL THEY BREAK.
...body ...hurts ...
IT'S OKAY... SOON ALL YOUR PAIN WILL PASS.
...
CHECKING IT OVER, MUTSUMI?
カッ
カッ
THAT'S GOOD. YOU CAN NEVER BE TOO CAREFUL, AFTER ALL.
EARLIER I SAW THAT THE ROPES WERE FAULTY. I REPLACED THEM ALL.
!
THE FAMILY MAY ENTER.
ガコン
ギィィイ

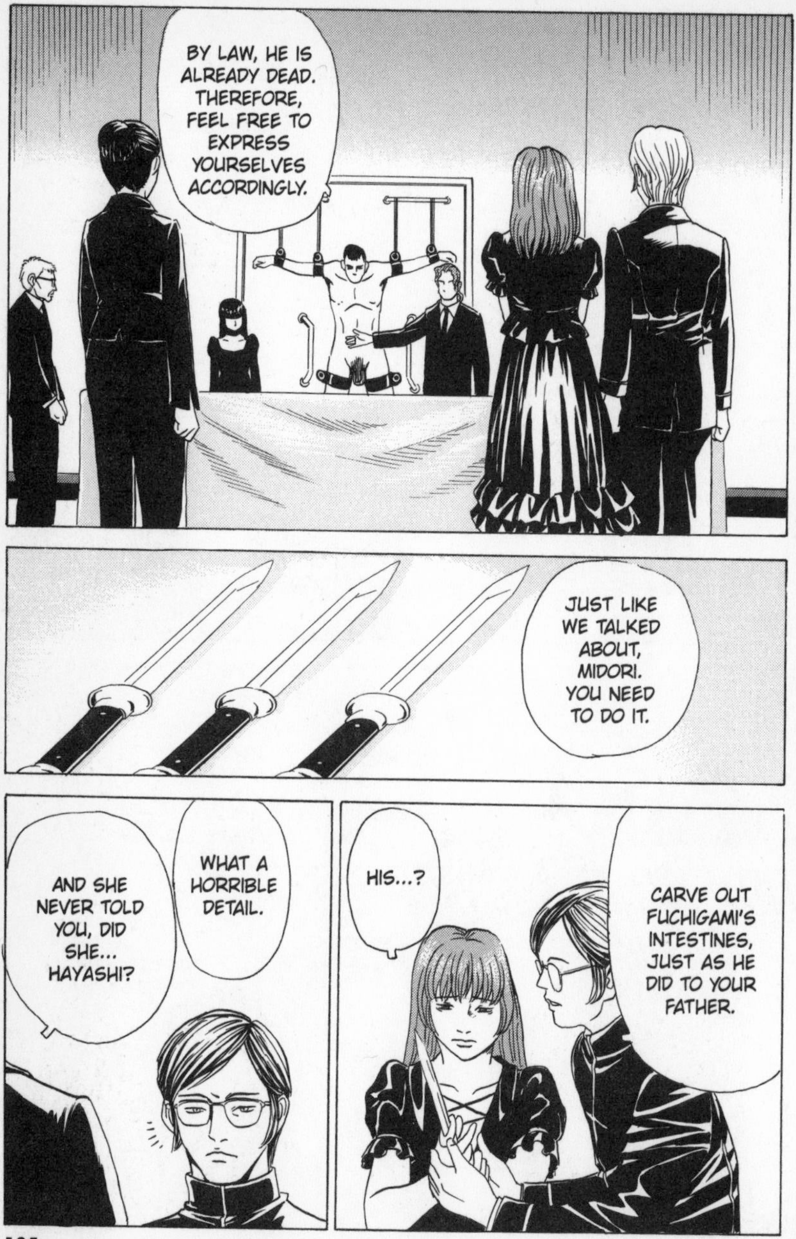
BY LAW, HE IS ALREADY DEAD. THEREFORE, FEEL FREE TO EXPRESS YOURSELVES ACCORDINGLY.
JUST LIKE WE TALKED ABOUT, MIDORI. YOU NEED TO DO IT.
CARVE OUT FUCHIGAMI'S INTESTINES, JUST AS HE DID TO YOUR FATHER.
HIS...?
WHAT A HORRIBLE DETAIL.
AND SHE NEVER TOLD YOU, DID SHE... HAYASHI?

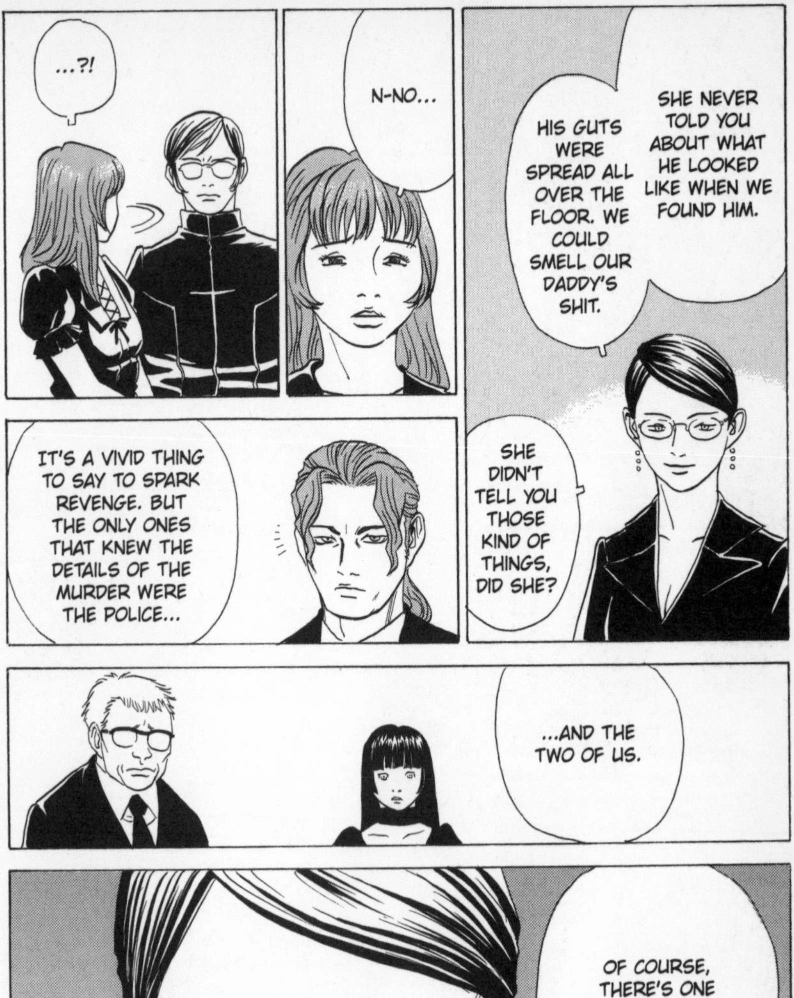
SHE NEVER TOLD YOU ABOUT WHAT HE LOOKED LIKE WHEN WE FOUND HIM.
HIS GUTS WERE SPREAD ALL OVER THE FLOOR. WE COULD SMELL OUR DADDY'S SHIT.
SHE DIDN'T TELL YOU THOSE KIND OF THINGS, DID SHE?
N-NO...
...?!
IT'S A VIVID THING TO SAY TO SPARK REVENGE. BUT THE ONLY ONES THAT KNEW THE DETAILS OF THE MURDER WERE THE POLICE...
...AND THE TWO OF US.
OF COURSE, THERE'S ONE OTHER WAY A MAN WOULD KNOW.
IF THEY TOO HAD BEEN THERE THAT DAY.

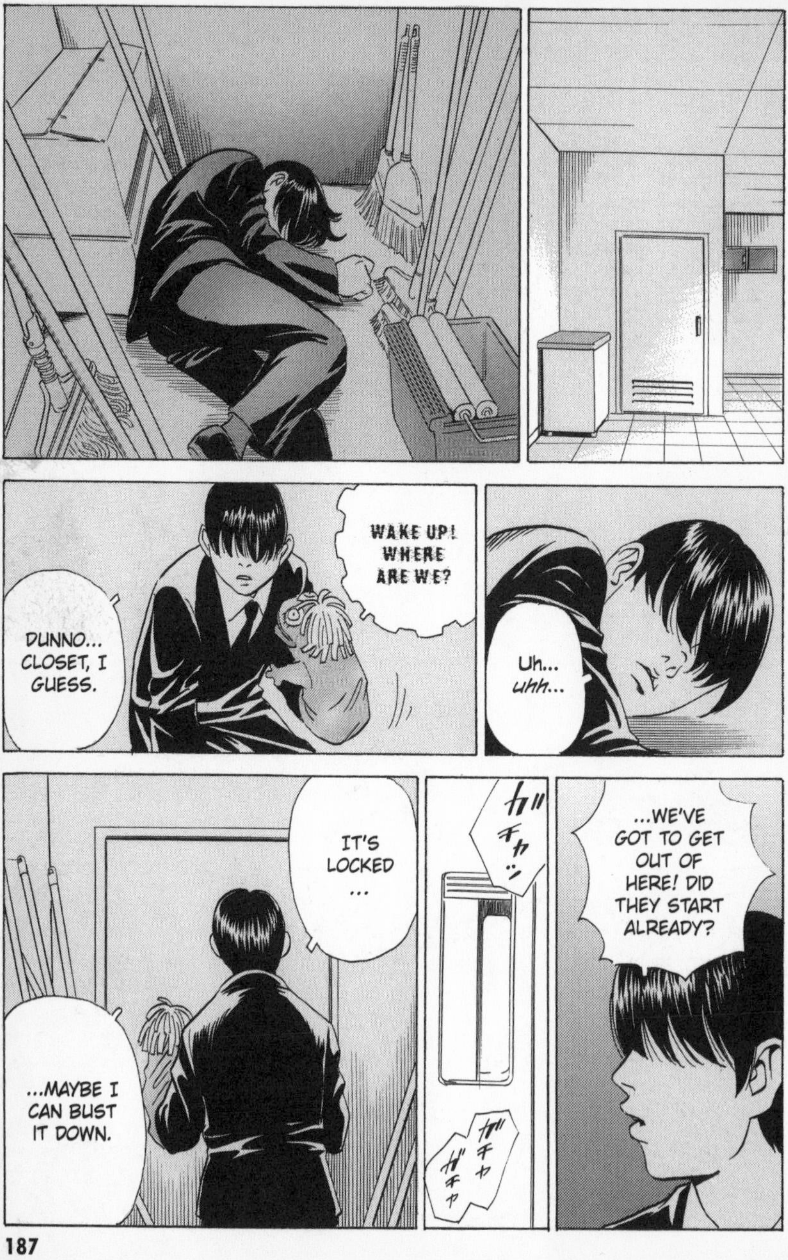
Uh... uhh...
WAKE UP! WHERE ARE WE?
DUNNO... CLOSET, I GUESS.
...WE'VE GOT TO GET OUT OF HERE! DID THEY START ALREADY?
ガチャッ
ガチャ ガチャ
IT'S LOCKED ...
...MAYBE I CAN BUST IT DOWN.

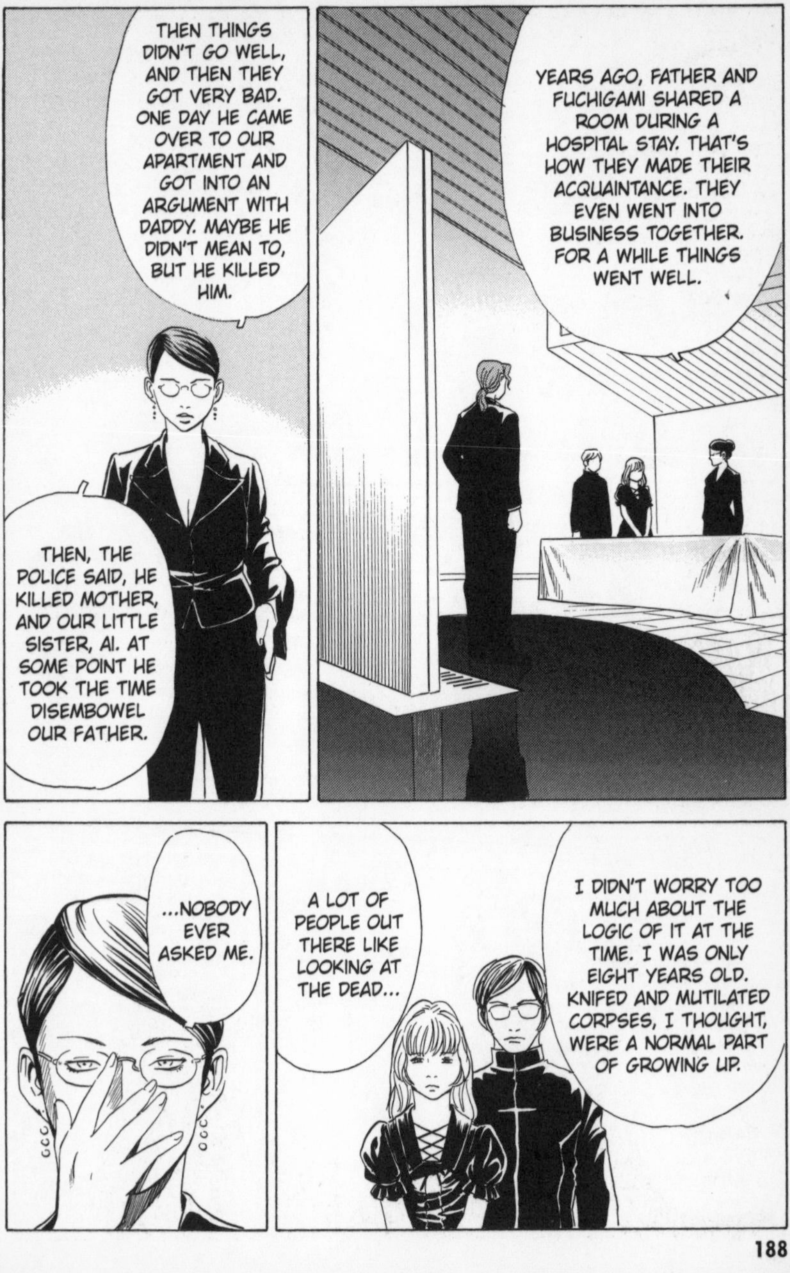
YEARS AGO, FATHER AND FUCHIGAMI SHARED A ROOM DURING A HOSPITAL STAY. THAT'S HOW THEY MADE THEIR ACQUAINTANCE. THEY EVEN WENT INTO BUSINESS TOGETHER. FOR A WHILE THINGS WENT WELL.
THEN THINGS DIDN'T GO WELL, AND THEN THEY GOT VERY BAD. ONE DAY HE CAME OVER TO OUR APARTMENT AND GOT INTO AN ARGUMENT WITH DADDY. MAYBE HE DIDN'T MEAN TO, BUT HE KILLED HIM.
THEN, THE POLICE SAID, HE KILLED MOTHER, AND OUR LITTLE SISTER, AI. AT SOME POINT HE TOOK THE TIME DISEMBOWEL OUR FATHER.
I DIDN'T WORRY TOO MUCH ABOUT THE LOGIC OF IT AT THE TIME. I WAS ONLY EIGHT YEARS OLD. KNIFED AND MUTILATED CORPSES, I THOUGHT, WERE A NORMAL PART OF GROWING UP.
A LOT OF PEOPLE OUT THERE LIKE LOOKING AT THE DEAD...
...NOBODY EVER ASKED ME.

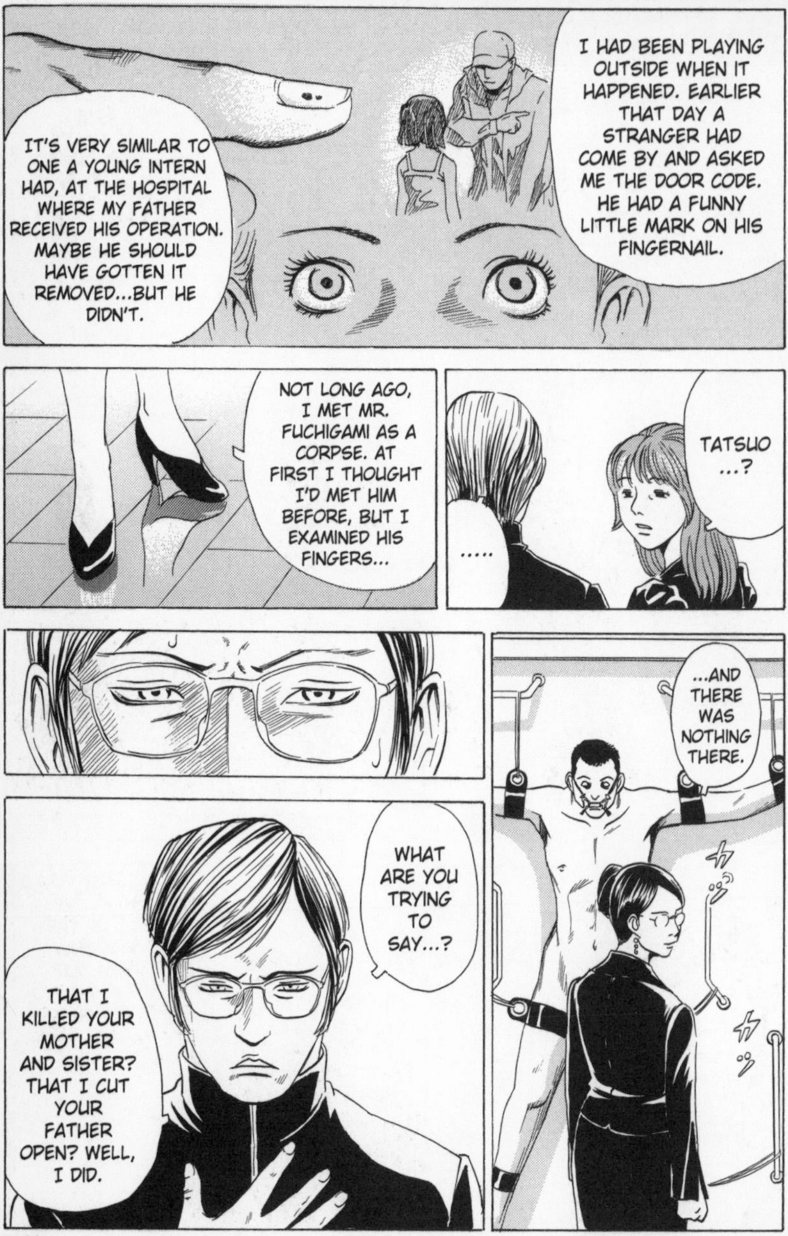
I HAD BEEN PLAYING OUTSIDE WHEN IT HAPPENED. EARLIER THAT DAY A STRANGER HAD COME BY AND ASKED ME THE DOOR CODE. HE HAD A FUNNY LITTLE MARK ON HIS FINGERNAIL.
IT'S VERY SIMILAR TO ONE A YOUNG INTERN HAD, AT THE HOSPITAL WHERE MY FATHER RECEIVED HIS OPERATION. MAYBE HE SHOULD HAVE GOTTEN IT REMOVED...BUT HE DIDN'T.
TATSUO ...?
.....
NOT LONG AGO, I MET MR. FUCHIGAMI AS A CORPSE. AT FIRST I THOUGHT I'D MET HIM BEFORE, BUT I EXAMINED HIS FINGERS...
...AND THERE WAS NOTHING THERE.
WHAT ARE YOU TRYING TO SAY...?
THAT I KILLED YOUR MOTHER AND SISTER? THAT I CUT YOUR FATHER OPEN? WELL, I DID.

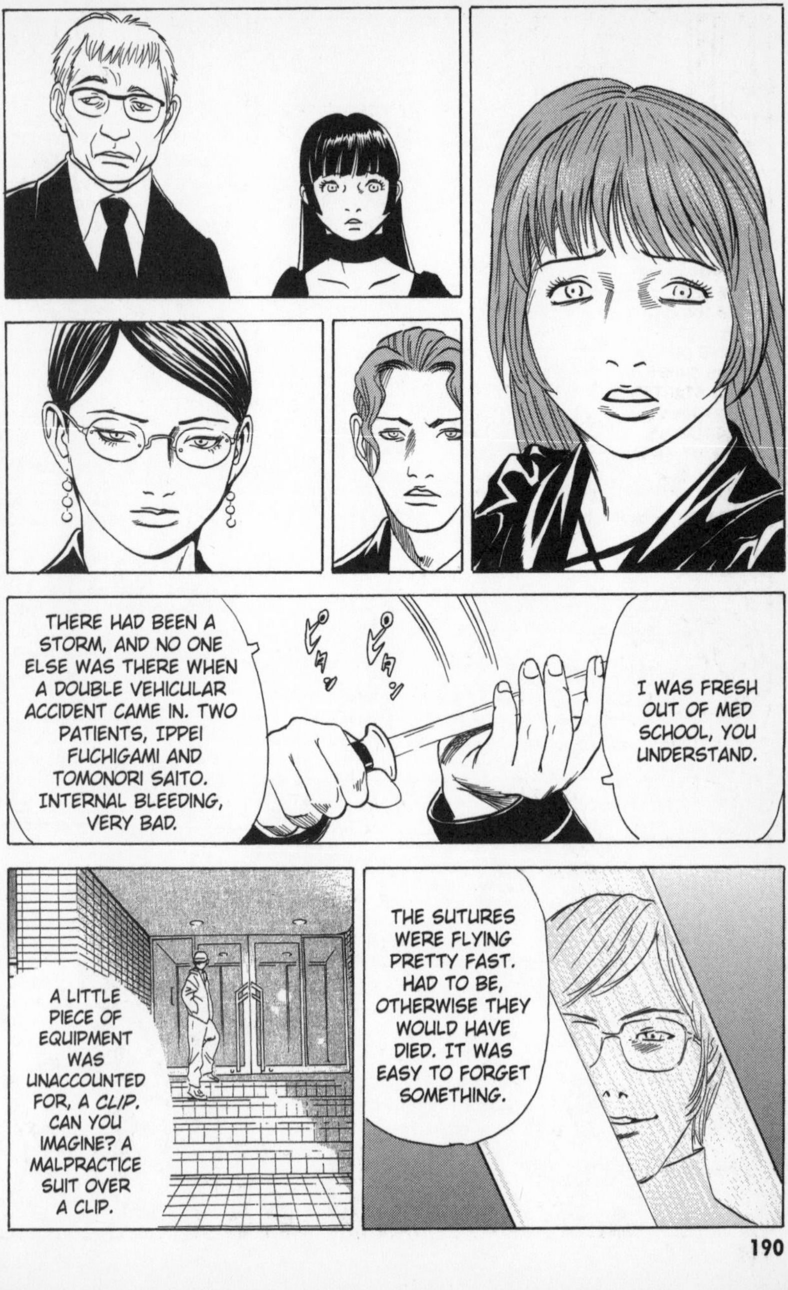
I WAS FRESH OUT OF MED SCHOOL, YOU UNDERSTAND.
THERE HAD BEEN A STORM, AND NO ONE ELSE WAS THERE WHEN A DOUBLE VEHICULAR ACCIDENT CAME IN. TWO PATIENTS, IPPEI FUCHIGAMI AND TOMONORI SAITO. INTERNAL BLEEDING, VERY BAD.
THE SUTURES WERE FLYING PRETTY FAST. HAD TO BE, OTHERWISE THEY WOULD HAVE DIED. IT WAS EASY TO FORGET SOMETHING.
A LITTLE PIECE OF EQUIPMENT WAS UNACCOUNTED FOR, A *CLIP*. CAN YOU IMAGINE? A MALPRACTICE SUIT OVER A CLIP.

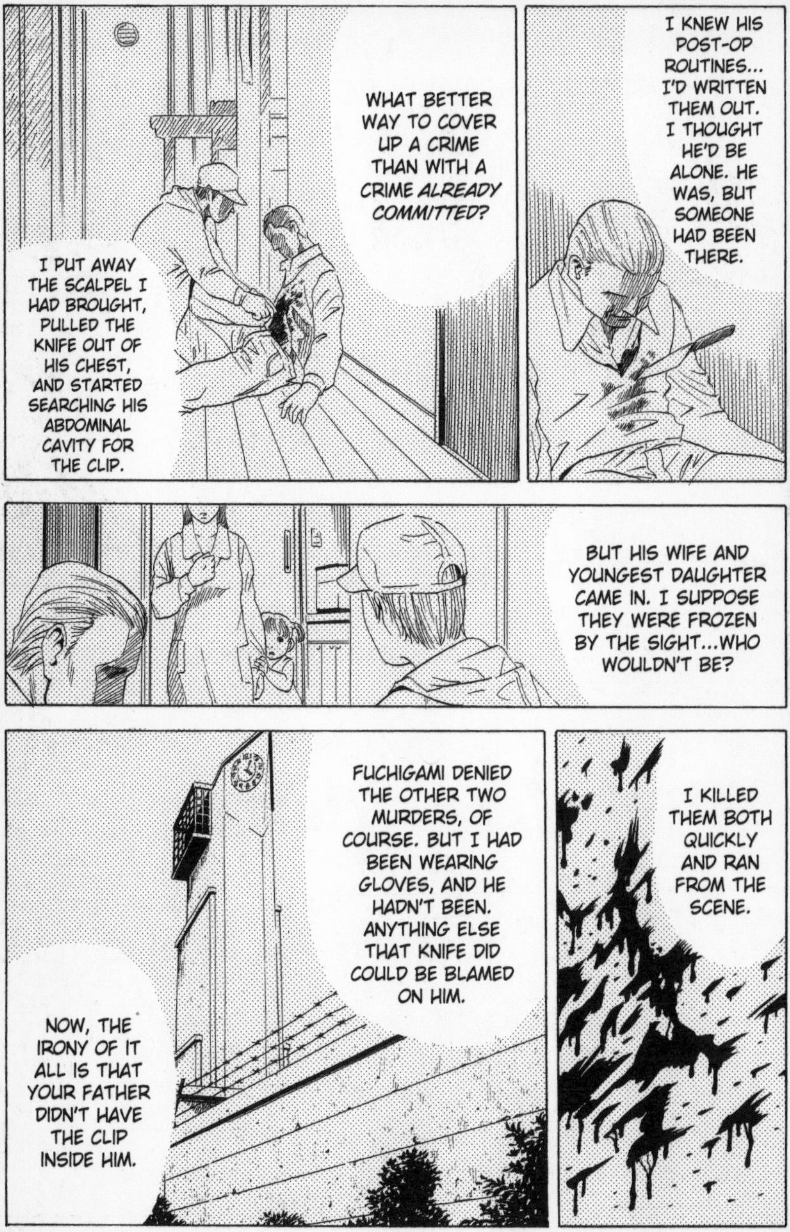
I KNEW HIS POST-OP ROUTINES... I'D WRITTEN THEM OUT. I THOUGHT HE'D BE ALONE. HE WAS, BUT SOMEONE HAD BEEN THERE.
WHAT BETTER WAY TO COVER UP A CRIME THAN WITH A CRIME *ALREADY COMMITTED*?
I PUT AWAY THE SCALPEL I HAD BROUGHT, PULLED THE KNIFE OUT OF HIS CHEST, AND STARTED SEARCHING HIS ABDOMINAL CAVITY FOR THE CLIP.
BUT HIS WIFE AND YOUNGEST DAUGHTER CAME IN. I SUPPOSE THEY WERE FROZEN BY THE SIGHT...WHO WOULDN'T BE?
I KILLED THEM BOTH QUICKLY AND RAN FROM THE SCENE.
FUCHIGAMI DENIED THE OTHER TWO MURDERS, OF COURSE. BUT I HAD BEEN WEARING GLOVES, AND HE HADN'T BEEN. ANYTHING ELSE THAT KNIFE DID COULD BE BLAMED ON HIM.
NOW, THE IRONY OF IT ALL IS THAT YOUR FATHER DIDN'T HAVE THE CLIP INSIDE HIM.

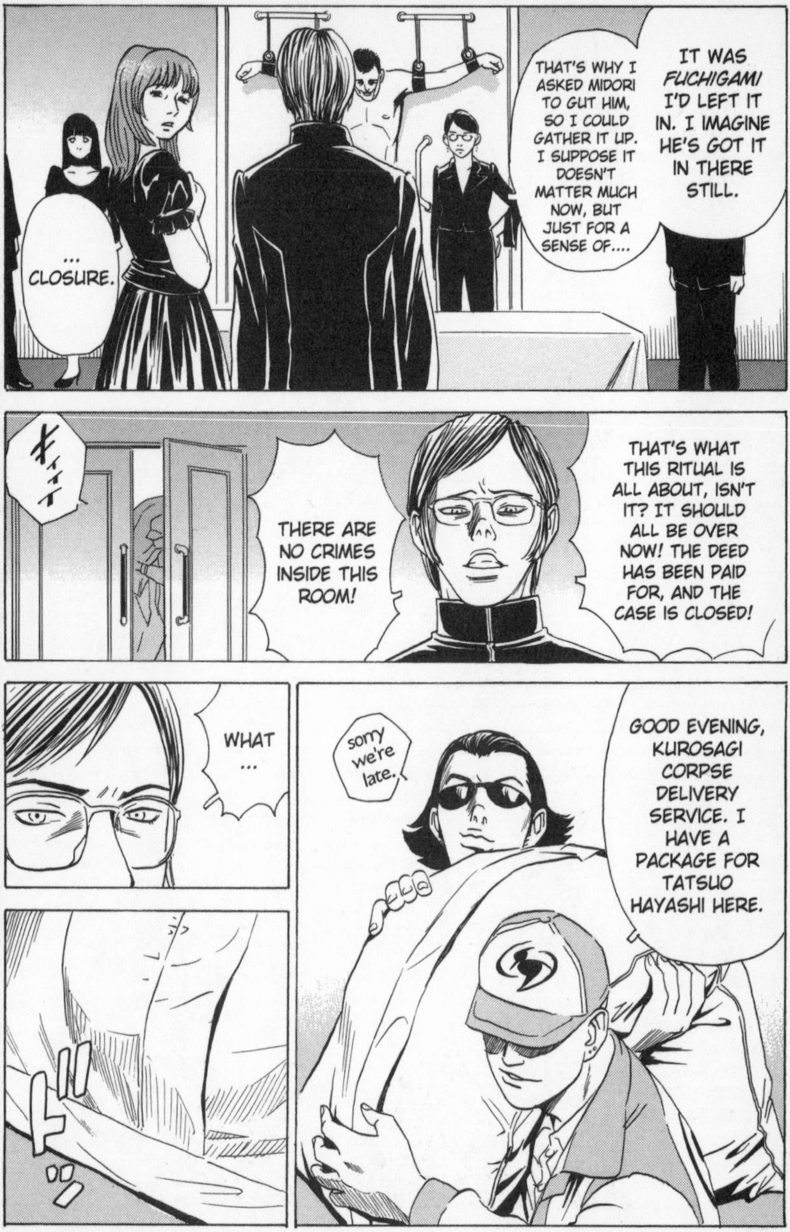
IT WAS *FUCHIGAMI* I'D LEFT IT IN. I IMAGINE HE'S GOT IT IN THERE STILL.
THAT'S WHY I ASKED MIDORI TO GUT HIM, SO I COULD GATHER IT UP. I SUPPOSE IT DOESN'T MATTER MUCH NOW, BUT JUST FOR A SENSE OF....
... CLOSURE.
THAT'S WHAT THIS RITUAL IS ALL ABOUT, ISN'T IT? IT SHOULD ALL BE OVER NOW! THE DEED HAS BEEN PAID FOR, AND THE CASE IS CLOSED!
THERE ARE NO CRIMES INSIDE THIS ROOM!
GOOD EVENING, KUROSAGI CORPSE DELIVERY SERVICE. I HAVE A PACKAGE FOR TATSUO HAYASHI HERE.
sorry we're late.
WHAT ...

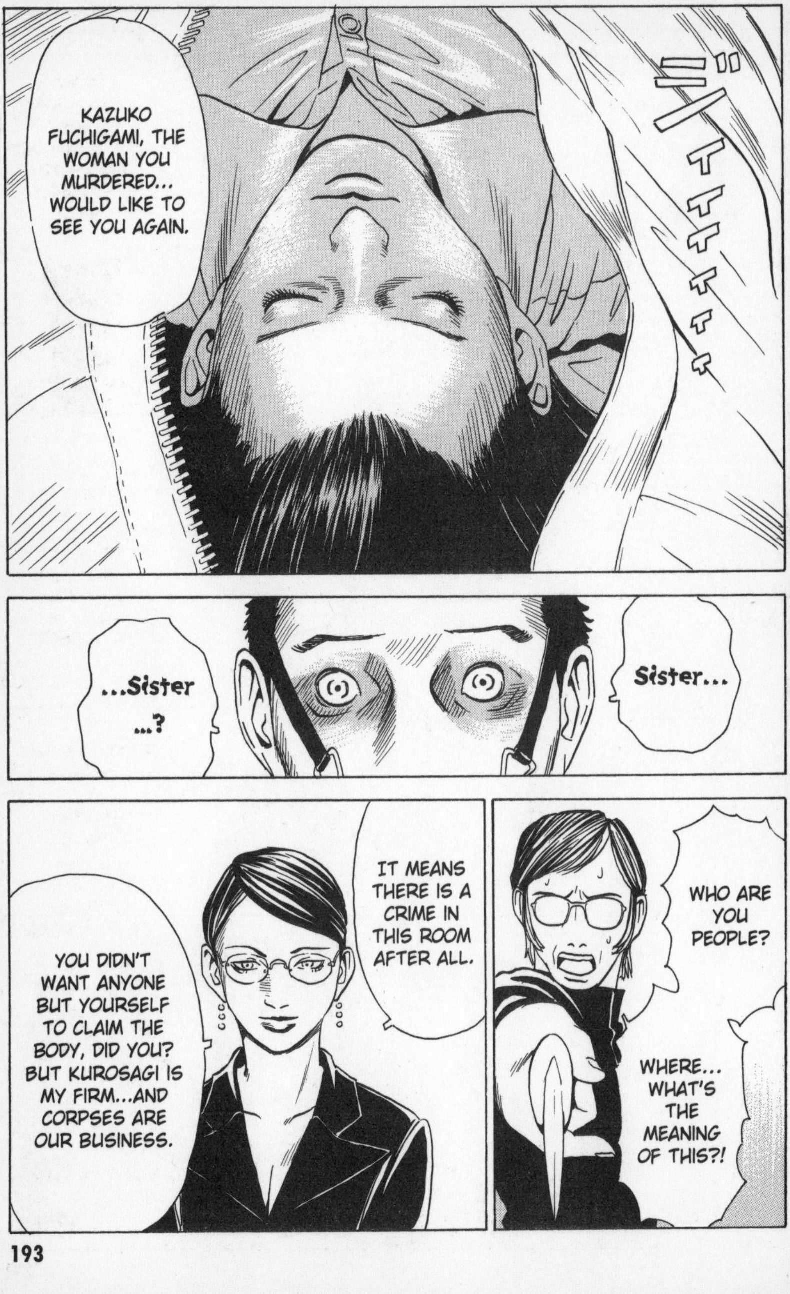
KAZUKO FUCHIGAMI, THE WOMAN YOU MURDERED... WOULD LIKE TO SEE YOU AGAIN.
Sister...
...Sister ...?
WHO ARE YOU PEOPLE?
WHERE... WHAT'S THE MEANING OF THIS?!
IT MEANS THERE IS A CRIME IN THIS ROOM AFTER ALL.
YOU DIDN'T WANT ANYONE BUT YOURSELF TO CLAIM THE BODY, DID YOU? BUT KUROSAGI IS MY FIRM...AND CORPSES ARE OUR BUSINESS.

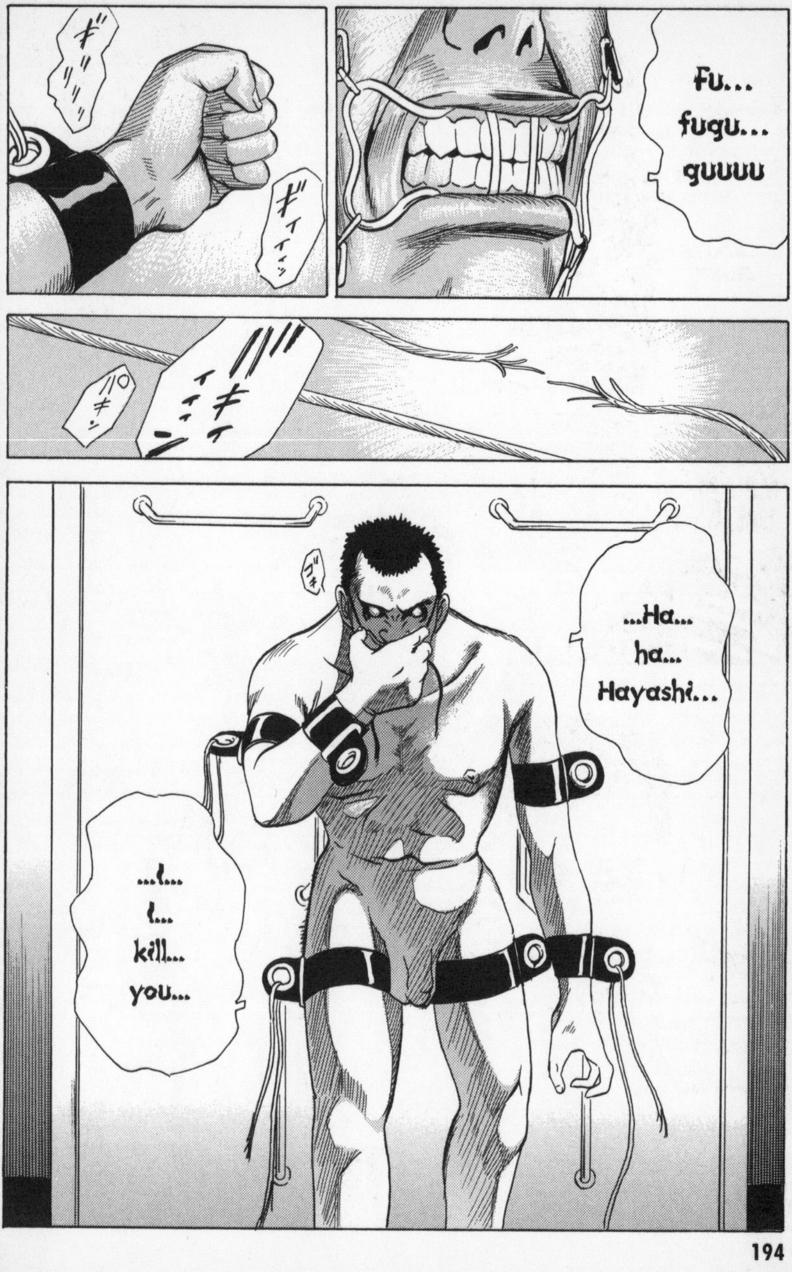
Fu... fugu... guuuu
ギイイィッ
ギィィィィン
パキン
ブチ
...Ha... ha... Hayashi...
...I... I... kill... you...

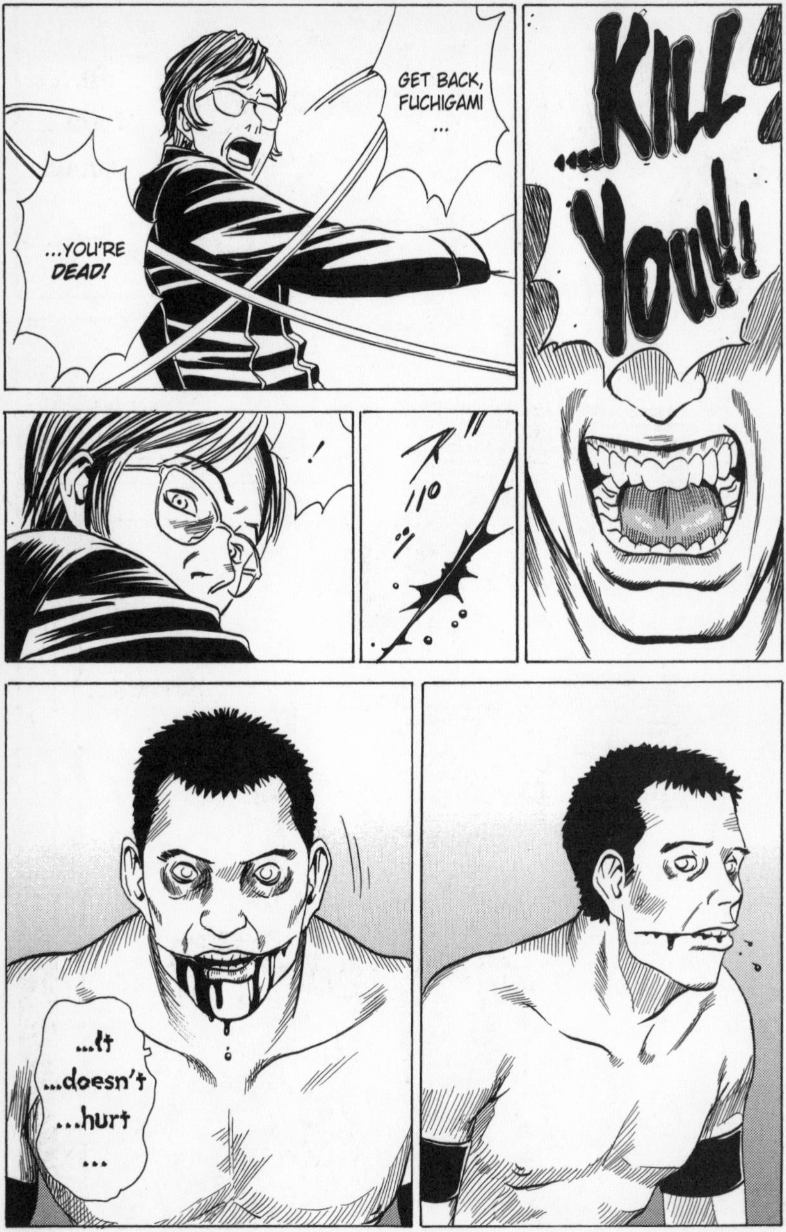
...KILL YOU!!
GET BACK, FUCHIGAMI ...
...YOU'RE DEAD!
!
...It ...doesn't ...hurt ...

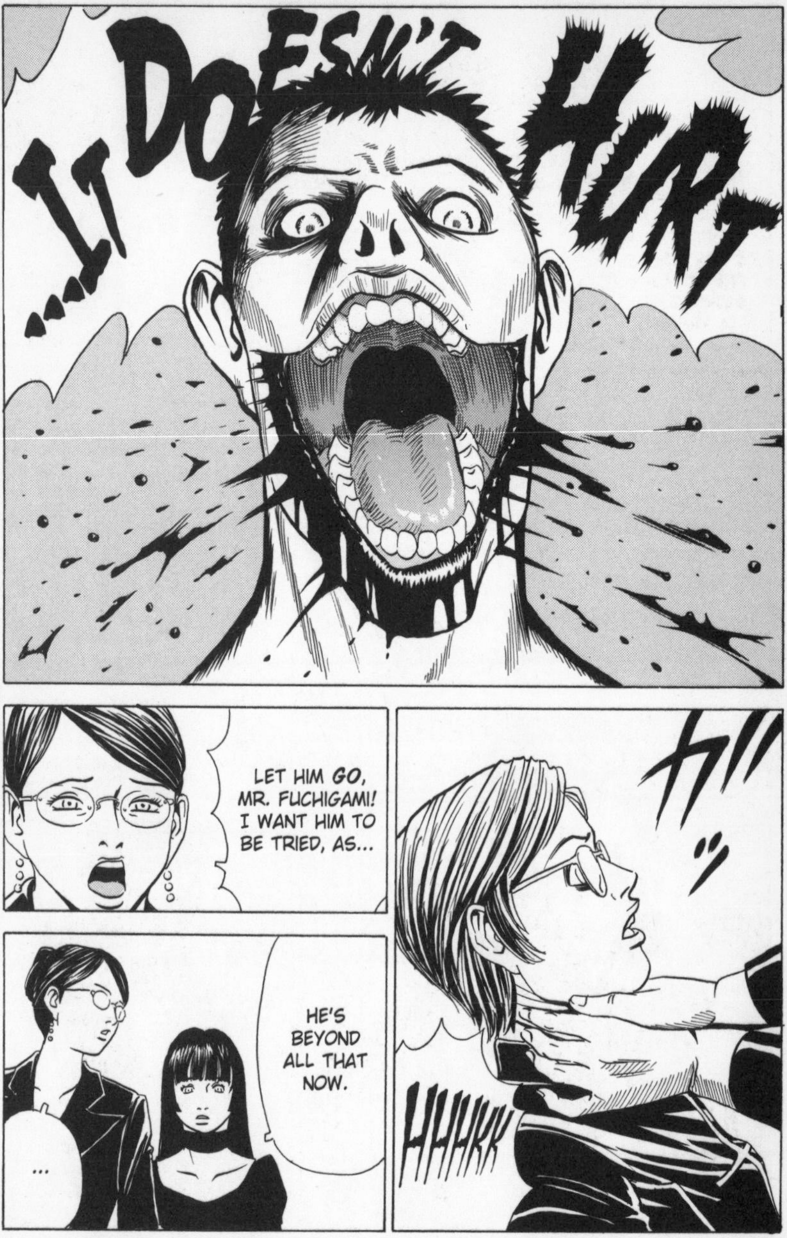
...IT DOESN'T HURT
ガッ
HHHKK
LET HIM GO, MR. FUCHIGAMI! I WANT HIM TO BE TRIED, AS...
HE'S BEYOND ALL THAT NOW.
...

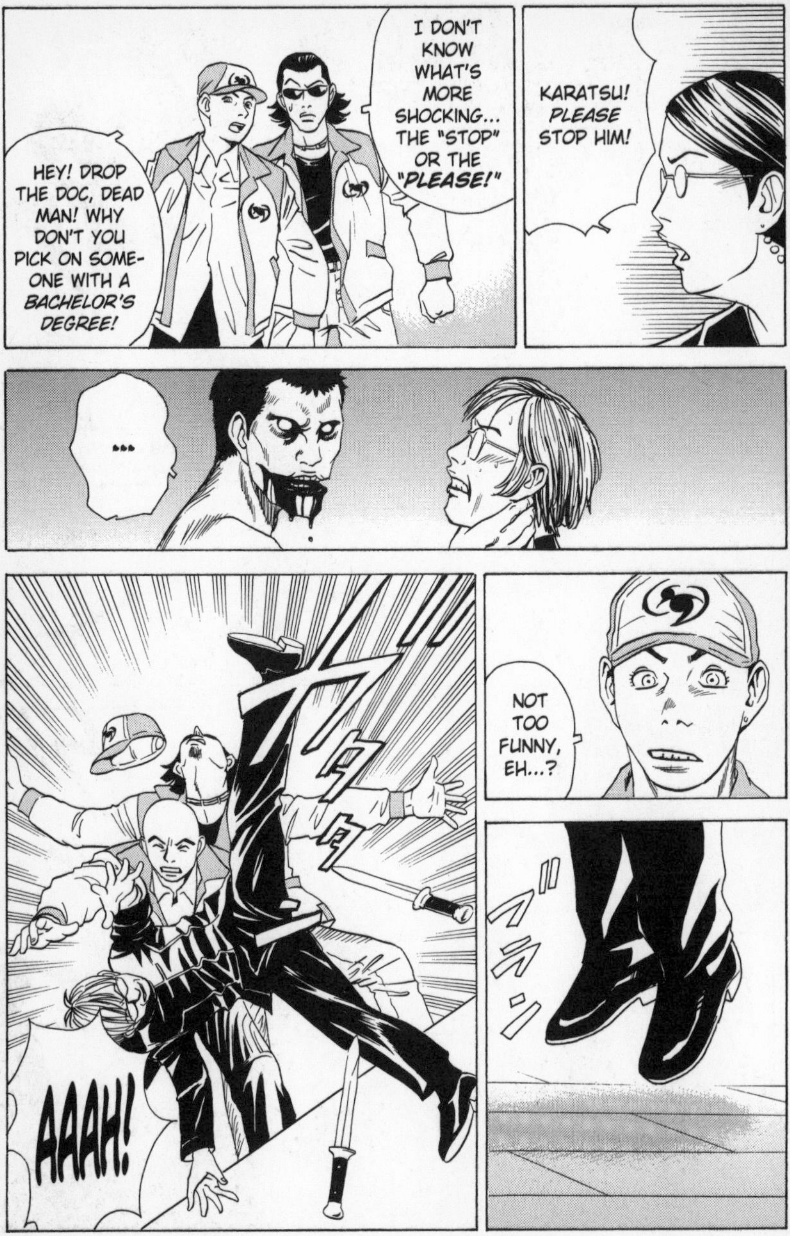
KARATSU! PLEASE STOP HIM!
I DON'T KNOW WHAT'S MORE SHOCKING... THE "STOP" OR THE "PLEASE!"
HEY! DROP THE DOC, DEAD MAN! WHY DON'T YOU PICK ON SOME-ONE WITH A BACHELOR'S DEGREE!
...
NOT TOO FUNNY, EH...?
AAAH!

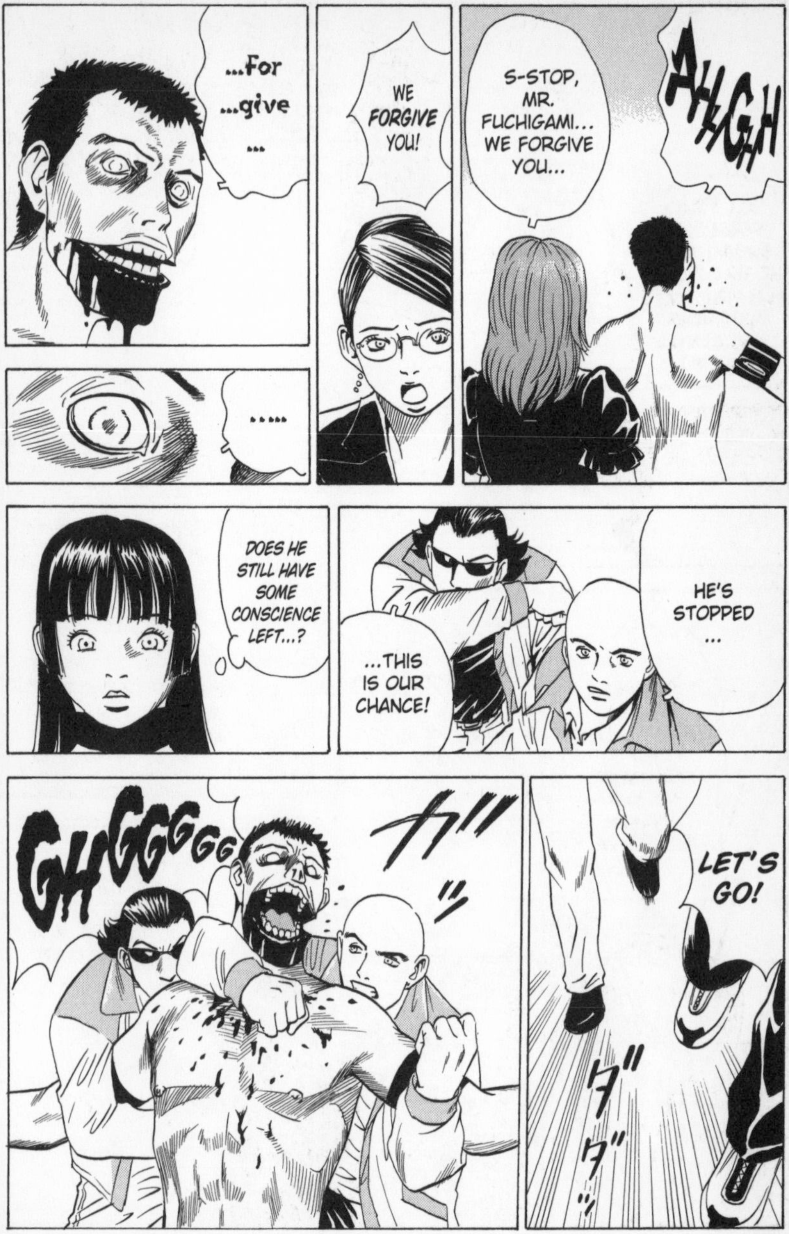
AHHGHH
S-STOP, MR. FUCHIGAMI... WE FORGIVE YOU...
WE FORGIVE YOU!
...For ...give ...
......
HE'S STOPPED ...
...THIS IS OUR CHANCE!
DOES HE STILL HAVE SOME CONSCIENCE LEFT...?
LET'S GO!
ダダッ
GHGGGGG
ガッ

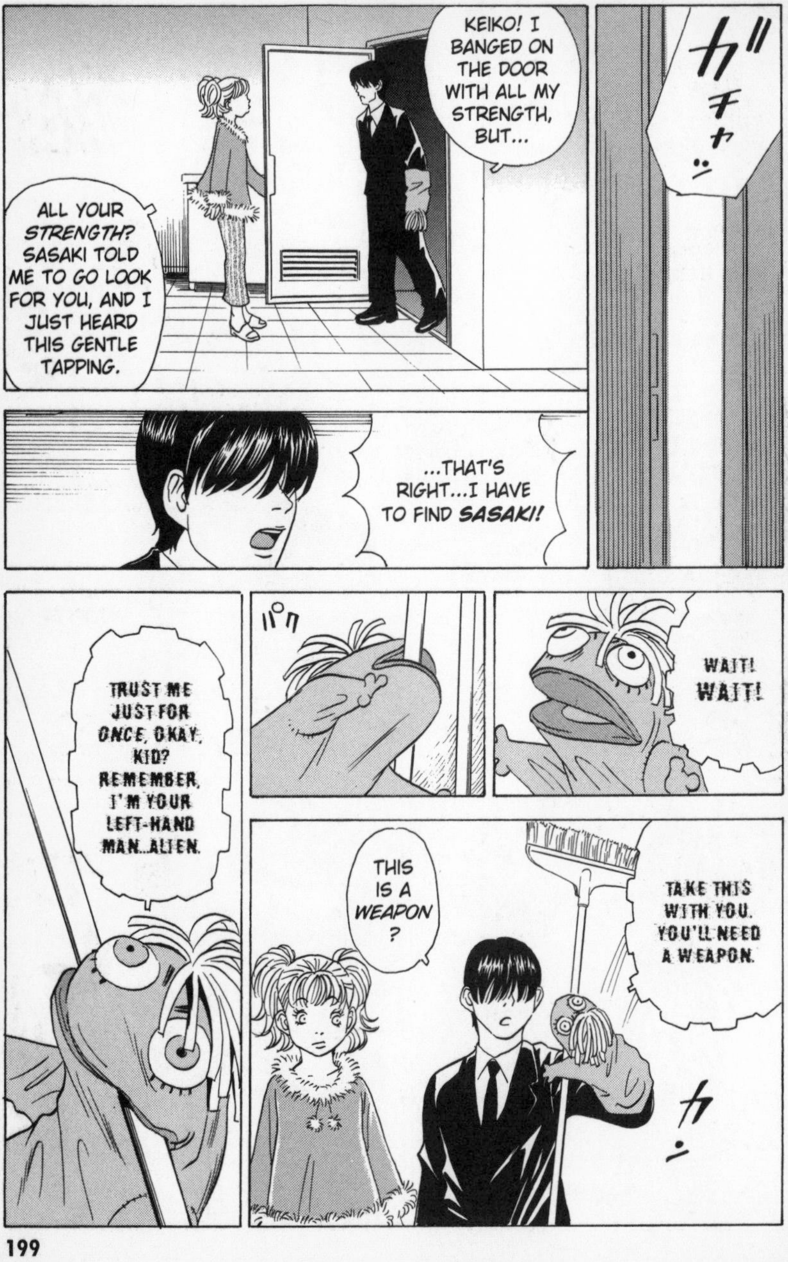
ガチャッ
KEIKO! I BANGED ON THE DOOR WITH ALL MY STRENGTH, BUT...
ALL YOUR *STRENGTH?* SASAKI TOLD ME TO GO LOOK FOR YOU, AND I JUST HEARD THIS GENTLE TAPPING.
...THAT'S RIGHT...I HAVE TO FIND **SASAKI!**
WAIT! WAIT!
パク
TAKE THIS WITH YOU. YOU'LL NEED A WEAPON.
THIS IS A *WEAPON*?
カン
TRUST ME JUST FOR *ONCE*, OKAY, KID? REMEMBER, I'M YOUR LEFT-HAND MAN...ALIEN.

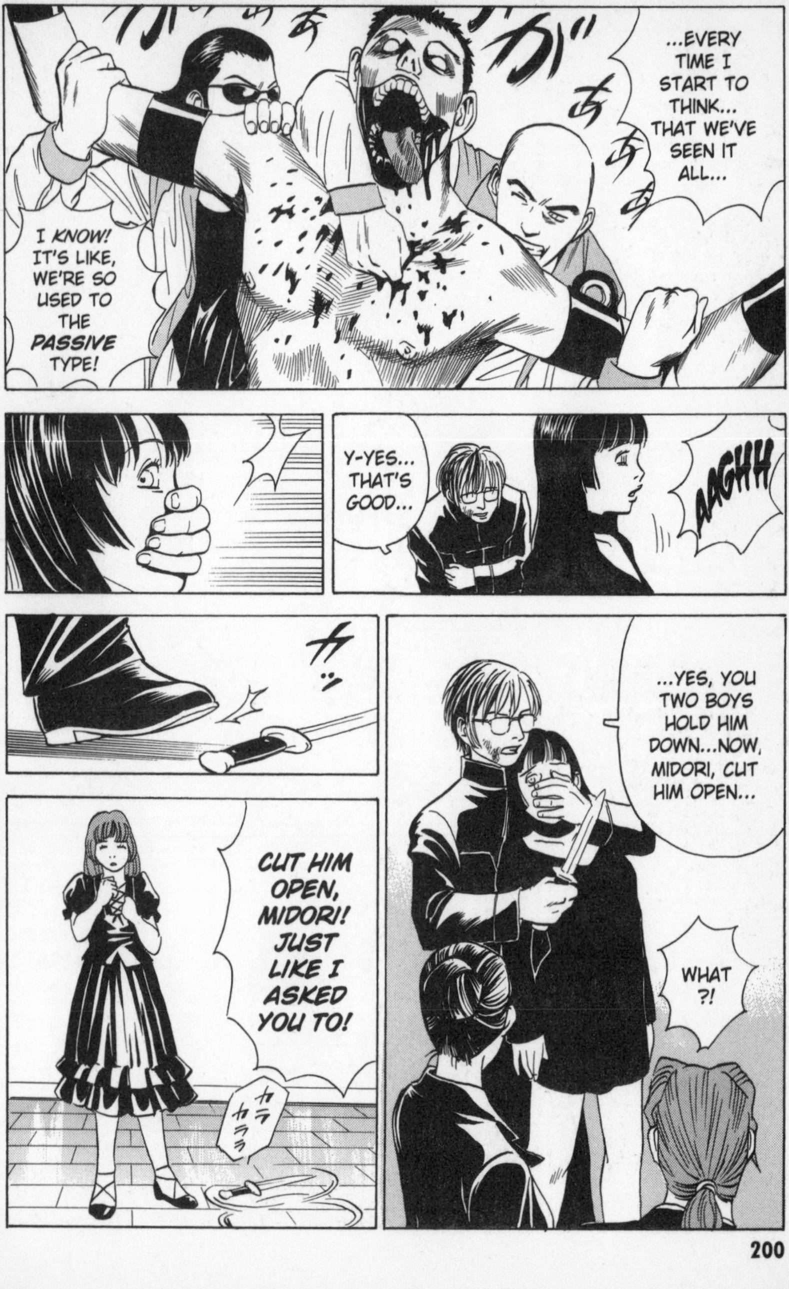
...EVERY TIME I START TO THINK... THAT WE'VE SEEN IT ALL...
I *KNOW!* IT'S LIKE, WE'RE SO USED TO THE *PASSIVE* TYPE!
AAGHH
Y-YES... THAT'S GOOD...
...YES, YOU TWO BOYS HOLD HIM DOWN...NOW, MIDORI, CUT HIM OPEN...
WHAT ?!
カッ
CUT HIM OPEN, MIDORI! JUST LIKE I ASKED YOU TO!
カラ カラ

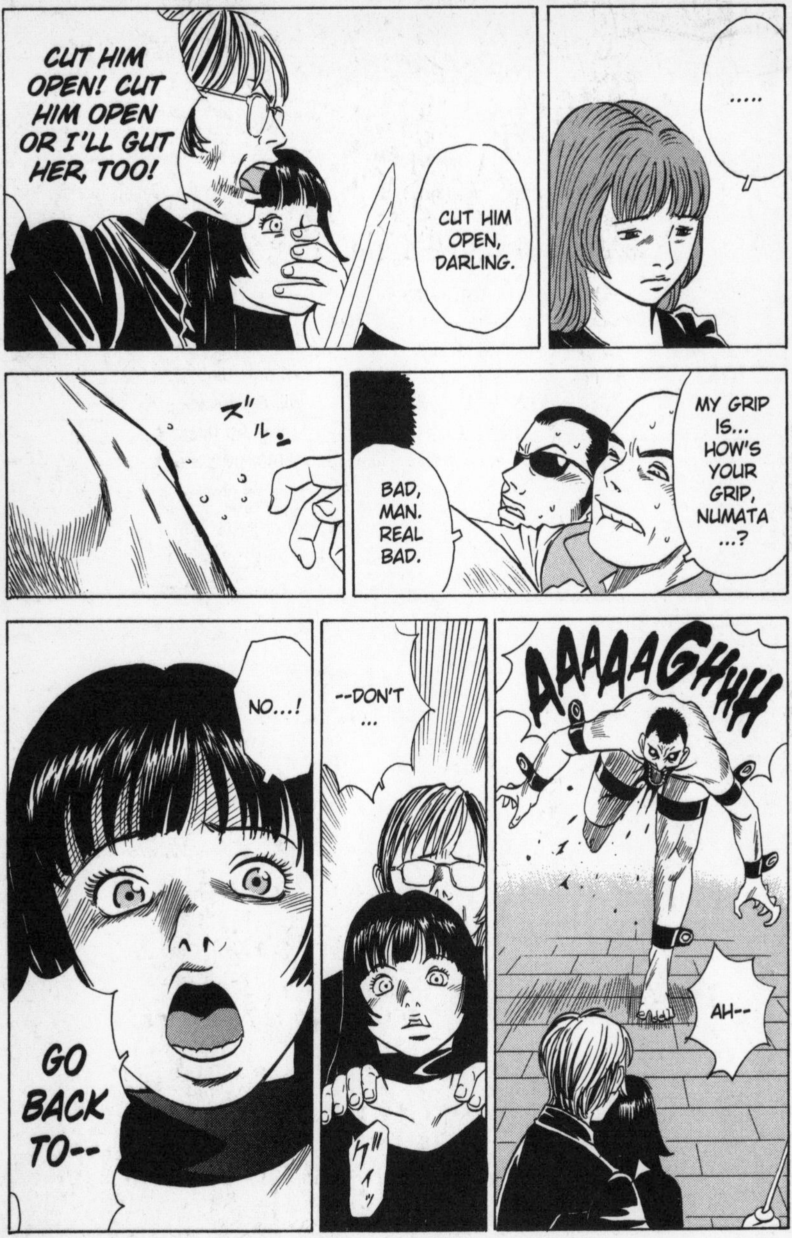
.....
CUT HIM OPEN! CUT HIM OPEN OR I'LL GUT HER, TOO!
CUT HIM OPEN, DARLING.
MY GRIP IS... HOW'S YOUR GRIP, NUMATA ...?
BAD, MAN. REAL BAD.
ズル
AAAAAGHHH
AH--
--DON'T ...
グイッ
NO...!
GO BACK TO--

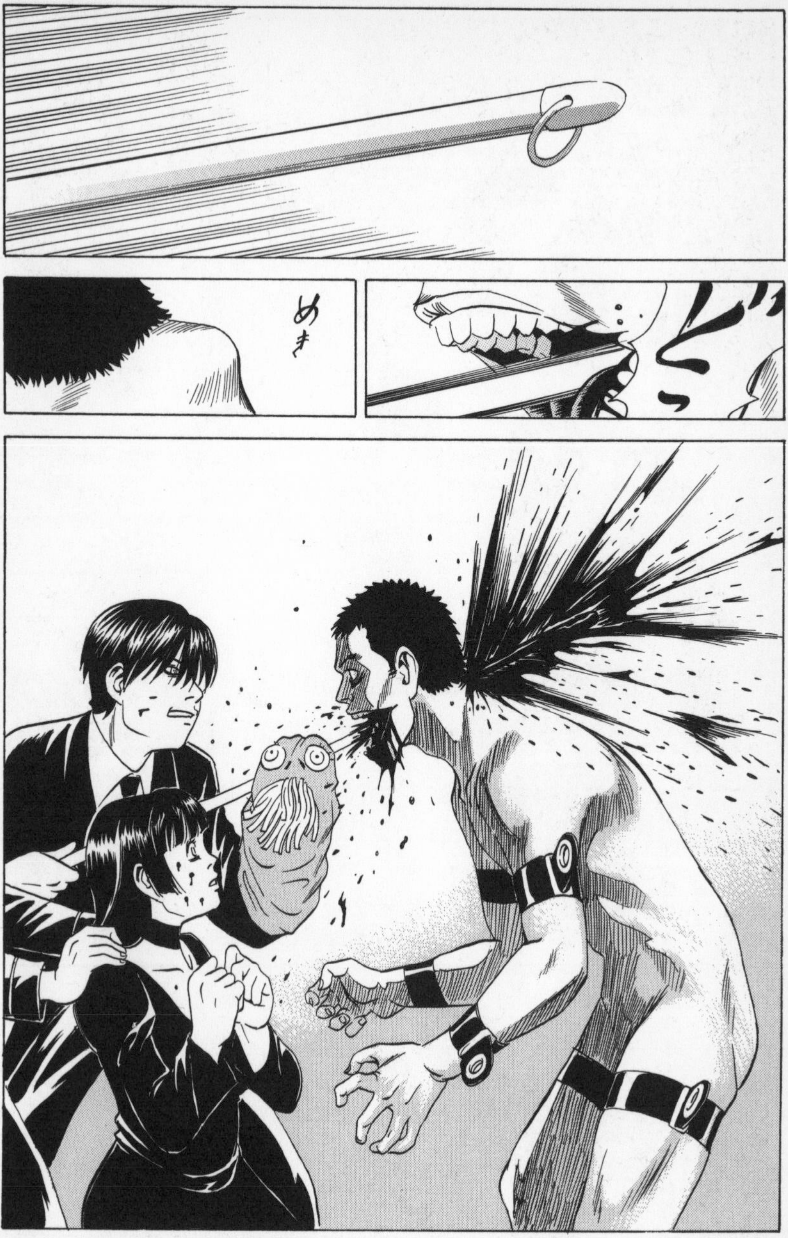
どっ
めき

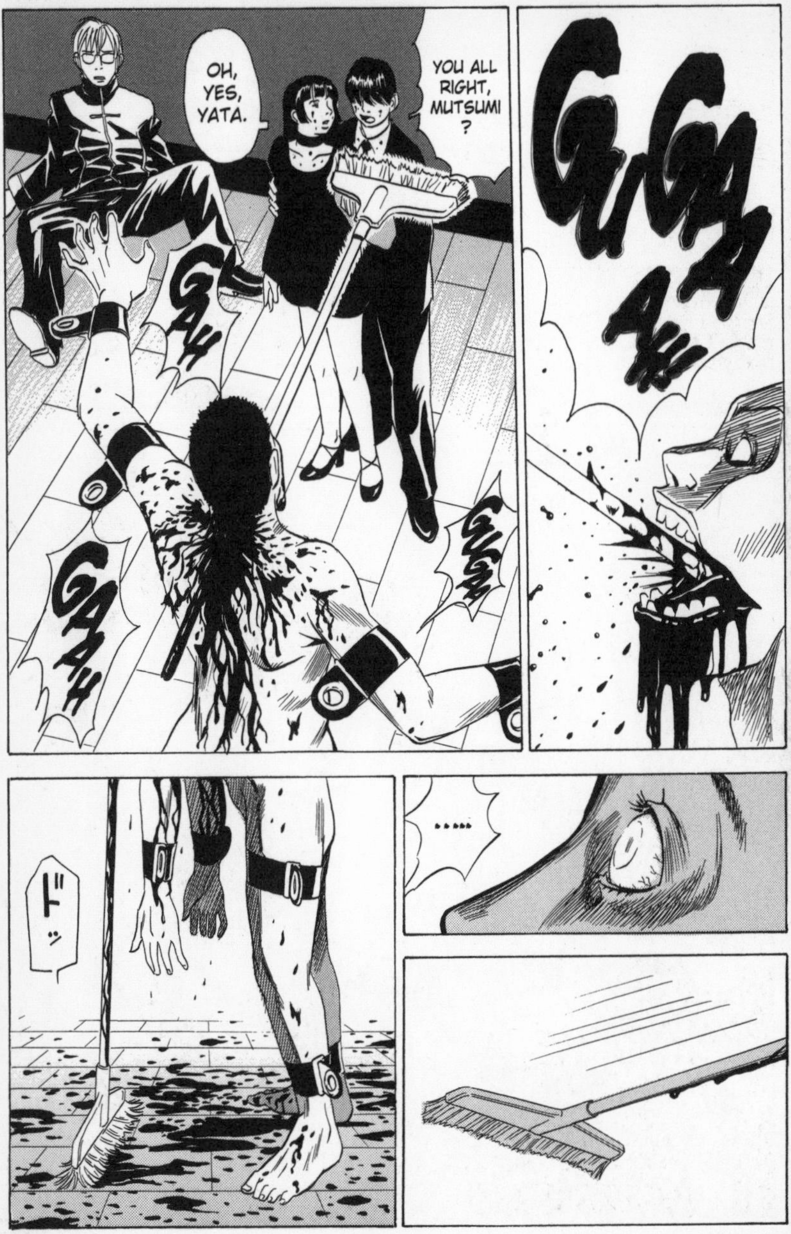
YOU ALL RIGHT, MUTSUMI?
OH, YES, YATA.
GAAH
GUGAH
GAAAH
.....
ドッ

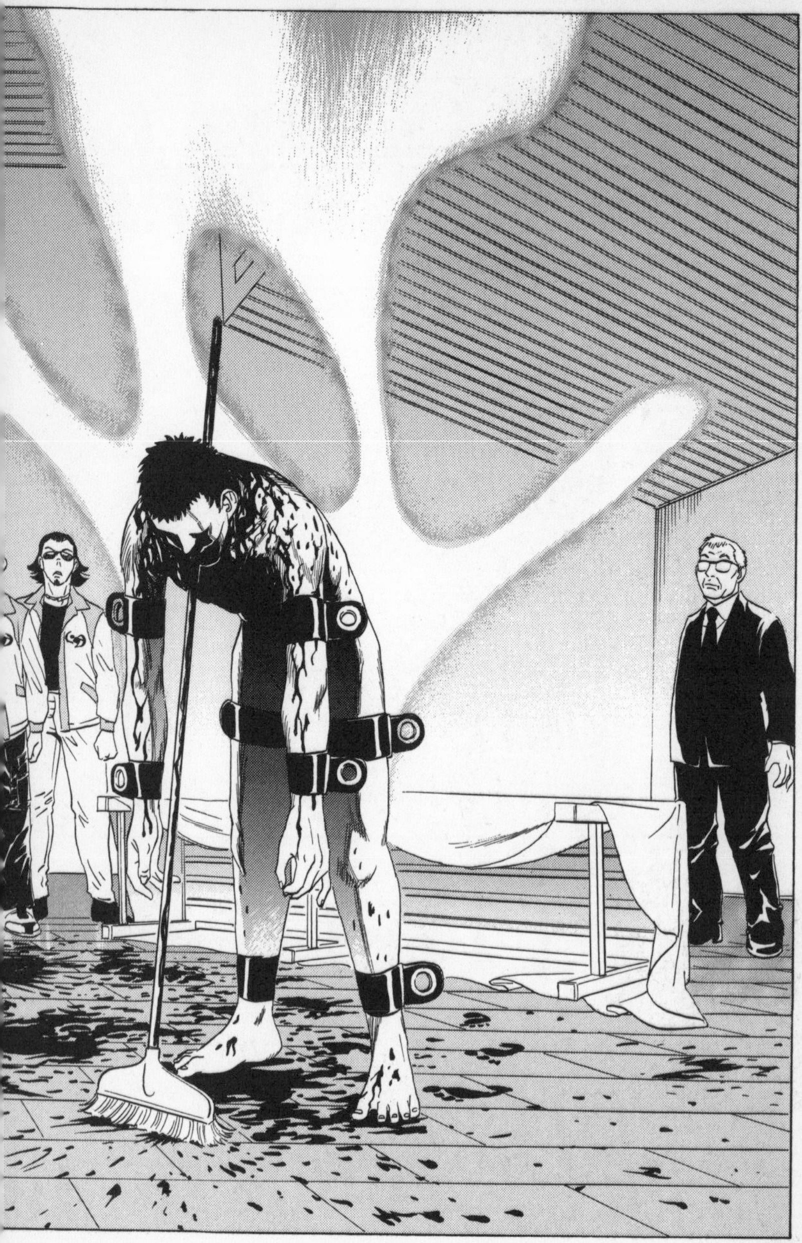

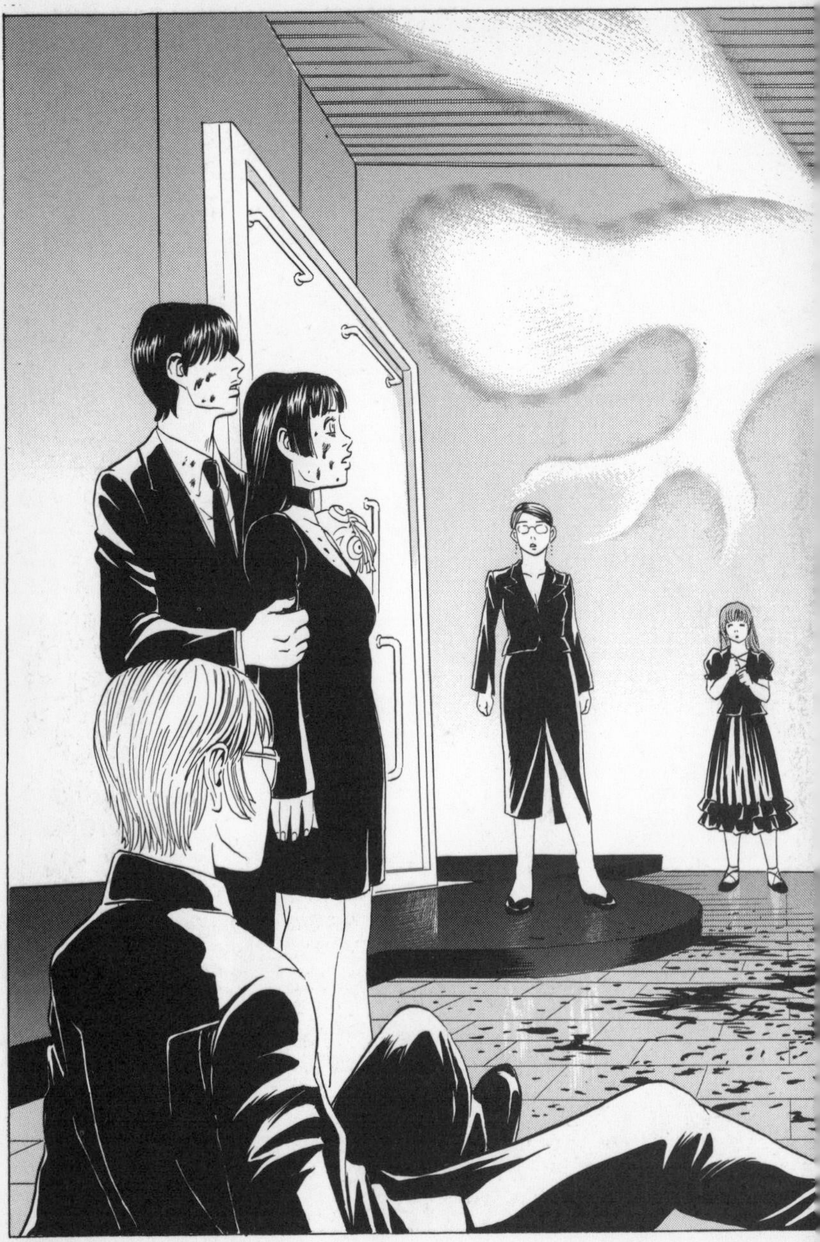

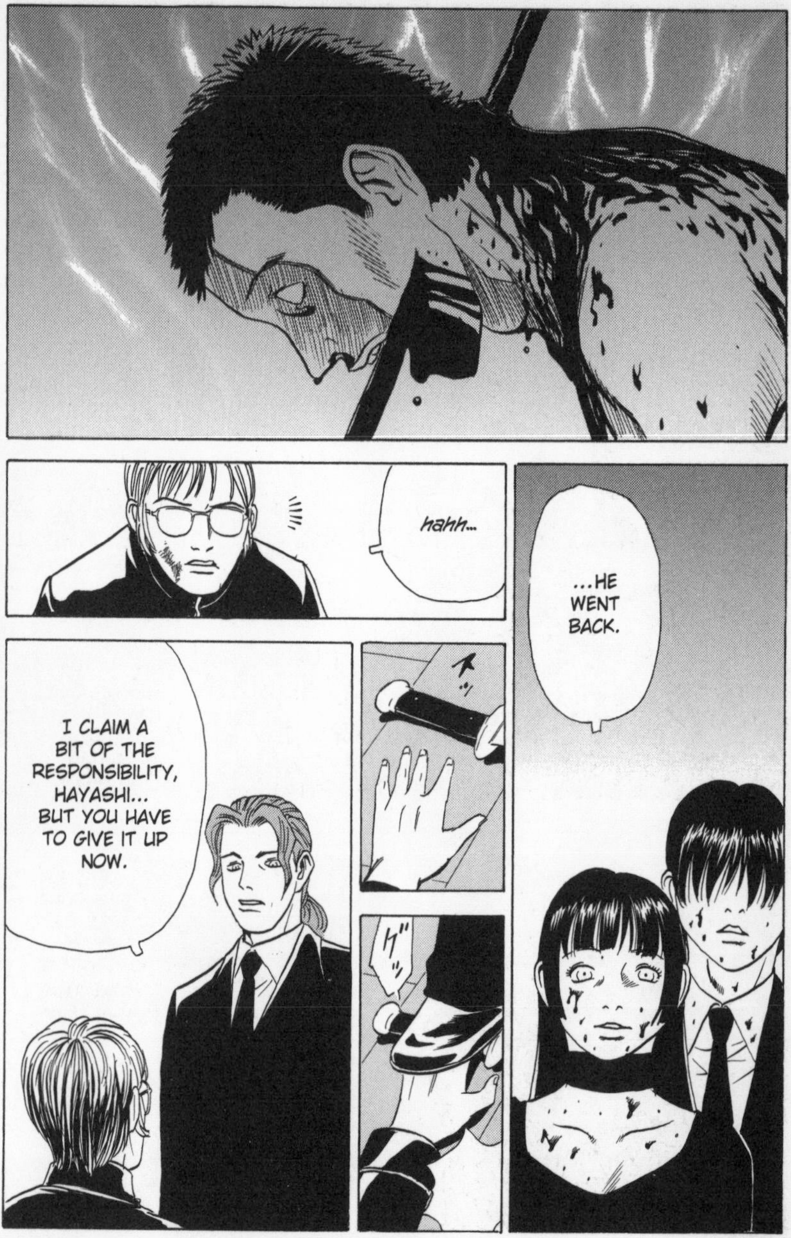
...HE WENT BACK.
hahh...
I CLAIM A BIT OF THE RESPONSIBILITY, HAYASHI... BUT YOU HAVE TO GIVE IT UP NOW.

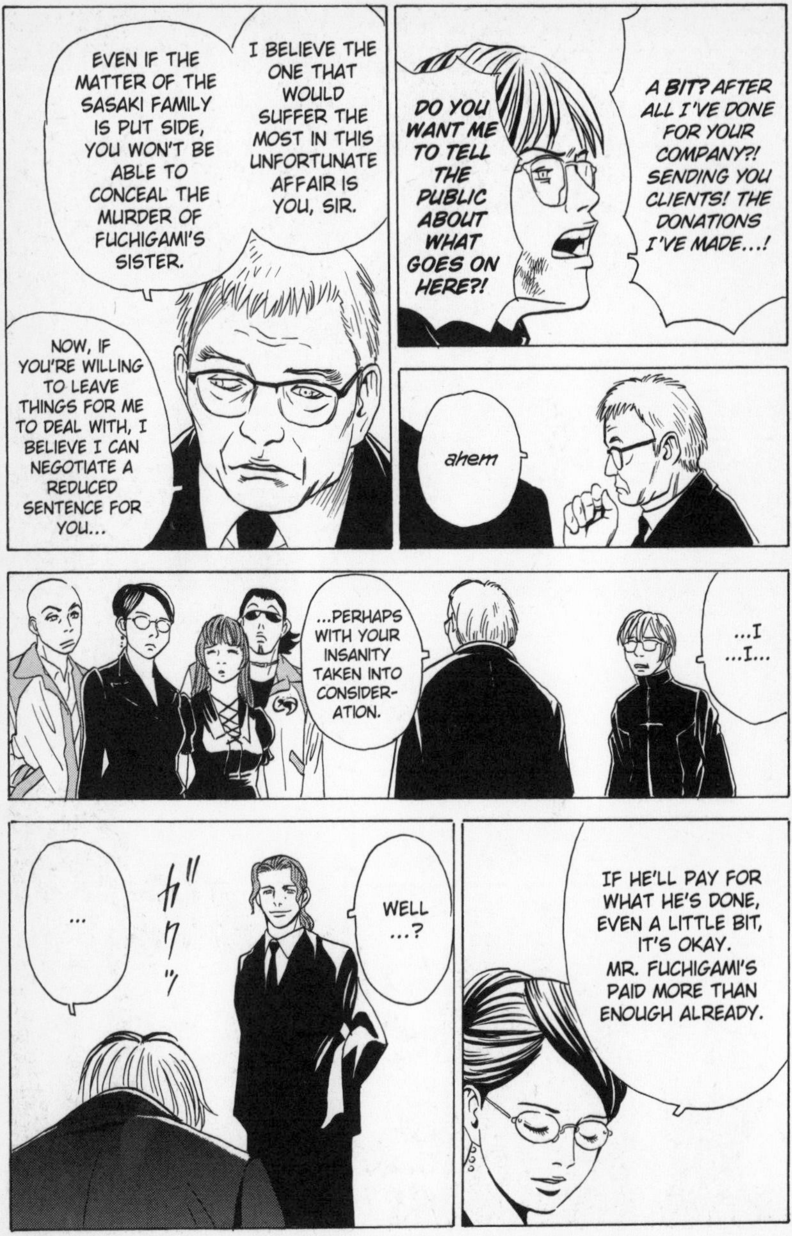
A BIT? AFTER ALL I'VE DONE FOR YOUR COMPANY?! SENDING YOU CLIENTS! THE DONATIONS I'VE MADE...!
DO YOU WANT ME TO TELL THE PUBLIC ABOUT WHAT GOES ON HERE?!
ahem
I BELIEVE THE ONE THAT WOULD SUFFER THE MOST IN THIS UNFORTUNATE AFFAIR IS YOU, SIR.
EVEN IF THE MATTER OF THE SASAKI FAMILY IS PUT SIDE, YOU WON'T BE ABLE TO CONCEAL THE MURDER OF FUCHIGAMI'S SISTER.
NOW, IF YOU'RE WILLING TO LEAVE THINGS FOR ME TO DEAL WITH, I BELIEVE I CAN NEGOTIATE A REDUCED SENTENCE FOR YOU...
...I ...I...
...PERHAPS WITH YOUR INSANITY TAKEN INTO CONSIDER-ATION.
IF HE'LL PAY FOR WHAT HE'S DONE, EVEN A LITTLE BIT, IT'S OKAY. MR. FUCHIGAMI'S PAID MORE THAN ENOUGH ALREADY.
WELL ...?
ガクッ
...

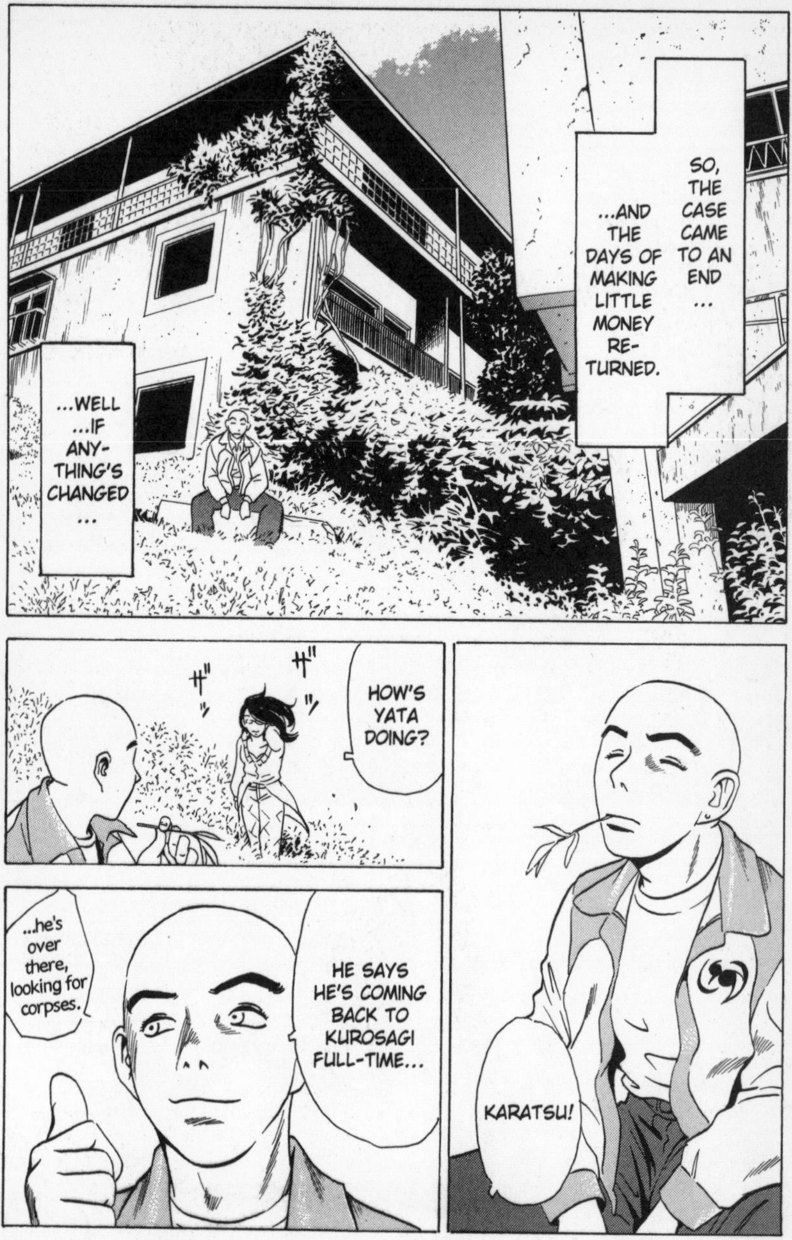
SO, THE CASE CAME TO AN END...
...AND THE DAYS OF MAKING LITTLE MONEY RE-TURNED.
...WELL ...IF ANY-THING'S CHANGED...
KARATSU!
ザッ
ザッ
HOW'S YATA DOING?
HE SAYS HE'S COMING BACK TO KUROSAGI FULL-TIME...
...he's over there, looking for corpses.

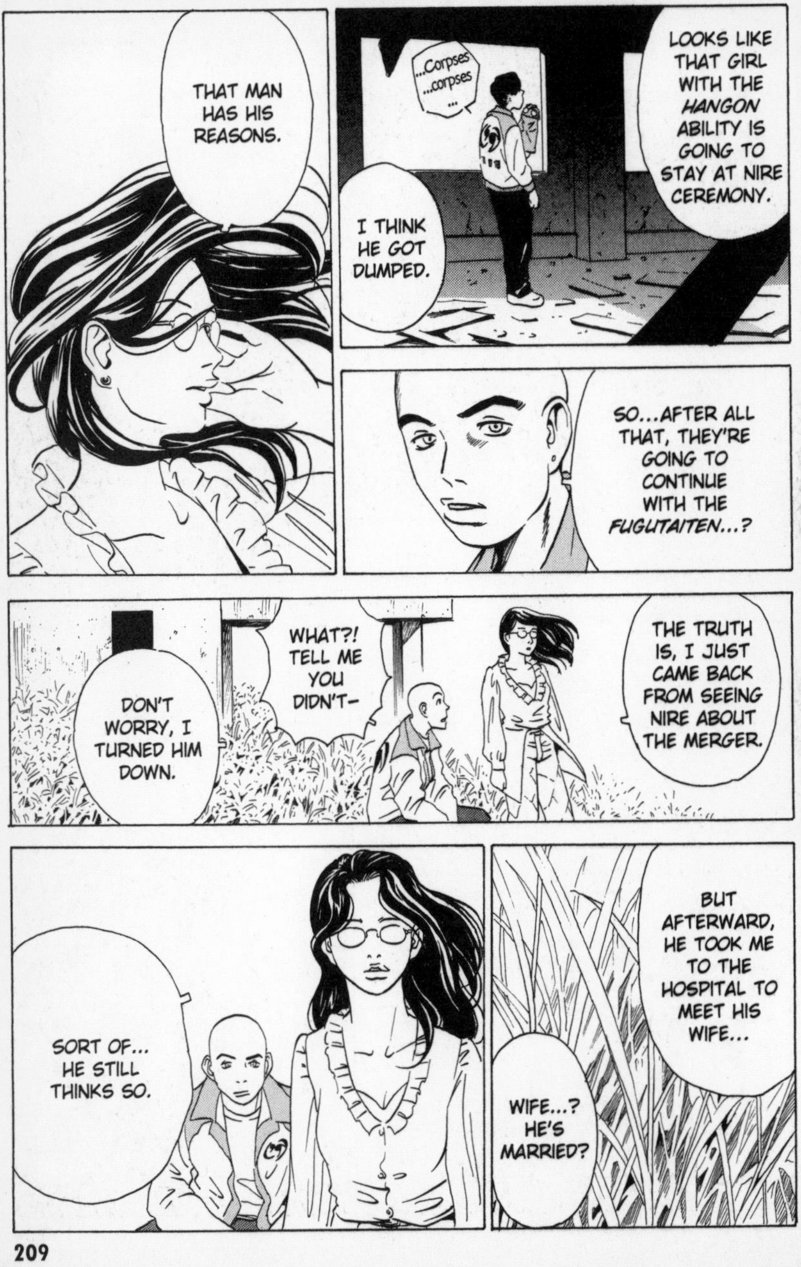
LOOKS LIKE THAT GIRL WITH THE *HANGON* ABILITY IS GOING TO STAY AT NIRE CEREMONY.
...Corpses ...corpses ...
I THINK HE GOT DUMPED.
SO...AFTER ALL THAT, THEY'RE GOING TO CONTINUE WITH THE *FUGUTAITEN*...?
THAT MAN HAS HIS REASONS.
THE TRUTH IS, I JUST CAME BACK FROM SEEING NIRE ABOUT THE MERGER.
WHAT?! TELL ME YOU DIDN'T-
DON'T WORRY, I TURNED HIM DOWN.
BUT AFTERWARD, HE TOOK ME TO THE HOSPITAL TO MEET HIS WIFE...
WIFE...? HE'S MARRIED?
SORT OF... HE STILL THINKS SO.

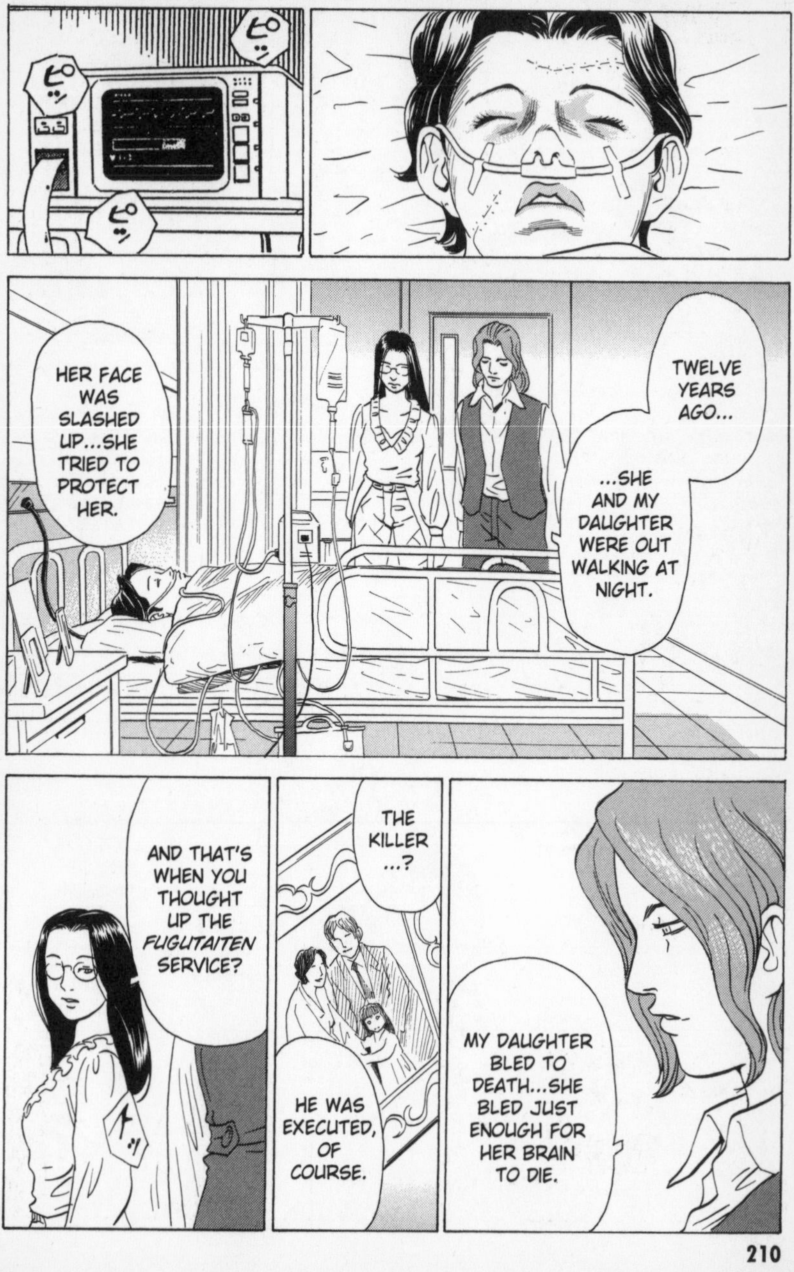
ピッ
ピッ
ピッ
TWELVE YEARS AGO...
...SHE AND MY DAUGHTER WERE OUT WALKING AT NIGHT.
HER FACE WAS SLASHED UP...SHE TRIED TO PROTECT HER.
MY DAUGHTER BLED TO DEATH...SHE BLED JUST ENOUGH FOR HER BRAIN TO DIE.
THE KILLER ...?
HE WAS EXECUTED, OF COURSE.
AND THAT'S WHEN YOU THOUGHT UP THE *FUGUTAITEN* SERVICE?

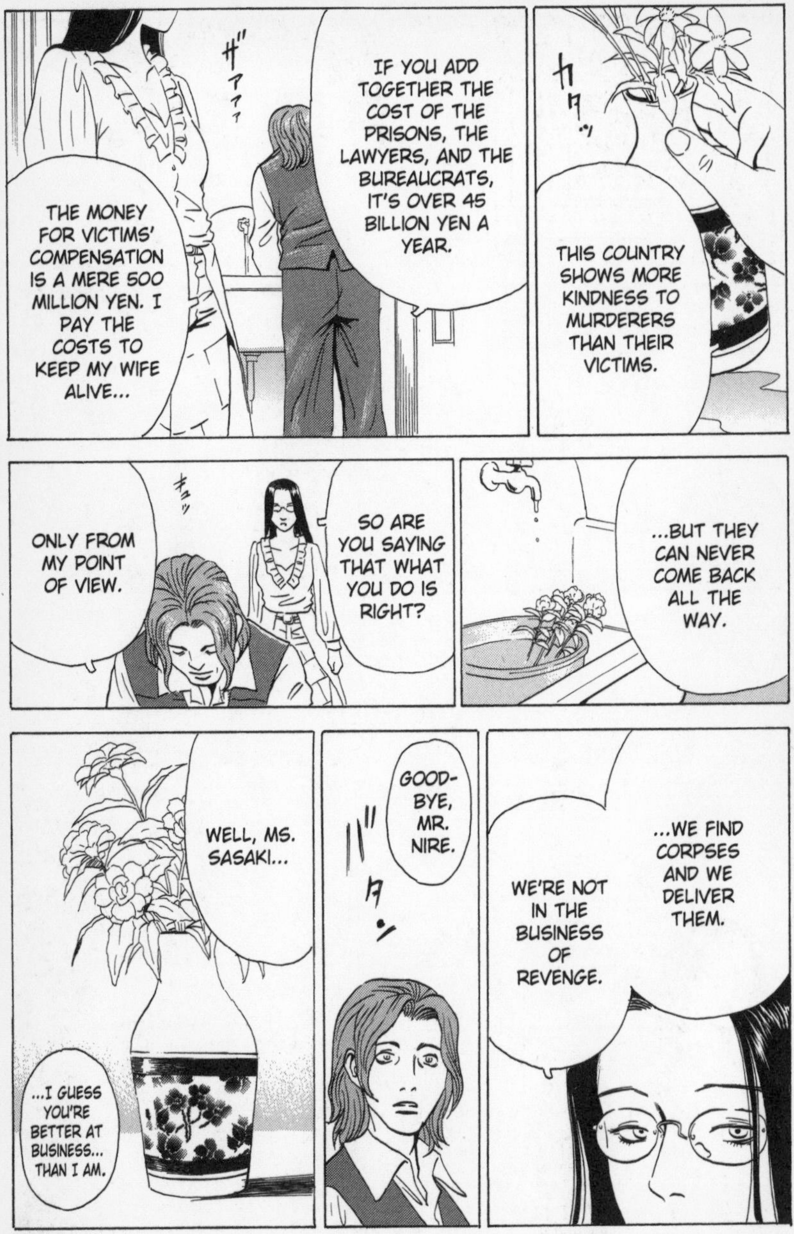
カタッ
THIS COUNTRY SHOWS MORE KINDNESS TO MURDERERS THAN THEIR VICTIMS.
IF YOU ADD TOGETHER THE COST OF THE PRISONS, THE LAWYERS, AND THE BUREAUCRATS, IT'S OVER 45 BILLION YEN A YEAR.
ザァァァ
THE MONEY FOR VICTIMS' COMPENSATION IS A MERE 500 MILLION YEN. I PAY THE COSTS TO KEEP MY WIFE ALIVE...
...BUT THEY CAN NEVER COME BACK ALL THE WAY.
SO ARE YOU SAYING THAT WHAT YOU DO IS RIGHT?
キュッ
ONLY FROM MY POINT OF VIEW.
...WE FIND CORPSES AND WE DELIVER THEM.
WE'RE NOT IN THE BUSINESS OF REVENGE.
GOOD-BYE, MR. NIRE.
バタッ
WELL, MS. SASAKI...
...I GUESS YOU'RE BETTER AT BUSINESS... THAN I AM.

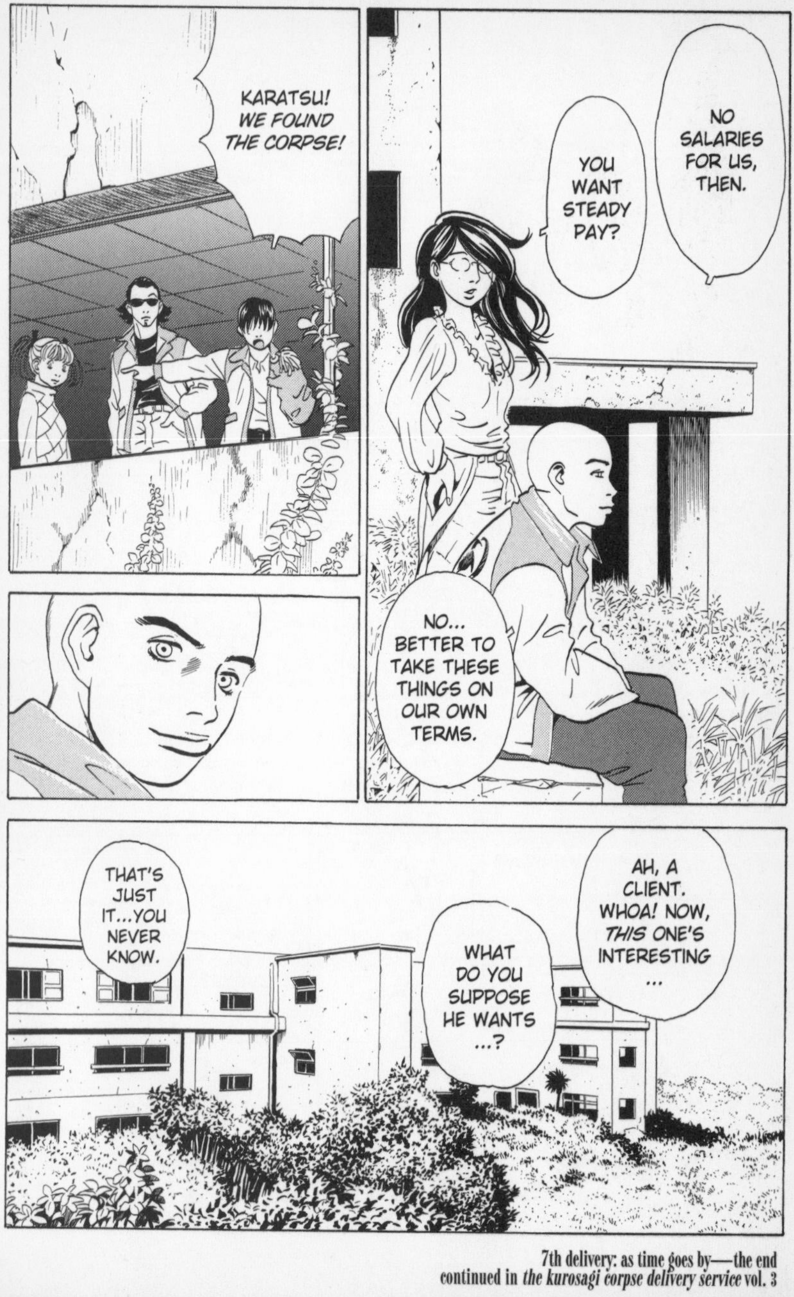
NO SALARIES FOR US, THEN.
YOU WANT STEADY PAY?
NO... BETTER TO TAKE THESE THINGS ON OUR OWN TERMS.
KARATSU! WE FOUND THE CORPSE!
AH, A CLIENT. WHOA! NOW, *THIS* ONE'S INTERESTING ...
WHAT DO YOU SUPPOSE HE WANTS ...?
THAT'S JUST IT...YOU NEVER KNOW.

7th delivery: as time goes by—the end
continued in *the kurosagi corpse delivery service* vol. 3

AFTERWORD FROM THE AUTHOR

AFTERWORD BY THE AUTHOR

My father died of cancer the January just before I graduated college. The doctors said he had very little time to live, and so my family and I went to the hospital to be there in his last days. But his death lasted longer than they had thought, and so, the strain upon those lying by his side, waiting for it.

I awoke one morning just before daybreak on one of the cots the hospital provides. My mother and sister were asleep upon another, and so I was the first to know that my father had passed during the night. I didn't check him or take his pulse; I just knew. I didn't call the nurse nor wake the rest of my weary family; what would have been the point? Let them sleep a little longer; let me sleep again now, too.

My mother died twenty years after—not too long ago. Due to work and other troubles, I couldn't visit her before; I couldn't even make the funeral. Sometimes these things can't be helped as a writer. But the truth is I hadn't seen her in several years, and my sister's family had become worn out from her care, so what I felt was again relief.

Recently things came full circle from my college days, when I went to visit the grave of my old anthropology professor, Tokuji Chiba, with the classmates I hadn't seen in a generation. It was in the professor's will that his old students be notified only after he had been buried. When we came to the site, we saw he'd even left his name off the headstone—and we all agreed that this was just like him. Then we started wondering what the proper procedure was to burn incense at a grave, and how ironic it was that students of anthropology weren't sure. We said, well, we're the kind of students the professor raised.

It hit me later that both my parents and my mentor had now all passed on. I find myself thinking that in few years, the time may come for the first of our generation to be buried.

The Kurosagi Corpse Delivery Service is a story I created out of my desire to write an orthodox horror story. I thought it was odd how the walking dead had become such a normal sight in movies and video games—how much the idea of a zombie had been taken for granted. I wanted to get back to the fear any real person would feel, should death's work appear to be unfinished.

The office I work for comes up with plans for dozens of manga every year, but only a few ever actually get made. In most cases, it's the problem of not being able to find a manga artist that fits the plans, but fortunately for *Kurosagi*, I was paired up with Housui Yamazaki, and together we were able to express this concept as I had hoped.

With most of the readers being desensitized to corpses and zombies from pop culture, I would like to voice how wonderful it is to be able to work with an artist who can depict a sense of fear as Yamazaki can do by simply making the dead move in the way that he does.

Serialized in *Kadowaka Mystery,* a companion title to *Shonen Ace*, this is a series that seems to have a hard time finding a permanent home, but I have an entire story ready to explain why the members have those strange powers, so I hope it can see the light of day in some publication soon. (Editor's note: *Kurosagi* did return, this time to *Shonen Ace* magazine itself, in October of 2006).

See you in Volume Three.

— eiji otsuka

the KUROSAGI corpse delivery service
黒鷺死体宅配便

eiji otsuka 大塚英志 housui yamazaki 山崎峰水

designer **HEIDI FAINZA**
editorial assistant **RACHEL MILLER**
art director **LIA RIBACCHI**
publisher **MIKE RICHARDSON**

English-language version
produced by Dark Horse Comics

THE KUROSAGI CORPSE DELIVERY SERVICE VOL. 2

Published by
Dark Horse Manga
A division of Dark Horse Comics, Inc.
10956 SE Main Street
Milwaukie, OR 97222
www.darkhorse.com

To find a comics shop in your area,
call the Comic Shop Locator Service
toll-free at 1-888-266-4226

First edition: January 2007
ISBN-10: 1-59307-593-6
ISBN-13: 978-1-59307-593-4

1 3 5 7 9 10 8 6 4 2

PRINTED IN CANADA

DISJECTA MEMBRA

SOUND FX GLOSSARY AND NOTES ON KUROSAGI VOL. 2 BY TOSHIFUMI YOSHIDA
introduction and additional comments by the editor

TO INCREASE YOUR ENJOYMENT of the distinctive Japanese visual style of this manga, we've included a guide to the sound effects (or "FX") used in this manga adaptation of the anime film. It is suggested the reader not constantly consult this glossary as they read through, but regard it as supplemental information, in the manner of footnotes. If you want to imagine it being read aloud by Osaka, after the manner of her lecture to Sakaki on hemorrhoids in episode five, please go right ahead. In either Yuki Matsuoka or Kira Vincent-Davis's voice—I like them both.

Japanese, like English, did not independently invent its own writing system, but instead borrowed and modified the system used by the then-dominant cultural power in their part of the world. We still call the letters we use to write English today the "Roman" alphabet, for the simple reason that about 1600 years ago the earliest English speakers, living on the frontier of the Roman Empire, began to use the same letters the Romans used to write their Latin language, to write out English.

Around that very same time, on the other side of the planet, Japan, like England, was another example of an island civilization lying across the sea from a great empire, in this case, that of China. Likewise, the Japanese borrowed from the Chinese writing system, which then as now consists of thousands of complex symbols—today in China officially referred to in the Roman alphabet as *hanzi*, but which the Japanese pronounce as *kanji*. For example, all the Japanese characters you see on the front cover of *The Kurosagi Corpse Delivery Service*—the seven which make up the original title and the four each which make up the creators' names—are examples of kanji. Of course, all of them were hanzi first; although the Japanese did later invent some original kanji of their own, just as new hanzi have been created over the centuries as Chinese evolved.

Note that whereas both kanji and hanzi are methods of writing foreign words in Roman letters, "kanji" gives English speakers a fairly good idea of how the Japanese word is really pronounced—*khan-gee*—whereas "hanzi" does not—in Mandarin Chinese it sounds something like *n-tsuh*. The reason is fairly simple: whereas the most commonly used method of writing Japanese in Roman letters, called the Hepburn system, was developed by a native English speaker, the most commonly used method of writing Chinese in Roman letters, called the Pinyin system, was developed by native Mandarin speakers. In fact Pinyin was developed to help teach Mandarin pronunciation to speakers of other Chinese dialects; unlike Hepburn, it was not intended as a learning tool for English speakers *per se*, and hence has no particular obligation to "make sense" to English speakers or, indeed, users of other languages spelled with the Roman alphabet).

Whereas the various dialects of Chinese are written entirely in hanzi, it is impractical to render the Japanese language entirely in them. To compare once more, English is a notoriously difficult language in which to spell properly, and this is in part because it uses an alphabet designed for another language, Latin, whose sounds are different. The challenges the Japanese faced in using the Chinese writing system for their own language were even greater, for whereas spoken English and Latin are at least from a common language family, spoken Japanese is unrelated to any of the various dialects of spoken Chinese. The complicated writing system Japanese evolved represents an adjustment to these differences.

When the Japanese borrowed hanzi to become kanji, what they were getting was a way to write out (remember, they already had ways to say) their vocabulary. Nouns, verbs, many adjectives, the names of places and people—that's what kanji are used for, the fundamental data of the written language. The practical use and processing of that "data"—its grammar and pronunciation—is another matter entirely. Because spoken Japanese neither sounds nor functions like Chinese, the first work-around tried was a system called *manyogana*, where individual kanji were picked to represent certain syllables in Japanese (a similar method is still used in Chinese today to spell out foreign names).

The commentary in *Katsuya Terada's The Monkey King* (also available from Dark Horse, and also translated by To-shifumi Yoshida) notes the importance that not only Chinese, but Indian culture had on Japan at this time in history—particularly, Buddhism. It is believed the Northeast Indian *Siddham* script studied by Kukai (died 835 AD), founder of the Shingon sect of Japanese Buddhism, inspired him to create the solution for writing Japanese still used today. Kukai is credited with the idea of taking the manyogana and making the shorthand versions of them now known simply as *kana*. The improvement in efficiency was dramatic—a kanji, used previously to represent a sound, that might have taken a dozen strokes to draw, was now reduced to three or four.

Unlike the original kanji it was based on, the new kana had *only* a sound meaning. And unlike the thousands of kanji, there are only 46 kana, which can be used to spell out any word in the Japanese language, including the many ordinarily written with kanji (Japanese keyboards work on this principle). The same set of 46 kana is written two different ways depending on their intended use; cursive style, *hiragana*, and block style, *katakana*. Naturally, sound FX in manga are almost always written out using kana.

Kana works somewhat differently than the Roman alphabet. For example, while there are separate kana for each of the five vowels (the Japanese order is not A-E-I-O-U as in English, but A-I-U-E-O), there are, except for "n," no separate kana for consonants (the middle "n" in the word ninja illustrates this exception). Instead, kana work by grouping together consonants with vowels: for example, there are five kana for sounds starting with "k," depending on which vowel follows it—in Japanese vowel order, they go KA, KI, KU, KE, KO. The next set of kana begins with "s" sounds, so SA, SHI, SU, SE, SO, and so on. You will observe this kind of consonant-vowel pattern in the FX listings for *Kurosagi* Vol. 2 below.

Katakana is almost always the kind that gets used for manga sound FX, but on occasion (often when the sound is one made by a person) hiragana are used instead. In *Kurosagi* Vol. 2 you can see one of several examples on page 55, panel 6, when Mutsumi exhales with a "FUU" sound, which in hiragana style is written ふうっ. Note its more cursive appearance compared to the other FX. If it had been written in katakana style, it would look like フウツ.

To see how to use this glossary, take an example from page 4: "4.1 FX: GA-KON—sound of trap door dropping open." 4.1 means the FX is the one on page 4, in panel 1. GAKON is the sound these kana—ガコン—literally stands for. After the dash comes an explanation of what the sound represents (in some cases, such as this one, it will be more obvious than others). Note that in cases where there are two or more different sounds in a single panel, an extra number is used to differentiate them from right to left; or, in cases where right and left are less clear (for example, 4.2.1 and 4.2.2) in clockwise order.

The use of kana in these FX also illustrates another aspect of written Japanese—its flexible reading order. For example, the way you're reading the pages and panels of this book in general: going from right-to-left, and from top to bottom—is

the order in which Japanese is also written in most forms of print: books, magazines, and newspapers. However, if you examine those kana examples given above, you'll notice something interesting. They read "Western" style—left-to-right! In fact, many of the FX in *Kurosagi* (and manga in general) read left-to-right. On page 23 you can find the direction switching from right-to-left (23.3) to left-to-right (23.4) in two successive panels. This kind of flexibility is also to be found on Japanese web pages, which usually also read left-to-right. In other words, Japanese doesn't simply read "the other way" from English; the Japanese themselves are used to reading it in several different directions.

As might be expected, some FX "sound" short, and others "sound" long. Manga represent this in different ways. One of many examples of "short sounds" in *Kurosagi* Vol. 2 is to be found in the example 55.6 given above: FUU. Note the small つ mark it has at the end. This is ordinarily reprsents the sound "tsu" (the katakana form, more commonly seen in manga FX, is ツ) but its half-size use at the end of FX like this means the sound is the kind which stops or cuts off suddenly; that's why the sound is written as FUU and not FUUTSU—you don't "pronounce" the TSU in such cases.

Note the small "tsu" has another occasional use *inside*, rather than at the end, of a particular FX, as seen in 23.3's TA TTA TA—running sound—here it's at work between two "TA" タ sounds to indicate a doubling of the consonant sound that follows it.

There are three different ways you may see "long sounds"—where a vowel sound is extended—written out as FX. One is with an ellipsis, as in 21.1's GOTO. Another is with an extended line, as in 50.3's PIN-POON PINPOON. Still another is by simply repeating a vowel several times, as in 17.4's ZUZUUU. You will note this last example also has an ellipsis at its end; the methods may be combined within a single FX. As a visual element in manga, FX are an art rather than a science, and are used in a less rigorous fashion than kana are in standard written Japanese.

The explanation of what the sound represents may sometimes be surprising; but every culture "hears" sounds differently. Note that manga FX do not even necessarily represent literal sounds. Such "mimetic" words, which represent an imagined sound, or even a state of mind, are called *gitaigo* in Japanese. Like the onomatopoeic *giseigo* (the words used to represent literal sounds—i.e., most FX in this glossary are classed as giseigo), they are also used in colloquial speech and writing. A Japanese, for example, might say that something bounced by saying PURIN, or talk about eating by saying MUGU MUGU. It's something like describing chatter in English by saying "yadda yadda yadda" instead.

One important last note: all these spelled-out kana vowels should be pronounced as they are in Japanese: "A" as *ah*, "I" as *eee*, "U" as *ooh*, "E" as *eh*, and "O" as *oh*.

3   People are sometimes surprised to hear that the death penalty still exists in Japan, or that it is carried out by hanging (one might expect something more high-tech, like a laser beam). About two or three people on average are hung every year in Japan—the penalty is given in recent decades only for multiple murders or murder under aggravated circumstances; perhaps the most infamous prisoners on death row in Japan are several members of the cult Aum Shinri Kyo, for their participation in the Japanese nerve-gas terrorist attacks of 1995, and the serial killer Tsutomu Miyazaki, whose arrest in 1989 sparked condemnation of otaku (it was later understood that the media had exaggerated his participation in otaku culture). In Japan, both the defense and the prosecution can appeal a death sentence—that is, the prosecution can argue to a higher court that a person sentenced to life in prison should have their sentence "upgraded" to death!

3.5   **FX: KOKU**—nodding sound

4.1   **FX: GAKON**—sound of trap door dropping open

4.2.1   **FX: BAN**—body convulsing back and forth

4.2.2   **FX: BATAN**—body convulsing

4.3   **FX: GAKU GAKU**—fingers twitching

4.4   **FX: HEKO BEKO**—sound of chest trying to move/convulsing

4.5   **FX: GI GI**—legs twitching

5.1   **FX: PURAN**—legs hanging limp

6 All the chapters in Vol. 2 are titles of songs by Kenji Sawada, known to his fans as "Julie" (it's a little hard to explain). Sawada was the lead singer of The Tigers, one of the most famous of Japan's 1960s GS ("Group Sounds") bands, which, inspired by the Beatles, emphasized guitar and harmonies (Isao Takahata's classic anime film *Only Yesterday* features a brief glimpse of the scene). Today Sawada is a successful actor, appearing in such films as Takashi Miike (who directed the TV adaptation of Eiji Otsuka's *MPD Psycho*)'s *The Happiness of the Katakuris*.

8.2 FX: DODODODODO—sound of the bus engine

8.3 FX: ZA ZA—footsteps

10.5.1 "Alien hand syndrome" is a genuine neurological disorder where one of a person's hands acts in a way that is apparently not under the person's control, as in the movie *Dr. Strangelove*. The joke, of course, is that the puppet on Yuji's left hand actually *is* supposed to be (channeling) an alien.

10.5.2 FX: MOZO MOZO GOSO GOSO—sound of the puppet digging around in Yata's jacket.

11.1 FX: PASA—sound of paper being flipped open

12.2 FX: GACHA—sound of door opening

13.2 FX: GOTOTO—tires coming to a stop

13.3 FX: GACHA—door opening

13.4 FX: HENAA—sound of the two slumping lifelessly.

14.1 FX: DOBOBOBO—pouring hot water

14.3 FX: PACHIN—snapping chopsticks apart

14.5 FX: BARI BORI KARI—sound of crunching still-hard instant noodles. In other words, Kuro is so hungry he didn't even bother to take the pitcher of boiling water from Numata for his chicken ramen; he just starts crunching them dry. In 15.2 you can see that he's got most of the "brick" between his chopsticks.

14.7 FX/balloons: KAKO KAKOKO KOKO—keyboard sounds

16.5 *Nire* (said "nih-reh"—please see note on vowel pronunciation above) is the Japanese word for an elm tree. As with *Kurosagi* ("black heron") it has generally been left untranslated in the script.

17.2 FX: KAKOKO KOKO KAKOKO KAKOKO—keyboard sounds

17.4 FX: ZUZUUU—sound of photo printer

17.5 FX: PASARI—sound of photo hitting floor

18.1 FX/balloon: KATA—putting beer can on table

19.1 In case you think the editor learned about the Internet from a CD-ROM he got in the mail, that is what it said in the original; literally, the phrase *yuuga meeru!* written in katakana. The translator, by the way, was the first person the editor ever met who had a Sony VAIO.

21.1 FX: GOTO—putting down box

22.6 **FX: GOTO**—putting down heavy coffin

23.3 **FX: TA TTA TA**—running sound

23.4 **FX: ZURI**—dragging sound

23.5 **FX/balloon: BAN**—slamming door shut

24.1 **FX: BATAM**—closing car door

24.2 **FX: BURORO**—car starting up

24.3 **FX: GWOOO**—car speeding along. You may have already noticed this in Vol. 1, but naturally they don't drive around with their *full* company name written on the outside of the van; if you compare it with the front cover, you'll notice it's missing the two critical kanji for "corpse," and hence to the public they're just "The Kurosagi Delivery Service."

24.4 **FX: WOOO**—car speeding along

25.2 As you might observe, the sign on the hearse says "Nire Ceremony."

25.3 **FX: FUBA**—sound of the wind as the two cars pass by each other

27.2 **FX: GWOOO**—car sound

27.3 **FX: YURA YURA**—sound of pendulum swinging

28.1 **FX: GOTO GATA GOTO GATA**—sound of car hitting bumps in road

28.6 **FX/balloon: KEEE**—sound of brakes

28.7 **FX: CHAKA CHAKA CHAKA**—sound of the hazard lights blinking

29.1 **FX: HYUN HYUN HYUN**—sound of pendulum swinging

29.3 **FX/balloon: BA**—sound of the two looking back

33.4 **FX: SU**—reaching out with his hand

35.6 **FX: BOBON**—exhaust backfire as the engine starts

36.1 **FX/balloon: DORURURUN**—car engine sound

37.2 **FX/balloon: KWOOOO**—sound of approaching car

39.2 **FX: GOTO**—putting down coffin

39.4 **FX/Makino:** It's just a corpse right? Boring.

39.6 **FX: PASA**—pulling out a page of the paper

45.4 **FX: KACHA**—opening door

45.5 **FX: BATAN**—door slamming

50.3 **FX: PINPOON PINPOON**—doorbell sounds

50.5 **FX: GACHA**—sound of opening door

51.1 **FX/balloon: KOTO**—sound of cup being put on to plate

51.5 The peculiarities of how capital punishment is administered in Japan make this scenario not as bizarre as it may seem, as indicated by Hayashi's remarks on the system in page 130.

52.2 **FX/balloon: DON GARA GARA DOCHA**—sound of many things falling over

53.6 **FX: POTA POTA POTA**—sound of dripping blood

54.1 **FX/balloons: POTA POTA**—drip drip

   FX/balloon: POTA—drip

55.1 **FX/balloon: DOSARI**—sound of cat being tossed down

55.4 **FX: HITA**—hand touching cat

55.5 **FX/balloon: SUUUU**—inhale of air

55.6 **FX: FUU**—soft exhale

56.1 **FX: ZAWA ZAWA ZAWA ZAWA ZAWA**—sound of the leaves moving in the wind

56.2 **FX: ZA ZA ZA ZA ZA**—leaves being blown around by a gust of wind

57.1 **FX/balloon: KASA**—sound of leaves moving under paw

57.2 **FX/balloons: BIKU BIKU**—sound of mouth twitching

57.3 **FX/balloon: PACHI**—sound of eye opening

57.5 **FX: SUKU**—sound of cat getting up

58.2 **FX/balloon: PERO PERO**—sound of cat licking paw

58.3 **FX: GASA**—sound of cat moving off

59.3 Pronounced "keh-reh-ell-is." Bullmark (the logo, appropriately enough, was of a charging bull) made soft vinyl and die-cast toys based on such series as *Godzilla* and *Ultraman* between 1969 and 1977. If this really is his/Yata's/its hobby, it's a relatively expensive one; the originals can sell for several hundred dollars each.

60.2 **FX: KO KO**—footsteps

60.3 **FX: GASA**—something moving in the bushes

61.2 **FX: PURAN PURAN**—wiggling sausage

61.4 **FX: BABA**—sound of cat attacking

62.1 **FX: KUCHA BARI GUCHA**—chomping and bone cracking sounds

62.3 **FX: SHITA SHITA**—quiet cat footsteps

62.4.1 **FX: SHITA SHITA**—more cat footsteps

62.4.2 **FX/balloon: PERON**—licking mouth sound

63.1 **FX: BA**—sound of cat jumping

63.3 **FX: GATSU GATSU**—biting sounds

63.6 **FX: BAKI DOKA**—sound of hitting wall with cat

64.1 **FX: DOKA GA DOKA GA**—repeatedly hitting wall with cat

64.2 **FX: DOTA**—thud

64.4 **FX: MUKO**—sound of cat getting up

64.5 **FX: NU**—sound of spirit leaving cat's body

65.1 **FX: DO**—sound of lifeless cat hitting ground

65.2 **FX: FU**—sound of the spirit fading away

66.4 **FX: KACHA**—opening door

67.1 **FX: BASA BASA**—newspapers being tossed onto the floor

68.6 **FX: PAKU PAKU**—sound of puppet's mouth flapping. Notice Kereellis is now wearing a tie as well, presumably so as to help Yata not look out of place on the job.

70.3 **FX: BATAN**—door closing

71.2 **FX: PIRA**—sound of paper being held up

71.3 It is very common for a Japanese

to use as a form of personal ID when dealing with government records (taxes, registrations, etc.) a *jitsuin*—an ink seal carved with the individual's name. The person makes an impression with it, and registers it on file with a government office, who can then bring it out for comparison when the person brings the seal in on any future occasion. An an acceptable alternative, as Numata alluded to in 69.3, might be a signature (probably in conjunction with a personal identification number), or a thumbprint.

73.5 **FX: JAN CHAN JA JACHACHACHA CHAN**—ringtone playing

74.3 **FX: TSUU TSUU TSUU**—dial tone

75.1 In the original "joke," Karatsu misheard it as *nira*, meaning "leek." In the extremely unlikely event you haven't yet seen Orihime from *Bleach* spin a leek to the tune of the nostalgic Finnish song *Eva's Polka*, go directly to leekspin.com for the looped experience.

76.3 **FX/balloon: TOPOPO**—pouring tea

77.3 **FX: HO**—sigh of relief

78.3 **FX: KYUKYU**—sound of a squeaky wheel

78.4 **FX: KYU KYU**—more squeaks

79.4 **FX: GACHA**—opening door

80.3 **FX: PEKORI**—bowing sound

80.5 **FX: GATA**—getting up

80.6 **FX: KACHA**—putting cup down on plate

82.1 **FX: KON KON**—knock knock

82.3 **FX: KACHI**—door opening

82.7 **FX: KACHA**—cup being put down

83.6 **FX: GA**—getting up

85.4 **FX: ZA**—turning to leave

85.6.1 **FX/black: KACHA**—door opening

85.6.2 **FX/white: BATAN**—door slamming

86.2 **FX: BATAM**—closing car door

87.4 **FX: SU**—starting to turn to leave

88.1 **FX: BUUUN**—fluorescent light buzzing

88.2 **FX: CHIKA CHIKA CHIKA**—fluorescent light flickering

88.3 **FX/balloon: PA**—light turning on

89.3 **FX: KO**—footstep

90.3 **FX: FUUU**—exhale sound

90.8 **FX: GO**—pulling on door

93.1 **FX: RIRII RIRII RII**—sound of crickets

93.3 **FX: GACHA**—door opening

93.4 **FX: KO KO GO GO**—several footsteps

94.4 **FX: KO KO**—footsteps walking up

98.1 **FX: PAKU PAKU**—sound of mouth moving

99.1 **FX: PAKU PAKU**—flapping mouth sound

101.1 **FX: GATAN**—pulling chair out

101.3 **FX: SU**—sliding envelope forward

101.6 Sasaki is commenting on the casual nature of how Hayashi is calling her name without any honorifics such as -*san*, -*chan*, or -*kun*.

102.3 In other words, no longer the addresses of their respective original families. The translator notes that in Japan, one's official record (the "family register") almost always uses the address of the residence your family lived in when you were born. His is still the same, even though the actual house was torn down long ago and four new houses were erected on the property. Only on rare occasions is the registered address ever changed.

102.5 **FX: SHA SHA**—sound of the pen on paper

103.1 **FX: GATA**—getting up

104.1 **FX/balloon: KOOOO**—car engine sounds

104.4 **FX: KEEE**—sound of brakes

105.1 The ubiquitous roadside or sidewalk vending machines, where you can buy hot or cold food and drinks (as well as alcohol and cigarettes) any time of day or night, are one of the great charms of Japan. As with the remark about gun violence in Vol. 1's "Disjecta Membra," the disturbing scenes portrayed in this volume should perhaps be balanced against the simple remark that such outdoor vending machines can exist in Japan without being vandalized into oblivion; Japan has a much lower crime rate than the U.S.

105.3 **FX/balloon: PI**—pressing button

FX/balloon: GARA GOSHON—sound of bottle dropping

105.4 **FX: SU**—taking bottle out

106.1 **FX: PI**—pressing bottle against cheek

106.3 **FX: GOKYU**—gulp

106.7 **FX: BASA**—sound of map dropping

106.8 **FX: GON**—head slumping onto window

107.2 **FX/balloon: DOTA**—puppet falling onto armrest

107.4 **FX/balloon: SHA**—moving curtain aside. Note the hinged doors on the coffin so that the face of the dead can be viewed.

107.5 **FX: GOTO**—sound of crowbar being put down on coffin

108.2 **FX/balloons: DON DON DADAN DON**—banging on door

108.3.1 **FX/balloons: DON DON**—banging

108.3.2 **FX/balloon: BAN**—banging

109.1 **FX/balloon: GACHA**—opening door

109.4.1 **FX/balloon: GABU**—biting sound

109.4.2 **FX/balloon: BAKI**—sound of breaking bones

110.7 **FX/balloon: BURORORO**—car engine sound

112.1 **FX: BASA**—sound of newspaper being tossed onto table

112.5 **FX: BOSO**—mumbling sound effect

113.3 **FX/balloon: BATAN**—door slam

116.1 **FX: GACHA**—opening car door

116.2 **FX: BAN**—car door being shut

116.3 **FX/balloon: KUI**—pointing at driver seat

116.4 **FX/balloon: BAN**—car door shutting

116.6 FX: KYUTOTOTO—engine turning over

116.7 FX/balloon: BUROROORON—engine starting

117.1 FX/balloon: PIPAPII PIPAPIPA PIIPAPAAPII—ringtone

117.2 FX/balloon: PI—answering cell phone

118.6 FX: KO KO—footsteps

119.1 FX: PINPOON PINPOON—doorbell

119.3 FX/balloon: GACHA—door opening

119.5 FX/balloon: KACHI BO—sound of turning on a gas stove and the fire igniting

120.5 FX: KACHA—putting down coffee cups

121.2 FX: KOTO—putting video down

121.4 FX: TATA—running off

121.5 FX: BATAN—door closing

122.2 FX: TATATATA—running sound

123.1 FX: SU—sound of tape being taken out of sleeve

123.2 FX: GAKON—putting tape in

123.4 FX: WHEEEN—VCR starting up

125.3 FX: GAKON—sound of the trap door opening

126.5 FX: SU—picking up remote to stop tape

126.7 *Fugutaiten* means having to take revenge against another even if it means one's own death. The kanji literally mean that one person cannot live under the same heavens if the other is to stay alive.

127.1 FX: PA—sound of the screen changing

130.6 FX: GATA—getting up

131.4 FX: KO KO—footsteps

132.1 FX: KYU KYUKYU—sound of squeaky wheels

132.4 FX: JYARI—sound of footsteps in gravel

133.4 FX: PAKU PAKU—mouth flapping

137.3 FX: PINPOON PINPOON—doorbell

137.4 FX: GARA—sliding door opening

138.5 FX: GAPA—rice cooker being opened

139.2 FX/balloon: KU—putting ring on

139.3 FX: CHARA—letting pendulum drop

139.4 FX: SUUU—reaching out with his arm

139.5 FX: HYUN HYUN HYUN—pendulum beginning to swing

140.2 FX: GI—grabbing handle

140.3 FX: GIIIII—door being opened

142.4 FX: GACHA—opening door

143.4 FX/balloon: GASHA—loading videotape

143.5 FX/balloon: ZAAA—static

143.6 FX/balloon: PA—screen turning on

145.2 FX: FUU FUU—heavy breathing

145.3 FX/box: DOSU BYU—stabbing then spurting sound

145.5 FX/box: GACHA GACHA—rattling against restraints

146.2 FX/box: ZAKU—stab

146.4 FX/box: DOKA—thud

146.7.1 FX/box: KOTSU KOTSU—footsteps

146.7.2 FX/box: KOTSU—footstep

147.1 FX/box: DOSU GUCHU—stab then wet stabbing sound

147.2 In the original, Yata refers to the myth of the *Hangon* ritual, meaning "half a spirit," supposedly able to reanimate the dead.

148.1 FX/balloon: GATA—getting up angrily

148.4 FX: GA—grasping shoulder

152.2 FX/balloons: PI PO PA—dialing cell phone

153.1 FX/balloon: PIII—hanging up cell

153.2 FX: PATAN—closing flip phone

153.4 FX: KUSHA—crushing business card

153.5 FX/balloon: KORO—sound of balled up card rolling

154.2 FX/balloon: PA—lights coming on

154.3 FX/balloon: ZAAAA—static on TV

155.3 The term as used in Western culture comes from Matthew 27:7, alluding to the practice of soils full of clay (and thus useful to potters) being also used for graveyards—although the Japanese term was *choshinda*, meaning "forsaken ground."

156.1 FX/balloon: KU—lifting up chin

157.6 FX/balloon: BATAN—door closing

158.1 FX: GWOOOO—car sound

159.1 FX: GATA GOTO GOTON GATAN—sound of the rattling inside the car

159.2 FX: GOGO AGO GOGO—vibrations inside car

159.3 FX: GOGOGOGOGO—vibrations

161.1 FX: SU—touching sound

162.1 FX: GOGO GOGO GOGO—car sound

164.2 FX: GACHA—door opening sound

165.5.1 FX: GATAN—getting up

165.5.2 FX/balloon: DOSA—putting laptop into bag

165.7 FX: BATAAN—door slamming

167.1 FX/balloon: KASHAN—putting in key

167.3 In the West, a corpse might be laid out in formal dress, but the equivalent Japanese practice is to clothe them in a white kimono.

167.7 FX/balloon: BATAN—door closing

168.1.1 FX/balloon: KOTSU—footstep

168.1.2 FX/balloon: KOTSU—footstep

169.1 FX: SUU—inhale

169.2 FX: FUUU—exhale

169.3.1 FX/balloon: PIKU—eye twitch

169.3.2 FX/balloons: PIKU PIKU—more twitching

169.4 FX/balloon: PACHI—eyes snapping open

170.2 FX: PAKU PAKU—mouth flapping

170.4 FX: KACHA—opening door

170.5 **FX/balloon: KACHA**—opening door

171.5 **FX/balloon: BASA**—sound of raincoat falling

172.4 **FX/balloons: TOKU TOKU**—chloroform being poured onto handkerchief

172.5 **FX: BA**—hand jerking up

172.6 **FX: SA**—hand going over mouth and nose

173.2 **FX/balloon: YORO**—stagger

173.3 **FX: DOTA**—sound of Yata falling

174.3 **FX/balloon: PACHIN**—snapping open knife

174.4 **FX: GIRI GIRI**—putting cuts into wire

174.6 **FX: CHIKA**—small LED lighting up

176.1 **FX: TON TON**—straightening papers

176.6 **FX/balloon: GAA**—sound of automatic doors sliding open

177.4 **FX/balloon: BAMUN**—car door closing

177.5 **FX/balloon: VWOON**—engine revving

178.4.1 **FX/balloon: PIIPAPI HOPAP-IPAA PIIPAAPI**—ringtone

178.4.2 **FX/balloon: PIIPAPI HOPAP-IPAA PIIPAA**—ringtone

178.5.1 **FX/balloon: KYUKO**—sound of shower being turned off

178.5.2 **FX/balloon: PIIPAPI HOPAP-IPAA PIIPAAPI**—ringtone

178.6 **FX/balloon: PI**—answering phone

179.2 **FX: SU**—picking up glasses

179.6 **FX: PASA**—sound of towel falling

181.1 **FX/balloon: KIII**—brake sound

181.2 **FX/balloons: KACHA BAN**—door opening and closing

181.5 **FX/balloon: KUI**—gesturing with head

187.7 **FX/balloons: KO KO KO**—sound of footsteps

183.2 **FX/balloon: PECHI PECHI**—light slapping on face

184.4 **FX: KA KA**—footsteps

184.7 **FX: GAKON GEEE**—doors being unlatched and creaking open

187.6.1 **FX/balloon: GACHA**—rattling doorknob

187.6.2 **FX/balloon: GACHA GACHA**—more rattling

189.4 **FX: KATSU KATSU**—walking toward Fuchigami

190.5 **FX: PITAN PITAN**—slapping knife blade against palm

192.2 **FX/balloon: KII**—door creaking open

192.5 **FX: DO**—putting body down

193.1 **FX: JIIII**—sound of zipper being pulled down

194.2.1 **FX/balloon: GIIII**—sound of straining wire

194.2.2 **FX/balloon: GIRIRIRI**—more straining

194.3.1 **FX/balloon: BAKIIIN**—wire breaking

194.3.2 **FX/small: PAKI**—twang of wire

195.3 **FX: ZUPAA**—sound of slicing flesh

196.2 **FX: GA**—sound of neck being grasped

197.5 **FX: BURAN**—sound of Hayashi's legs hanging off the ground

197.6 **FX: GATATAN**—sound of everyone falling as Hayashi's body is thrown

198.7 **FX: DADA**—running sound

198.8 **FX: GA**—grabbing sound

199.1 **FX: GACHA**—door being opened

199.5 **FX: PAKU**—biting down on broom handle

199.6 **FX: KAN**—sound of the broomstick hitting floor

200.1 **FX: GAAAAAA GAAAAAH**—screaming

200.5 **FX: KA**—kicking knife

200.6 **FX/balloon: KARA KARARA**—sound of knife spinning on floor

201.4 **FX: ZURU**—hand slipping

201.6 **FX/balloon: GUI**—pushing Mutsumi forward

202.2 **FX: DO**—sound of broomstick hitting back of throat

202.3 **FX: MEKI**—sound of the neck/spine starting to break

203.5 **FX/balloon: DON**—tip of broom hitting floor

206.4 **FX: SU**—reaching for knife

206.5 **FX/balloon: GU**—stepping on hand

207.6 **FX: GAKUN**—slumping in defeat

208.3 **FX: ZA ZA**—walking thought field sound

210.2.1 **FX/balloon: PI**—beep

210.2.2 **FX/balloon: PI**—beep

210.2.3 **FX/balloon: PI**—beep

210.6 **FX/balloon: SU**—moving away

211.1 **FX: KATA**—picking up vase

211.2 **FX: ZAA**—sound of running water

211.4 **FX: KYU**—closing tap

211.6 **FX: BATAN**—door closing